THE WATCHTOWER FILES:

Dialogue with a Jehovah's Witness

THE WATCH~TOWER FILES:

Dialogue with a Jehovah's Witness

DUANE MAGNANI
with Arthur Barrett

BETHANY HOUSE PUBLISHERS
MINNEAPOLIS, MINNESOTA 55438
A Division of Bethany Fellowship, Inc.

Scripture quotations are from the New American Standard Bible, © The Lockman Foundation 1960, 1962, 1963, 1968, 1971, 1972, 1973, 1975, 1977.

Published by Bethany House Publishers
A Division of Bethany Fellowship, Inc.
6820 Auto Club Road, Minneapolis, MN 55438

Printed in the United States of America

Library of Congress Cataloging in Publication Data

Magnani, Duane.
The Watchtower files.

Bibliography: p.
Includes indexes.
1. Jehovah's Witnesses—Controversial literature—Addresses, essays, lectures. I. Barrett, Arthur, 1953- . II. Title.
BX8526.5.M34 1985 289.9'2 84-28318
ISBN 0-87123-816-0

ACKNOWLEDGMENT

This work is due to the encouragement of David Merrick, who believed in its wide distribution. The authors would like to gratefully acknowledge his desire that Christians should have "witnessing tools" to aid in making a defense of the true Gospel. It is our prayer that the Lord will raise up many more, like David, who have a heart for seeing the captives of false religions set free in Christ.

THE AUTHORS

DUANE MAGNANI was a member of the Jehovah's Witnesses for eighteen years. After he became a Christian in 1974, he founded Witness, Inc., an organization dedicated to bringing Jehovah's Witnesses to Christ. Duane and his wife live in California.

ARTHUR BARRETT is a student of Christian apologetics at Golden Gate Theological Seminary in San Francisco. He has been active in the ministry of Witness, Inc., since 1975. He is married and they make their home in California.

CONTENTS

SECTION I: AUTHORITY OF THE WATCHTOWER

1. Inspiration—Part I: Is God Responsible for the Watchtower? 13
2. Inspiration—Part II: God's Supreme Court 19
3. Who is the Watchtower's Faithful and Wise Servant? 25
4. Worshiping Pastor Russell 35
5. C. T. Russell *v.* the Organization 42
6. The Power of the Watchtower President—Part I: A Look at Charles Taze Russell 50
7. The Power of the Watchtower President—Part II: A Look at the Next Three Presidents 57
8. Watchtower Prophecy Analysis 63

SECTION II: MAJOR DOCTRINE

Introduction 101

9. The Resurrection of Christ—Analysis 102
   - *Jesus—Spirit or Man?* 109
   - *Who Rose from the Dead?* 112
   - *Was Thomas Deceived?* 112
   - *What Happened to the Body?* 116
10. The Godhead (The Trinity)—Analysis 118
    - *One God or Many?* 123
    - *The Trinity—Misrepresented* 126
    - *"Trinity"—That's Not in the Bible!* 146
11. The Deity of Christ—Analysis 156
    - *Is Jesus Christ Worthy of Worship?* 161
    - *Relative Worship—Can Jesus Receive Indirect Worship?* 166
    - *Jesus, the God of Thomas* 178
    - *Jesus—"Our God and Savior"* 180
    - *John 1:1 and the Two Gods* 184
    - *John 1:1 and the Watchtower Rule* 185
    - *John 1:1—Clearing Up the Difficulty* 190

The "Perfect" Translation—John 8:58 207
Jews Don't Stone Angels—John 8:58 215
Ego Eimi, Ho On, and the KIT—John 8:58 218
Who Is the Alpha and the Omega? 221
12. The Holy Spirit—Analysis 228
Is the Holy Spirit a Person? 228
Is the Holy Spirit God Himself? 231
13. Salvation—Analysis 232
The Distinction Between Watchtower Believers 244
Is Jehovah God Your Heavenly Father? 246
Born Again. Can Jehovah's Witnesses Be "Born Again"? 250
Who Is the Christ—A Person or a Group? 252

SECTION III: MINOR DOCTRINE

14. The Cross—Analysis 257
Dialogue on the Christian Cross 260
15. Christmas—Analysis 263
Should We Celebrate the Birth of Christ? 264
Does the Christmas Date Matter? 269
16. Blood Transfusions—Analysis 274
Does the Bible Forbid Blood Transfusions? 278
17. Military Service—Analysis 282
War and Jehovah's Witnesses—Part I 283
War and Jehovah's Witnesses—Part II 291
Bibliography 295
Scripture Index 299
Subject Index 301

INTRODUCTION

From small beginnings in 1881 to a multi-million dollar corporation today, the Watchtower Bible and Tract Society has expanded its outreach around the world. Among some of their teachings is the doctrine that Jehovah has a prophet-class on earth today. Individual Witnesses are further led to believe that this prophet speaks only through the publications of the Watchtower Society. Therefore, they feel it is vital for one to remain in close association with the organization of Jehovah. Indeed, if God does have a prophet-class on the earth today, the sincere Christian would want to be in touch with them and adhere to what God has said through that group. But if a prophet is false, the Christian's duty is to expose that fact (Eph. 5:11). The material in this book will help you do just that.

Jehovah's Witnesses were once very willing to speak with the Christian and aggressively defend their position. They were confident and willing to debate the Christian whom they believed had fallen prey to pagan myths. But today, many who desire to share Christ with the Jehovah's Witnesses find the situation is much different. In the last few years they have changed their tactics. The Watchtower has lost its confidence and is very conscious of losing members, as even secular news sources are reporting. *Newsweek*, October 15, 1984, reported:

> Many dissident and former members are becoming militant in their criticism of the society; last week, in an unprecedented public protest, 50 of them showed up outside the Witnesses' Brooklyn home, waving placards, complaining of oppression and demanding the resignation of the Governing Body. More important, dissidents have formed networks of former Witnesses who have been shunned by families and friends. One result is a growing body of damning literature, much of it compiled from Watch Tower files, depicting a closed, almost Orwellian society.

Not only was the Society discouraged over their failure to see the 1975 prediction of the world's end come to pass, but even more disturbing to the Society is the fact that Christians are taking action! For as ministries reaching out to Jehovah's Witnesses increase, so are the number of Christians preparing themselves to effectively evangelize the Witnesses.

The Watchtower's method of proselytizing has been literally turned around in recent years. Christians armed with the Word of God and prayer are now looking upon Jehovah's Witnesses as a veritable mission field on their doorstep. Preparing themselves much as they would before entering any mission field, these Christians are trying to understand things as the Witness sees them and then to reach out to him in ways to which he is most likely to respond positively. Many Witnesses have already shaken off the shackles of Watchtower theology and found a new life in Jesus Christ. As Christians begin to reach out, we can see the Society seeming to prefer that JWs turn their backs to informed individuals. The alternative, of course, is to run the risk of losing more of its followers.

How can we reach Jehovah's Witnesses for the Lord? The Lord works through many means, but some seem to be more effective than others. Leighton Ford, associate evangelist of the Billy Graham Evangelistic Association, notes, "The typical method of evangelism in the Acts, in dealing with both Jews and 'God-fearing' Gentiles, was to preach the Word of God out of the scriptures."[1] But what of those who do not share our respect for the authority of the Word, and persons of other faiths? Ford says this:

> Paul on Mars' Hill is an example. Beginning with common religious ground and longing, pointing to their altars and idols and quoting their poets, he went on to declare Jesus and the resurrection. (Acts 17:22–31)[2]

This approach of the Apostle Paul is the one we suggest. We hope this book will help concerned Christians effectively communicate what the Bible has to say on many vital subjects and expose the false doctrines of the Watchtower Bible and Tract Society.

This book, *The Watchtower Files*, contains many compact suggested dialogues with Jehovah's Witnesses. The dialogues examine many different subjects, ranging from major doctrinal differences to points of Watchtower policies and prophetic schemes. Because of the need to *prove* each point and expose the Watchtower Society's false statements, supporting photo-documentation follows each dialogue.

Even after the Witness leaves the authority of the Watchtower organization, and accepts Jesus as Lord and Savior, he will have

---

[1]Leighton Ford, *Christian Persuader* (New York: Harper & Row, 1976), p. 96.
[2]Ibid., pp. 96, 97.

questions, more questions, and even more questions for his new Christian friends. This is because almost all of the doctrines of Jehovah's Witnesses are totally opposed to those of historical Christianity. The major value of *The Watchtower Files* is in the definitive answers provided to Jehovah's Witnesses on a great variety of subjects.

Duane Magnani and Arthur L. Barrett

SECTION ONE

AUTHORITY OF THE WATCHTOWER

Chapter One

INSPIRATION—PART I: IS GOD RESPONSIBLE FOR THE WATCHTOWER?

In our dialogue Chris, a Christian, and Jay, a Jehovah's Witness, talk about the Watchtower Society and inspiration from God.

Jay: Say, Chris, why are you always criticizing the Watchtower Society for its mistakes? After all, they're just human.

Chris: True, but what bothers me is that the Society is always claiming to be God's "means of communication to His people." (See p. 15.) That sounds to me like they are blaming Jehovah himself for their mistakes.

Jay: Well, it's true that the Watchtower Society interprets the Bible for us, but they don't claim to be inspired.

Chris: What do *you* mean by "inspired"?

Jay: I mean that *The Watchtower* is written by men who are imperfect; if it was written by God, then it would be inspired, like the Bible.

Chris: Then you don't blame Jehovah for the doctrinal errors over the years?

Jay: No, of course not. It would be different if *The Watchtower* claimed He was directly responsible for the information.

Chris: Then, you'd better prepare for a shock. Your leaders have claimed Jehovah *is* responsible for all the information in *The Watchtower*.

Jay: I've gotta *see* this!

Chris: Here goes. In a 1943 court case, Watchtower Vice-President Fred Franz was asked the following:

Q. . . . Jehovah God is now the editor of the paper, is that right?

A. He is today the editor of the paper.

Q. How long has He been editor of the paper?

A. Since its inception He has been guiding it. (See p. 16.)

Jay: I've never heard that before!

Chris: I didn't think so. In the same court case, President Nathan Knorr was asked about the importance of *The Watchtower* magazine:

Q. In fact, it is set forth directly as God's word, isn't it?

A. Yes, as His word.

Q. Without any qualification whatsoever?

A. That is right. (See p. 17.)

Jay: I can't believe he said that!

Chris: But, Jay, this is why *The Watchtower* says, "The interpretation of prophecy, therefore, is not from man, but is from Jehovah. . . . (See p. 18.) And they claim not to be inspired! Jay, you see they are actually blaming God for their mistakes!

Jay: Do you have more information on this?

Chris: Yes. I'll show you how the Watchtower gets its information. You won't believe your eyes!

keep out of jail. The case is now pending before the Court of Appeals of New York.

Other cases involving the right to attend school without stifling conscience to salute a flag are pending on appeal in the Supreme Court of Florida and the Texas Court of Civil Appeals.

"THE WATCHTOWER"

It should be expected that the Lord would have a means of communication to his people on the earth, and he has clearly shown that the magazine called *The Watchtower* is used for that purpose. During the year *The Watchtower* has published in each issue some further enlightenment of Jehovah's prophecies, which publication has been of great aid and comfort to those who have devoted themselves to the kingdom of God. The subscription list has greatly increased during the year, as it should be expected. The remnant have been constant readers of *The Watchtower,* and more recently the "other sheep", or Jonadabs, have come to clearly see that they need *The Watchtower.* It is therefore strongly urged that all of the Jonadabs avail themselves of *The Watchtower* and attend the studies that are held in each company, and that they participate therein that they may more fully see and appreciate their privileges of now serving God and Christ his King.

"CONSOLATION"

During the year the magazine *Consolation,* which took the place of the *Golden Age* magazine, has been published and its subscription list has marvelously increased. It is published not only in English, but in five other languages, to wit: German, Hungarian, Polish, Spanish, and Ukrainian.

BRITAIN

For the past few years it has been said by some that the work in Great Britain had reached its peak; that there was no more room for additional publishers, and

1939 Yearbook of Jehovah's Witnesses, p. 85.

2596 *Fred W. Franz—For Defts.—Cross*

Q. Didn't you state that on October 15, 1931, the Watch Tower discontinued the naming of an editorial committee and then Jehovah God became the editor? A. I didn't say Jehovah God became the editor. It was appreciated that Jehovah God really is the One who is editing the paper, and therefore the naming of an editorial committee was out of place.

Q. At any rate, Jehovah God is now the editor of the paper, is that right? A. He is today the editor of the paper.

2597 Q. How long has He been editor of the paper? A. Since its inception he has been guiding it.

Q. Even before 1931? A. Yes, sir.

Q. Why did you have an editorial committee up to 1931? A. Pastor Russell in his will specified that there should be such an editorial committee, and it was continued down till then.

Q. Did you find that the editorial committee was in conflict with having the journal edited by Jehovah God, is that it? A. No.

Q. Was the policy in opposition to what your conception of an editing by Jehovah God was?

2598 A. It was found on occasions that some of these on the editorial committee were preventing the publication of timely and vital, up-to-date truths and thereby hindering the going of those truths to the people of the Lord in His due time.

By the Court:

Q. After that, 1931, who on earth, if anybody, had charge of what went in or did not go in the magazine? A. Judge Rutherford.

Q. So he in effect was the earthly editor-in-chief, as he might be called? A. He would be the visible one to take care of that.

Olin Moyle v. *WTBTS*, 1943, Sections #2596–2597.

to look up these Scriptures and study them in their own Bibles in their own homes.

Q. But you don't make any mention in the fore part of your Watch Tower that "We are not infallible and subject to correction and may make mistakes"? A. We have never claimed infallibility.

Q. But you don't make any such statement, that you are subject to correction, in your Watch Tower papers, do you? A. Not that I recall.

4421 Q. In fact, it is set forth directly as God's Word, isn't it? A. Yes, as His word.

Q. Without any qualification whatsoever? A. That is right.

Q. Do you subscribe to this statement that has been made in court, that Christ suffered for the obedient ones? A. Yes, I do.

Q. Do you recall this part of the Scriptures in Romans, 5, 6, that "* * * in due time Christ died for the ungodly"? A. Yes.

Q. Is that a truth? A. Yes, it is a truth.

Q. Well, now, don't you find in the Bible that
4422 there are different considerations that can be
placed on different wordings and sentences in
the Bible? A. I believe that when you are studying any subject in the Bible you should bring
all the Scriptures together under one heading
and get the general thought of all those Scriptures.

Q. Well, you know different considerations can be placed on the Bible, don't you? A. If you take an isolated Scripture, yes.

Q. And it is very possible for these infallible people in the Watch Tower to take the wrong

Olin Moyle v. *WTBTS*, 1943, Section #4421.

The entire picture shows that what is there described is fulfilled when the Lord Jesus is at the temple of Jehovah for judgment, and this fixes the time when the work of scattering the fire by the man in linen must be done. 'Jehovah is in his holy temple, Jehovah's throne is in heaven; his eyes behold, his eyelids try, the children of men. Jehovah trieth the righteous; but the wicked, and him that loveth violence, his soul hateth. Upon the wicked he shall rain snares, fire and brimstone, and an horrible tempest; this shall be the portion of their cup.' (Ps. 11:4-6; Jude 14, 15; Mal. 3:1-3) When the Lord is at the temple for judgment, the glory of Jehovah is over the house. 'When Jehovah shall build up Zion, he shall appear in his glory.' (Ps. 102:16) The vision of Ezekiel discloses the Lord Jesus Christ at the temple for judgment, accompanied by his corps of officers made up of cherubim, seraphim and angels, and employing both animate and inanimate parts of the great organization to carry forward God's purposes; and these are symbolized by wheels and the cherubim and other living creatures.

The foregoing scriptures lay the foundation for the conclusion that, following the year 1918, which marks the coming of the Lord to his temple, the prophetic vision of Ezekiel here described began to be fulfilled, and until that time the prophecy could not be understood.

The commandment to the man clothed in linen was to go in between the wheels, under the cherubim, thus showing that the "servant" class on earth is under the direction of the higher officers of God's organization and are to work with both animate and inanimate parts of the organization in obedience to the commandments. "And it came to pass, that when he had commanded the man clothed with linen, saying, Take fire from between the wheels, from between the cherubims; then he went in, and stood beside the wheels. And one cherub stretched forth his hand from between the cherubims unto the fire that was between the cherubims, and took thereof, and put it into the hands of him that was clothed with linen; who took it, and went out." (Ezek. 10:6, 7) This shows that God makes all provision necessary to carry out all his judgments of fiery indignation upon Satan's organization. It is thrilling and awesome for the "servant" class of Jehovah to realize that they are permitted to work under the guiding hand of God's great officers that are invisible to their eyes. This helps them to appreciate the fact that, the "servant" trusting implicitly in Jehovah and not following his own selfish course, but being always joyfully obedient to Jehovah, his ways are directed of Jehovah and therefore cannot fail. (Prov. 3:5, 6) "The steps of a good man [God's ideal man, the 'faithful servant'] are ordered by the Lord; and he delighteth in his way."—Ps. 37:23.

The actual burning or destruction by fire is done by the officers of Jehovah that are invisible to human eyes, that is, the cherubim, seraphim and angels; but it seems clear that the cherubim have charge over fire or that which destroys. These invisible ones Jehovah uses to put in the hands of his "faithful servant" class, that is, the man clothed with linen, the fiery message from his Word, or judgments written, and which is to be used as directed. The resolutions adopted by conventions of God's anointed people, booklets, magazines, and books published by them, contain the message of God's truth and are from the Almighty God, Jehovah, and provided by him through Christ Jesus and his underofficers. This shows the grand and glorious organization working in exact harmony, as indeed it must work. These instruments being provided by Jehovah, and placed in the hand of the remnant, the remnant or "servant" class is commanded to use the same.

The interpretation of prophecy, therefore, is not from man, but is from Jehovah; and Jehovah causes events to come to pass in fulfillment of the prophecy in due time. It is his truth, and not man's; and when men attempt to give the honor and glory for the message of truth to a man or men, such make fools of themselves. Jehovah provides the machinery, the printing presses, and all material for the purpose of preparing his fiery message that must be poured out or scattered upon "Christendom", and this is done by his "faithful servant" class. The Devil tries to induce men to believe that the Watch Tower Bible and Tract Society is engaging in a bookselling scheme. Only the Devil is capable of manufacturing such a lie. God's "servant" class, pictured by the man in linen, is commanded to do the work of declaring the vengeance of Jehovah, and only those who obey this commandment can and will maintain their integrity toward God. The "servant", or remnant class, will not be deceived or discouraged by the slanderous statements of enemies that they are engaged in a bookselling scheme. They carry the message of truth to the people in printed form; and this is done under the commandment of Jehovah, and is the greatest privilege that has ever been granted the followers of Christ on earth. The remnant delights to do this work and continually sings the praises of Jehovah while doing it.

It is easy to be seen that the remnant must do a twofold work, as pictured by the work of Ezekiel, in this: They go from house to house, carrying the message of truth in printed form of books and magazines and by phonograph with discs; they first deliver an introductory message to the one whom they address; they do not open their testimony with a denunciation of the wicked, but first speak of the message of the goodness of God that gives hope to those who will hear, and comfort those that mourn. This is the commission of the remnant.

At the same time the remnant must declare or tell the people of God's judgment of fiery indignation

The Watchtower, May 1, 1938, p. 143.

Chapter Two

INSPIRATION—PART II: GOD'S SUPREME COURT

In our dialogue Chris, a Christian, and Jay, a Jehovah's Witness, discuss the Watchtower Society and its claim of special revelation.

Jay: Chris, when you showed me that the Watchtower claims God himself is *responsible* for their writings, you said this means their mistakes are blamed on God. This is so hard for me to accept. You promised to show me how they claim to get their information.

Chris: Sure, let me explain. Have you ever heard of the heavenly Supreme Court?

Jay: No. What is it?

Chris: Not *what*, Jay, but *who*! *The Watchtower* says of Jehovah, "He is therefore the Supreme Court in Himself." (See p. 21.) Then they claim *no* organization on earth is the interpreter of His Word. (See p. 22.)

Jay: But, if the Watchtower Society doesn't *interpret* the Bible, how does the information get into *The Watchtower*?

Chris: They say God uses the Watchtower organization to "publish the interpretation after the Supreme Court by Christ Jesus reveals it." (See p. 23.) They claim the Watchtower is able to understand world events when God reveals the interpretation. But do you know how these events are understood?

Jay: No, how?

Chris: *Angels* deliver the correct information.

Jay: What! I don't believe that!

Chris: I know, but the Watchtower explains that:

> These angels are invisible to human eyes and are there to carry out the orders of the Lord. No doubt they first hear the instruction which the Lord issues to his remnant and then these invisible messengers pass such instruction on to the remnant. (See p. 24.)

Now you know, Jay. The Watchtower says it gets information from God's Supreme Court through the invisible angels. Looking at their records of false prophecies, lies, and cover-ups, there must be a big communication breakdown! Do you really believe Jehovah directly interprets His own prophecies in *The Watchtower*? Do you really believe that God's angels deliver information to the Watchtower Society?

Jay: Well, what can I say?

What do you say?

The WATCHTOWER
ANNOUNCING JEHOVAH'S KINGDOM
VOL. LXIV JULY 1, 1943 No. 13

SUPREME COURT INTERPRETS

"Thou hast magnified thy word above all thy name. All the kings of the earth shall praise thee, O Lord, when they hear the words of thy mouth."—Ps. 138:2, 4.

JEHOVAH is the Supreme Judge or Justice. "For Jehovah is our judge, Jehovah is our lawgiver, Jehovah is our king; he will save us." (Isa. 33:22, *Am. Rev. Ver.*) Not by virtue of any constitution drawn up by creatures to organize a national or world government is Jehovah the Most High Judge, nor is He limited or held in check by what is written down in any state-making document on earth. He is the First and Most High Judge in his own right, by his own power and wisdom, and according to his own ever-existent being and his creatorhood. He is the source of the supreme law, which law is perfect and hence righteous. "The law of Jehovah is perfect, restoring the soul." (Ps. 19:7, *A.R.V.*) He is the Creator of the written Constitution which governs his visible organization on earth. "From his right hand went a fiery law for them. Yea, he loved the people; all his saints are in thy hand: and they sat down at thy feet; every one shall receive of thy words."—Deut. 33:2, 3.

[2] Jehovah needs no associate judge or justices with whom to consult or to qualify or overrule his own rulings, judgments and decisions. "Who hath directed the spirit of the LORD [Jehovah], or being his counsellor hath taught him? With whom took he counsel, and who instructed him, and taught him in the path of judgment, and taught him knowledge, and shewed to him the way of understanding?" (Isa. 40:13, 14) The answer to this challenging question is, No one. He is therefore the Supreme Court in Himself.

[3] In human or worldly processes of law the nation's supreme court is the tribunal of last appeal in most cases; it is the court of last resort. Decisions of such court may appear to have infallibility and to be beyond recall, yet such human supreme court is not infallible. It makes mistakes, and at times reverses itself. Heaven's Supreme Court is infallible; its decisions are unchangeable. Rightly, it is the court of first appeal. To go aright and to be guided in the way of divine approval and of life in peace and prosperity all creatures should appeal first to Its decisions and abide by them. "Let us hear the conclusion of the whole matter: Fear God, and keep his commandments: for this is the whole duty of man. For God shall bring every work into judgment, with every secret thing, whether it be good, or whether it be evil."—Eccl. 12:13, 14.

[4] Jehovah God created and took into association with himself another judge, but not of equal power and authority with himself. That Associate Judge is a just and perfect one, God's beloved and only begotten Son. Such action was only after God's supreme law had been put in issue throughout the universe. The appointment of such Associate Judge was only after the Son of God had proved himself inflexibly loyal and obedient to the law and judgments of the universal Supreme Judge. The Great Judge sent his Son to earth as a man nineteen centuries ago. He sent him to this earth where the supreme law is ignored, held in contempt and continually violated by imperfect, sinful humankind. With few exceptions, the whole race lies under the power of the wicked first violator of divine law, namely, Satan the Devil. In the midst of this world of lawbreakers the One whom Jehovah would appoint to be his Associate Justice and to execute his judgments toward law violators must be tested as to perfect keeping of God's commandments. He must put God's law first and must obey it rather than laws and practices which are popular among sinful men. To prove his unbreakable devotion to God's righteous standard and judgments the Son must never turn aside from doing his Father's will, even under the hate, reproach, and violent oppositions of those who despise God's law and word.

[5] By thus keeping integrity under test the Son would prove himself trustworthy and reliable, both to God and to all other creatures. To him God would confidently entrust the heavenly judgeship with Him-

1. By virtue of what is Jehovah the Supreme Judge, and, as such, of what is he the source and creator?
2. Why does Jehovah need no associate in judgeship, and what is he in himself?
3. Why should Heaven's Supreme Court be man's court of first appeal?
4. Whom did Jehovah take into association with himself as judge, and after meeting what requirements and qualifications?
5. By keeping integrity under test, what did the Son of God prove respecting himself as to judgeship, and how did God reward him?

The Watchtower, July 1, 1943, p. 195.

the Bible, nor could it be the divinely guided interpreter of that inspired Word.

[31] The claim of any individual or religious organization to be the interpreter of God's sacred Word is false and misleading. No creature or organization on earth can truly presume to sit as the supreme tribunal of interpretation of the Holy Bible. Jehovah God, the Supreme Judge, has set up no such supreme court of interpretation upon our planet. His Associate Judge, Christ Jesus, has appointed no so-called "vicar" or "vicegerent" to act for him as interpreter to His church. In ancient time the faithful Hebrew Joseph said: "Do not interpretations belong to God?" When called before Pharaoh of Egypt to give an interpretation he said: "It is not in me: God shall give Pharaoh an answer of peace." (Gen. 40:8; 41:16) Centuries thereafter the apostle Peter related how God caused the fulfillment of prophecy to take place respecting Christ Jesus and how thereby God gave the interpretation of the prophecy. Then the apostle Peter added: "We have also a more sure word of prophecy; whereunto ye do well that ye take heed, as unto a light that shineth in a dark place, until the day dawn, and the day star arise in your hearts: knowing this first, that no prophecy of the scripture is of any private interpretation. For the prophecy came not in old time by the will of man: but holy men of God spake as they were moved by the holy [spirit]."—2 Pet. 1:19-21. (See also Acts 15:5-18.)

[32] Jehovah God is therefore the only Supreme Court of interpretation of His inspired Word. Regarding God's exclusive place Christ Jesus his Son said in the prophecy concerning the end of the world and the time of the final war of Armageddon: "Heaven and earth shall pass away: but my words shall not pass away. But of that day and that hour knoweth no man, no, not the angels which are in heaven, NEITHER THE SON, but the Father." (Mark 13:31,32) The heavenly Father chose to call into his service his beloved Son as his divinely inspired Interpreter of the whole Word of God. He foretold his Son acting in such capacity. In the prophetic drama of Job God used Job to portray how the faithful remnant today of the Christian church would suffer great affliction, reproach and persecution at the hands of the Devil and his religious dupes on earth. In the drama God then raised up the young man Elihu. God inspired Elihu to utter a prophecy concerning the end of the world, the time when Jehovah's witnesses would be hated of all nations and would be in great affliction and in need of enlightenment on the Bible. "Yea, his soul draweth near unto the grave, and his life to the destroyers. If there be a messenger with him, an interpreter, one among a thousand, to shew unto man his uprightness: then he is gracious unto him, and saith, Deliver him from going down to the pit: I have found a ransom." (Job 33:22-24) That messenger and interpreter and ransom is Christ Jesus, Jehovah's Judge at the temple.

MANNER OF INTERPRETATION

[33] The Scriptures prophesied that Jehovah's Messenger, Interpreter and Judge would come to the spiritual temple of God. Many facts in fulfillment of prophecy prove that he came thither in A.D. 1918, spring. (See Malachi 3:1-4; Revelation 11:18,19.) Malachi's prophecy shows that Christ Jesus would sit as a refiner of silver, that is, of the Word of God. Not that the written Word of God is impure, but that those seeking to understand God's Word had unwittingly commingled so many impurities of religion with their beliefs. Therefore those fully consecrated to God and dedicated to his service needed purification from all soils and taints of religion. Such defiling had attached to them from the great religious confusion that set in shortly after the death of the apostles and their faithful associates. (Acts 20:28-31; 2 Thess. 2:2-12) At Christ's coming to the temple in 1918 he gathered before him for judgment all professing Christians, because "judgment must begin at the house of God". (1 Pet. 4:17) He foretold that he would judge them by his word, which is the Word of God. This Christ Jesus does by acting as Interpreter of God's Word and making clear the meaning and message of the Bible, to magnify Jehovah's name and purpose and His Theocratic Government or Kingdom.—Isa. 42:19-21.

[34] The time of Christ's coming into his kingdom and then coming to the temple is a time for the grand fulfillment of the prophecies telling of the establishment of The Theocracy and the end of Satan's world organization. It is accordingly the time of revealing and publishing the truth, and hence the time of interpreting the prophecies. (Dan. 12:1-4) In ancient days Jehovah God used some visible channel for making known his truth and interpretations to his consecrated people. Jehovah God does not change his rule of action, and he uses a like channel at this end of the world. What is that channel or visible agency? Christ Jesus described it when giving his prophecy on the visible evidences that would mark the end of Satan's uninterrupted rule and the setting up of the Theocratic Government. Our inspired Master and Interpreter said: "Who then is a faithful and wise servant, whom his lord hath made ruler

31. What Scriptural facts show that the claim of any individual or religious organization to be the Bible interpreter is false?
32. (a) What did Jesus say as to Jehovah's exclusive place respecting interpretation? (b) Whom did Jehovah take into the interpreter service, and how did God foretell such in the prophetic drama of Job?
33. When did Jehovah's Messenger and Interpreter come to the temple, and how has he sat and acted as a refiner of silver?
34. (a) The time of Christ's coming to the temple is the time for what treatment of the truth, and what does God use for that purpose? (b) Under what prophetic expression did Jesus describe that visible agency?

The Watchtower, July 1, 1943, p. 202.

over his household, to give them meat in due season? Blessed is that servant, whom his lord when he cometh shall find so doing. Verily I say unto you, That he shall make him ruler over all his goods." (Matt. 24:45-47; see also Luke 12:42-44) Whom do the facts of our day prove to be that "faithful and wise servant"?

[35] Aside from Christ Jesus, divine prophecy foretells no individual man. In times past prophetic figures such as Elijah, Elisha, and others, were used to foreshadow a company or society of faithful, devoted servants of God, who should be Jehovah's witnesses at the end of the world, where we are at present. Likewise, the expression "faithful and wise servant" does not picture any man or individual on earth now, but means the faithful remnant of Jehovah's witnesses who are begotten of His spirit and gathered into a unity unto Him and His service. They are part of his Theocratic organization and are subject to Theocratic rule, which means, the divine will as to organization and work. They act as a unit or society, together doing Jehovah's "strange work" as he reveals it to them. (Isa. 54:13; Ps. 25:14) Such "society" is not a legal society or corporation, chartered according to the laws of some state or nation, but is a society or association formed by the Creator, Jehovah God, and composed of his spiritual remnant approved by Christ Jesus at the temple judgment. Such society, however, may use as their earthly instrumentality or servant a legal corporation, such as the Watch Tower Bible and Tract Society; and they do so, since A.D. 1884. Christ Jesus is the Chief Servant of Jehovah God, and he is the invisible or heavenly Head of the "faithful and wise servant" class.—Isa. 42:1; Matt. 12:15-21.

[36] To such remnant of faithful servants of Jehovah God Christ Jesus has entrusted all "his goods", or earthly interests of the Kingdom. This does not signify that the faithful remnant or society of Jehovah's anointed witnesses are an earthly tribunal of interpretation, delegated to interpret the Scriptures and its prophecies. No; Christ Jesus the King has not entrusted that office to them. THE SUPREME COURT STILL INTERPRETS, thank God; and Christ Jesus, the Court's official mouthpiece of interpretation, reserves to himself that office as Head of Jehovah's "faithful and wise servant" class. He merely uses the "servant" class to publish the interpretation after the Supreme Court by Christ Jesus reveals it. How does the Lord God make known the interpretation? By causing the facts to come to pass visibly which are in fulfillment of the prophecy or dark saying or misunderstood scripture. Thereafter "in due season" he calls such fulfillment or clarification of prophecy and scripture to the attention of his "faithful and wise servant" class. Thereby he makes them responsible to make known the meaning of such scriptures to all members of the household of faith and to all persons of good-will. This constitutes giving them the "meat in due season".

[37] In bygone days those now composing the "faithful and wise servant" class or remnant of Jehovah's witnesses have believed many things which were not strictly correct according to the Scriptures. They continued to hold on to such beliefs even for some time after A.D. 1918, when Christ Jesus arrived at the temple. Today they see and understand differently, with Scripture backing. Does this mean that God is the Author of confusion or that they are not of His Theocratic organization? No; Jehovah God is not the author of confusion, but is the remover of confusion from his devoted people who both pray and seek to know his truth. Although the understanding of his "servant" class has cleared up and has been corrected, yet the text of God's infallible Word has not changed and its information has been there all the time from days of old.

[38] After Jehovah's royal Associate Judge came to the temple for judgment and the purification of his people, Jehovah God used his Messenger and Interpreter to cleanse away, little by little and point by point, any misunderstanding, which misunderstanding was due to their having been in contact with religion in the past or due to not having the fulfilled facts at hand because it was not yet God's due time. Thus Jehovah by Christ Jesus continues to this day to lead them in the path of truth, and they follow the revealed decisions of the Supreme Court of Interpretation and walk on in the light. Such increase of light is in fulfillment of God's promise: "The path of the just is as the shining light, that shineth more and more unto the perfect day." (Prov. 4:18) The light continues to grow brighter, and the perfect day is at hand, as we walk on where our Guide and Interpreter leads us.—Ps. 25:9.

[39] Thus the great Supreme Interpreter magnifies now his infallible Word. Shortly, at the battle of Armageddon, Jehovah by his Associate Judge and Executioner will vindicate that Word. He will also magnify his holy name and destroy all opposing kings of this world. For that reason his faithful remnant, who are in line to be "kings and priests" with Christ Jesus, bow toward Jehovah God, who is representatively in his holy temple by Christ Jesus. Their beloved earthly companions bow with them,

35. (a) Whom does that "faithful and wise servant" picture? (b) Is a legal corporation meant, or what part does a legal corporation play therein?
36. (a) The Lord's entrusting "all his goods" to the "servant" class has what connection with interpretation of the Scriptures? (b) How does the Lord God make known the interpretation, and what responsibility thereafter falls upon the "servant" class?

37. Why does difference of understanding today from that held previously not prove God the author of confusion or prove that the remnant of Jehovah's witnesses are not of His organization?
38. How, then, do we explain Scripturally the change of understanding since the Lord's coming to the temple?
39. What is the Supreme Interpreter thereby doing respecting his Word? and for that cause what do the remnant and their faithful companions do respecting Jehovah God?

The Watchtower, July 1, 1943, p. 203.

heaven-sent messenger, his guide. The vision is a very intimate one of the Lord to his servant, but the remnant whom Ezekiel pictured are commanded to tell others of God's people about it. In obedience to this commandment the faithful have been telling others about the temple of Jehovah.

It was in the spring of 1918 that the Lord Jesus, as the representative of Jehovah, appeared at the temple, and from that time forward the glory of Jehovah has been there. "And I heard him speaking unto me out of the house; and the man stood by me." (43:6) When Ezekiel heard the Lord speaking to him the man stood by him. "The man" was the heavenly messenger, and this pictures the heavenly messengers or angels of the Lord now used by the Lord in behalf of the remnant. These angels are invisible to human eyes and are there to carry out the orders of the Lord. No doubt they first hear the instruction which the Lord issues to his remnant and then these invisible messengers pass such instruction on to the remnant. The facts show that the angels of the Lord with him at his temple have been thus rendering service unto the remnant since 1919. The Lord from his holy temple speaks: "Hear, all ye people; hearken, O earth, and all that therein is: and let the Lord God be witness against you, the Lord from his holy temple." (Mic. 1:2) The faithful remnant in 1922 began to hear and to respond: "Also I heard the voice of the Lord, saying, Whom shall I send, and who will go for us? Then said I, Here am I; send me. And he said, Go and tell this people, Hear ye indeed, but understand not; and see ye indeed, but perceive not." —Isa. 6:8, 9.

Vindication, Vol. 3, 1932, p. 250.

Chapter Three

WHO IS THE WATCHTOWER'S FAITHFUL AND WISE SERVANT?

The Watchtower teaches that Jesus Christ prophesied that a special servant of God would come in these last days to be God's "channel of communication" (see p. 27). It bases the teaching on an unusual interpretation of Matt. 24:45, which reads, "Who then is a faithful and wise servant, whom his Lord hath made ruler over his household, to give them meat in due season?" (KJV). For the Watchtower this Faithful and Wise Servant is very important, and there are a few things we should all understand:

1. This Servant was to come in these, the last days (see p. 28).
2. This Servant is not one person, but a group or "class" of individuals (see p. 28).
3. This Servant is to be God's spokesman, who alone can understand the Bible and teach Jehovah's Witnesses (see p. 29).
4. Today, this Servant is the source for the Watchtower's authority over the lives of Jehovah's Witnesses (see p. 30). In other words, this Servant "class" is absolutely essential to Jehovah's Witnesses!

The founder of the Watchtower Society was Charles Taze Russell. Years ago, many believed that he alone was the Faithful and Wise Servant. Today, the Watchtower teaches that Russell never claimed to be the Faithful and Wise Servant himself, but that he believed this Servant was a "class of people" (see pp. 31 & 32). Yet, when we check the writings of Russell, we find that although he originally taught that the Faithful and Wise Servant was a class, some years later he changed his mind. He came to believe and teach that he alone was the Faithful and Wise Servant. One of many examples is found in *The Watchtower*, where Russell said:

> . . . The Lord at the time indicated would specially use one member of his church as the channel or instrument through which he would send the appropriate messages. . . . (See p. 33.)

Upon his death, *The Watchtower* claimed:

> Thousands of the readers of Pastor Russell's writings believe that he filled the office of "that faithful and wise servant." . . . His modesty and humility precluded him from *openly* claiming this title, *but he admitted as much in private conversation.* (See p. 34, italics mine.)

The Watchtower leaders have gone to great lengths to cover up the fact that Russell did claim to be the Faithful and Wise Servant. After all, if Jehovah's Witnesses find this out, they would realize the Watchtower has deceived them. Why do you think the Watchtower is doing this?

with Jehovah's people helps him to understand that Jehovah has, not only a heavenly, but also an earthly, visible organization of people doing his will. Jesus foretold that among his people there would be a "faithful and discreet slave" class who would be providing the spiritual food to God's family of devoted servants on earth, acting as his channel of communication and overseeing the carrying out of the Kingdom interests world wide. (Matt. 24:45-47) These anointed overseers serve as though being guided in their activities by the right hand of Christ. They take the same viewpoint as Jesus had when he said to Jehovah, "Let, not my will, but yours take place." (Luke 22:42) To illustrate the harmony that would prevail in Jehovah's organization, Jesus likened it, in John 15:1-10, to a vine with branches. Jehovah is the Great Cultivator, Jesus is the vine and those coming into spiritual union with him are the branches. Clearly this necessitates a recognition of Jehovah's organization in the earth today. This vine is a productive one bearing fruit that will last through Armageddon.—Heb. 13: 7, 17.

15 What kind of fruit is it that those attached to the vine must bear in order to have God's favor and to avoid being pruned off as unproductive sprouts? Actually the Scriptures mention two kinds of fruitage that a Christian would endeavor to cultivate. One is the fruitage of the spirit, including love, joy, peace, long-suffering, kindness, goodness, faith, mildness and self-control. (Gal. 5:22, 23) To stay in harmony with Christ and to be pleasing to Jehovah, these qualities must be produced. But we want to see such fruitage, not only in ourselves, but also in others. Those who are disciples of Christ understand that it is Jehovah's will that they make disciples of others also. As Proverbs 11:30 says, "The fruitage of the righteous one is a tree of life, and he that is winning souls is wise." This was the work to which Paul and the early Christians devoted themselves. Paul wrote to the Romans (1:13) that he hoped to come to minister among them that he 'might acquire some fruitage also among them even as among the rest of the nations.' By this he referred to Kingdom fruitage or Christian disciples. Each one who dedicates himself to Jehovah has a responsibility in this regard to endeavor to acquire fruitage by discipling people of the nations.

16 Paul felt so strongly about this responsibility, that he said: "If, now, I am declaring the good news, it is no reason for me to boast, for necessity is laid upon me. Really, woe is me if I did not declare the good news!" (1 Cor. 9:16) This work is not one we do just in our own strength, but we can be assured of the assistance of Jehovah's spirit as long as we prepare and do our part. It is Jehovah who brings the fruitage and the increase as a result of the activities of his servants throughout the earth. Each one who dedicates himself to Jehovah has a serious responsibility before his Creator. As Ezekiel 33: 8 says, if "you actually do not speak out to warn the wicked one from his way, he himself as a wicked one will die in his own error, but his blood I shall ask back at your own hand." How much happier a course to share actively in giving the warning and as a result have the joy of rescuing many honest-hearted ones for life in Jehovah's paradisaic new system! To such ones Jesus declared: "I say, then, to you, Everyone that confesses union with me before men, the Son of man will

15. What good fruits should all Christians endeavor to produce?

16. How do the Scriptures point out a Christian's responsibility and the wise course to follow?

The Watchtower, Jan. 15, 1969, p. 51.

hardships can be borne. Peter told fellow believers: "Beloved ones, do not be puzzled at the burning among you, which is happening to you for a trial, as though a strange thing were befalling you. On the contrary, go on rejoicing forasmuch as you are sharers in the sufferings of the Christ."—1 Pet. 4:12, 13.

Jehovah and his "messenger of the covenant," Jesus Christ, came to inspect the spiritual temple in 1918 C.E. Judgment then began with the "house of God" and a period of refining and cleansing commenced. (Mal. 3:1-3; 1 Pet. 4:17) Something else also occurred. Men manifesting the marks of an "evil slave" came forward and figuratively began 'beating' their fellow slaves. Jesus Christ had foretold how such ones would be dealt with. At the same time he showed that a "faithful and discreet slave" class would be in evidence, dispensing spiritual food.—Matt. 24:45-51.

The identity of the "faithful and discreet slave," or "faithful and wise servant" (*King James Version*), was a matter of quite some concern back in those years. Much earlier, in 1881, C. T. Russell wrote: "We believe that every member of this body of Christ is engaged in the blessed work, either directly or indirectly, of giving meat in due season to the household of faith. 'Who then is that *faithful* and *wise servant* whom his Lord hath made ruler over his household,' to give them meat in due season? Is it not that 'little flock' of consecrated servants who are *faithfully* carrying out their consecration vows—the body of Christ—and is not the whole body individually and collectively, giving the meat in due season to the household of faith—the great company of believers?"

So it was understood that the "servant" God used to dispense spiritual food was a class. With the passing of time, however, the idea adopted by many was that C. T. Russell himself was the "faithful and wise servant." This led some into the snare of creature worship. They felt that all the truth God saw fit to reveal to his people had been presented through Brother Russell, that nothing more could be brought forth. Annie Poggensee writes: "This caused a great sifting out of those who chose to stay back with Russell's works." In February 1927 this erroneous thought that Russell himself was the "faithful and wise servant" was cleared up.

Shortly after Brother Rutherford became president of the Watch Tower Society, a real conspiracy developed. The seed of rebellion was planted and then the trouble spread, as explained below.

C. T. Russell had seen the need to send someone from headquarters to Britain to strengthen the Bible Students there after the outbreak of World War I.

1975 Yearbook of Jehovah's Witnesses, p. 88.

can always find excuses, plausible reasons for not accepting the accountability that belief will bring upon him. As the apostle Paul well said: "Faith is not a possession of all people." (2 Thess. 3:2) But the Beroeans had the will to believe. They considered what they heard with a receptive frame of mind. As a result, "many of them became believers, and so did not a few of the reputable Greek women and of the men."—Acts 17:12.

Jesus' disciples wrote many letters to Christian congregations, to persons who were already in "the way of the truth." (2 Pet. 2:2) But nowhere do we read that those brothers first, in a skeptical frame of mind, checked the Scriptures to make certain that those letters had Scriptural backing, that the writers really knew what they were talking about.

OUR VIEW OF THE "SLAVE"

We can benefit from this consideration. If we have once established what instrument God is using as his "slave" to dispense spiritual food to his people, surely Jehovah is not pleased if we receive that food as though it might contain something harmful. We should have confidence in the channel God is using. At the Brooklyn headquarters from which the Bible publications of Jehovah's Witnesses emanate there are more mature Christian elders, both of the "remnant" and of the "other sheep," than anywhere else upon earth.

True, the brothers preparing these publications are not infallible. Their writings are not inspired as are those of Paul and the other Bible writers. (2 Tim. 3:16) And so, at times, it has been necessary, as understanding became clearer, to correct views. (Prov. 4:18) However, this has resulted in a continual refining of the body of Bible-based truth to which Jehovah's Witnesses subscribe. Over the years, as adjustments have been made to that body of truth, it has become ever more wonderful and applicable to our lives in these "last days." Bible commentators of Christendom are not inspired either. Despite their claims to great knowledge, they have failed to highlight even basic Bible truths —such as the coming Paradise earth, the importance of God's name, and the condition of the dead.

Rather, the record that the "faithful and discreet slave" organization has made for the past more than 100 years forces us to the conclusion that Peter expressed when Jesus asked if his apostles also wanted to leave him, namely, "Whom shall we go away to?" (John 6:66-69) No question about it. We all need help to understand the Bible, and we cannot find the Scriptural guidance we need outside the "faithful and discreet slave" organization.

THE SCYTHIAN

WHEN stressing that fleshly distinctions do not affect a Christian's standing as a member of Christ's body, the apostle Paul wrote: "There is neither Greek nor Jew, circumcision nor uncircumcision, foreigner, Scythian, slave, freeman, but Christ is all things and in all." (Col. 3:11) The inclusion of the Scythians is noteworthy, as these fierce, nomadic people were regarded as the worst of barbarians. However, through the power exerted by God's holy spirit, even they could put on a Christlike personality, discarding their former ways. (Col. 3:9, 10) How powerful is the spirit of God!

The Watchtower, Feb. 15, 1981, p. 19.

INFORMANT

NOVEMBER, 1943 "More than conquerors through him that loved us."—Rom. 8: 37 BROOKLYN, N. Y.

"Trust Your Proved Faithful Brethren"

Keep in Line with Organization

Faithfulness Required

At this time it seems well to consider the blessings that the Lord has poured upon His people during the past year, and particularly to do so in the light of the slogan for this month: "Trust your proved faithful brethren." How do we show that we trust our faithful brethren? Why should we trust them? What blessings have resulted from applying this Theocratic precept?

We show that we trust our faithful brethren when we send contributions to the Society; when we engage in the house-to-house work; when we make back-calls and conduct book studies; when we participate in the magazine work; and when we carry on all these activities according to organization instructions. We show that we trust our faithful brethren by enrolling as pioneers; by accepting appointments such as servants in a company and as special pioneers; and by faithfully discharging the obligations of such appointments. During November we are going to manifest our trust in our faithful brethren by pushing the work with *"The Truth Shall Make You Free"* and *Freedom in the New World,* on a contribution of 25c, in united activity with our faithful brethren. Yes, we will accept any and all of these provisions as coming from the Lord through His "faithful and wise servant", whom we trust because it is the Lord's choice.

These service requirements are not advocated for any personal reward, but, like Jephthah of old, your faithful brethren rejoice to have a share in the vindication of Jehovah's name and to see Him gain the victory, and they want to see their brethren share in that victory. Our faithful brethren 'pay their vows' unto Jehovah; for they not only preach activity in the field and the giving of one's all, but they practice what they preach, and by such "fruits" we know them.

What blessings have resulted from trusting our faithful brethren whom the Lord has appointed to direct the work in the earth?

Informant, Nov. 1943.

merely entertain themselves by reading it as sacred literature. Bible study classes apart from the Sunday Schools and churches of Christendom were formed and progressed in the understanding of the fundamental truths of the Sacred Scriptures. The sincere unselfish ones among these Bible students were eager to share these vital portions of spiritual food with others. They had the faithful spirit of the "slave" appointed to give the "domestics" the needed spiritual "food at the proper time." They were "discreet" in discerning that it was then the right and proper time and what were the best means for serving the food. They endeavored to serve it.

30 A "ransom for all" was one of those basic doctrines of the Bible, and a great danger began to loom up that this vital dish on the spiritual table of God-fearing persons would be taken away by the devotees of higher criticism and the evolution theory. At what can now be appreciated as "the proper time" there appeared an uncompromising champion of Christ's "ransom for all." It was in the form of a brand-new magazine for Bible lovers, *Zion's Watch Tower and Herald of Christ's Presence,* its first issue being that of July, 1879, with an initial edition of 6,000 copies. Its editor and publisher was a member of the Pittsburgh, Pennsylvania, Bible study group, namely, Charles Taze Russell. This studious Christian took note of Jesus' illustration of the "faithful and wise servant" (Matthew 24:45, *Authorized Version*) and published his understanding of it in the *Watch Tower* issue of November, 1881, page 5. In the fourth- and fifth-last paragraphs of the article "In the Vineyard," he said:

> We believe that every member of this body of Christ is engaged in the blessed work, either directly or indirectly, of giving meat in due season to the household of faith. "Who then is that *faithful* and *wise servant* whom his Lord hath made ruler over his household," to give them meat in due season? Is it not that "little flock" of consecrated servants who are *faithfully* carrying out their con-

30. (a) What danger then existed with regard to the doctrine of a "ransom for all," but what champion thereof was raised up at the "proper time"? (b) What did the editor of the *Watch Tower* publish about the "faithful and wise servant" back in 1881?

God's Kingdom of a Thousand Years Has Approached, p. 345.

secration vows—the body of Christ—and is not the whole body individually and collectively, giving the meat in due season to the household of faith—the great company of believers?

Blessed is that servant (the whole body of Christ) whom his Lord when he has come (Gr. *elthon*) shall find so doing. "Verily, I say unto you, that he shall make him ruler over all his goods." "He shall inherit all things."

[31] From this it is clearly seen that the editor and publisher of *Zion's Watch Tower* disavowed any claim to being individually, in his person, that "faithful and wise servant." He never did claim to be such.* However, he did continue to edit the *Watch Tower* magazine down to the day of his death on October 31, 1916. He organized Zion's Watch Tower Tract Society in the year 1881 and got it incorporated under State of Pennsylvania law in December, 1884. He also authored and published the six volumes of *Studies in the Scriptures* during the years 1886-1904, as well as published many booklets on Bible themes and engineered the world-famous Photo-Drama of Creation, which began to be shown in January of 1914 and was thereafter displayed around the earth. He delivered innumerable public lectures all around the globe. His death occurred during his last public lecture tour across the United States of America. It cannot be successfully disputed that, till his death in 1916, he lovingly served as a part of the "faithful and discreet slave" class in giving to the Master's domestics "their food at the proper time."

[32] Since the "slave" of Jesus' illustration is not just one Christian man but is the anointed congregation of Christ's disciples, the "faithful and discreet slave" class continued to serve on after the death of C. T. Russell. However, the sense of appreciation and indebtedness toward Russell moved many of his associates to view him as the fulfillment of the "faithful

* See the book *The Battle of Armageddon,* published in 1897, page 613, under the heading "Dispensing of Food to the Household.—Matt. 24:45-51; Luke 12:42-46."

31. (a) What must be said as to whether C. T. Russell claimed to be the "faithful and wise servant"? (b) What record proves that he served as a faithful part of that "servant" class?
32. After Russell's death, how did a sectarian trend toward him develop, but when was this halted, and how?

God's Kingdom of a Thousand Years Has Approached, p. 346.

quiet coming, unostentatious, unknown, without heralds or any commotion likely to disturb. The breaking up of the strong man's house—the breaking up of present institutions, civil, religious, political, financial—is already under way, just as the knocking for his servants is in process. The entire social structure is under control of the new Prince. He is marshaling his forces, and will cause even the wrath of man to praise him and to work out his purposes in the overthrow of every known institution built upon selfishness Great will be the fall thereof—"a time of trouble such as was not since there was a nation"; but upon the ruins the King of kings and Lord of lords will rear the grand Kingdom of the Lord, for which all who are his already pray, "Thy Kingdom come," and which, when it shall come to be instituted by the Lord, will be indeed the "desire of all nations."—Haggai 2:7.

"IN SUCH AN HOUR AS YE THINK NOT."

The essence of this lesson is summed up in the 40th verse, "Be ye also ready; for in an hour ye think not the Son of man cometh." No one will be aware of the hour of the Son of man's coming; it is not a matter that is left in such a form as to be speculated upon in advance. His knock will be the first intimation of his presence. And so it has been fulfilled: none of us knew in advance when the Lord's coming would take place; it was after it had occurred that we heard the knock—his voice through the prophets of the Old Testament, declaring to us that we are already in the harvest time and in the days of the presence of the Son of man. Here we have fulfilled the words of the Lord in Matthew 24:37, "As the days of Noah were, so shall also the *parousia* [presence] of the Son of man be." The text shows that the thought is that as the world was ignorant of coming events in Noah's days, and, being ignorant, was eating and drinking and planting and building, so it will be in the days of the presence of the Son of man: the world will be ignorant of the fact of his presence, and the ordinary affairs of life will be progressing as usual. Only "ye brethren" who hear the knock will discern the presence and get the blessing.

Peter inquired whether or not this parable was applicable only to the twelve apostles, or to all those who were disciples in a general sense. Our Lord measurably ignored the question in his reply, "Who then is the faithful and wise steward whom his lord shall set over his household, to give them their portion of food in due season?" The implication seems to be that when the right time should come for understanding the parable, it would be clearly set forth: that at the time of the parable's fulfilment the Lord would appoint a servant in the household to bring these matters to the attention of all the servants, and that certain responsibilities would rest upon such a one respecting the dispatch of his duties. If faithfully performed a great blessing would be his reward, and if unfaithful to his charge severe penalties would be inflicted. The implication would be also that if faithful the servant would be continued in his service, and if unfaithful he would be dismissed and another take the position and its responsibilities.

"THE FAITHFUL AND THE WISE STEWARD."

We would naturally enough endeavor to interpret our Lord's words as signifying a composite steward—that is that a certain number or class of brethren together would constitute the steward of this parable. In endeavoring to make such an interpretation we are met with several difficulties, however.

(1) To suppose such a class in the Church would be to recognize what is elsewhere denied—to recognize a clerical or authoritative class as distinct and separate from the remainder of the Church, because this steward is to dispense the meat in due season to the household, to the fellow-servants. The Church of Christ, we hold, is not composed of clergy and laity, but "ye are all one in Christ Jesus, and one is your Master, even Christ." There would be no violation of principle, however, in supposing that the Lord at the time indicated would specially use one member of his Church as the channel or instrument through which he would send the appropriate messages, spiritual nourishment appropriate at that time; because at various times in the past the Lord has used individuals in such a manner. For instance, Peter used the "keys" of the Kingdom of heaven at Pentecost, and again at the home of Cornelius, and in both places he was used as a special servant in connection with the dispensing of special truths. This did not constitute Peter a lord over the other apostles or over the Church, but merely a servant.

(2) However much we might endeavor to apply this figure to the Lord's people collectively, the fact would still remain that the various items stated would not fit to a company of individuals. For instance, in the 42nd verse, in the common version it is rendered, *that* faithful steward; the revised version, *the* faithful steward; as though a particular one were meant and the term not used indefinitely for a number. Turning to the Greek text we find that the emphasis is there also and in double form—the faithful, the wise steward. If it were a case in which we could apply this text to Christ, there would be no difficulty, or if it were a case in which it could be applied to the whole body of Christ, there could be no difficulty, in harmonizing the one with the many members of the one body of Christ; but since the servant mentioned is to dispense food to the other members of the body, his fellow-servants, the term seems to be limited to some particular individual. However, just as we said of Peter, that he was not by reason of special use made a lord over the brethren, so we say of whoever is meant

The Watchtower, April 15, 1904, p. 125.

Paradise and made fit as a place habitable for perfect man; that man, fully restored to perfection, will inhabit the beautified earth in all the ages to come.

HIS WORK

Seeing that God has such a wonderful Plan for the blessing of mankind, Pastor Russell gave all of his power and energy to making known these great truths to the world. He never took a vacation; he worked until the day of his death.

Like other Christians he was looking for the Second Coming of Christ. Between 1872-6 he discovered that the Scriptures clearly teach that the Lord would not return in a body of flesh, but would return as a spirit being, invisible to human eyes, and that His second presence was due in the autumn of 1874. This led to the publishing of a booklet entitled, "The Object and Manner of Our Lord's Return," which had a phenomenal circulation.

Many students of the Bible throughout the United States and Canada responded to the information derived from that book, and his correspondence became voluminous. Realizing the necessity of keeping the Truth before the minds of those who had begun to investigate, in 1879 he began the publication of THE WATCH TOWER AND HERALD OF CHRIST'S PRESENCE, and was its sole Editor to the time of his death. This journal is issued semi-monthly; it never publishes advertisements, but is devoted exclusively to religious topics. Among the English speaking people in the United States, Canada and Great Britain, its semi-monthly circulation is 45,000 copies. It is also published in German, French, Swedish, Dano-Norwegian and Polish, reaching a large number of subscribers in America and Europe.

He was President of the WATCH TOWER BIBLE AND TRACT SOCIETY from its organization in 1884 until his death. He was also President of the PEOPLES PULPIT ASSOCIATION, organized in 1909, and the INTERNATIONAL BIBLE STUDENTS ASSOCIATION, incorporated in London, in 1913, both of the latter corporations being adjuncts to the WATCH TOWER BIBLE AND TRACT SOCIETY. Through these religious corporations, as well as by word of mouth, he promulgated the Gospel of Messiah's Kingdom. He was the author of the following publications, issued between the years 1881 and 1914, each having phenomenal circulation, as given below:

FOOD FOR THINKING CHRISTIANS	1,450,000
TABERNACLE SHADOWS	1,000,000
DIVINE PLAN OF THE AGES	4,817,000
THE TIME IS AT HAND	1,657,000
THY KINGDOM COME	1,578,000
BATTLE OF ARMAGEDDON	464,000
THE ATONEMENT	445,000
THE NEW CREATION	423,000
WHAT SAY THE SCRIPTURES ABOUT HELL	3,000,000

He was also the author of WHAT SAY THE SCRIPTURES ABOUT SPIRITISM, OLD THEOLOGY TRACTS, et cetera, et cetera. He was the author of the PHOTO-DRAMA OF CREATION, which had been exhibited prior to his death to more than nine million persons. He wrote and published the SCENARIO of the PHOTO-DRAMA OF CREATION, which has had a very wide circulation. His publications were translated into thirty-five different languages. At the same time he was Pastor of more than 1,200 congregations of Bible Students, in different parts of the world. These he visited and taught as often as possible.

He organized and conducted a Lecture Bureau which constantly employed seventy Bible lecturers, who traveled and delivered lectures on the Scriptures He organized and managed an auxiliary lecture bureau of seven hundred men who gave a portion of their time to lecturing on Bible teachings. Each year he wrote practically all of the copy for the BIBLE STUDENTS MONTHLY, the annual distribution of which amounted to approximately fifty million copies.

His weekly sermons were handled by a newspaper syndicate. More than 2,000 newspapers, with a combined circulation of fifteen million readers, at one time published his discourses. All told, more than 4,000 newspapers published these sermons.

The Continent, a publication whose editor often opposed Pastor Russell, once published the following significant statement concerning him:

> "His writings are said to have greater newspaper circulation every week than those of any other living man; a greater, doubtless, than the combined circulation of the writings of all the priests and preachers in North America; greater even than the work of Arthur Brisbane, Norman Hapgood, George Horace Lorimer, Dr. Frank Crane, Frederick Haskins, and a dozen other of the best known editors and syndicate writers put together."

HARVEST WORK

Pastor Russell adhered closely to the teachings of the Scriptures. He believed and taught that we are living in the time of the second presence of our Lord, and that His presence dates from 1874; that since that time we have been living in the "time of the end"—the "end of the Age," during which the Lord has been conducting His great Harvest work; that, in harmony with the Lord's own statement, this Harvest work is separating true Christians designated as "wheat," from merely professing Christians, designated as "tares," and gathering the true saints into the Kingdom of the Lord. It is here interesting to note that Jesus said, "Who then is a faithful and wise servant, whom his Lord hath made ruler over His Household, to give them meat in due season? Blessed is that servant, whom his Lord, when He cometh, shall find so doing! Verily I say unto you that He shall make him ruler over all His goods." Thousands of the readers of Pastor Russell's writings believe that he filled the office of "that faithful and wise servant," and that his great work was giving to the Household of Faith meat in due season. His modesty and humility precluded him from openly claiming this title, but he admitted as much in private conversation. For a more detailed account of his work, reference is made to THE WATCH TOWER of June 1st, 1916.

In 1910 Pastor Russell visited Palestine and Russia. He there orally delivered lectures to thousands of orthodox Jews on the regathering of Jews to Palestine. In 1911 he was one of a committee of seven who made a journey around the world and especially examined into the conditions of missionary work in Japan, China, Korea and India. On the same occasion he again visited the Jews in Palestine and Galatia, explaining to them that the prophecies teach that the Jews at an early date will again be established in Palestine. On his return to America he was given a great ovation at the New York City Hippodrome by thousands of Jews, his discourse on this occasion being published by Hebrew papers both in America and in Europe.

During the 42 years of Pastor Russell's Christian work he never directly or indirectly solicited money. No collection was ever taken at any meeting addressed by him or by any of his associates. He had faith that the Lord would supply sufficient money to carry on His work; that the work was the Lord's, and not man's. The fact that voluntary contributions were liberally made by many persons throughout the world proved that his conclusions were correct.

He devoted his private fortune entirely to the cause to which he gave his life. He received the nominal sum of $11.00 per month for his personal expenses. He died, leaving no estate whatsoever.

Thus closed the career of a most remarkable man. He was loved most by those who knew him best.

The Watchtower, Dec. 1, 1916, p. 357.

Chapter Four

WORSHIPING PASTOR RUSSELL

Did you know that for many years the Watchtower's first president, Pastor Russell, was actually worshiped by Jehovah's Witnesses? This is news to many. But if you were a Jehovah's Witness living in the 1920s, you would have been among those who worshiped him.

For many years, all Witnesses believed Russell was the special Servant sent from God to teach the Church (see p. 37). The Watchtower's history book claims:

> The insistence that Russell had been "that servant" led many to regard Russell in what actually amounted to creature worship. (See p. 38.)

The *1975 Yearbook of Jehovah's Witnesses* adds:

> . . . the idea adopted by many was that C. T. Russell himself was the "faithful and wise servant." This led some into the snare of creature worship. (See p. 39.)

Who was responsible for the teaching that Russell was this special Servant? A modern Watchtower book gives us the answer:

> This view was prominently featured in the book published in July of 1917 by People's Pulpit Association. . . . This book was called "The Finished Mystery". . . . Such a book and religious attitude tended to establish a religious sect centered around a man. (See p. 40.)

Who was responsible for establishing a religious sect around Russell? The Watchtower puts the blame squarely on the People's Pulpit Association. Who were they? We are informed

> a corporation came into legal existence February 23, 1909, and was named People's Pulpit Association. Thirty years later, in 1939, the name was changed to its present one, Watchtower Bible and Tract Society, Inc. (See p. 41.)

The People's Pulpit Association was the Watchtower Society! The Watchtower itself promoted the idolatrous worship of Pastor Russell for many years. Now they try to hide the facts. Do you believe an organization that actually worshiped a man can be God's representative? God's Word clearly condemns idolatry. The Apostle Paul might as well have been speaking of the Watchtower Society when he said in Romans 1:25: "For they exchanged the truth of God for a lie, and worshiped and served the creature rather than the Creator. . . ." *Jesus* is the Creator. He loves you.

or positive opposition. If the person holding the doubt takes himself too seriously, thinking more highly of his own importance than he should think (Romans 12: 3), or where he permits bitterness to abide in his heart, darkness is almost certain to ensue.

Agitation concerning the error in chronology has continued to increase throughout the year, and some have turned into positive opposition to that which has been written. This has resulted in some of the Lord's dear sheep becoming disturbed in mind and causing them to inquire, Why does not THE WATCH TOWER say something? Is not its silence tantamount to an admission that our chronology is wrong?

From time to time the question of publishing something in this journal has been considered. Each time the Lord has seemed to interfere, until now. Why should such be the case? Our opinion is that the Lord has permitted the delay in the reviewing of the question of chronology since the agitation was begun in order to give those who had the wrong condition of heart an opportunity to manifest themselves, and to give the others an opportunity to have their faith tested.

FAITHFULNESS IS LOYALTY

To be faithful means to be loyal. To be loyal to the Lord means to be obedient to the Lord. To abandon or repudiate the Lord's chosen instrument means to abandon or repudiate the Lord himself, upon the principle that he who rejects the servant sent by the Master thereby rejects the Master.

There is no one in present truth today who can honestly say that he received a knowledge of the divine plan from any source other than by the ministry of Brother Russell, either directly or indirectly. Through his prophet Ezekiel Jehovah foreshadowed the office of a servant, designating him as one clothed with linen, with a writer's inkhorn by his side, who was delegated to go throughout the city (Christendom) and comfort those that sighed by enlightening their minds relative to God's great plan. Be it noted that this was a favor bestowed not by man, but by the Lord himself. But in keeping with the Lord's arrangement he used a man. The man who filled that office, by the Lord's grace, was Brother Russell.

Jesus clearly indicated that during his second presence he would have amongst the church a faithful and wise servant, through whom he would give to the household of faith meat in due season. The evidence is overwhelming concerning the Lord's second presence, the time of the harvest, and that the office of "that servant" has been filled by Brother Russell. This is not man-worship by any means. It matters not who Charles T. Russell was—whether he was a doctor, a hod-carrier or a seller of shirts. St. Peter was a fisherman; St. Paul a lawyer. But these matters are immaterial. Above all, these men were the chosen vessels of the Lord. Regardless of his earthly avocation, above all, Brother Russell was the Lord's servant. Then to repudiate him and his work is equivalent to a repudiation of the Lord, upon the principle heretofore announced.

FULL TEST OF FAITH

But every one who has a desire in his heart to shine at the expense of the reputation of the Lord's chosen servant, or who meditates the building for himself of a reputation amongst men that it may be said of him that he was particularly wise — such a one is almost certain to have an opportunity to attempt to realize his desires. Every one of the consecrated who has the inclination of heart to follow such self-constituted leaders is almost certain to have an opportunity to have a full test of his faith. For this cause there arise from time to time conditions which operate as a test of the faith of God's people.

Again the test is on. This time it is on chronology. And following this lead, it will be found that the road of doubt and opposition will carry one into doubting the second presence of the Lord, the time of the harvest, the office of "that servant" and the one who filled it, the evidences of the end of the world, the inauguration of the kingdom, the nearness of the restoration of man, and finally to a repudiation of God and our Lord Jesus Christ and the blood with which we were bought.

The opening crevice for the enemy thus to blast at the Rock of Ages is now made by the raising of the question concerning the gentile times. Some thus impressed with their own wisdom begin to hold forth the argument that the gentile times began with the beginning of the reign of Nebuchadnezzar in the year 625 B. C.; hence could not end in 1914; hence the present work of the church is wrong, and the course of action should be reversed. The holding of such views blinds one to the present events, minimizes the importance of the tremendous evidences of the end of the age, causes those who have been active to cease to be witnesses for the Lord, and being thus led away by the error of the wicked one, they fall away from steadfastness.—2 Peter 3:17, 18.

With gratitude to God for what he has done for us, with supreme love for him, with a heart's sincere desire to be led by him, with humble and sincere supplication that he hold us by the hand and keep us in the light, let us come to an honest examination of the facts.

"TIMES"

The word "gentile" is a term used to distinguish the nations of earth aside from the Jews, the Jews being God's chosen people, with whom he made a covenant. The "gentile times" is a period of time during which the gentiles shall exercise imperial or kingly power over the affairs of earth. God constituted Israel his chosen people above all other peoples. (Exodus 19:6) This favor they were to enjoy provided they remained obedient to the Lord Jehovah. For their disobedience he permitted them to be punished from time to time, the punishment being inflicted by other nations. (Judges

The Watchtower, May 1, 1922, p. 132.

In course of time this view was lost sight of, and attention was focused more upon an individual man.° The view generally held, that Pastor Russell himself was the "faithful and wise servant" of Matthew 25:45-47, created considerable difficulty for some years. The insistence that Russell had been "that servant" led many to regard Russell in what amounted actually to creature worship. They believed that all the truth God had seen fit to reveal to his people had been revealed to Russell, and now nothing more could be brought forth because "that servant" was dead. This attitude caused Rutherford to root out any remnants of creature worship that might be left in the organization. For that reason he did not seek the favor of men and, because of the course many had taken in times past, he was suspicious of those who seemed to be working to curry favor with him. This attitude led to an unusual directness in dealing with his associates.

After Rutherford was elected president, it soon began to appear that there were some in the organization who were not in favor of the arrangement. A few believed that they should have been given this position and they went so far as to endeavor to wrest the administrative control from Rutherford's hands. This feeling began to develop early in 1917, within a few months after Rutherford was elected.

A SEED OF REBELLION IS PLANTED

TOM: Was this a sort of conspiracy or an "every-man-for-himself" controversy?

JOHN: The seed of rebellion seemed to germinate in one man, but soon spread and finally did develop into a real conspiracy. This is the way it started.

Pastor Russell had recognized the need for someone from the Society's headquarters to go to Britain to strengthen the brothers there after World War I broke out. He had intended sending P. S. L. Johnson, born a Jew, who had forsaken Judaism to become a Lutheran minister before he came to a knowledge of the truth. Johnson had served as a speaker for the Society and was a man of recognized ability. This brilliance finally led to his downfall.

Because of Russell's expressed wish, the committee that served before Rutherford's election sent Johnson to England for this proposed task. When he arrived in London he began to assume an authority the Society had not given him, and began to oppose the Society's policy and the Society's Branch servant in the London office. He gave talks to the brothers in England to the effect that he, Johnson, was Pastor Russell's successor, indicating that the mantle of Pastor Russell had fallen upon him just as the prophet Elijah's cloak had fallen upon Elisha.

In the weeks that followed, he tried to take complete control of the British field and make himself the most prominent one in Britain. Without authority he even attempted to dismiss certain members of the London Bethel family. The work was so disrupted and such confusion developed that the Society's Branch servant was forced to complain to Brother Rutherford, the president of the Society. Immediately Brother Rutherford appointed a commission of several prominent brothers in London, not members of the headquarters staff, to hear the facts in this case and report directly to him. The commission met and after due consideration recommended that Johnson be recalled to the United States for the good of the work in Britain.

Brother Rutherford acted upon this committee's recommendation and instructed

° *The Battle of Armageddon*, of 1897, pp. 613, 614; *The Finished Mystery*, of 1917, pp. 53, 125, 237, 416-423; *W* 1916, p. 377; *W* 1917, pp. 323, 324; *W* 1919, p. 103; *W* 1923, pp. 67, 68.

Jehovah's Witnesses in the Divine Purpose, 1959, p. 69.

hardships can be borne. Peter told fellow believers: "Beloved ones, do not be puzzled at the burning among you, which is happening to you for a trial, as though a strange thing were befalling you. On the contrary, go on rejoicing forasmuch as you are sharers in the sufferings of the Christ."—1 Pet. 4:12, 13.

Jehovah and his "messenger of the covenant," Jesus Christ, came to inspect the spiritual temple in 1918 C.E. Judgment then began with the "house of God" and a period of refining and cleansing commenced. (Mal. 3:1-3; 1 Pet. 4:17) Something else also occurred. Men manifesting the marks of an "evil slave" came forward and figuratively began 'beating' their fellow slaves. Jesus Christ had foretold how such ones would be dealt with. At the same time he showed that a "faithful and discreet slave" class would be in evidence, dispensing spiritual food.—Matt. 24:45-51.

The identity of the "faithful and discreet slave," or "faithful and wise servant" (*King James Version*), was a matter of quite some concern back in those years. Much earlier, in 1881, C. T. Russell wrote: "We believe that every member of this body of Christ is engaged in the blessed work, either directly or indirectly, of giving meat in due season to the household of faith. 'Who then is that *faithful* and *wise servant* whom his Lord hath made ruler over his household,' to give them meat in due season? Is it not that 'little flock' of consecrated servants who are *faithfully* carrying out their consecration vows—the body of Christ—and is not the whole body individually and collectively, giving the meat in due season to the household of faith—the great company of believers?"

So it was understood that the "servant" God used to dispense spiritual food was a class. With the passing of time, however, the idea adopted by many was that C. T. Russell himself was the "faithful and wise servant." This led some into the snare of creature worship. They felt that all the truth God saw fit to reveal to his people had been presented through Brother Russell, that nothing more could be brought forth. Annie Poggensee writes: "This caused a great sifting out of those who chose to stay back with Russell's works." In February 1927 this erroneous thought that Russell himself was the "faithful and wise servant" was cleared up.

Shortly after Brother Rutherford became president of the Watch Tower Society, a real conspiracy developed. The seed of rebellion was planted and then the trouble spread, as explained below.

C. T. Russell had seen the need to send someone from headquarters to Britain to strengthen the Bible Students there after the outbreak of World War I.

1975 Yearbook of Jehovah's Witnesses, p. 88.

and discreet slave." This view was prominently featured in the book published in July of 1917 by People's Pulpit Association of Brooklyn, New York. This book was called "The Finished Mystery" and furnished a commentary of the Bible books of Revelation and Ezekiel and The Song of Solomon. On its Publishers page the book was called the "Posthumous Work of Pastor Russell." Such a book and religious attitude tended to establish a religious sect centered around a man. Such a drift toward sectarianism was halted, however, by the publication early in 1927 of the articles "The Son and Servant" and "Servant—Good and Evil," in *The Watch Tower* under date of February 1 and 15, 1927. These articles showed that the "servant" of Matthew 24:45 was a composite one.—Isaiah 43:10-12.

[33] Later in the year 1927 any remaining stocks of the six volumes of *Studies in the Scriptures* by Russell and of *The Finished Mystery* were disposed of among the public. But did this leave the Lord's "domestics" or "household staff" without spiritual "food at the proper time"? Not by any means! Why not, we shall shortly see.

THE "HAPPY" SLAVE

[34] Did Jesus, in Matthew 24:45, raise the question regarding the "slave" that was appointed over his master's "domestics" to feed them and how this "slave" would prove his faithfulness and discreetness? In the very next verse (Matthew 24:46) Jesus also answers that question, saying: "Happy is that slave if his master on arriving [Greek: *elthòn*] finds him doing so." He proved his faithfulness to his master and his prudence by continuing to do what his master appointed him to do until his return, namely, "to give [the domestics] their food at the proper time." This was to result in great happiness for the "slave" at his master's return.

---

33. Did disposal of remaining stocks of Russell's books and of *The Finished Mystery* leave Christ's "domestics" with no "food"?
34. Who raised the question regarding the "faithful and discreet slave," and who answered it. and how?

God's Kingdom of a Thousand Years Has Approached, 1973, p. 347.

the chronological proof and the physical facts indicating that the "Gentile times" were due to end in the fall of 1914.

2 But to undertake an all-out campaign of world-wide proportions the Society's twenty-year-old four-story "Bible House" headquarters in Allegheny (Pittsburgh) were inadequate and not strategically located for world shipping and communication. So in 1908 J. F. Rutherford, who by this time had become the Society's legal counselor and also a pilgrim traveling from city to city to give public lectures, and other Society representatives were sent to Brooklyn, New York, to negotiate the purchase of more desirable quarters. They obtained the old "Plymouth Bethel," 13-17 Hicks St., Brooklyn, and the old Beecher home located at 124 Columbia Heights. To hold this new property in New York state satisfactorily and to do business within this state as a religious body it was necessary to form another corporation. Such a corporation came into legal existence February 23, 1909, and was named Peoples Pulpit Association. Thirty years later, in 1939, the name was changed to its present one, Watchtower Bible and Tract Society, Inc.

3 From 1909 onward a monthly tract called "Peoples Pulpit" and then later "The Bible Students Monthly" was widely distributed by the millions, warning the Gentiles of the fateful year 1914. And so for a number of years the society of witnesses became known as the International Bible Students Association, and, in 1914, the same identical work was organized under an association incorporated under the laws of Great Britain, under the name and style of International Bible Students Association.

4 The Watch Tower Society now in the Brooklyn headquarters was equipped to keep abreast with the gigantic publishing work that was then under way. The years from 1909 to 1914 saw an ever-increasing output of tracts, pamphlets and bound volumes running into the millions. The 1914 warning work was augmented by the organizing of an international newspaper syndicate service that sent Russell's sermon for each week to approximately three thousand newspapers in the United States, Canada and Europe. It is estimated that ten million people were reached each week in this manner.

5 The public platform was also geared to an expanded witness for the nearing year of 1914. In the year 1911 alone, it is reported, 12,113 public and semipublic lectures were given

Qualified to Be Ministers, 1955, p. 309.

Chapter Five

C. T. RUSSELL *V.* THE ORGANIZATION

In discussions with Jehovah's Witnesses, one topic nearly always comes up. They almost always try to prove that God has an organization. Just what do they mean by "organization"? The Watchtower Society says:

> Jehovah's organization is theocratic. This means that it is ruled by the direct administration of God, and all who desire to serve in association with the organization must respect the theocratic arrangement of things. (See p. 44.)

The *earthly* leaders of this organization are called the "Governing Body." *The Watchtower* says:

> . . . recognition of that governing body and its place in God's theocratic arrangement of things is necessary for submission to the headship of God's Son. (See p. 45.)

In light of these Watchtower claims, we will look at what the first Watchtower leader, Charles T. Russell, had to say about an organization. Did he believe a governing body should set rules for our lives? We think you will find his thoughts most interesting. Russell warned:

> Beware of "organization." It is wholly unnecessary. The Bible rules will be the only rules you will need. Do not seek to bind others' consciences, and do not permit others to bind yours. Believe and obey so far as you can understand God's Word today. . . . (See p. 46.)

He also said:

> . . . it is plain that the forming of a visible organization of such gathered out ones would be *out of harmony* with the spirit of the divine plan. . . . (See p. 47, italics mine.)

Therefore, for Russell, the Watchtower's founder, God's Church should *not* be an organization. Ironically, since Russell refused to recognize a central governing body of human leaders, he would certainly be kicked out of the Jehovah's Witnesses today! Yes, Charles Russell would not qualify as a Christian in the eyes of today's Watchtower leaders. But Russell would not understand their reasoning. He declared:

> There is no *organization* to-day clothed with such divine authority to imperiously command mankind . . . though we are well aware that many of them in theory claim that they *ought* to be permitted to do so. . . . (See p. 48.)

So we see a great battle between the thinking of present-day Watchtower leaders and their founder.

Early in his career Russell was asked this question:

> Would not an earnest, aggressive organization (or sect), built upon scriptural lines, be the best means of spreading and publishing the *real* Good Tidings?

He answered:

> The natural man can see that a visibly organized body, with a definite purpose, is a thing of more or less power. . . . But the natural man cannot understand how a company of people, with no organization which they can see, is ever going to accomplish anything. (See p. 49.)

We have quoted Russell, not to show he was right in his theology, for we believe he also was a false prophet. But we wish to illustrate how the Watchtower's first president would argue that today's Watchtower organization has no right to even exist! Would it not be well for Watchtower leaders to read the advice of Jesus who dealt with the pride of His own disciples. He said, "If any one wants to be first, he shall be last of all, and servant of all" (Mark 9:35).

recognize, and how do the Scriptures show this? (b) What attitude should we all have toward this organization?

Study 95

THEOCRATIC SOCIETY IN OPERATION

1 Jehovah's organization is theocratic. That means that it is ruled by the direct administration of God, and all who desire to serve in association with the organization must respect the theocratic arrangement of things. They must submit to Jehovah God as the Universal Sovereign and they ought to give full cooperation to those whom he has put in positions of responsibility. It is vital that each one appreciate the position occupied by Jesus Christ as Head of the Christian congregation, as the Ransomer and now as King empowered by God. (Acts 4:12; Rev. 19:16) So, too, they must show proper regard for those on earth who have been appointed by holy spirit as overseers of God's people, and, even within the family, they must work in harmony with the principle of theocratic headship.—Acts 20:28; 1 Cor. 11:3.

2 The modern-day organization of Jehovah's witnesses functions in harmony with the pattern found in the early Christian congregation. In accord with the example set by Jesus Christ and his apostles, they look to the Bible as the inspired word of God. In order to govern his congregation on earth, Jehovah caused the Bible to be written. Although written mostly by men, it is not from a visible source, but is inspired from heaven. Its instructions are theocratic, from God to his creatures. It applies earth-wide and takes precedence over anything humans may say. (1 Pet. 1:24, 25; 2 Pet. 1:21) The Creator knows how to operate his organization and what are the best procedures for it to employ.

3 At the time of Pentecost, 33 C.E., Jesus Christ, to whom his disciples looked as their master, appointed his spirit-anointed followers as a class as "the faithful and discreet slave," responsible to provide spiritually for the individual members of the household of faith. (Matt. 24:45-47, *NW*) A few were moved by holy spirit to write portions of the Christian Greek Scriptures. Others were shepherds and teachers; all were active ministers of God who shared in various ways, not only in preaching to unbelievers but in building up their fellow Christians.—Eph. 4:16.

4 That "faithful and discreet slave" is still with us today, being made up of all those of the remnant of Christ's

Qualified to Be Ministers, 1967, p. 380.

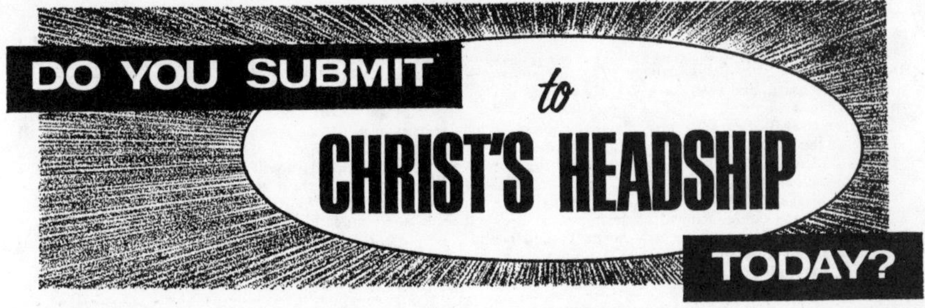
DO YOU SUBMIT
to
CHRIST'S HEADSHIP
TODAY?

IN THE first century of our Common Era Jesus Christ gave the apostle John a divine revelation. In it he revealed his active headship over Christian congregations at that time. The revelation showed that Christ was personally carrying on inspection of conditions within the congregations. He was concerned as to their spiritual health, their Christian works and activity. But he was not only inspecting. He was prepared to take appropriate *action* according to what his inspection revealed concerning the response to his counsel.—Revelation chapters 1 to 3; see also *The Watchtower* of December 15, 1971, page 751.

Christ Jesus continues to exercise full headship of the true Christian congregation earth wide today. And, just as he did back then, he uses earthly agencies to express that headship. The first-century Christian congregation had a governing body composed of apostles and elders at Jerusalem. A similar body of anointed Christians functions now. This governing body is the administrative part of a "faithful and discreet slave" or "steward" class concerning which Jesus promised: "His master . . . will appoint him over all his belongings." (Matt. 24:45-47; Luke 12:42-44) So, recognition of that governing body and its place in God's theocratic arrangement of things is necessary for submission to the headship of God's Son.

LOCAL BODIES OF ELDERS IN HARMONY

As was true in the first century, however, each congregation has its local body of elders. Of such men, the apostle Paul wrote Christians in his day: "Be obedient to those who are taking the lead among you and be submissive, for they are keeping watch over your souls as those who will render an account." (Heb. 13:17) Or, rendering the Greek word used by the apostle more literally, they should be obeying the ones "governing" them. (See *Kingdom Interlinear Translation.*) Does this mean that each local body of elders formed a separate governing body operating independently of the governing body of the 'faithful and discreet steward' class?

No, that could not be. Why not? Because that would mean disconnecting themselves from the headship of Christ Jesus. The connection of all those composing the Christian congregation with their Head, Christ Jesus, is likened to the ways the members of a human body are joined to the head. Of Jesus, the apostle writes: "From him all the body, by being harmoniously joined together and being made to cooperate through every joint that gives what is needed, according to the functioning of each respective member in due measure, makes for the growth of the body for the building up of itself in love." (Eph. 4:16) So, the Head, Christ Jesus, has various arrangements for 'joining' the individual members of the congregation to

The Watchtower, Dec. 15, 1972, p. 755.

not, Daniel, for from the first day that thou didst *set thine heart* to understand, and *to chasten thyself before thy God*, thy words were heard, and I am come *for thy words*."—Dan. 10: 2, 3, 10–12.

Even so shall it ever be with all the beloved of the Lord: at the beginning of our supplications God begins to set in operation the influences and to shape the circumstances which are designed to work out the intended blessing for us—if we faint not, but continue instant in prayer, thereby evincing our continued earnestness of desire, and if we confess our sins, and set our hearts to understand, and chasten ourselves before him. How many prayers are not heard or are hindered because the one who asks does not first purify himself of evil in his own heart? "Ye ask, and receive not, because ye ask amiss, that ye may consume it upon your lusts;" *i. e.*, you ask selfishly and without regard to the will of God. (Jas. 4: 3.) But to the chastened and sanctified comes the promise—"Before they call [reading the desire of the heart even before it finds expression in words] I will answer [will begin so to shape events as to bring the answer soon or later]; and while they are yet speaking I will hear." (Isa. 65: 23, 24.) While this is in connection with a prophecy relating to the Lord's people in the Millennial age, it nevertheless is true of all his faithful ones of this age. Praise the Lord for all his loving kindness to even the least of his lowly children!

CONCERNING PROFITABLE MEETINGS.

WE have received a number of requests from friends of the truth for advice as to the most profitable methods of conducting meetings. One Brother writes:

"A few brethren who have been reading DAWN express their willingness to meet somewhere to study in consecutive order, and I ask suggestions for a plan suited to beginners. Pray for us, that we may commence this study in the right way, and be the recipients of many blessings.

"Yours in the faith, J. W. MCLANE."

Another Brother recently removed to a new neighborhood says:

"I find in this locality a fine field for labor. Several here to whom I have given tracts already manifest interest. I have conversed freely with them on Bible subjects, and have their promise to attend meetings at my house. So if you can aid me by suggestions I will be thankful.

"I am, dear brother, yours in the service of the Master, "JOSHUA L. GREEN."

Another Brother writes:—

"We have a number of persons here who wish to assemble themselves together for worship. We would be pleased to have some instructions from you as to how to go about it.

"I hope you can give us some way which will be satisfactory. Some of us have left the churches and are now free from all precepts of men. To speak for myself, I left the Presbyterian church.

"Yours in Christ, C. C. FLEMING."

We are glad to note the increasing desire for the study of God's plan of the ages; and also to see that the importance of method and order are recognized in this. We give our advice as follows:—

(1) You would best first re-read some things already written which bear upon this subject—in our issues of May 1, '93, page 131; Sept. '93, page 259; Oct. 15, '93, page 307; Mar. 1, '94, page 73; April 1, '95, page 78; May 1. '95, page 109.

(2) Beware of "organization." It is wholly unnecessary. The Bible rules will be the only rules you will need. Do not seek to bind others' consciences, and do not permit others to bind yours. Believe and obey so far as you can understand God's Word to-day, and so continue growing in grace and knowledge and love day by day.

(3) The Bible instructs you whom to fellowship as "brethren;"—only believers who are seeking to walk, not after the flesh, but after the spirit. Not believers of any and every thing, but believers of the Gospel record—that mankind is *fallen* into sin and its penalty, death, and that only in Christ is there salvation, "through faith in his blood" "shed for the remission of sins", as "a *ransom* [a corresponding price] for all." Any who merely believe in Christ as a noble and good person, a grand example of righteous living, etc., may be agreeable as neighbors or business acquaintances, but they are not "believers," and hence are not "brethren," any more than are Jews, Mohammedans, Infidels, publicans and sinners—for practically these also so acknowledge him.

(4) You come together, then, as God's children, bought back from sin and death with the great price, and resolved henceforth to live not unto yourselves, but unto him who died for you. (2 Cor. 5: 15.) Your meetings should have certain objects in view, viz:—

(a) Worship, praise and prayer.

(b) Mutual helpfulness in waging victorious warfare against the world, the flesh and the devil within and without.

(c) And to these ends you meet also for the study of God's Word, which he provided for our instruction and help in the narrow way which leads to those blessings prepared by him for those who love him and who demonstrate their love by their efforts to serve, honor and obey him.

(5) Thus seen, a *knowledge* of doctrines is not our ultimate object in meeting, but the building up of characters, which, as attempted copies of the character of God's dear Son, will be "accepted in the Beloved." But God declares that *knowledge* of the doctrines which he has revealed in his Word will be of great value to us in our endeavors to grow in his grace.

Hence, after worship, praise and prayer, Bible study should be recognized in its two parts,—(a) The study of God's plan,—what he tells us he is doing for us and for the world; what he has done; and what he will yet do; that we may be enabled as sons to enter into the very spirit of the great work of God and be intelligent co-workers with him. (b) The study of our duties and privileges in God's service, toward each other and toward those that are without, to the end that we may build up such characters as would be pleasing and acceptable to God now and in the age to come.

And since for general convenience these meetings should not last much longer than from one and a half to two hours, it will generally be found best to have at least two meetings per week, one for the consideration of Christian graces and testimony and mutual helpfulness; and the other for Bible study. And at every meeting our songs and prayers of thankful worship should ascend as in-

The Watchtower, Sept. 15, 1895, p. 216.

fleshly or spiritual, which are judged unworthy of the grace of God, because they cast it from them. The judgment upon condemned fleshly Israel was a terrible overthrow in the midst of harrowing scenes of war and desolation and famine, leaving them utterly desolate and scattering them as fugitives among all nations; while that which is shortly to come upon nominal spiritual Israel is described as a time of unparalleled trouble, such as never has been and never again shall be.

Another point of contrast which this lesson suggests is that between the Lord's methods for the harvest work of the Jewish age and the subsequent methods of the inspired Apostles, equally under the Lord's direction and supervision, which not only winnowed the grain of that harvest, but also sought to systematically store it. The wheat of that dispensation was to form the nucleus of the Christian Church—the embryo kingdom of heaven—which as a compact and sympathetic body subject toChrist, imbued with his spirit, and representing his truth, was to stand before the world as a living testimony to his truth and to the power of his grace for nearly two thousand years. It was necessary, therefore, as believers multiplied in the days of the apostles, to adopt some simple method of recognition which would serve to unify them and to make them helpful one to another as members of one body.

But as that work of organizing theChurch of the new Gospel dispensation was no part of the harvest work of the old Jewish dispensation, so the present harvest work or reaping of the Gospel dispensation is also separate and distinct from the work of the new Millennial dispensation now drawing on. But there is this difference between our days and those of the apostles: the wheat of the Gospel age is not to form the nucleus of another Church for the Millennial age; and those gathered out from among the tares are not beginning, but are finishing their course on earth, and the time of their sojourn in the flesh is very short and cannot go beyond the twenty years of harvest yet remaining. Their organization for the work of the new dispensation will be beyond the vail, when they are changed to the glorious likeness of the Lord.

In view of these facts and also of the nature of the harvest work, and the additional fact that each one so gathered is expected to enter into the harvest work as a reaper, and will do so to the extent of his ability and opportunity, it is plain that the forming of a visible organization of such gathered out ones would be out of harmony with the spirit of the divine plan; and, if done, would seem to indicate on the part of the Church a desire to conform to the now popular idea of organization or confederacy. (See Isa. 8:12.) The work now is not organization, but division, just as it was in the Jewish harvest proper (Matt. 10:34–36.) And this harvest, as illustrated by the natural, is the busiest time of all the age, because the time is short and the "winter" is fast approaching. What is to be done must be done quickly. and there is abundant room in the great field for every member of the body of Christ to reap.

While, therefore, we do not esteem a visible organization of the gathered ones to be a part of the Lord's plan in the harvest work, as though we expected as an organization to abide here for another age, we do esteem it to be his will that those that love the Lord should speak often one to another of their common hopes and joys, or trials and perplexities, communing together concerning the precious things of his Word, and so help one another, and not forget the assembling of themselves together as the manner of some is; and so much the more as they see the day approaching.—Mal. 3:16; Heb. 10:25.

Let us, then, give ourselves diligently to the great harvest work, observing and carefully following the providential lines for the guidance of the work as indicated by the Lord of the harvest—the same Lord, and just as truly present and active in this harvest as in the Jewish harvest, though invisible to mortal sight. What dignity and grandeur and blessed inspiration does the realization of this truth give our humble services! Truly it is not a glory which the world can discern, but faithfulness to the end of our course will bring an exceeding and eternal weight of glory which will appear to all God's intelligent creatures of every name and order; for in the ages to come he will show forth the exceeding riches of his grace in his loving kindness toward us who are in Christ Jesus (Eph. 2:7); and, praise the Lord! our exaltation and glory will be for a grand and benevolent service—even the privilege of scattering universal blessings.

The Watchtower, Dec. 1, 1894, p. 384.

or of a political party, have a right to withdraw and form a new organization. The Protestant theory of the Church is that of an aggregation of individuals, 'who can rearrange themselves at will, and thus create new churches at every re-arrangement.' (*Ewer.*) The Catholic theory, on the other hand, is that it is an organization which God Almighty has founded once for all, to last to the end of time, and into which he invites men: it is his family, his household, his kingdom, his city. Its officers are commissioned by him and hold their authority as teachers only from him. In a word, the Catholic Church is not a democracy but an empire, not a republic but a kingdom. As such, its comes to man with divine authority: its officers are under oath to the Eternal King, and they are to minister to man in his name, and for him."—*The Living Church.*

In presenting the true view of the Church, we labor under the disadvantage that for fifteen hundred years people have been taught one or the other of the above views, or combinations of both, while the *true* idea has been generally lost sight of since the second century. The true view, as we conceive it, is as follows:—

God's Church, when completed and *organized*, will be all that is given above as the Catholic or Episcopal view. But it is not yet completed, and hence not yet *organized.* When organized, it will be clothed with power, and will be, "not a democracy, but an empire; not a republic, but a kingdom. As such it [*will*] come to *man* [the world—during the Millennium] with *divine authority* [and with power to back up that authority]. Its officers are [then to be] under oath to the Eternal King, and they are to minister to man in his name, and for him." All this, it is to be noted, fits exactly to the coming *reign* of the Church, when it shall "bless all the families of the earth;" but it does not fit at all to the present state or condition. There is no *organization* to-day clothed with such divine authority to imperiously command mankind. There is no *organization* doing this to-day; though we are well aware that many of them in theory claim that they *ought* to be permitted to do so; and many more would like to do so.

This was the fatal mistake into which the Church began to fall in the second century; and the effort to realize this false conception culminated in the boastful, imperious counterfeiting of the *coming* Kingdom in Papacy, which for centuries sought to dominate the world, by claimed "divine authority." This idea has more or less pervaded and poisoned the ideas of all the Protestant "clergy" as well; who, copying Papacy's false ideas of the Church, claim also that the Church of Christ *is now organized*, though they make less boastful claims to "divine authority," to teach and rule mankind in general, than Papacy does.

God's Church is not yet *organized.* On the contrary, the Gospel age has been the time for *calling out and testing* the volunteers willing to sacrifice and suffer with their Lord now, and thus prove themselves worthy (Rev. 3:4, 5, 21; 2 Tim. 2:11, 12; Rom. 8:17) to be organized as joint-heirs in his Kingdom at the close of the Gospel age, when he shall "set up" or organize his Kingdom in power and great glory, to bless and rule the world with "divine authority."

In the meantime, these *unorganized* but merely called out ones, who are seeking to make their calling and election sure, that they may obtain a share in the Kingdom (2 Pet. 1:10; 2 Cor. 5:9), are "*a voluntary association of believers,*" drawn together for mutual assistance in seeking to know and to do the Master's will, that they may be accounted worthy the honors and glories promised, and not now to rule men by divine authority; for they have as yet no such authority. In this "*voluntary* association" of the consecrated there is no imperial authority of one over another; and no lording over God's heritage should be permitted; for the one and only Lord has left the instruction, "Be not ye called Rabbi; for one is your Master, even Christ, and *all ye are brethren.*"—Matt. 23:8.

Instead of the kingly and lordly rule prevailing in the customs of the world, the Master gave all another and an opposite rule, saying, "Ye know that they which are accounted to rule over the Gentiles exercise lordship over them; and their great ones exercise authority upon them. But so shall it not be among you; but whosoever will be great among you, shall

The Watchtower, Sept. 1, 1893, p. 266.

QUESTIONS AND ANSWERS

Q. Wherein consists the difference between "the Bride" and the great company if both have spiritual bodies?

A. Angels are spiritual bodies; but "unto which of the angels said God at any time, Thou art my Son; this day have I begotten thee?" (Heb. 1:5.) But "when he bringeth the first-born (Jesus) into the world (first-born from the dead, to the divine nature, at his resurrection) he saith, Let all the angels of God worship him"—render the homage due to his nature and office. (Heb. 1:5, 6.) He became a partaker of the divine nature, and it is fitting that all other forms of life should worship divinity. "God hath highly exalted him (Jesus) and given him a name which is above every name, that at the name of Jesus every knee should bow, of things in heaven (heavenly beings—angels) and things in earth, (men) and things under the earth, (the dead when raised to life) and that every tongue should confess that Jesus Christ is Lord (master, ruler) to the glory of God the Father." (Phil. 2:9-11.) From 1 Cor. 15:40, 41 we learn that there are different degrees of glory on the celestial, or spiritual plane, illustrated by sun, moon, and different stars, just as verse 39 calls attention to the fact there are different degrees of glory on the terrestrial, or earthly plane.

Though both companies will be spiritual beings, the Bride is joint-heir with her Lord, who is "appointed heir of all things; being made so much better than the angels, (other spiritual beings) as he hath by inheritance obtained a more excellent name than they." (Heb. 1:2-4.) Thus, though the "great company" will be the companions of the Bride, spiritual beings, (Psa. 45:14; Rev. 7:15) there will be a very great difference in the degrees of glory.

Q. What is the work of the Bride in making herself ready?

A. The Bride, as we have seen, is a company composed of many members. Paul says, "Ye are the body of Christ and members in particular:" and again, "Ye are members one of another:" and one is not to say to another, I have no need of you: The foot member must minister to the hand and the hand to the foot, and all, by a mutual and vital union of spirit with the Head, are to build each other up. (Jude, verse 20.) All the members have one aim, one joyful hope, one work of preparation—adorning for the marriage. She is to put on the spotless robe of Christ's righteousness (imputed to her by faith in the ransom) and to keep the same "unspotted from the world." And not only so, but she is to adorn it with fine "needle work." (Psa. 45:14.) The Christ-like character is to be wrought out in her life. As Paul expresses it, she is to *"add to her faith"* the various Christian graces. We must help one another in this important work.

Each member has a work to do in the making ready: Some may travel and preach, some may write, some publish the grace of God by printing it, some may teach more privately, some may publish it by furnishing of the Lord's funds entrusted to their care, some may seek out the *"meek"* (see Isa. 61:1) and put words in their ears and reading into their hands, and the work of all is thus to build up yourselves in the most holy faith. It is thus that the "Bride makes herself ready." It was by the faithfulness of some of the other members that these "glad tidings" ever reached your ears and gladdened and sanctified your heart: and now you, *if a member* of that company, are doing what you can to "make ready" others. To be ready to help each other, we must diligently hearken and incline our ear to the Word of truth, forget the world and worldly associations. (Psa. 45:10.) "So shall the King greatly desire thy beauty: for he is thy Lord." (Verse 11.)

Q. Please explain 1 Pet. 3:19, 20. I have not gotten clearly in mind what becomes of the spirits of men from death until the resurrection.

A. (By Bro Smith.) Does not the Scripture you quote state the condition of "spirits in prison?" The first question that would naturally occur, in examining this passage, would be: *When* did Christ preach to them? We find the answer in verse 20: "When once the patience of God waited *in the days of Noah.*" Gen. 6:3 refers to Noah's days: "The Lord said, My spirit shall not always strive with man." It is not unreasonable, then, to say he was at that time striving with man.

The general belief, that Christ preached to these spirits during his death, we think, unscriptural, for then other spirits than those of Noah's day could have heard him.

None knew better than Jesus that Scripture: "There is no knowledge nor device in the grave;" hence he would never go there to preach. Isa. 42:7; 49:9 and 61:1 state that Christ is to deliver death's prisoners. He did not do so at his first advent (excepting the temporary deliverance of Lazarus and a few others), but will in due *time* set at liberty all the captives and open the prison doors of *hades* (the tomb) to all captives.

Our understanding, then, of 1 Pet. 3:19, 20 is this: Those of Noah's day who were disobedient, and to whom Christ preached by Noah, are NOW *in prison.* If any Scripture teaches otherwise, we shall be glad to have our attention called to it.

Q. "Would not an earnest, aggressive organization (or sect), built upon Scriptural lines, be the best means of spreading and publishing the *real* Good Tidings? We must have fellowship and sympathy. Union is strength. It is not the skirmishers that win the battle, but the disciplined and solid battalions."

A. We believe that a visible organization, and the adopting of some particular name, would tend to increase our numbers and make us appear more respectable in the estimation of the world. The natural man can see that a visibly organized body, with a definite purpose, is a thing of more or less power; therefore, *they esteem* the various organizations, from which we have come out, in obedience to the Master's call. But the natural man cannot understand how a company of people, with no organization which they can see, is ever going to accomplish anything. As they look upon us, they regard us simply as a few scattered skirmishers—a "peculiar people"—with very peculiar ideas and hopes, but not worthy of special notice.

But, though it is impossible for the natural man to see our organization, because he cannot understand the things of the Spirit of God, we trust that you can see that the true Church is most effectually organized, and in the best possible working order. (See the plan of our organization, as stated in October issue, under the caption "The Ekklesia.") The Apostle Paul urges all to unity of faith and purpose (Phil. 3:15, 16—*Diaglott.*) All led by the *same Spirit* may and do come to a knowledge of the *same truth.* Under our Captain, all the truly sanctified, however few or far separated in person, are closely united by the Spirit of Christ, in faith, hope and love; and, in following the Master's command, are moving in solid battalions for the accomplishment of his purposes. But, bear in mind, God is not dependent upon numbers (See Judges 7, as an illustration).

Recognizing this organization, which is of the Spirit, and desiring no assimilation whatever with the worldly, who cannot see or understand it, we are quite willing to bear the reproach of a peculiar people. We always refuse to be called by any other name that that of our Head—Christians—continually claiming that there can be no division among those continually led by his Spirit and example as made known through his Word.

We disown none of our Lord's dear children. The weakest child of the household of faith (in Christ, our Redeemer) we gladly recognize as our brother. Some, in ignorance of their privilege of the communion of saints, are mixed with the various worldly organizations, to their great detriment. Though we cannot follow them there, we gladly welcome them when they come among us. Wherever we have hope of finding any such, in the various nominal Churches, etc., we tell them the "good tidings of great joy," and, by word and example, say, "Come out from among them (the worldly, though professing Christians) and be ye separate." How could we deliver this message if we were not obeying it? We have unbounded faith in our Captain; and this perfect organization, invisible to the world, marches on to certain and glorious victory.

"From victory unto victory,
His army he shall lead;
'Till every foe is vanquished,
And Christ is Lord indeed."

THE INSPIRATION OF THE BIBLE

Extracts from a lecture by H. L. Hastings before the Massachusetts Annual Convention of Y. M. C. Associations.

The question as to the inspiration of the Bible is not a question raised by me. It is a question that is already up for discussion through the length and breadth of this land. What are we to do with this book? How are we to regard it? Is it the best book in the world, or the worst? Is it a true book, or is it a false one? Is it God's book, or man's?

Over and over again this Book says, "Hear ye the word of the Lord." Now, the message *is* the word of the Lord, or it is a lie. It is the Word of the Lord, as it professes to be, or else it is a cheat, a swindle, a humbug, a fraud.

The Watchtower, March 1883, p. 6.

Chapter Six

THE POWER OF THE WATCHTOWER PRESIDENT—PART I:

A Look at Charles Taze Russell

We have spent much time talking about the reason Jehovah's Witnesses believe the things they do. It is clear that for Jehovah's Witnesses, the Watchtower is a guide for their lives; following it means life, ignoring it means *death*. Whoever has responsibility for the teachings in the Watchtower has *spiritual control* over the lives of all Jehovah's Witnesses.

Watchtower believers are told they must recognize that God has established a small group of men in Brooklyn, N.Y., as a "governing body" over Jehovah's Witnesses (see p. 52). Has this been the group in control of Watchtower teaching for the past one hundred years? We think the *facts* will prove otherwise. Who really has been in control of Jehovah's Witnesses?

To answer this question it is necessary to go back to the time of Charles Russell, the first Watchtower president. Did Russell recognize the authority of a group called the "governing body"? The answer is clearly *no*. Russell knew *nothing* of a governing body. He said in the April 1904 edition of *The Watchtower*, p. 126, that the Lord would use ". . . one member of his church as the channel. . ." (see p. 53). The facts show that Russell, as Watchtower president, was in total control, by *himself*. He made himself president of the New York corporation for life, even though the other officers had to be elected each year (see p. 54).

The record shows that all Jehovah's Witnesses in his day were considered his "followers" (see p. 55). In fact, it was even claimed in the September 15, 1922 edition of *The Watchtower:*

> God gave Brother Russell to the church to be as a mouthpiece for him; and those who claim to have learned the truth apart from Brother Russell and his writings have been manifested by the Lord as deceivers. . . . (See p. 56.)

Charles Russell was a one-man show. In him we see the first-fruits of the power of Watchtower presidency over the lives of Jehovah's Witnesses. Russell died in 1916 and Joseph Rutherford took over. In the following chapter we will examine his presidency and also that of his successors.

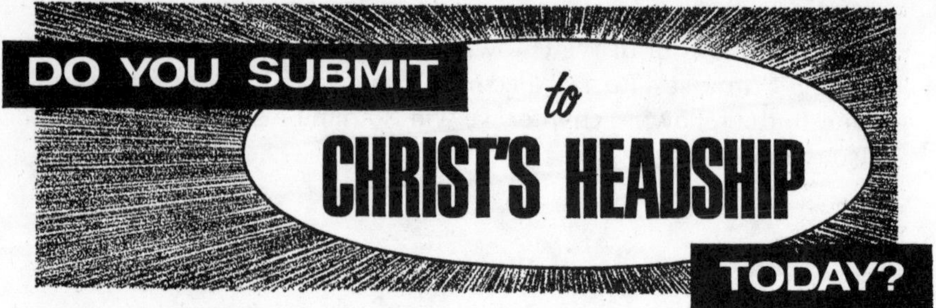
DO YOU SUBMIT
to
CHRIST'S HEADSHIP
TODAY?

IN THE first century of our Common Era Jesus Christ gave the apostle John a divine revelation. In it he revealed his active headship over Christian congregations at that time. The revelation showed that Christ was personally carrying on inspection of conditions within the congregations. He was concerned as to their spiritual health, their Christian works and activity. But he was not only inspecting. He was prepared to take appropriate *action* according to what his inspection revealed concerning the response to his counsel.—Revelation chapters 1 to 3; see also *The Watchtower* of December 15, 1971, page 751.

Christ Jesus continues to exercise full headship of the true Christian congregation earth wide today. And, just as he did back then, he uses earthly agencies to express that headship. The first-century Christian congregation had a governing body composed of apostles and elders at Jerusalem. A similar body of anointed Christians functions now. This governing body is the administrative part of a "faithful and discreet slave" or "steward" class concerning which Jesus promised: "His master . . . will appoint him over all his belongings." (Matt. 24:45-47; Luke 12:42-44) So, recognition of that governing body and its place in God's theocratic arrangement of things is necessary for submission to the headship of God's Son.

LOCAL BODIES OF ELDERS IN HARMONY

As was true in the first century, however, each congregation has its local body of elders. Of such men, the apostle Paul wrote Christians in his day: "Be obedient to those who are taking the lead among you and be submissive, for they are keeping watch over your souls as those who will render an account." (Heb. 13:17) Or, rendering the Greek word used by the apostle more literally, they should be obeying the ones "governing" them. (See *Kingdom Interlinear Translation.*) Does this mean that each local body of elders formed a separate governing body operating independently of the governing body of the 'faithful and discreet steward' class?

No, that could not be. Why not? Because that would mean disconnecting themselves from the headship of Christ Jesus. The connection of all those composing the Christian congregation with their Head, Christ Jesus, is likened to the ways the members of a human body are joined to the head. Of Jesus, the apostle writes: "From him all the body, by being harmoniously joined together and being made to cooperate through every joint that gives what is needed, according to the functioning of each respective member in due measure, makes for the growth of the body for the building up of itself in love." (Eph. 4:16) So, the Head, Christ Jesus, has various arrangements for 'joining' the individual members of the congregation to

The Watchtower, Dec. 15, 1972, p. 755.

ination, and from the four quarters of the earth, as well as from all the ecclesiastical systems, those who really love the Lord. It must be conceded, then, that this work of the Lord is done in an orderly way. He could do it in no other way except in an orderly way. If it is conceded that he began his work in an orderly way, the burden of proof is on the objectors to show that he would afterward change his course and do that work in a disorderly way. The presumption must be indulged that he would continue it in an orderly way, even to a completion.

[7]In connection with his presence and the harvest work, the office of that "faithful and wise ser nt" is important, and is made so by the Lord himself. The one who fills that office is made *ruler* over all the Lord's goods during the time of his incumbency in office. The office of that "faithful and wise servant" therefore *is a part* of *the orderly manner* in which the Lord carries on his work during his second presence. The *office* is of far greater importance than the *individual* who fills the office; for if the officer placed in the office should fail to fill it properly, the office would still exist, and the Lord could easily appoint or assign some one else to fill that office.

[8]We believe that all who are now rejoicing in present truth will concede that Brother Russell faithfully filled the office of special servant of the Lord; and that he was made ruler over all the Lord's goods. Discussing this question of "that servant" himself in THE WATCH TOWER (April 15, 1904), Brother Russell said:

[9]"'Who then is the faithful and wise steward whom his Lord shall set over his household, to give them their portion of food in due season?' The implication seems to be that when the right time should come for understanding the parable, it would be clearly set forth: that at the time of the parable's fulfilment the Lord would appoint a servant in the household to bring these matters to the attention of all the servants, and that certain responsibilities would rest upon such a one respecting the dispatch of his duties. If faithfully performed, a great blessing would be his reward; and if unfaithful to his charge, severe penalties would be inflicted. The implication would be also that if faithful the servant would be continued in his service, and if unfaithful he would be dismissed and another take the position and its responsibilities.

[10]". . . There would be no violation of principle, however, in supposing that the Lord at the time indicated would specially use one member of his church as the channel or instrument through which he would send the appropriate messages, spiritual nourishment appropriate at that time; because at various times in the past the Lord has used individuals in such a manner."—WATCH TOWER REPRINTS, pages 3355, 3356.

[11]If Brother Russell filled that office, then it must be conceded that he did so *under* the *supervision* of the Lord. "The steps of a good man are ordered by the Lord." (Psalm 37:23) *Acting under the supervision* of the Lord, Brother Russell organized the *Watch Tower Bible & Tract Society*. In expressing his reason why the Society was organized, he said:

[12]"It seems tolerably certain that some of the saints will be in the flesh during a great part at least of the 'time of trouble'; and if so, there will be need of printed matter, tracts, etc., as much then, perhaps, as now, and possibly will be more heeded; for when the judgments of the Lord are 'in the earth the inhabitants of the world will learn righteousness.' (Isaiah 26:9) Should *those at present prominently identified* with the work [undoubtedly referring to himself] not be the LAST to be 'changed,' some interruption of the work might result; but this may be obviated by having a legal standing, granted by a State Charter."—WATCH TOWER REPRINTS, page 671.

[13]In modest phrase Brother Russell here clearly indicated that it was his thought that *the Society*, as organized in an orderly manner, would carry on the work begun by him and finish that which had been committed to him personally. Often when asked by others, Who is that faithful and wise servant?—Brother Russell would reply: "Some say I am; while others say the Society is." Both statements were true; for Brother Russell was in fact the Society in a most absolute sense, in this, that he directed the policy and course of the Society without regard to any other person on earth. He sometimes sought advice of others connected with the Society, listened to their suggestions, and then did according to his own judgment, believing that the Lord would have him thus do.

[14]Since Brother Russell's "change" some who believe that he filled the office of "that servant" have said that the Lord has cast off the Society. Is such a conclusion either reasonable or Scriptural? Brother Russell's own thought was that the Society would continue to do the Lord's work as above indicated. Besides, if the Lord was pleased to have this organization *started originally* for *his purposes*, why should he cast it off? Why not continue to direct the servants therein according to his own will or supply other servants? Such is the reasonable conclusion.

[15]Do not the facts prove beyond a doubt that the Lord has been doing some harvest work during the past six years and since the death of Brother Russell? During that time have not many been gathered to the Lord, even out from the world, and have manifested every evidence of acceptance with the Lord? If the Lord, then, has been doing a work and is still doing it, is it reasonable to conclude that he is doing it in an orderly manner? If the Society is not being used to fulfil the office in carrying out the work, then who is? Can any of the murmurers or objectors point to another arrangement the Lord has in which he is carrying out his work? If any of them know of any other arrangement, let them come forward and name it. If there is any such other arrangement that the Lord has, all the saints will want to be in harmony with it and serve in the Lord's way, and not man's way.

WHAT CONSTITUTES THE SOCIETY?

[16]The word *Society* as used herein is a generic term applied to the body of consecrated, anointed Christians throughout the world engaged in the work of represent-

The Watchtower, March 1, 1923, p. 68.

following; A President, who shall be elected by the Board of Directors at the first meeting thereof, and shall hold his office for life and whose duties shall be to preside at the meetings of the Corporation or of the Board of Directors, and have the general supervision and control and management of the business and affairs of said Corporation; a Vice-President, and a Secretary who shall also be Treasurer. Such officers, except the President, shall be chosen annually, from among the Board of Directors, on the first Saturday of each year, by an election, by ballot, to be held at the principal office of the Corporation in the City of Brooklyn, New York. The members of the Board of Directors, except the President who shall always be a member of said Board of Directors, shall be chosen by, and from among, the members of the corporation, by an election, by ballot, to be held annually on the first Saturday of each year, at the principal office of the Corporation in the city of Brooklyn New York. They shall hold office until their successors are duly elected and installed. Vacancies in the Board of Directors, arising from any cause, shall be filled by a majority vote of the remaining members of the Board, who shall meet within thirty days

Charter of the People's Pulpit Association, 1909, Art. 9.

done since the days of the Reformation. Efforts to throttle the press to prevent the publication of his sermons have repeatedly been made. Why this opposition? Why would any one oppose investigation or revelation and searching the Scriptures? Why? What right has any one to prevent free thought, free speech, or the freedom of the press? What manner of men are we? Let men, preachers or what not, beware of blocking the way of such a man. Jesus said, 'And whosoever shall offend one of these little ones that believe in Me, it is better that a millstone were hanged about his neck, and he were cast into the sea.' Mark 9:42. Better be like Gamaliel in the days of the Apostles, when St. Peter and others were on trial. Gamaliel rose up and said, 'Refrain from these men, and let them alone, for if this work be of men it will come to naught; but if it be of God, ye cannot overthrow it, for ye fight against God.' "—Prof S. A. Ellis..

To the four angels.—The church in the flesh, the Harvest workers.—Matt. 24:31.

To whom it was given.—By completing the Harvest work and thus releasing the restraints on the evil spirits.

To hurt the earth.—Throw order-loving peoples into desperation.

And the sea.—So enrage the masses, not under religious restraint, as to make it impossible to control them.

7:3. **Saying, Hurt not the earth.**—Do not complete the Harvest work too soon, and thus allow the demons to invade the minds of men until the appointed time. (Many writers claim that this has already happened to the ex-Czar of Russia, to Kaiser Wilhelm and to the chief of modern "evangelists.")

Neither the sea.—I will see to it that the work of Harvest shall hold in check those not under religious restraint until the work of Harvest is finished and the demons are released, when, maddened by the obsession of the evil spirits, there are no lengths to which the godless will not presume to go. All Bible Students, followers of Pastor Russell, know how urgently he has warned for forty years that this deluge of evil spirits is sure to come.

Nor the trees.—See Rev. 8:7. Have you enjoyed this work thus far? Are you convinced it is of the Lord—prepared under His guidance? Have you carefully and prayerfully read the comments on Rev. 7:1? Then brace yourself for the truth that it is evidently God's purpose soon to allow the minds of many of His little ones to become an open battle ground, upon which the fallen angels shall be judged, and the manner in which we meet the tests will prove our worthiness of crowns at the same

The Finished Mystery, 1917, p. 126.

presence; and the time prophecies showed them God's purpose of gathering his people into unity. These have not been disturbed in mind by any of these things.

The church, the faithful, joined heart to heart, said: "My times are in thy hand; my God, I wish them there." The church realized God had begun a work, and that he would care for it and them; and they waited for the manifestation of his will. All such were made stronger in faith by reason of the tests which the loving Father permitted to come upon them, or into which he brought them. And this will continue until the end of the way; for it is by such exercise of faith that the faithful are strengthened. The manifestation of God's favor is not seen through ever continuous outward blessings, but in growth of grace, in clarity of understanding, and in strength of character.

During this time of special favor to the church Satan has had favorable opportunities and has mingled among the sons of God. Naturally he has made use of the tests which God has permitted to come upon the church, and has endeavored to turn them into temptations. We regret to say that he has had a certain measure of success. He has succeeded in beclouding the eyes of some and in leading them astray. In some cases he has had so much success as to make his dupes believe that the whole church has gone wrong, and that the Lord was no longer in control. No child of God should allow himself to believe such a thing could be possible or that God would cease to lead his people. It is not a proper nor a reasonable expectation. Such a thing would mean that Satan had become leader of the Lord's hosts; that the church had forgotten the voice of its Master, and was listening to that of a charmer. But Jesus said: "My sheep know my voice, and they follow me." The Lord would not permit Satan to become leader of his people, nor could he afford to do so: they must be sure of their Guide. All who succumb to such temptation either have not understood or have forgotten that God is gathering his people together in order that he may do a great work on earth, and that they may be ready for an entrance into the kingdom.

THE TEST OF LOYALTY

One of the chief temptations to the church has been in respect to loyalty to God's arrangements for it. Since the days when in the providences of God our late beloved leader came into prominence as the chief representative of the Lord's people and stood before them as "that servant" who had charge of his Master's goods, every indication of the Lord's providence has shown that God gave Brother Russell to the church to be as a mouthpiece for him; and those who claim to have learned the truth apart from Brother Russell and his writings have been manifested by the Lord as deceivers, ready to lead the flock of God in their way.

Since Brother Russell's death the evidence of God's favor upon the Society, which was organized by Brother Russell for the furtherance of the Lord's work, has been manifested as clearly as it was previously upon him. Satan has attempted by many attacks upon this fact to break it down; to cause the Lord's people to believe: (1) that Brother Russell was *not* the only channel by which the Lord would lead his people; and (2) that the Society in its organized capacity could not be a channel for the Lord. If Satan could accomplish his object, he had a great chance of leading a large number of the Lord's people aside from their path, and away from the work of the Lord, which he hates so much since it tells of his own dethronement and the overthrow of his kingdom.

Some have allowed themselves to be tempted astray on the plea of liberty. This is Satan's own cry. Without doubt he was the first who called out for liberty. He has always wanted to make out that God's laws are a restraint of the proper liberty of the subject. The law of love makes no appeal to him, nor does it to any who seek to break away from arrangements made by God. For thirty years this cry has been raised in the church. But those who have accepted the Lord's arrangements feel no bondage; they are the freest, happiest people on earth. Theirs is the liberty of the King's high-road. Those who leave the Lord's work on the plea of bondage, tie themselves up in their own ideas: they become bound hand and foot, having neither work to do nor place wherein to labor.

TESTS THROUGH FALSE LEADERS

Again, because the witness of the church in this day is to the downfall of his empire and the establishment of the kingdom of righteousness, Satan hates both the message and those who deliver it. He seeks to destroy both it and them by every means in his power. He has persuaded some that personal holiness is the end of all desire, and that love for the brethren is the final test.

In England a holiness movement, which became associated with Keswick in Cumberland, led many professing Christians to feel that they had at last obtained the acme of Christian experience; but we do not know of any who were associated with that movement who are not in some measure opponents of the truth. They sought a mystic union with Christ, but would not listen to their Master's voice through his messenger. Some who have been persuaded to this idea have separated themselves from their brethren. Little companies meet together to build up each other in love! Self predominates; the true labor of the church is lost sight of; the unity of fellowship is gone. Such forget the purpose of God, and ignore the fact of the Lord's providences and of Jesus' presence in the harvest field as Chief Reaper. There is no real difference between their position and that of those who lived in the days preceding the presence; and, indeed, the darkness of the dark ages begins to creep over them.

Of late some have been led astray from the Lord's

The Watchtower, Sept. 15, 1922, p. 279.

Chapter Seven

THE POWER OF THE WATCHTOWER PRESIDENT—PART II:

A Look at the Next Three Presidents

In the previous chapter we discussed the power of the Watchtower president over the lives of Jehovah's Witnesses. We examined the fact that the first president, Charles Russell, was *alone* considered God's mouthpiece to Watchtower followers of his day. He recognized no other person as speaking directly for God, and there was no central governing body over Jehovah's Witnesses.

In this section we will look at Russell's successors. Did they have the same power he had enjoyed? Were they also God's "mouthpieces" to Jehovah's Witnesses? What about Joseph Rutherford? To Jehovah's Witnesses, he was known as the "Judge." As the next Watchtower president, he had certainly chosen a good title for himself, as we will see.

In Rutherford's day, there had been an *editorial* committee, five men whose function was to determine all doctrine to be printed in *The Watchtower*. In effect, they were a governing body for Jehovah's Witnesses. But in 1931, this editorial committee was disbanded. Why? Today's Watchtower president, Fred Franz, explained the reason in a court case in 1943. Sworn to tell the truth, he said the following:

> A. It was found on occasions that some of these on the editorial committee were preventing the publication of timely and vital, up-to-date truths and thereby hindering the going of those truths to the people of the Lord in His due time.
>
> Q. After that, 1931, who on earth, if anybody, had charge of what went in or did not go in the magazine?
>
> A. Judge Rutherford. (See p. 59.)

(He was also asked:)

Q. You say that the board of directors gave Mr. Rutherford the power to write the articles in the "Watch Tower"?
A. No, sir.
Q. Who gave him the power?
A. The Lord. (See p. 60.)

Yes, Joseph Rutherford was the "Judge"—the judge of all things Jehovah's Witnesses were to believe. Then came Nathan Knorr. Watchtower leader Fred Franz, under oath in a Scotland trial, stated that all Bible interpretation was personally approved by President Knorr (see p. 61). In 1977 Fred Franz became Watchtower president. (He is the one who said Rutherford had all power, yet later stated that Nathan Knorr determined what Jehovah's Witnesses believe.)

Raymond Franz, nephew of President Fred Franz and a member of the select Governing Body of Jehovah's Witnesses from 1971 to 1980, revealed that as of January 1, 1976, a major change in the power structure took place. Up until that time he claims the president had more power than a pope over Roman Catholics. In 1976, the Governing Body voted to take control of the operation of Jehovah's Witnesses worldwide. In that year Raymond Franz said, "The power of the presidency was decimated and virtually disappeared, that office now serving an almost purely legal function.[1]

Raymond Franz also reveals that during 1975, Fred Franz tried to convince the Governing Body that it was *God's will* to keep the power in the hands of one man; he was most upset when the other members of the Governing Body didn't agree and voted against his wishes.[2] Ironically, Fred Franz, who had served under three Watchtower dictators and supported their power as Watchtower presidents, now was just "one of the boys" on the Governing Body!

---

[1]Raymond Franz, *Crisis of Conscience* (Atlanta, Ga.: Commentary Press, 1983), pp. 91–92.

[2]Ibid. See the chapter: "Internal Upheaval and Restructure."

2596 *Fred W. Franz—For Defts.—Cross*

Q. Didn't you state that on October 15, 1931, the Watch Tower discontinued the naming of an editorial committee and then Jehovah God became the editor? A. I didn't say Jehovah God became the editor. It was appreciated that Jehovah God really is the One who is editing the paper, and therefore the naming of an editorial committee was out of place.

Q. At any rate, Jehovah God is now the editor of the paper, is that right? A. He is today the editor of the paper.

2597 Q. How long has He been editor of the paper? A. Since its inception he has been guiding it.

Q. Even before 1931? A. Yes, sir.

Q. Why did you have an editorial committee up to 1931? A. Pastor Russell in his will specified that there should be such an editorial committee, and it was continued down till then.

Q. Did you find that the editorial committee was in conflict with having the journal edited by Jehovah God, is that it? A. No.

Q. Was the policy in opposition to what your conception of an editing by Jehovah God was?

2598 A. It was found on occasions that some of these on the editorial committee were preventing the publication of timely and vital, up-to-date truths and thereby hindering the going of those truths to the people of the Lord in His due time.

By the Court:

Q. After that, 1931, who on earth, if anybody, had charge of what went in or did not go in the magazine? A. Judge Rutherford.

Q. So he in effect was the earthly editor-in-chief, as he might be called? A. He would be the visible one to take care of that.

Olin Moyle v. *WTBTS*, 1943, Section 2598.

letter going out from Headquarters to find out about any communications respecting Mr. Moyle to these various companies out in Wisconsin? A. I know nothing about such.

Q. These letters all came to you voluntarily as far as you know from— A. I don't know.

Q. You don't know how they came in? A. No, sir.

The Court: As a matter of fact, as I understand your testimony, Judge Rutherford had some of them on his desk or 2696
table and you so indicated?

The Witness: Yes, sir.

The Court: You didn't see the letters at all. The only time you heard this letter read, and you heard Judge Rutherford's statement concerning it.

The Witness: Yes, sir.

The Court: Is that the correct understanding?

Mr. Covington: Yes.

Q. You say that the board of directors gave 2697
Mr. Rutherford the power to write the articles in the "Watch Tower"? A. No, sir.

Q. Who gave him the power? A. The Lord.

The Court: He made him President of the Corporation and gave him the right to supervise or—

The Witness: The Board of Directors have nothing to do with the doctrinal matters. This is a legal corporation and they take care of the legal matters.

Q. So the Lord was writing the magazine in 1939? A. He is guiding it.

Olin Moyle v. *WTBTS*, 1943, Section 2697.

A it was a calculation which is no longer acoppted by the
Board of Directors of the Society? A. That is correct.
Q. So that am I correct, I am just anxious to canvas the
position; it became the bounden duty of the Witnesses to
accept this miscalculation? A. Yes. Q. In what form
B was the miscalculation corrected? A. When we reached
the date 1914 and the world developments went forward,
then we say that we had not understood some of the
prophecies correctly. Therefore, we saw that there was
a need for a review of our beliefs respecting how the
C prophecies would be fulfilled. Q. Was that matter
considered first by the editorial committee or was it
considered by the Board of Directors of the
Pennsylvania Society? A. I was not at Brooklyn
Headquarters to know. Q. But that has throughout
D your experience been the usual way of issuing
authoritative interpretations or corrections? A. That
is right. Q. In your experience which body is it
which issues authoritative interpretations or corrections
of the same; I mean, is it the editorial committee or
E is it the Board of Directors of the Pennsylvania
Society? A. The editorial committee does the
research work, and then it comes finally under the
review of the President of the Society, the Chairman
of the Board of Directors. He issues the final
F approval and sends it to press. Q. Does it come
before the Board of Directors? A. Not as a Board in
session/

Douglas Walsh Trial, Scotland, 1954, p. 105, 1958 ed.

A session met. Q. How does it come before them? A. In
the manner that I described. It comes through the
editorial committee and finally reaches the Chairman of
the Board of Directors. Q. But am I right that the
Board of Directors do at some stage consider it?
B A. They all consider it. Q. And vote upon it if need
be? A. They express their opinions upon it. Q. And
vote upon it if need be? A. There is no voting upon
it. If it is published it is accepted. Q. But before
it is published how is it decided upon if there be a
C difference of view in the Board of Directors about the
interpretations? A. There is no difference of view
in the Board of Directors. Q. Never? A. After the
matter is published there is agreement. Q. I am not
concerned with after publication / but before publication
D is effected? A. The matter proceeds as I have
explained. The editorial committee does the research
work. It finally goes to the President, the Chairman
of the Board of Directors, and he approves it, if it
meets with his agreement, and he sends the matter to
E press. Q. I thought, correct me if I am wrong, that
you had agreed that between the matter being considered
by the editorial committee and finally by the President
it was a matter of consideration by the Board of
Directors, am I right in that? A. The Board of
F Directors read the publications and they conform to
them./

Douglas Walsh Trial, Scotland, 1954, p. 106, 1958 ed..

Chapter Eight

WATCHTOWER PROPHECY ANALYSIS

What is a false prophet? Jeremiah was a true biblical prophet who warned God's people about those who claimed to be prophets, yet who were not truly inspired by God. Jeremiah 23:16 says, "Do not listen to the words of the prophets who are prophesying to you. They are leading you into futility; they speak a vision of their own imagination, not from the mouth of the Lord."

The Watchtower magazine claims that God has a prophet to "declare things to come," the Jehovah's Witnesses' organization (see p. 68). *The Watchtower* also declares that this modern prophet has been commissioned just as Ezekiel was (see p. 69), and that God himself interprets His own prophecies in *The Watchtower* magazine (see p. 70). How do the Watchtower leaders receive these prophecies? The answer is given in *The Watchtower*, of course. It says of Jesus: "He merely uses the 'servant' class to publish the interpretation after the Supreme Court by Christ Jesus reveals it" (see p. 71). So the interpretation of the prophecies are claimed to be given by Jesus Christ himself. Do the prophecies really come from heaven?

Let's take a look at one from the Watchtower book, *The Time Is at Hand*. "The 'battle of the great day of God Almighty' (Rev. 16:14), which will end in A.D. 1914 with the complete overthrow of earth's present rulership, is already commenced" (see p. 72). Did anyone notice Armageddon in 1914?

Interestingly, the Watchtower itself has spoken out against false prophets. However, the following statements clearly condemn the Watchtower itself as a false prophet! From *Awake!* magazine:

> True, there have been those in times past who predicted an "end to the world," even announcing a specific date. . . . Yet, nothing happened. The "end" did not come. They were guilty of false prophesying. . . . Missing from such people were God's truths and the evidence that he was guiding and using them. (See p. 73.)

The warning should be clear to all: it is impossible to get clear direction (not to mention good doctrine) from a false prophet!

The nature of these prophetic claims is clear: the Watchtower Society claims to speak for God. Furthermore, they say: "Whom has God actually used as his prophet? . . . Jehovah's witnesses are deeply grateful today that the plain facts show that God has been pleased to use them" (see p. 74). Can this be true? The Apostle Paul instructs us to "examine everything carefully" (1 Thess. 5:21). We will follow that advice in this chapter. We will examine the Watchtower's record of predicting events for the years 1874 and 1914.

In the book, *The Battle of Armageddon*, 1897, it was claimed that Jesus' second coming happened invisibly in the year 1874 (see p. 75). In 1922 *The Watchtower* said: "No one can properly understand the work of God at this present time who does not realize that since 1874, the time of the Lord's return in power, there has been a complete change in God's operations" (see p. 76). And then in 1924 *The Watchtower* said: "Surely there is not the slightest room for doubt in the mind of a truly consecrated child of God that the Lord Jesus is present and has been since 1874" (see p. 77). Today, not one Jehovah's Witness believes this false prophecy about Christ coming in 1874.

The Watchtower was also predicting the end of the world by 1914! In 1892 *The Watchtower* claimed that Armageddon began in 1874 and would end in 1914 (see p. 78). Two years later, in 1894, *The Watchtower* said 1914 was God's date, and that they couldn't change their prediction even if they wanted to (see p. 79). In a book entitled *Pastor Russell's Sermons*, the Watchtower president said that World War I "is the beginning of the Armageddon of the Scriptures" (see p. 80). Clearly 1914 was a false prophecy which led many astray.

We will conclude our brief examination of Watchtower prophecy by examining their claims about the date 1925 and World War II. But before we do this, let's look at how the Watchtower itself defines a false prophet. From the 1930 *The Watchtower*:

> If he is a false prophet, his prophecy will fail to come to pass. . . . The difference between a true and a false prophet is that the one is speaking the word of the Lord and the other is speaking his own dreams and guesses. . . . Their prophecies did not come true. Therefore they are false prophets; and the people should no longer trust them as safe guides. (See pp. 81–83.)

With these warnings in mind, let us examine what the Watchtower said about 1925 and World War II and see if they themselves are "safe guides."

To answer the question, "What happened in 1925?", let us pretend that we are Jehovah's Witnesses living in the early 1920s. Our message is: Millions Now Living Will Never Die! That is also the title of a book we distribute door to door. The book tells us that Abraham, Isaac, and Jacob will rise from the dead soon, in 1925 (see pp. 84, 85). The Watchtower Society says we should put our own interests aside and spend more time preaching this "good news." We don't have time to do other things—the end is so very near!

Isn't it strange how some people can doubt the Watchtower's predictions about the year 1925? After all, *The Watchtower* of April 1, 1923, said, "1925 is definitely settled by the Scriptures. . . . As to Noah, the Christian now has much more upon which to base his faith than Noah had . . . upon which to base his faith in a coming deluge" (see p. 86). And again, here in *The Watchtower* of July 15, 1924, we read, "The year 1925 is a date definitely and clearly marked in the Scriptures, even more clearly than that of 1914" (see p. 87).

Finally 1925 arrives; we can hardly wait to open our January issue of *The Watchtower*! Here on page 3 it says, "The year 1925 is here. With great expectation Christians have looked forward to this year. Many have confidently expected that all members of the body of Christ will be changed to heavenly glory during this year." Oh yes, this is truly our hope, based on the Watchtower's interpretation of the Scriptures to us! Now, let's read on. The Society says, "This may be accomplished. It may not be" (see p. 88). It may not be? What? Didn't the Society say it was the Scriptures that foretold the year 1925? Oh no! Many of us have sold our homes, others have quit school to do this work full time! What will our friends and neighbors think?

Yes, the Watchtower misled many to believe that 1925 was a Bible date indicating the return of the ancient Hebrew princes. When individual Jehovah's Witnesses became upset and demanded an explanation for the failure of these princes to arrive on time, *The Watchtower* (Sept. 1, 1925) said this, "It is to be expected that Satan will try to inject into the minds of the consecrated the thought that 1925 should see an end of the work, and that therefore it would be needless for them to do more" (see p. 89). Yes, Satan did tell Jehovah's Witnesses that 1925 would witness an end to the work—and he used the Watchtower to print it! Jesus Christ warned about false prophets who would try to keep the truth from us.

The Watchtower Society not only met with prophetic disaster in 1914 and 1925, but during World War II as well. As you may already know, the Watchtower misrepresented the chaos of WWI by claiming it was Armageddon. But what about WWII? At the present time, the Watchtower denies that it prophesied the end during WWII as they had during WWI. They claim:

> During World War I God's people expected it to lead directly into Armageddon, but Jehovah prevented such a climax at that time. We didn't succumb to such an expectation during World War II. (See p. 90.)

Is this a true statement? Or, could the Watchtower Society be covering up the historical facts? In October, 1941, the Watchtower said:

> Meantime the German people are awakening to their horrible predicament . . . the near future will bring and is already hastening to bring to them—Armageddon, the battle of that great day of God Almighty. (See p. 91.)

The evidence is clear. The Watchtower *did* connect WWII with Armageddon. They predicted the destruction of Germany, not by the Allied nations, but by Jehovah God! In *The Watchtower's* December issues for 1941, they were extremely specific and made these points:

1. WWII will not end in decisive victory for either side because the Bible prophecy will not allow it. (See p. 92.)
2. America and England will turn into dictatorships. (See p. 92.)
3. The end of Nazi rule will mark the end of demon rule. In other words, God will rule when the Nazis are defeated. (See p. 93.)

All of these prophecies deceived many. Today, the Watchtower claims not to have linked WWII with Armageddon. Yet, as we have seen, they are covering up their history—and for good reasons: the facts brand them as false prophets.

There were other things that the Watchtower said about WWII as well. The booklet "Judge Rutherford Uncovers Fifth Column" said in 1940 that the Nazis would destroy the British Empire (see p. 94). They said in *The Watchtower* in 1941 it was just a matter of "the remaining months before Armageddon" (see p. 95). As we have already seen, the Society prophesied the return of Abraham, Isaac and Jacob for 1925. Few people are aware of the fact, however, that the Society fell into the same false teaching during WWII. But according to the Society in 1942, these ancient Hebrew princes were due to return from the dead "any day now" (see p. 96). It would certainly seem that their day and Armageddon are long overdue!

The most recent prophetic disaster to befall the Watchtower Society was their ill-fated prediction concerning the year 1975 (see p. 97). Though later admitted by even the Society itself to be a false prediction, the tragic effects that this latest travesty had upon the lives of individual Jehovah's Witnesses can best be summed up in the following dialogue with accompanying documentation:

Lois: John, have you read the latest *Watchtower*—the one for August, 1968?

John: Of course!

Lois: Do you believe what *The Watchtower* is saying about 1975 in the article "Why Are You Looking Forward to 1975?" (See p. 97.)

John: Of course I do. *The Watchtower* speaks for Jehovah!

Lois: John, what should we do? The end is so very close!

John: I don't know. I've got an opportunity for a promotion at work if I can get a little night-school in. But, we'd better *wait* and *see* what the Society says.

Several months passed and Lois found the answer in a Watchtower publication.

Lois: John, I've found what we should do about your job and school. The Society says in the June, *Kingdom Ministry:*

> In view of the short time left, a decision to pursue a career in this system of things is not only unwise but extremely dangerous. . . . Many young brothers and sisters were offered scholarships or employment that promised fine pay. However, they turned them down and put spiritual interests first. (See p. 98.)

John: But, what should we do to "put spiritual interests first"?

Again, *The Watchtower* had the answer. Lois found it in the *Kingdom Ministry* of May, 1974.

Lois: Listen John, the Society says:

> . . . the end of this system is so very near! Is that not reason to increase our activity? . . . Reports are heard of brothers selling their homes and property and planning to finish out the rest of their days in this old system in the pioneer service. Certainly this is a fine way to spend the short time remaining before the wicked world's end. (See p. 99.)

John and Lois took the Society's advise, sold their home, and went to work selling *Watchtower's* door to door. 1975 finally arrived *but* the end of the world didn't. John and Lois were upset and had every right to be.

At this point we must return to the Society's claim and their invitation in *The Watchtower* for April 1, 1972.

> Of course, it is easy to say that this group acts as a "prophet" of God. It is another thing to prove it. The only way that this can be done is to review the record. What does it show? (See p. 68.)

The record clearly destroys any claims to the prophetic authority of the Watchtower Bible and Tract Society.

'They shall know that A PROPHET was among them'

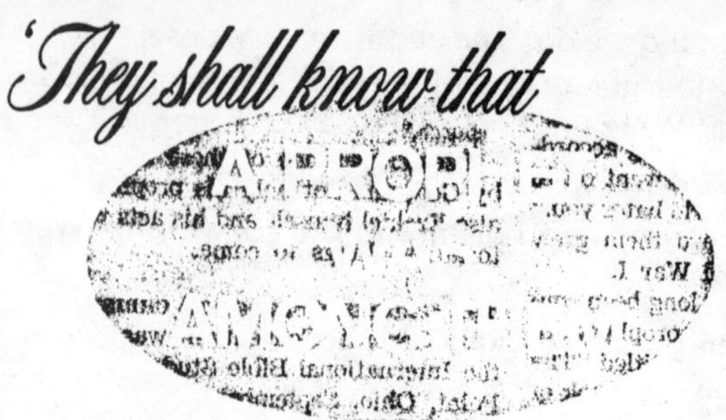

JEHOVAH GOD is interested in having people know him. Though he is invisible to human eyes, he provides various ways by which they can know his personality. They can know what to expect from him and what he expects of them.

One can come to understand that Jehovah is a God of surpassing wisdom by observing creation. This also reveals the loving care with which he designed things for man's welfare and enjoyment. A second way to know God is through his Word of truth, the Bible. Herein one finds the full expression of Jehovah's purpose toward mankind—why man is on the earth and the blessings that God has in store.

A third way of coming to know Jehovah God is through his representatives. In ancient times he sent prophets as his special messengers. While these men foretold things to come, they also served the people by telling them of God's will for them at that time, often also warning them of dangers and calamities. People today can view the creative works. They have at hand the Bible, but it is little read or understood. So, does Jehovah have a prophet to help them, to warn them of dangers and to declare things to come?

IDENTIFYING THE "PROPHET"

These questions can be answered in the affirmative. Who is this prophet? The clergy of the so-called "Christian" nations hold themselves before the people as being the ones commissioned to speak for God. But, as pointed out in the previous issue of this magazine, they have failed God and failed as proclaimers of his kingdom by approving a man-made political organization, the League of Nations (now the United Nations), as "the political expression of the Kingdom of God on earth."

However, Jehovah did not let the people of Christendom, as led by the clergy, go without being warned that the League was a counterfeit substitute for the real kingdom of God. He had a "prophet" to warn them. This "prophet" was not one man, but was a body of men and women. It was the small group of footstep followers of Jesus Christ, known at that time as International Bible Students. Today they are known as Jehovah's Christian witnesses. They are still proclaiming a warning, and have been joined and assisted in their commissioned work by hundreds of thousands of persons who have listened to their message with belief.

Of course, it is easy to say that this group acts as a "prophet" of God. It is another thing to prove it. The only way that this can be done is to review the record. What does it show?

During the World War I period this group, the International Bible Students, was very active in preaching the good news of God's kingdom, as their Leader Jesus Christ had set this work before them in his prophecy at Matthew 24:14. They took literally Jesus' words to the Roman governor Pontius Pilate: "My kingdom is no part of this world." (John 18:36) They also took to heart Jesus' words to his fol-

197

The Watchtower, April 1, 1972, p. 197.

Covenant of the League of Nations was made a part of that peace treaty.

When the League of Nations was proposed as an international organization for world peace and security, the bloodstained religious organizations backed it, seizing upon this circumstance as an opportunity to "save face." The Church of England and the churches of Canada supported the League, since Great Britain was the League's proposer and chief backer. In the United States of America there was the Federal Council of the Churches of Christ in America (superseded in 1950 by the National Council of the Churches of Christ in the U.S.A., a federation of 33 Protestant and Orthodox churches). On December 18, 1918, this Council sent its adopted Declaration to the American president and urged him to work for the League. The Declaration said, in part:

> "Such a League is not a mere political expedient; it is rather the political expression of the Kingdom of God on earth. . . . The Church can give a spirit of good-will, without which no League of Nations can endure. . . . The League of Nations is rooted in the Gospel. Like the Gospel, its objective is 'peace on earth, good-will toward men.'"

By accepting the League of Nations as "the political expression of the Kingdom of God on earth," the members of the Federal Council of churches were really accepting a counterfeit "Kingdom of God on earth." Why? Because Jesus Christ, the Head of the church, when on trial for his life before the Roman governor Pontius Pilate, in 33 C.E., said: "My kingdom does not belong to this world. If it did, my followers would be fighting to save me from arrest by the Jews. My kingly authority comes from elsewhere." (John 18:36, *New English Bible*) The fact that they were not, as a body, a commissioned messenger of God was made clear and their hypocrisy exposed when, twenty years later, the League of Nations was knocked out of business by the outbreak of World War II. The churches again entered into this war with all their might, encouraging their members to take part.

WHAT IS REQUIRED OF GOD'S MESSENGER

Therefore, when it came time for the name of Jehovah and his purposes to be declared to the people, along with God's warning that Christendom is in her "time of the end," who qualified to be commissioned? Who was willing to undertake this monumental task as Jehovah's "servant"? Was there anyone to whom Jehovah's heavenly "chariot" could roll up and whom it could confront? More accurately, was there any group on whom Jehovah would be willing to bestow the commission to speak as a "prophet" in His name, as was done toward Ezekiel back there in 613 B.C.E.? What were the qualifications?

Certainly such a messenger or "servant" group would have to be made up of persons who had not been defiled with bloodguilt as had Christendom and the rest of Babylon the Great, the world empire of false religion, by sharing in carnal warfare. In fact, they would be a group that had come out from the religious organizations of Babylon the Great. More than that, they would be persons who not only saw the hypocrisy and God-defaming action of these religions, but in addition actually rejected them and turned to Jehovah God in true worship of him as set forth in the Bible. Who would they be?

In identifying the group that is truly commissioned as God's messenger, these are points for us to consider seriously. God does not deal with persons who ignore his Word and go according to their own independent ideas. Nor does he recognize those who make a profession of serving him and at the same time associate with religions that teach God-dishonoring doc-

The Watchtower, March 15, 1972, p. 189.

Joshua to that of David Jehovah fought their battles for them and ultimately the accursed Canaanites were subjugated. Some served the priests at the temple as "hewers of wood and drawers of water". (Josh. 9:23) During the peaceful reign of Solomon all the Canaanites who had not been destroyed or driven out of the promised land were subject to a tribute of bond-service. "And all the people that were left of the Amorites, Hittites, Perizzites, Hivites, and Jebusites, which were not of the children of Israel, their children that were left after them in the land, whom the children of Israel also were not able utterly to destroy, upon those did Solomon levy a tribute of bondservice unto this day." (1 Kings 9:20,21) Thus the descendants of Shem, whose God was Jehovah, possessed the land once occupied by the descendants of Ham and the accursed Canaan, who did not acknowledge Jehovah as their God but worshiped idols and false gods. They were either destroyed or reduced to a condition of servitude.

The name "Shem" means "name, renown, fame", and through his lineage came many men of valor. Their fame as men of faith in Jehovah, the God of Shem, is made known in the eleventh chapter of Hebrews. Another statement concerning Shem which, if true, would greatly enhance his fame and renown, is that made by many scholars that Shem and Melchizedek were one and the same person. Melchizedek is the first one mentioned in the Scriptures as a man who ruled any people by divine right. Undoubtedly he was of Shem's line, and it is quite probable that he was Shem. Shem was living at the time Abraham met Melchizedek and paid tithes to him. In fact, he lived up till within twenty-five years of Abraham's death. "Shem was an hundred years old, and begat Arphaxad two years after the flood: and Shem lived after he begat Arphaxad five hundred years."—Gen. 11:10,11.

If the peoples of earth today would receive the blessings of the Lord, some of which were prophetically foretold through Shem, let them follow a course of action that says, in effect, "Blessed be Jehovah, the God of Shem."

RESOLUTION

We, the Hot Springs (Ark.) company of Jehovah's witnesses, knowing that we must pass through much tribulation before entering the Kingdom, do adopt and make this our resolution:

As Jehovah's witnesses we are commissioned to comfort all that mourn, as stated in Isaiah 61:1,2; that Jehovah has enthroned Christ Jesus as King of The Theocracy and he has now begun his reign amidst his enemies, and that now is the time to defeat persecution; that the time is now here when the people have a right to hear discussed the great truths concerning the establishment of the great Theocracy as expressed in His Word, the Bible.

That it is our duty to fear only God, and not man, and that we must and will obey His supreme command in preference to man's command the same as the faithful that have gone before us have suffered for and obeyed The Theocracy and rejoiced in that privilege.

Therefore, be it resolved, that we, as Jehovah's witnesses, will, by His grace, be faithful to our covenant and that we are determined not to slack the hand and therefore not yield to the Devil's side of the issue. We, therefore, will stand unitedly, shoulder to shoulder in the fight for The Theocracy on Jehovah's side and be "fighters for the New World". That we will not break our covenant because of arrests, persecution or imprisonment and will push on in the work Jehovah through Christ Jesus has commissioned us to perform until "the cities be wasted" and Armageddon is on. We rejoice in the opportunity of bearing the reproach that fell on the Perfect One and to be counted worthy to suffer for his name, and that, by God's grace, we will not stop preaching this gospel of the Kingdom, regardless of the fact that we are classed as "peddlers" by some city ordinance passed by men.

Further, be it resolved, that we are united with those at Bethel by the spirit of Jehovah and that we will continue so and to recognize Jehovah's channel to give us "meat in due season".

Unanimously adopted.

(*Continued from page 114*)

cherished freedoms for preservation of which Jehovah's witnesses are putting up a splendid fight on the "home front" everywhere. *Fighting for Liberty on the Home Front* shows, with much evidence, who is the enemy of liberty, and why the fight therefor must continue on after the global war ends. A copy will be mailed to you, postpaid, on your contribution of 5c.

MEMORIAL

The date Scripturally arrived at for 1943 for celebrating the memorial to Jehovah's name and to the faithful death of his King, Christ Jesus, is Monday, April 19. After 6 p.m., Standard Time, of that date each Christian company should assemble, and the anointed ones thereof celebrate the Memorial, their companions as the Lord's "other sheep" being present as observers. If no competent person is present to deliver a brief discourse immediately before partaking of the emblems, then appropriate paragraphs may be read from the Memorial articles appearing in the March 1 and 15, 1943, issues of *The Watchtower* to those assembled. Since the breaking of the bread and the drinking of the wine both picture Christ's death, in which also his body members partake, it follows that both emblems should be served together at partaking, and not separately. The emblems should be unleavened bread and real red wine. Jesus and his apostles most certainly used real red wine in symbol of his blood, and the anointed remnant should follow their lead. Report your celebration and its total attendance and partakers of the emblems to the Society, as instructed also in the *Informant*.

"THE WATCHTOWER"

The Watchtower is a magazine without equal in the earth, and is conceded this rank by all that have been faithful readers thereof during its more than sixty years of publication. *The Watchtower* has increased in importance with the progress of the years, and never has it been more valuable than today, at this world crisis, when the destiny of each intelligent human creature is being decided. The getting of correct information and instruction, just such as is required for the times, to decide your course wisely to a happy destiny, was never more vital than now, for "where there is no vision, the people perish". Informed persons well acquainted with the consistent contents of *The Watchtower* agree that those who want to gain life in peace and happiness without end should read and study it together with the Bible and in company with other readers. This is not giving any credit to the magazine's publishers, but is due to the great Author of the Bible with its truths and prophecies, and who now interprets its prophecies. He it is that makes possible the material that is published in the columns of this magazine and who gives promise that it shall continue to publish the advancing truths as long as it continues to exist for the service of the interests of his Theocratic Government. Carefully and prayerfully read this issue of *The Watchtower*. Then do not delay to mail in your subscription, that you may receive it regularly, twice a month, twenty-four copies the year. It is $1.00 in the United States; $1.50 elsewhere.

The Watchtower, April 15, 1943, p. 127.

over his household, to give them meat in due season? Blessed is that servant, whom his lord when he cometh shall find so doing. Verily I say unto you, That he shall make him ruler over all his goods." (Matt. 24:45-47; see also Luke 12:42-44) Whom do the facts of our day prove to be that "faithful and wise servant"?

35 Aside from Christ Jesus, divine prophecy foretells no individual man. In times past prophetic figures such as Elijah, Elisha, and others, were used to foreshadow a company or society of faithful, devoted servants of God, who should be Jehovah's witnesses at the end of the world, where we are at present. Likewise, the expression "faithful and wise servant" does not picture any man or individual on earth now, but means the faithful remnant of Jehovah's witnesses who are begotten of His spirit and gathered into a unity unto Him and His service. They are part of his Theocratic organization and are subject to Theocratic rule, which means, the divine will as to organization and work. They act as a unit or society, together doing Jehovah's "strange work" as he reveals it to them. (Isa. 54:13; Ps. 25:14) Such "society" is not a legal society or corporation, chartered according to the laws of some state or nation, but is a society or association formed by the Creator, Jehovah God, and composed of his spiritual remnant approved by Christ Jesus at the temple judgment. Such society, however, may use as their earthly instrumentality or servant a legal corporation, such as the Watch Tower Bible and Tract Society; and they do so, since A.D. 1884. Christ Jesus is the Chief Servant of Jehovah God, and he is the invisible or heavenly Head of the "faithful and wise servant" class.—Isa. 42:1; Matt. 12:15-21.

36 To such remnant of faithful servants of Jehovah God Christ Jesus has entrusted all "his goods", or earthly interests of the Kingdom. This does not signify that the faithful remnant or society of Jehovah's anointed witnesses are an earthly tribunal of interpretation, delegated to interpret the Scriptures and its prophecies. No; Christ Jesus the King has not entrusted that office to them. THE SUPREME COURT STILL INTERPRETS, thank God; and Christ Jesus, the Court's official mouthpiece of interpretation, reserves to himself that office as Head of Jehovah's "faithful and wise servant" class. He merely uses the "servant" class to publish the interpretation after the Supreme Court by Christ Jesus reveals it. How does the Lord God make known the interpretation? By causing the facts to come to pass visibly which are in fulfillment of the prophecy or dark saying or misunderstood scripture. Thereafter "in due season" he calls such fulfillment or clarification of prophecy and scripture to the attention of his "faithful and wise servant" class. Thereby he makes them responsible to make known the meaning of such scriptures to all members of the household of faith and to all persons of good-will. This constitutes giving them the "meat in due season".

37 In bygone days those now composing the "faithful and wise servant" class or remnant of Jehovah's witnesses have believed many things which were not strictly correct according to the Scriptures. They continued to hold on to such beliefs even for some time after A.D. 1918, when Christ Jesus arrived at the temple. Today they see and understand differently, with Scripture backing. Does this mean that God is the Author of confusion or that they are not of His Theocratic organization? No; Jehovah God is not the author of confusion, but is the remover of confusion from his devoted people who both pray and seek to know his truth. Although the understanding of his "servant" class has cleared up and has been corrected, yet the text of God's infallible Word has not changed and its information has been there all the time from days of old.

38 After Jehovah's royal Associate Judge came to the temple for judgment and the purification of his people, Jehovah God used his Messenger and Interpreter to cleanse away, little by little and point by point, any misunderstanding, which misunderstanding was due to their having been in contact with religion in the past or due to not having the fulfilled facts at hand because it was not yet God's due time. Thus Jehovah by Christ Jesus continues to this day to lead them in the path of truth, and they follow the revealed decisions of the Supreme Court of Interpretation and walk on in the light. Such increase of light is in fulfillment of God's promise: "The path of the just is as the shining light, that shineth more and more unto the perfect day." (Prov. 4:18) The light continues to grow brighter, and the perfect day is at hand, as we walk on where our Guide and Interpreter leads us.—Ps. 25:9.

39 Thus the great Supreme Interpreter magnifies now his infallible Word. Shortly, at the battle of Armageddon, Jehovah by his Associate Judge and Executioner will vindicate that Word. He will also magnify his holy name and destroy all opposing kings of this world. For that reason his faithful remnant, who are in line to be "kings and priests" with Christ Jesus, bow toward Jehovah God, who is representatively in his holy temple by Christ Jesus. Their beloved earthly companions bow with them,

35. (a) Whom does that "faithful and wise servant" picture? (b) Is a legal corporation meant, or what part does a legal corporation play therein?
36. (a) The Lord's entrusting "all his goods" to the "servant" class has what connection with interpretation of the Scriptures? (b) How does the Lord God make known the interpretation, and what responsibility thereafter falls upon the "servant" class?
37. Why does difference of understanding today from that held previously not prove God the author of confusion or prove that the remnant of Jehovah's witnesses are not of His organization?
38. How, then, do we explain Scripturally the change of understanding since the Lord's coming to the temple?
39. What is the Supreme Interpreter thereby doing respecting his Word? and for that cause what do the remnant and their faithful companions do respecting Jehovah God?

The Watchtower, July 1, 1943, p. 203.

and the living saints, as well as many of the world, are now being used as the Lord's soldiers in overthrowing errors and evils. But let no one hastily infer a *peaceable conversion* of the nations to be here symbolized; for many scriptures, Such as Rev. 11:17, 18; Dan. 12:1; 2 Thes. 2:8; Psalms 149 and 47, teach the very opposite.

Be not surprised, then, when in subsequent chapters we present proofs that the setting up of the Kingdom of God is already begun, that it is pointed out in prophecy as due to begin the exercise of power in A. D. 1878, and that the "battle of the great day of God Almighty" (Rev. 16:14.), which will end in A. D. 1914 with the complete overthrow of earth's present rulership, is already commenced. The gathering of the armies is plainly visible from the standpoint of God's Word.

If our vision be unobstructed by prejudice, when we get the telescope of God's Word rightly adjusted we may see with clearness the character of many of the events due to take place in the "Day of the Lord"—that we are in the very midst of those events, and that "the Great Day of His Wrath is come."

The sword of truth, already sharpened, is to smite every evil system and custom—civil, social and ecclesiastical. Nay, more, we can see that the smiting is commenced: freedom of thought, and human rights, civil and religious, long lost sight of under kings and emperors, popes, synods, councils, traditions and creeds, are being appreciated and asserted as never before. The internal conflict is already fomenting: it will ere long break forth as a consuming fire, and human systems, and errors, which for centuries have fettered truth and oppressed the groaning creation, must melt before it. Yes, truth—and widespread and increasing knowledge of it—is the sword which is perplexing and wounding the heads over many countries. (Psa. 110:6.)

The Time Is at Hand, 1888 (1911 ed.), p. 101.

A TIME TO 'Lift Up Your Head' in CONFIDENT HOPE

THE evidence that we are far along in the "last days" can be either good news or bad news to you, depending on the position you take. If you long to be free from a rule that has proved both unsatisfactory and unrighteous and that is torn more and more by discord and confusion; if you really love what is right and have a sincere desire to do the will of your Creator, then this evidence should make you rejoice. Why? Because, as Jesus Christ said: "As these things start to occur, raise yourselves erect and lift your heads up, because *your deliverance is getting near.*"—Luke 21:28.

A perfect government, heaven-based and with heaven's blessing and heaven's power backing it up, will soon take complete control of this earth. In this way God will answer the prayer: "Let your kingdom come." What better news could there be?

Still some persons may say: "How can you be sure? Maybe it is later than many people think. But maybe it is not as late as some persons claim. People have been mistaken about these prophecies before."

The Difference

True, there have been those in times past who predicted an "end to the world," even announcing a specific date. Some have gathered groups of people with them and fled to the hills or withdrawn into their houses waiting for the end. Yet, nothing happened. The "end" did not come. They were guilty of false prophesying. Why? What was missing?

Missing was the full measure of evidence required in fulfillment of Bible prophecy. Missing from such people were God's truths and the evidence that he was guiding and using them.

But what about today? Today we have the evidence required, *all of it.* And it is overwhelming! All the many, many parts of the great sign of the "last days" are here, together with verifying Bible chronology.

Take a simple illustration: Suppose on a hot day at the beginning of summer, someone told you that winter was coming within a week because he had seen some trees without leaves. But those trees could have died from disease or age. So, by itself that would not be enough evidence that winter was approaching. Especially so when none of the other trees had shed their leaves, when the heat continued day after day, and when the calendar told you it was just the beginning of summer. You

Awake!, Oct. 8, 1968.

claims. We should appeal to the facts. Let facts speak for themselves. Consult the factual record of Christendom's religious systems, Catholic and Protestant, not to speak of Jewry. More than that, examine also what those religious systems are doing today. Then consult the record of the one religious organization that all Christendom's religious organizations and Jewry strenuously opposed during World War I and have opposed since. Everybody knows that this opposed organization of Christians is Jehovah's witnesses. Consult the newspaper reports or magazine articles, the police and judicial court records, yes, consult the homes of the millions of people who have been visited by these witnesses of Jehovah, apart from their own annual reports and the *Yearbooks* of Jehovah's witnesses. Ask all these what the witnesses have been doing since 1919 till this very hour. The combined answer will be that they have been preaching by all the means and channels of publicity. They have specialized on preaching just one thing, and that is, God's kingdom of good news. This they have preached, as Jesus commanded, "for the purpose of a witness to all the nations," including the nations behind the Iron Curtain.

[13] The fact that decides the answer to the question is, not, Do all the clergy of Roman Catholicism and of Protestantism agree that Jehovah's witnesses have been and are God's prophet to the nations? but, Who discerned the divine will for Christians in this time of the world's end and offered themselves to do it? Who have undertaken God's foreordained work for this day of judgment of the nations? Who have answered the call to the work and have done it down till this year 1958? Whom has God actually used as his prophet?

13, 14. (a) What fact decides the answer to the question? (b) As regards the answer, why are Jehovah's witnesses grateful today, and why have they become happy?

[14] By the historical facts of the case Christendom is beaten back in defeat. Jehovah's witnesses are deeply grateful today that the plain facts show that God has been pleased to use them. All the preaching and all the Bible educational work that they have done till now in 175 countries and islands of the sea they confess has been, not by help of a military army, nor by human power, but by God's spirit, his invisible active force. (Zech. 4:6, *AV*) It has been because Jehovah thrust out his hand of power and touched their lips and put his words in their mouths. It has evidently been because he commissioned them to be over the nations and over the kingdoms. Happy are all those who have seen what the work of Jehovah God for now is and who have volunteered to do it.

TWO KINDS OF DIVINE WORK

[15] Individuals have not been foreordained for God's work, as in Jeremiah's case. The work was the thing foreordained. Christendom may fail to do the foreordained work, but it will be done just the same. We must harmonize with the work, not decide for ourselves what God's work should be at this time and then ask his divine blessing on what we decide. This latter course is one of lawlessness against God, no matter how loudly and insistently one claims to be a Christian. God offers the foreordained work to Christians, as these claim to have given themselves to him through Christ to do the divine will. Thus God lets Christians live up to their claims, if they want to, by accepting the work he foreordained for Christians in this day. Regardless of the names of the individuals, a remnant of consecrated, anointed witnesses of Jehovah rejoiced to be freed from their captivity during World

15. (a) What was it that was foreordained? (b) How, then, must Christians live up to their claims, and which "Christians" have done so?

The Watchtower, Jan. 15, 1959, pp. 40, 41.

lated out of the power of darkness into the Kingdom of God's dear Son.—Col. 1:13.

This *submission* for over eighteen centuries to the violence of dominant evil has not been because of lack of power on the part of our risen, ascended and glorified Lord to protect his people; for after his resurrection he declared,—"All power is given unto me in heaven and in earth." (Matt. 28:18.) The exercise of the power is delayed for a purpose. In the Father's plan there was a "due time" for the great sacrifice for sins to be given, and another due time for the Kingdom to be set up in power and great glory to rule and bless the world: and these were far enough apart to permit the calling and preparing of the "elect" Church to be joint-heirs of the Kingdom with Christ. The evil influences and opposition of sinners have been *permitted* for the purifying, testing and polishing of those "called" to be members of the Kingdom class. As with the Head, so with the body, it is God's design that each member shall as a new creature be "made perfect through suffering."—Heb. 5:9.

But now we are in the end of this Gospel age, and the Kingdom is being established or set up. Our Lord, the appointed King, is now present, since October 1874, A. D., according to the testimony of the prophets, to those who have ears to hear it: and the formal inauguration of his kingly office dates from April 1878, A. D.: and the first work of the Kingdom, as shown by our Lord, in his parables and prophecy (the gathering of "his elect"), is now in progress. "The dead in Christ shall rise *first*," explained the Lord through the Apostle; and the resurrection of the Church shall be in a moment.* Consequently the Kingdom, as represented in our Lord, and the sleeping saints already fitted and prepared and found worthy to be members of

* VOL. III. Chap. 6.

The Battle of Armageddon, Studies in the Scriptures, Series IV, 1897, p. 621.

are assembled in heaven with their Head and Master and presented faultless before the throne of God. There is now, we feel sure, a closer bond existing between the consecrated throughout the world than has existed for a long while, due to the fact of increased zeal and love for the Lord and his cause and for each other. It is a blessed thing for them to meet together now. How much more blessed will it be in the kingdom! Well has the poet expressed this thought in these lines:

"Oh, that glorious heav'nly city!
Oh, that New Jerusalem!
How 'twill shine in all its beauty!
'Twill be gorgeous as a gem.
We shall meet in that fair city;
We shall meet in that fair city—
In the New Jerusalem."

TESTS AND TEMPTATIONS

"The Lord thy God led thee these forty years ... to prove thee, to know what was in thine heart." "We are not ignorant of his devices."—Deuteronomy 8:2; 2 Corinthians 2:11.

A SHARP difference between tests and temptations must be noted. Tests are from God, very frequently by his providences, but sometimes, through an apparent withholding of himself from his servant. God tries his children, but does not tempt them. If the Scripture says God tempted Abraham, it is not to be understood as if it said God was tempting Abraham astray. God was trying Abraham's faith to give him an opportunity of strengthening himself in God, and also that God himself might refer to Abraham as a man of faith. Tests are always for our development and, as in Abraham's case, that God may be justified in all his ways.

GOD TESTS; SATAN TEMPTS

God tests; Satan tempts. God is always kind in his tests; Satan has always a murderous spirit in his temptations. All temptations are more or less directly from Satan. He seeks to break down the faith of God's people, and to that end uses many devices. He plays upon every weakness of the flesh, and by subtlety seeks to lead the mind away from the Hope. Every saint knows this enemy, and feels the cunning of Satan's attacks; but the saints of God are armed by knowledge, for to be forewarned is to be forearmed; and they know that their Lord is stronger than all that can be against them. No temptation is permitted to come upon the believer greater than he is able to bear, and no pressure beyond endurance is allowed by him who loves his own and watches for their every need. In these last days of the church upon earth Satan is particularly pressing upon the followers of the Lord Jesus. He would wear out the saints. To everyone come temptations to slackness; temptations to think too highly of himself; temptations to pride and to take his own viewpoint of the Lord's work. This day of the world's sore trouble is also the hardest in the experience of the church.

Both tests and temptations are usually considered in relation to an individual, but these come also upon the church as a whole. And this is specially the case in these the last days of the church's human history. Just as it is true that when God begets a son according to the spirit Satan tries to destroy the child of grace, so it is true respecting the church. God has now gathered his church as one family. Satan seeks to take advantage of this fact and, if he could, would destroy the church as a whole.

No one can properly understand the work of God at this present time who does not realize that since 1874, the time of the Lord's return in power, there has been a complete change in God's operations. Previous to that time God's people were not gathered together; the consecrated were scattered in the various systems. But since that time God has been gathering his consecrated into one family; and since then both his blessings and his testings have come upon the church collectively, as well as individually.

The blessings of God on the church since the time of the Lord's parousia have been multitudinous. Each of the consecrated has been privileged to have fellowship such as the church of God has not experienced except in the first few days of hallowed blessedness of joy and service just after Pentecost. God has now gathered the outcasts of Israel. (Psalm 147:2) But Satan seeks to take advantage of this fact, and has sought the destruction of the many, endeavoring to use God's blessings for his church to their hurt. In this new experience God has brought his *church* into testing, and of course, for their help.

TESTS STRENGTHEN THE FAITHFUL

There have been many tests; but out of all of them strength has come to the faithful, for these have been blessed with increased faith and understanding. The imprisonment of the leaders of the Lord's work in 1918 was such a test. The continuance of the sharp slanders upon our late beloved Brother Russell has proved a test. Changes of method of harvesting have also been used to the same end. God has, of course, a perfect right to permit untoward circumstances to come upon his church even as he has to permit them to come upon each individual member of the body of Christ. And the same result is always apparent; there is always gain. Those who are loyal are blessed; the faithful are preserved; their joy in the Lord increases. Those who were faithful in past testings, waiting upon God, ever ready to do his work, kept a clear understanding of the Lord's

The Watchtower, Sept. 15, 1922, p. 278.

[14]"Pentecost, that is, the fiftieth day, or Harvest Feast, or Feast of Weeks, may be regarded as a supplement to the Passover. It lasted only for one day; but the modern Jews extend it over two. The people, having at the Passover presented before God the first sheaf of the harvest, departed to their homes to gather it in, and then returned to keep the harvest-feast before Jehovah. From the sixteenth of Nisan seven weeks were reckoned inclusively, and the next or fiftieth day was the Day of Pentecost, which fell on the sixth of Sivan (about the end of May) (Exodus 23:16, 34:22; Leviticus 23:15-22; Numbers 28:26-31; Deuteronomy 16:9-12; 2 Maccabees 12:32; Acts 2:1, 20:16; 1 Corinthians 16:8). The intervening period included the whole of the grain harvest, of which the wheat was the latest crop. Its commencement is also marked as from the time when 'thou beginnest to put the sickle to the corn.' The Pentecost was the Jewish harvest-home; and the people were especially exhorted to rejoice before Jehovah with their families, their servants, the Levite within their gates, the stranger, the fatherless, and the widow, in the place chosen by God for His name, as they brought a freewill-offering of their hand to Jehovah their God.—Deuteronomy 16:10, 11."

[15]If we assume that the harvest of the wheat class, namely, the saints, began with the beginning of the second presence of our Lord in 1874, then would it be unreasonable to conclude that the harvest must continue for fifty symbolic days, or fifty literal years? If so, then we might expect the harvest to end fifty years after 1874, or with the year 1924. If this be true, what a wonderful incentive for the saints to be watchful, prayerful, active, and rejoicing in their privileges to have a part in the Lord's work in these concluding days of the harvest. That would mean that the selection of the royal family would be completed with the end of 1924. If this be true, then surely with confidence the saints now on earth can announce with the opening of this year, "The kingdom of heaven is at hand," because all the members of the royal line are about completed for the kingdom.

ITS MEANING TO THE CHURCH

[16]Surely there is not the slightest room for doubt in the mind of a truly consecrated child of God that the Lord Jesus is present and has been since 1874; that the harvest has been in progress during that time; that most of the saints have now been gathered. Therefore, can there be a reasonable doubt about the early completion of the church and its glorification in view of the fulfilment of prophecy? Do not all the physical facts about us indicate just exactly what we expected during the concluding hours of the church's earthly pilgrimage?

[17]Then should we expect the closing days of the harvest work and witnessing for the Lord to be all joy and no trials? To answer this question we must take into consideration the words of Jesus relative to the last work of the church. It seems quite clear that the last work of the church while in the flesh is to be that of proclaiming the good news that Satan's empire is falling; that the kingdom of heaven is here, and the blessing that the people will reap from that kingdom. Concerning this Jesus said: "And this gospel of the kingdom shall be preached in all the world for a witness unto all nations; and then shall the end come." (Matthew 24:14) The root word from which the word "end" is taken in this text is *"telos"*; and the meaning given to it by Doctor Strong is: "The point aimed at, as a limit, final or uttermost."

[18]The Lord's words here then, we would understand, mean to say: The point aimed at, as a limit of the work of the church while in the flesh, the final and uttermost part of that work, is and will be that of proclaiming the good tidings of the end of the old order and that the kingdom of heaven is here and of the blessings it will bring; and this should be done as a witness to the nations; that when this work of witnessing is done, that is, the end or final point aimed at, then will follow the great tribulation that will completely wreck all the nations.

[19]Necessarily there must be much joy in the heart of the Christian while proclaiming this blessed message, because it means the bringing to the people that which will comfort and console them in the hour of distress. It means to tell the groaning creation that the time for their deliverance is at hand. At the same time the words of Jesus in the context show that this final work to be done will be accompanied by many severe tests and trials. In verse thirteen he says: "He that endures unto the end, the same shall be saved." Here the word "end" is translated from the same Greek word *"telos."* Therefore we conclude that the endurance must relate to the same time that this message is to be delivered. If those who endure to the end are to be saved, the converse of the statement is true: That those who do not endure to the end will not be of the royal family. Since the endurance to the end and the preaching of the gospel of the kingdom referred to the same time, then it follows that there will be much to endure. The word "endure" means to bear trials, have fortitude, patiently suffer and persevere. Persevere means to persist in any business or enterprise undertaken, to maintain a purpose in spite of counter influences, opposition or discouragement; not to give over or abandon what is undertaken. The inference is, therefore, that there will be a great temptation to relax, to become discouraged, to yield to opposing influences and to give over or abandon the final work.

[20]The only conclusion to be drawn from these texts is that having put our hand to the plow we must keep on; that since the Lord has committed to his people the interests of his kingdom and commanded that these interests can be properly cared for by proclaiming the message of his kingdom, then a failure or refusal to do so would preclude one from being of the royal line. Strange as it may seem, many of these fiery trials, which will tend to discourage, will come from amongst the consecrated. St. Peter concerning this said: "Beloved, think it not strange concerning the fire that is among you to try you, as though some strange thing had happened unto you." Many of these trials will be due to

The Watchtower, Jan. 1, 1924, p. 5.

ers, evangelists and philanthropists—better, if they but realized it, than any foreign mission field we saw. And these emigrants, let us remember, although generally poor, are not always either ignorant or vicious. Some of them are God's consecrated saints whom he is sending here to be blessed and sealed with present truth, which he gives us the privilege of ministering to them.

True, the food of the lower classes of Europe would not be satisfactory to the average mechanic and laborer in the United States, who, accustomed to larger pay and unaccustomed to frugality, spends probably six times as much on his stomach, eating not only finer and more nutritious foods, but also much more of them, and wasting often through improvidence as much as or more than he eats. However, the European laborer seems to enjoy himself as much as or more than his artisan brother here, and on the whole there is more of an appearance of contentment on the faces of all the people there—the poor, the middle class and the rich—than on faces met in the streets here.

Intelligence without the grace of God to back it up brings discontent: only when it is backed by godliness, does it bring contentment, peace and joy. For this reason it is that the greater general intelligence and greater liberty of the people of the United States bring them, not more contentment, but less than their less favorably circumstanced European brothers. And this leads us to expect as stirring times in the United States as elsewhere when the "time of trouble" shall reach its height.

While the growing intelligence of Europeans is fast preparing them for the trouble and anarchy which God's Word predicts, it cannot reasonably be expected for some years yet. This is further in harmony with prophecy, though out of harmony with the expectations of many who look every day for a declaration of war in Europe, which they suppose will be the *battle* of the great day of God Almighty. Even should a war or revolution break out in Europe sooner than 1905, we could not consider it any portion of the severe trouble predicted. At most it could only be a forerunner to it, a mere "skirmish" as compared with what is to come. Indeed, in our judgment, based upon our observations, nothing could precipitate the great anarchistic trouble upon Europe, which the Scriptures predict, sooner than the date named, except a *famine* or some such unusual occurrence which would bring the people to feel that they have nothing to lose, but all to gain, by a general uprising.

While it was an agreeable surprise to us (in view of the contrary sensational accounts so often published) to find the situation in Europe as we here describe it—in harmony with what the Scriptures had led us to expect—yet so great is our confidence in the Word of God and in the light of present truth shining upon it, that we could not have doubted its testimony whatever had been the appearances. The date of the close of that "battle" is definitely marked in Scripture as October, 1914. It is already in progress, its beginning dating from October, 1874. Thus far it has been chiefly a battle of words and a time of organizing forces —capital, labor, armies and secret societies.

Never was there such a general time of banding together as at present. Not only are nations allying with each other for protection against other nations, but the various factions in every nation are organizing to protect their several interests. But as yet the various factions are merely studying the situation, testing the strength of their opponents, and seeking to perfect their plans and power for the future struggle, which many, without the Bible's testimony, seem to realize is the inevitable. Others still delude themselves, saying, Peace! Peace! when there is no possibility of peace until God's Kingdom comes into control, compelling the doing of his will on earth as it is now done in heaven.

This feature of the battle must continue with varying success to all concerned; the organization must be very thorough; and the final struggle will be comparatively short, terrible and decisive—resulting in general anarchy. In many respects the convictions of the world's great generals coincide with the predictions of God's Word. Then "Woe to the man or nation who starts the next war in Europe; for it will be a war of *extermination.*" It will be abetted not only by national animosities, but

The Watchtower, Jan. 15, 1892, p. 22.

ZION'S WATCH TOWER

AND

HERALD OF CHRIST'S PRESENCE.

PUBLISHED TWICE A MONTH.

TOWER PUBLISHING COMPANY, { "BIBLE HOUSE" ARCH STREET, ALLEGHENY, PA., U. S. A.

C. T. RUSSELL, EDITOR; MRS. C. T. RUSSELL, ASSOCIATE.

SUBSCRIPTION PRICE, $1.00 A YEAR, IN ADVANCE,

By Express Order, Postal Money Order, Bank Draft, or Registered Letter. Foreign only by *Foreign Money Order.*

FREE TO THE LORD'S POOR.

N. B.—Those of the *interested*, who by reason of old age or accidents, or other adversity, are unable to pay, will be supplied FREE, if they will send a Postal Card each December, stating their case and requesting the paper.

CAN IT BE DELAYED UNTIL 1914?

Seventeen years ago people said, concerning the time features presented in MILLENNIAL DAWN, They seem reasonable in many respects, but surely no such radical changes could occur between now and the close of 1914: if you had proved that they would come about in a century or two, it would seem much more probable.

What changes have since occured, and what velocity is gained daily!

"The old is quickly passing, and the new is coming in."

Now, in view of recent labor troubles and threatened anarchy, our readers are writing to know if there may not be a mistake in the 1914 date. They say that they do not see how present conditions can hold out so long under the strain.

We see no reason for changing the figures—nor could we change them if we would. They are, we believe, God's dates, not ours. But bear in mind that the end of 1914 is not the date for the *beginning*, but for the *end* of the time of trouble. We see no reason for changing from our opinion expressed in the View presented in the WATCH TOWER of Jan. 15, '92. We advise that it be read again.

TRACT NO. 21.—DO YOU KNOW?

We published one hundred and fifteen thousand copies of this tract, and have sent samples to all our TOWER readers. It seems to give general satisfaction, and orders from all quarters are large. We advise the circulation of this tract by all of you—on street cars, steam cars, at hotels and depots, and Sundays on the street-corners,—until everyone within your reach has been supplied. Order all that you will *agree to use*. Never mind the money. Many have opportunity for distributing sample copies of Old Theology Tracts who have no money to spare to pay for their printing, etc., but others, again, who have less opportunity for distributing tracts, take delight in meeting the publishing expenses, and thus help to preach the "good tidings of great joy, which shall be unto all people."

The first edition, although large, is already exhausted; but we have another edition of over two hundred thousand under way which will be ready in about ten days. Send in your order and have a share in this feature of the harvest work. There should be a million copies of this tract in circulation within a year.

ALLEGHENY CHURCH MEETINGS.

Our meetings are held in Bible House Chapel, Arch st., Allegheny, Pa. Readers and friends will be warmly welcomed. Preaching every Sunday at 3:30 P. M.

The Watchtower, July 15, 1894, p. 226.

are bound, not for Purgatory, but for eternal torment. So a devout Catholic has great fears of being a heretic. Thus we find but comparatively few Catholics even today who dare to read the Bible.

How much trouble all this nonsense has caused! The Bible foretold it all. The Apostle Paul declared that "many would depart from the faith, giving heed to seducing spirits and doctrines of devils." (1 Tim. 4:1-3; Acts 20:29, 30.) It is upon these seducing spirits that we lay the blame—Satan and his fallen angels. We are not claiming that our Catholic and Episcopalian friends have intended to perpetrate a fraud, nor any of the others. But with the Apostle Paul we claim that they were deceived by the great Adversary. We are beginning to see that a God of Love would never have such a Plan for His creatures as is taught by the creeds. We are living in a day when more light than ever before is due upon God's Word. We are living at the dawning of the glorious New Dispensation. We are nearing the time when, according to the Bible, "all the blind eyes shall be opened and the deaf ears unstopped." Thank God!

ARMAGEDDON NEAR—GOD'S KINGDOM TO FOLLOW

The present great war in Europe is the beginning of the Armageddon of the Scriptures. (Rev. 16:16-20.) It will eventuate in the complete overthrow of all the systems of error which have so long oppressed the people of God and deluded the world. All iniquity of every kind will go down. The glorious Kingdom of Messiah is about to be set up in the earth, for the deliverance of the world and the establishment of permanent righteousness. We believe the present war cannot last much longer until revolution shall break out. The nations are rapidly impoverishing themselves.

Great Britain has already expended thirteen billions of dollars in the war, and her minister of finance says that another year of war will require nine billions more. That will make twenty-two billions. At five per cent interest

Pastor Russell's Sermons, 1917.

God-given message with boldness and fearlessness at all times.

God used holy men to write the Bible, and gave them an understanding of what he wished them to write, by giving them special visions and revelations of his will and purpose. This special revelation of his will and purpose is called "inspiration", and is mentioned by Peter as follows: "The prophecy came not in old time by the will of man: but holy men of God spake as they were moved by the holy spirit." —2 Pet. 1:21.

These holy prophets were used by God to foretell his purpose and his work, as well as certain events that pertained to God's people who lived in the days when the prophecies were made, and also to his people who would live in the future. They foretold many things that had fulfilment at the first advent of the Lord, and many other things that are now in process of fulfilment and will be fulfilled in the near future. The many fulfilments of these prophecies at the first advent, which are now facts recorded in history, prove beyond any question that the men who uttered these prophecies were God's holy prophets and had the divine approval. Yet there are men in our day who dare to sneer at and criticize these prophets.

In addition to the Old Testament prophets, Jesus and the apostles were likewise prophets, because they gave to us a message from Jehovah God and foretold many events to occur at the second advent of the Lord. Since the Bible was completed, this *special* "inspiration" from God through visions and revelations has ceased, for the reason that it is no longer necessary. To one who has a proper faith in God and his Word, the Bible is sufficient. He does not need special revelation to bolster up his faith. Anyone who lacks faith in God's Word, and needs some special demonstration or evidence that God is true, cannot be pleasing to God. God is testing the faith of his own people now, their faith in his Word and the promises recorded therein.

Many professed people of God lack a proper faith, and are constantly seeking some outward signs or evidences of divine approval and acceptance. The apostle mentions these as follows: "The god of this world hath blinded the minds of them which *believe not,* lest the light of the glorious gospel of Christ . . . should shine unto them." (2 Cor. 4:4) Jesus rebuked his disciples for their lack of faith, saying: "O fools, and slow of heart to believe all that the prophets have spoken!" (Luke 24:25) God is dealing with his people now "according to their faith"; and a person who must depend upon his emotions or upon spiritistic, hypnotic or mesmeric revelations in order to know what the will of God is has no proper or acceptable faith in the revealed Word of God; and so Satan uses spiritism, mesmerism and other occult deceptions to blind his mind to the truth. Those agents of Satan who use these methods of deception to blind the minds of the Lord's people are called false prophets.

The Bible is sufficient and needs no outside support or signs to demonstrate its truthfulness. Paul says: 'The holy scriptures are able to make thee wise unto salvation, through faith which is in Christ Jesus.' 'All scripture inspired by God is profitable for doctrine, for reproof, for correction, for instruction in righteousness: that the man of God may be perfect, thoroughly furnished unto every good work.' If this text is true, then any man who denies any portion of the inspired Word is a false prophet.

Some parts of the Bible are not inspired, however. Satan's words to mother Eve, of course, are not inspired. The words of the hypocritical scribes and Pharisees are not inspired. The words of the three men who accused Job are not inspired, neither are the words of the prophets of Baal, the enemies of Israel, nor of Pilate, Herod, or those men and women who were possessed of demons. The text just quoted says: 'All scripture *inspired of God* is profitable.' It is the *inspired* scriptures that were written by holy men. It is these scriptures that honor and magnify the name of Jehovah God; they harmoniously proclaim his attributes; they contain no contradictions; they correctly state God's law or rule of action; and every prophetic utterance found in these *inspired* scriptures is sure of fulfilment.

Since the Bible was completed, and "inspiration" is no longer necessary, a true prophet is one who is faithfully proclaiming what *is written* in the Bible. Such a one is declaring that the Bible is the Word of God, and that it is true and contains no contradictions. He is constantly telling the people of a coming kingdom of righteousness which will bless all the families of earth, both living and dead.

Since the Bible was completed, and special "inspiration" is no longer necessary, a false prophet is one who denies that the Bible is the Word of God; denies that it is inspired; denies the virgin birth of Jesus; denies the necessity for the death of Jesus; denies the story of creation, sin, and the fall. These false prophets seize upon some new-found fossil remains, some old bones recently dug up, and try their best to undermine faith in the Bible and to give the lie to the same by proclaiming some wild theory or guess of their own, and then call these guesses by the high-sounding name of "science".

But it may be asked, How are we to know whether one is a true or a false prophet? There are at least three ways by which we can positively decide: (1) If he is a true prophet, his message will come to pass exactly as prophesied. If he is a false prophet, his prophecy will fail to come to pass. This rule is laid down by God himself, through Moses, as follows: "If thou say in thine heart, How shall we know the word

The Watchtower, May 15, 1930, p. 154.

which the Lord hath *not* spoken? When a prophet speaketh in the name of the Lord, if the thing follow not, nor come to pass, that is the thing which the Lord hath not spoken, but the prophet hath spoken it presumptuously."—Deut. 18:21, 22.

(2) Any prophet whose message tends to turn people against God and his Word or to plant doubts in their hearts, or who denies or contradicts the Word of God, is a false prophet. In Deuteronomy 13:5 are these words: "That prophet . . . shall be put to death; because he hath spoken to turn you away from the LORD your God."

(3) All God's holy prophets have been, and still are, persecuted for their faithfulness in telling the message God has given them to tell, while the false prophets have never yet been persecuted. The reason for this is obvious. God's holy prophets foretell the destruction of all false prophets, the destruction of all wickedness and of all wicked people. Of course, this arouses the anger of the false prophets' father, the Devil; and he instigates all manner of persecution against God's prophets, and uses his dupes to do the persecuting. God's prophets never persecute anybody, not even their enemies. All persecution is of Satan.

Judged by these three tests, Moses, Samuel, Job, Isaiah, Jeremiah, Ezekiel, and all the minor prophets of the Old Testament, as well as Jesus and the apostles, were true prophets. Every one of these uttered prophecies which have already come true, and others which are to be fulfilled in the near future. Every one of them magnified the name of Jehovah God; every one of them believed in the Bible as the Word of God and honored and reverenced the same, and taught others to do likewise. They stood like adamant against the heathen gods and the doctrines and theories of men; and without exception they were persecuted for giving out their message.

The conclusion, therefore, is irresistible that they were God's holy prophets. The difference between a true and a false prophet is that the one is speaking the word of the Lord and the other is speaking his own dreams and guesses. This is most emphatically stated in Jeremiah 23:25-32, which reads: "I have heard what the prophets said, that prophesy lies in my name, saying, I have dreamed, I have dreamed. . . . yea, they are prophets of the deceit of their own heart; which think to cause my people to forget my name by their dreams . . . . The prophet that hath a dream, let him tell a dream; and he that hath my word, let him speak my word faithfully. . . . Behold, I am against them that prophesy false dreams, saith the Lord, . . . and cause my people to err by their lies, and by their lightness; yet I sent them not, nor commanded them."

The true prophet of God *today* will be telling forth what the Bible teaches, and those things that the Bible tells us are soon to come to pass. He will not be sounding forth man-made theories or guesses, either his own or those of others. He will be telling forth the good news of the coming kingdom of Christ, which will bless all the families of the earth. Why will he be telling of this kingdom? The answer is, Because all God's holy prophets spoke of it, including Jesus and his apostles.

In the New Testament, and in our day, the word "prophet" has a thought similar to that of our word "teacher", in the sense of a public expounder. Hence when the term "false prophet" is used, we shall get the correct thought if we think of a false teacher. The false prophets or teachers of our day are referred to in the New Testament as "antichrists", for the reason that the word "antichrist" means "against Christ". Every person who denies the statements of Jesus or of the holy prophets is against Christ, because he is teaching that which is against the truth, against Christ and against Jehovah God.

The false prophets of our day are the financial, political and clerical prognosticators. They assume to foretell future events; but their dreams or guesses never come true, and are always contrary to the teachings of God's holy prophets. Let us note some examples of false teachings which are contrary to the teachings of Jesus and his apostles and which are put forth by the three classes just mentioned; namely, politicians, clerics and financiers.

With united voice they declare that the world is getting better and will continue to get better until Christ comes. Now note what God's holy teachers or prophets say on this subject. These declare that the world will get worse and worse, and that Christ will come for the purpose of converting the world. In 1 John 2:18 we read: "Little children, it is the last time; and as ye have heard that antichrist shall come, even now are there many antichrists; whereby we know that it is the last time." This text tells us that in "the last time" the world will be filled with antichrists. This being true, of course it will not be converted, as the false teachers claim.

Again, in 1 Timothy 4:1, 2 we read: "Now the spirit speaketh expressly, that in the latter times some shall depart from the faith, giving heed to seducing spirits, and doctrines of devils; speaking lies in hypocrisy; having their conscience seared [as] with a hot iron." Again, in 2 Timothy 3:1-5 is the following statement: "This know also, that in the last days perilous times shall come. For men shall be lovers of their own selves, covetous, boasters, proud, blasphemers"; and then follows a long list of other sins which will prevail in the last days. This text proves again that those men who foretell things out of harmony with the Bible statements are false prophets.

In 1914-1918 these same three classes told the whole

The Watchtower, May 15, 1930, p. 155.

world that the great World War would end all wars and make the world safe for democracy; and that the young men who died on the field of battle would die sacrificial deaths as did Jesus and would go to heaven. Their prophecies did not come true. Therefore they are false prophets; and the people should no longer trust them as safe guides, but should look to the Lord through his revealed Word for their instructions as to what is to occur on the earth in the future.

The Apostle Peter warns us of these false prophets in the last days, saying: "But there were false prophets also among the people, even as there shall be false teachers among you, who privily shall bring in damnable heresies, even denying the Lord that bought them." (2 Pet. 2:1) There are many thousands of prominent religious leaders in our day who deny that the blood of Jesus bought the race; they claim that it was not necessary for Jesus to die; they go even further and claim that he did not die, but was really more alive than ever, when he was buried in Joseph's tomb. These are false prophets, because they contradict the Bible and the words of the holy prophets, and thus cast reproach on the Bible and lead people to doubt its truthfulness, and thus turn people away from God.

The words of God's true prophets on this subject are as follows: "Without shedding of blood is no remission." (Heb. 9:22) "Christ died for our sins according to the scriptures." (1 Cor. 15:3) "Ye are bought with a price." (1 Cor. 6:20) "Ye were not redeemed with corruptible things, as silver and gold, . . . but with the precious blood of Christ, as of a lamb without blemish and without spot."—1 Pet. 1:18, 19.

Several texts tell us that Jesus was dead, and was raised on the third day. (1 Cor. 15:4) The false teachers claim that Jesus was not dead, and hence did not need a resurrection. These false prophets claim that it is the body that will be resurrected. But Paul, one of God's holy prophets, speaking of the resurrection of the dead, says: "But some man will say, How are the dead raised up? and with what body do they come? Thou fool! . . . that which thou sowest, thou sowest not that body that shall be . . . ; but God giveth it a body as it hath pleased him."—1 Cor. 15:35-38.

The false prophets claim that the earth is to be burned up at some future time; but God's holy prophets emphatically state to the contrary. In Ecclesiastes 1:4 we read: "The earth abideth for ever." Again, in Isaiah 45:18 we read: "God himself . . . formed the earth and made it; he hath established it, he created it not in vain, he formed it to be inhabited."

These false prophets tell the people that God has provided a lake of fire and brimstone in which to torture for ever those who do not accept their teachings; others tell the people that many are in purgatory, and that it is possible to pray them out. They teach the people the doctrine of the trinity; namely, that 'God the Father, God the Son, and God the holy ghost are three persons in one, and all three equal in substance, in power and in eternity'. They tell the people that they need not study the Bible, 'because they cannot understand it'; and that if the people will follow the instructions of these false prophets they will not need to study the Bible. Without exception, these things are unscriptural and untrue, and tend to turn the people away from God and from Bible study.

These false prophets claim that the governments of earth, even though very wicked and corrupt, constitute God's kingdom on earth. They claim that all the saved will be in heaven, in face of hundreds of texts which say that the righteous shall inherit the land and dwell therein for ever. (Isa. 60:21) They discourage Bible study by telling the people that the "Bible is an old fiddle on which one can play any tune", that it is a book of mystery, and that God did not intend it to be understood. Such remarks turn people away from God and from the Bible, and brand the authors of such statements as being false prophets.

Why is it that the words of God's holy prophets are discredited, denied and sneered at, while the words of these false prophets are given the widest possible publicity, and approved by all great men of earth? The records of God's holy prophets, found in the Bible, show that Adam was the first man, and that he lived about 6,056 years ago. Quite recently a man found some bones in Nebraska, and broadcast to the world that they were the bones of a man who had lived in Nebraska over 5,000,000 years ago. His statement was wild, unreasonable and foolish; yet it could be published in the best magazines and newspapers, and retailed from the best pulpits and platforms in the world.

On the contrary, if any one should try to defend the accuracy of the Bible and prove that its authors were holy men sent of God, his copy would be refused by the best newspapers and magazines, and he would be denied the use of halls or pulpits to put forth his message. Should some paper be liberal enough to publish his defense, it would be so garbled as to discredit the author and hold him up to ridicule. Why is this true? The answer is that the false prophets, financial, political and religious, control the pulpit and the press; and that they desire to hold on to their positions of trust, influence and power. They do not want the truth, namely, that they are false prophets, to get out to the people; and so they use their power over the pulpit and press to keep the message from the people.

Anyone who will stand up to defend Jehovah God

The Watchtower, May 15, 1930, p. 156.

the hills; and people shall flow unto it. And many nations shall come, and say, Come, and let us go up to the mountain of the Lord, and to the house of the God of Jacob; and he will teach us of his ways, and we will walk in his paths: for the law shall go forth of Zion, and the word *of the Lord from Jerusalem. And he shall judge* among many people, and rebuke strong nations afar off; and they shall beat their swords into plowshares, and their spears into pruninghooks; nation shall not life up a sword against nation, neither shall they learn war any more. But they shall sit every man under his vine and under his fig tree; and none shall make them afraid; for the mouth of the Lord of hosts hath spoken it." —Micah 4:1-4.

EARTHLY RULERS

As we have heretofore stated, the great jubilee cycle is due to begin in 1925. At that time the earthly phase of the kingdom shall be recognized. The Apostle Paul in the eleventh chapter of Hebrews names a long list of faithful men who died before the crucifixion of the Lord and before the beginning of the selection of the church. These can never be a part of the heavenly class; they had no heavenly hopes; but God has in store something good for them. They are to be resurrected as perfect men and constitute the princes or rulers in the earth, according to his promise. (Psalm 45:16; Isaiah 32:1; Matthew 8:11) Therefore we may confidently expect that 1925 will mark the return of Abraham,

Millions Now Living Will Never Die, 1920, p. 89.

Isaac, Jacob and the faithful prophets of old, particularly those named by the Apostle in Hebrews chapter eleven, to the condition of human perfection.

RECONSTRUCTION

All the statesmen of the world, all the political economists, all the thoughtful men and women, recognize the fact that the conditions existing prior to the war have passed away and that a new order of things must be put in vogue. All such recognize that this is a period now marking the beginning of reconstruction. The great difficulty is that these men are exercising only human wisdom and have ignored the divine arrangement. We are indeed at the time of reconstruction, the reconstruction not only of a few things, but of all things. The reconstruction will not consist of patching up old and broken down systems and forms and arrangements, but the establishment of a new and righteous one under the great ruler Christ Jesus, the Prince of Peace. The Apostle Peter at Pentecost, speaking under divine inspiration, and referring to that time, said: "Times of refreshing shall come from the presence of the Lord; and he shall send Jesus Christ, which before was preached unto you: whom the heaven must receive [retain] until the times of restitution of all things, which God hath spoken by the mouth of all his holy prophets since the world began". —Acts 3:19 - 21.

Millions Now Living Will Never Die, 1920, p. 90.

The Apostle's argument in this text is, that as new creatures we must not be carnally minded, because in the new creature the holy spirit dwells; hence that we should cleanse ourselves from all filthiness of the flesh and of the mind, that we might be more and more made into the likeness of our Lord and Head. Following this instruction, it is to be seen that we should keep the body clean and in as healthy condition as possible, and that the clothing wherewith it is clothed should be always neat and clean, be it ever so common. Such things influence the mind toward cleanliness. An untidy, unclean thing has a tendency to lead the mind in the wrong direction.

Unselfish things, high and pure things, lead the mind in the right direction. Malice, hatred, ill-will, fault-finding, sensuality, selfishness, corrupt the mind; and if the mind is permitted to meditate and study upon such things, the tendency is to overthrow the will power to do right. On the contrary, when the mind is filled with good things the will of God is more clearly seen, thus enabling us to follow God's holy will.

The importance of proper thoughts was emphasized by St. Paul when he said: "Finally, brethren, whatsoever things are true, whatsoever things are honest, whatsoever things are just, whatsoever things are pure, whatsoever things are lovely, whatsoever things are of good report; if there be any virtue, and if there be any praise, think on these things." (Philippians 4: 8) The new creature, therefore, grows by concentrating his mind upon spiritual things, that is to say, by studying and meditating upon that which relates to God's character and to his plans and purposes for the deliverance of humanity into the realm of life and happiness. Thus using the mind, we ascertain what is the good and acceptable and perfect will of God concerning us and our course as Christians; and as we follow his will, the transformation progresses from one degree of glory to another, by the spirit of the Lord.

TEXT FOR MAY 2

"By one spirit are we all baptized into one body."—1 Corinthians 12: 13.

THE body of Christ is made up of many members. As soon as one is begotten of the holy spirit he is set or placed in the body of Christ by Jehovah, according to God's own pleasure. (1 Corinthians 12: 18) Each member of the body, then, has his separate functions to perform. This does not mean, however, that one member of the body is more important in its structure than others, and that some members may be ignored, as though there were no need for such in the body.

By one spirit, the holy spirit of God, each member is immersed into the body of Christ; and from that moment forward it becomes his privilege, yea his duty, to look well to his own spiritual interests and also to look out for the interests of other members of the body. There must be a real family or reciprocal love between the members of the body; and such love will, and does, exist in the heart of each one who appreciates the fact that he is a member of the body of Christ. This love draws them together and holds them together.

Futhermore, there must be an unselfish love of each member for every other member, which leads each to do good to his brother as opportunity offers. Thereby is the spirit of the Lord made manifest. Wherever the spirit of oneness exists amongst Christians and each one manifests the proper spirit toward the other, a division in the class is an impossibility. As there is no division in the body of Christ, even so all who are diligently putting aside selfishness and being transformed into the likeness of our Lord will desire to hold together and will hold together. Appreciating the proper relationship existing between the members of the body leads each one thus appreciating it to be loyal to every other member of the body. By one spirit, the spirit of love, each one is placed in the body; and all are held together, growing into the likeness of the Head.

QUESTION AND ANSWER

Question: Did the order go forth eight months ago to the Pilgrims to cease talking about 1925? Have we more reason, or as much, to believe the kingdom will be established in 1925 than Noah had to believe that there would be a flood?

Answer: It is surprising how reports get abroad. There was never at any time any intimation to the Pilgrim brethren that they should cease talking about 1925. Anyone who has made the statement that such an instruction was sent out has made it without any authority or excuse or cause.

Our thought is, that 1925 is definitely settled by the Scriptures, marking the end of the typical jubilees. Just exactly what will happen at that time no one can tell to a certainty; but we expect such a climax in the affairs of the world that the people will begin to realize the presence of the Lord and his kingdom power. He is already present, as we know, and has taken unto himself his power and begun his reign. He has come to his temple. He is dashing to pieces the nations. Every Christian ought to be content, then, to do with his might what his hands find to do, without stopping to quibble about what is going to happen on a certain date.

As to Noah, the Christian now has much more upon which to base his faith than Noah had (so far as the Scriptures reveal) upon which to base his faith in a coming deluge.

The Watchtower, April 1, 1923, p. 106.

The WATCH TOWER
AND HERALD OF CHRIST'S PRESENCE

VOL. XLV JULY 15, 1924 No. 14

OUR PRESENT DUTIES

"And I have put my words in thy mouth, and I have covered thee in the shadow of mine hand, that I may plant the heavens, and lay the foundations of the earth, and say unto Zion, Thou art my people."—Isaiah 51:16.

THE Lord lays certain duties and obligations upon his followers. Performance of these duties is not compulsory; but failure or refusal to perform them may cause one who has for some time been following him to fail and fall out. Faithful performance of our duties will surely result in attaining the promised blessings. This faithful performance must continue until the last. The Lord himself has said to his followers: "Be thou faithful unto death, and I will give thee a crown of life." And mere mental loyalty will not suffice; for "faith without works is dead." There must be an active demonstration of loyalty as opportunity is afforded.

²It will not do to say that 1925 is approaching and the work will not be finished during that year, and that therefore one can slack up for awhile and take on the work again some time later. Who knows that the work of the Church this side the vail may not be completed in 1925? It is unlike the Lord to tell his people just what day their work in any line will be completed and when they will enter another condition. He expects us to walk by faith, trusting him as to the result. But for the sake of argument, suppose that we assume the Church will not finish its work here in 1925. Would that be a just cause or excuse to slack the hand now? Could faithfulness be shown by ceasing for a time to advertise the King and his kingdom, and thus neglecting the interests committed unto us?

³Suppose the Lord should say to his people in 1925 words to the effect that several years more will be required to give the witness to the nations before all the body members shall be changed into glorious spirit beings. Would not the truly loyal ones respond in effect thus? "Gracious Lord, thy will be done. The place thou hast given me in thy cause to advertise thy kingdom is the most blessed one I have ever had or ever hope here to have. I love thee; and I am determined to be loyal to thee. Therefore gladly will I stay where thou requestest me to stay, and I will go when and where thou directest me to go. Whatsoever is thy will, that I shall do."

⁴How could any one be loyal to the Lord even unto death and take any other course? Let no one now be deceived by calculations as to just when the Lord will cease his work with the Church on earth. The year 1925 is a date definitely and clearly marked in the Scriptures, even more clearly than that of 1914; but it would be presumptuous on the part of any faithful follower of the Lord to assume just what the Lord is going to do during that year. Each day the faithful will do with his might what his hands find to do as though it is the last day; and he will look forward to being loyal to the Lord in continuing to do his holy will whether he be in the flesh many months or many years.

⁵The reports from the field show that there are not quite so many active workers in the field now as there were a year ago. The reports also show that those who are in the field are placing more books in the hands of the people, and are giving a more effectual witness and showing better results than they did a year ago. This proves conclusively that the withdrawal of some from the field is not due to slowing up of the work or that there is less to do; but it proves exactly the contrary. If some fail to do the work, the Lord will take away that which they have and commit it into the hands of others. The reports conclusively show that the Lord is blessing those who persist in advertising his kingdom.

⁶Of course, there may be some who are so handicapped by conditions over which they have no control that they cannot continue to engage actively in the field service. If one is doing what is within the reasonable scope of his power, and what he has opportunities to do, then surely that is pleasing to the Lord; and he would require no more. But the question is, Have some turned aside from advertising the King and his kingdom in order to gratify some earthly desire? Have some turned their minds to money-making, contrary to the admonition of St. Paul? (Hebrews 13:5, *Diaglott*) Examine the context of the Apostle's words in the text last cited; and it will be found to relate specifically to the time in which we are now living; hence indicating that some would yield to the temptations of this world and neglect faithfully to perform the duties devolving upon them as representatives of the Lord.

The Watchtower, July 15, 1924, p. 211.

The WATCH TOWER
AND HERALD OF CHRIST'S PRESENCE

VOL. XLVI JANUARY 1, 1925 No. 1

WORK FOR THE ANOINTED

"The Spirit of the Lord God is upon me; because the Lord hath anointed me to preach the good tidings unto the meek: . . . to proclaim . . . the day of vengeance of our God; to comfort all that mourn."—Isaiah 61:1, 2.

THE paramount duty devolving upon every intelligent creature is to glorify God. It is the expressed will of Jehovah that the unfolding and outworking of his plan shall be to his glory. When the divine program relating to man is complete, every feature thereof will reflect the dignity, majesty, and glory of God. Christians, being the chief recipients of Jehovah's favor, should always be eager to do something to the glory of God. Working in harmony with the divine plan, and being prompted so to do by unselfish devotion to the Lord and to his cause, will accomplish for the faithful this desired end.

[2]The year 1925 is here. With great expectation Christians have looked forward to this year. Many have confidently expected that all members of the body of Christ will be changed to heavenly glory during the year. This may be accomplished. It may not be. In his own due time God will accomplish his purposes concerning his own people. Christians should not be so deeply concerned about what may *transpire* during this year that they would fail to joyfully *do* what the Lord would have them to do.

[3]A Christian is one who is begotten and anointed of the holy spirit. He has agreed to do the will of God. The obligation devolves upon him to perform faithfully his part of the covenant. This he must do before he can enter the heavenly kingdom. The Lord is not taking men to heaven merely to save them, but that his purposes concerning the entire human family may be accomplished and that his own name may be glorified. There are some things for the Christian to do before he is taken to heaven. A failure or refusal to do those things would necessarily bar his entrance into the kingdom. Nor will the thing that the Christian actually does be the most important thing, but the spirit or motive by which he does it will be the deciding factor. That which should chiefly concern the Christian for this year then should be: Am I faithfully performing my covenant in the spirit of Christ?

The word "anointed", as related to the Christian, means his divinely-given commission or warrant of authority. A commission is a formal statement conferring power and authority upon one or more creatures authorizing or commanding the doing of certain things. One receiving such commission will, if he is discreet, from time to time consult the terms or provisions of that commission, and ascertain whether or not he is performing those duties.

[5]The anointed ones must hold fast to that which they have learned, to wit: That the Lord Jesus Christ, the Redeemer and Head of the Church, is now present and has taken his power and begun his reign; that the great fundamental truths of God's plan have been restored to the Church, which restoration was foreshadowed by the work of Elijah; that the Lord has come to his temple and is examining the members thereof; that the present work of the Church this side of the vail was foreshadowed by the work of Elisha, who did both a slaying and a comforting work; that the part of the commission given to the Church yet unfulfilled is: To declare the day of vengeance of our God, and to comfort all that mourn.

[6]An abundant entrance into the kingdom of our Lord and Savior is the sincere desire of each one of the anointed. To this end it is essential that he hold fast in these precious truths. He must hold fast with fortitude; he must increase in knowledge, hence the necessity for the study of the Word of God; he must exercise self-control and cheerfully drink the potion which the Lord has poured for him; he must grow in godliness, manifesting love for the brethren and an unselfish devotion to the Lord and his cause. The doing of these things will require the faithful performance of the obligations laid upon the Christian by his divinely given commission. The promise is, that if he gives diligence to the doing of these things he shall never fall, and he shall have an abundant entrance into the everlasting kingdom. It seems clear, therefore, that activity in proportion to opportunity is now required of all who will from this time forward enter into the kingdom.

[7]The commission to the Church shows there are two classes that are the objects of comfort, namely: (1)

The Watchtower, Jan. 1, 1925, p. 3.

the Lord has graciously provided his message in such printed form that each and every one of the anointed ones may have some opportunity in using this message to the glory of the Lord and thus to the carrying out of the Christian's commission.

DANGER OF DECEPTION

[24] Note the marginal reading of the text, 2 Chronicles 29: 11. It says: "My sons, be not now deceived." One who is negligent is deceived or ensnared by the Devil or by some of his agencies. The adversary will try to inject into the minds of some the thought that their physical condition will not warrant them in further activity in the Lord's service, and thereby will ensnare such a one. Most of the ailments that induce such to cease activity in the Lord's service are in the mind and not particularly physical ailments. Remember our consecration is to be faithful in service even unto death. Better by far would it be to die in the active service of the Lord than to imagine ourself ill and thereby be ensnared by Satan, who would lead us into such idleness and negligence which may result in the loss of everything. If the adversary can lull some to sleep on any pretext and cause them to become indifferent to their own course of action, indifferent to the giving of the testimony for the King and for Jehovah's cause, he will thereby gain the victory.

[25] It is to be expected that Satan will try to inject into the minds of the consecrated the thought that 1925 should see an end of the work, and that therefore it would be needless for them to do more. This conclusion is warranted by the words of the Master. Referring to these very perilous times in the end, Jesus said: 'If it were possible they would deceive the very elect.' It is not likely that any will now be deceived concerning the fundamental doctrines; these are clearly settled in the minds of the anointed ones. But it seems quite clear that there is danger of being lulled into a state of indifference, carelessness and negligence, both in conduct and in service of the Lord, and thereby being deceived by the adversary. Diligence now and to the end seems absolutely essential to victory.

[26] The anointed ones should now reason thus: 'I have gladly severed my connection with Satan's organization; I have fled to Christ for refuge; I have been received into the family of God; I am now a son of God and abiding in his temple; I know that my Lord and King is here; I have enlisted upon his side; I know that Satan is now seeking my destruction because I am striving to keep the commandments of my God and have the testimony that I am the Lord's; I know that my preservation and ultimate victory depend upon my faithfulness to him, not for a short time only but to the very end. Therefore with me time is no more. I am irrevocably and forever on the Lord's side, and by his grace I will stand before him and serve him and shall show forth his praises now, henceforth and forever.' It seems that the anointed in such an attitude would not be at all anxious about what may or may not transpire in 1925. They will see that they have everything to lose by becoming negligent and indifferent, and everything to gain by remaining stedfast, diligent and faithful.

[27] The Apostle Peter, addressing himself to the anointed, to whom the exceeding great and precious promises are given, says: "Brethren, give diligence to make your calling and election sure: for if ye do these things ye shall never fall." (2 Peter 1: 10, 11) It follows then that either negligence in our course of conduct or unfaithfulness in the Lord's service would cause us to fail in the race for the high calling and to miss the blessedness of the kingdom. Therefore diligence and fervency in spirit should mark the Christian's activity and course of conduct every day.

FEARLESSNESS

[28] He who is thus fervent and diligent will be without fear. Perfect love knows no fear, and perfect love means an unselfish devotion to the Lord and his cause. If the Christian is perfect in love he is like our Lord was when on earth. Jesus expresses this condition in these words: 'Of my own self I can do nothing. I came to do the will of my Father.' (John 5: 30) He did not mean that he had no power to do anything of himself. What he did mean was that he was so thoroughly devoted to his Father that he could not do anything contrary to his Father's will. He could not do violence to himself and to his covenant and do God's will at the same time.

[29] The Apostle Paul expressed the same thought when he said: "This one thing I do." As it was with Jesus so must it be now with the members of his body. They know nothing and can do nothing except what is commanded of the Lord. The words of our text thus come forcibly to us at this time: "My sons, be not now negligent." Each member of the body who will win the prize must now have in mind the one thing he must do, and that one thing is to diligently, earnestly and zealously press on, marking well his course as a follower in the footsteps of Jesus and joyfully proclaiming the message of the King and his kingdom.

[30] The church is now entering the portals of the new order under the great King of righteousness. The remaining members are the only witnesses on earth that Jehovah is God. All the nominal professed Christians have failed to give the witness that Jehovah is God. Great therefore is the privilege of those who are called out of darkness into the marvelous light of Jehovah, to testify that he is the Most High. The time has come for God to make for himself a name. The diligent, fervent and zealous ones will seize every opportunity to give the testimony to this fact. This testimony may be given by word of mouth or by the printed message which the Lord has put into our hands for that purpose.

[31] Having in mind then the responsibility of the position that we occupy by virtue of the Lord's favor,

The Watchtower, Sept. 1, 1925, p. 262.

ouster, until ten years afterward. However, all people alive then could easily recognize World War I as bringing great tribulation on mankind.

Of course, in our discussions the question came up, 'If the great tribulation is so closely connected with World War I, would World War II be considered a resumption of the tribulation?' No, that war was different. During World War I God's people expected it to lead directly into Armageddon, but Jehovah prevented such a climax at that time. We didn't succumb to such an expectation during World War II. Rather, in 1942 we learned that the war would end and that the beastly peace organization would be re-established. And that's just what occurred. But when the tribulation is resumed, it will definitely lead into Armageddon.

Some noted, though, that the same sentence in the book identified it as a "final" tribulation. Does that not mean that "tribulation" is restricted to Armageddon? No, Daniel 12:1 shows that this "time of distress" is associated with Jesus' standing up as king in 1914. The tribulation that began in that year was interrupted or "cut short." Soon it will start again when the political element turns on Babylon the Great and destroys her. The events thus initiated will reach a climax of tribulation on the nations at their Armageddon destruction. So, as a whole it will be the "final" tribulation on this wicked system of things. In its last part it will be a "tribulation such as has not occurred since the world's beginning . . . nor will occur again."—Matt. 24:21.

Another matter that we discussed with great interest was water baptism and its significance. What first got us thinking about this was the comment on page 90 to the effect that even as a babe Jesus was dedicated to God, being part of a dedicated nation. How did you react to that comment?

Thinking back, we could see how Jehovah dealt in a special way with the natural seed of Abraham. Isaac and Jacob were treated in a distinct way because they were in the line of the natural seed to which God had given the Promised Land. (Gen. 17:7, 8; 22: 15-18) With this promise in mind, He eventually redeemed the Israelites out of Egypt, taking them to himself as a special nation. (Ex. 6:6, 7; Deut. 7:6-11; 1 Chron. 17:21, 22) At Mt. Sinai they entered a formal, legal contract to be a nation dedicated to God. (Ex. 19:4-8; Josh. 24:16, 17) Did you think of some of those points when reflecting on the reason why the Jews could be considered a dedicated nation? With this as a basis, it was easy to see why Jesus' baptism was not a symbol of a recent dedication to God, but of a presentation of himself to do Jehovah's will at the due time.—Heb. 10:7.

Our discussions, though, also helped us to realize how this affected the other Jews. As long as the Law was valid, they were dedicated to God. What about after it came to an end in 33 C.E.? As foretold at Daniel 9:27, Jehovah continued to deal with them as a favored and unique people until 36 C.E. even though the legal contract was not in effect. For three and a half years he gave them exclusive opportunity to be the spiritual seed of Abraham. The baptism of any dedicated Jew during that period would be in symbol of a presentation to do God's will. But after 36 C.E. the natural Jews were put on an equal footing with the uncircumcised Gentiles and would have to make a personal dedication, and be baptized in symbol of it, if they wanted to be acceptable to God.—Rom. 11:25, 32.

Did you then begin thinking about John's baptism? So did we. Up until Pentecost 33 C.E., sinful Jews desiring to do God's will could be baptized by John the Baptist or by Jesus' disciples in symbol of repentance. (Luke 3:3; John 3:22-26; 4:2) After Jesus' resurrection he told his disciples to do baptizing in his name. So once the Christian congregation was established on Pentecost 33 C.E., baptism in the manner of John's baptism was no longer valid. Anyone baptized in "the baptism of John" after that would have to be rebaptized, as were some in Ephesus. (Acts 19:3-5) (See also "Questions from Readers" in *The Watchtower* of May 1, 1959.)

Did This Impress You?

While the book literally teems with interesting facts and comments on Bible texts

5

Kingdom Ministry, Jan. 1968, p. 5.

Simultaneously with Nazi declaration of war on Russia, *In Fact* has received information from London and from diplomatic officials in Washington telling the secret of Hess's flight, revealing the plot of British appeasers and Buchmanites to switch the war into an Anglo-German war against Russia, and the peace terms which Hitler offers to achieve this end.

Hess, third most important Nazi, it is confirmed, brought a proposal of war and peace: war against Russia which Britain was asked to join, and peace which would repay Britain for aiding Hitler.

The peace terms, *In Fact* learns from a Washington source which obtained them from the Jugoslav minister, are as follows:

1) Restoration of France with the exception of Alsace and Lorraine.

2) British Empire to be left intact.

3) Restoration to Germany of German East and German West Africa and certain other former colonies.

4) Britain to make peace with Germany and join in the offensive against Russia.

5) Hitler to be given a vast territory from Prussia to the Black Sea, including Kiev, and Ukraine granary, and Odessa.

(At the same time *In Fact* obtained these peace terms, June 22, the United Press Madrid correspondent obtained a similar set of terms which included "Division of Europe into German and British spheres of influence" and "German expansion eastward at Russia's expense".)

The Religionists Back Hitler

The religionists back Hitler. When put to the test, when did they ever fail to call for the release of Barabbas and for the death of Christ? Recently it was announced, after the bestowal of a big bunch of junk on a flock of Catholic priests, that 1,100 Protestant clergymen had been decorated with the Iron Cross second class and 710 other clergymen had won lesser honors as killers in various jobs. The whole outfit are entitled to the Order of the Double Cross, made of millstones; and much good will the stones do them at Armageddon.

Ion Antonescu, Hitler's clerk in Rumania, after cheerfully calling on his countrymen to go out and fight Hitler's battles for him, said, "May God help us especially in this fight." The story comes back that as winter was coming on the Rumanians wanted to return home, and Hitler gave them the same deal that he gave to General von Fritsch before Warsaw and several hundred thousand of them were massacred by the Russians.

The *Schwarze Korps* of June 8, official organ of Hitler's Blackshirts, refers to Almighty God and His Son Christ Jesus as "the terrible ruthless Jehovah of the Old Testament and His Crucified Son". What favor can the Rumanians, working for Hitler, hope to receive at the hands of Almighty God?

Douglas Miller, who speaks German fluently and married a German wife, wrote a book entitled *You Can't Do Business with Hitler*, and in it he said, "If Hitler wins in Europe, he will control the Pope, the Vatican, the overwhelming majority of the Catholic Church and its central organization. He will be in a position to exercise pressure through his power to confiscate schools, universities, orphanages, asylums, hospitals, monasteries, and other kinds of church property." This disturbed American Catholics very much, so American Catholic papers state.

They are disturbed at the display of toothpicks at the end of Paoelli's meal. The Jesuits have used and are using Hitler to try to swallow up the whole world, and if, as and when he does it he will be the greatest man in their eyes that ever lived, excepting always their self-made and self-honored "Vicar of Christ".

Meantime the German people are awakening to their horrible predicament. They no longer laugh as decent men and women were made to laugh, but their faces are white, pinched and filled with forebodings of what the near future will bring and is already hastening to bring to them—Armageddon, the battle of that great day of God Almighty.

Consolation, Oct. 29, 1941, p.11.

derstanding of what this image represents "shall be in the latter days". (Dan. 2:28) That is the present time. All the prophecy of Daniel, therefore, now begins to clarify in the minds of those who love and serve JEHOVAH.

³ The text first above cited from Daniel 2:44 says: "And in the days of these kings." What kings? The answer is, the combined ruling powers of the earth, all the kings of the earth, including both "the north" and "the south", described in the eleventh chapter of the prophecy. At the time when these kings are ruling they announce their purpose to rule the earth, that is, to exercise world domination contrary to Jehovah God. They are therefore in complete opposition to THE THEOCRACY. "In the days of these kings shall the God of heaven set up a kingdom." What is that kingdom which the God of heaven sets up? It is The THEOCRATIC GOVERNMENT, which is the government of Jehovah God by Christ Jesus, His King. Christ Jesus is now enthroned; hence THE THEOCRACY has come; and all the kings of earth are arrayed against THE THEOCRACY, and this will become more pronounced in the very near future. Will THE THEOCRACY, Jehovah's kingdom, be able to withstand the opposition of Satan's organization? Concerning THE THEOCRACY, his kingdom, Jehovah says: "Which shall never be destroyed." It is the "everlasting kingdom". (Dan. 7:27) It is invincible and shall stand forever.

⁴ Satan, the arch demon, has always operated his organization by wicked angels and demonized men, and always contrary to the will of God. Concerning THE THEOCRACY Jehovah says: "And the kingdom shall not be left to other people." No one in Satan's crowd will have anything to do with that kingdom. THE THEOCRACY shall be forever ruled from heaven by Christ Jesus; and those on earth who are representatives of that government will execute the judgments heretofore written. (Isa. 32:1) There will be no politics, commerce or religion in THE THEOCRACY. How will THE THEOCRACY affect the kingdoms of Satan's organization? Of THE THEOCRACY Jehovah says in this prophecy: "It shall break in pieces and consume all these kingdoms," that is, the ruling powers of Satan. That means the end of demon rule for ever, because Jehovah says of THE THEOCRACY: "And it shall stand for ever." Return now to the consideration of the prophecy of Daniel as related to "the king of the north" and "the king of the south", as set forth in the eleventh chapter of that prophecy.

⁵ As heretofore stated, after verse forty of that prophecy "the king of the south" disappears from the prophetic picture. Nowhere in the prophecy does it appear that "the king of the north", that is, the "Axis powers", shall be victorious in the present war between the two "kings", nor does the prophecy indicate that "the king of the south" will suffer defeat in battle at the hands of "the king of the north". "The king of the south" claims to be fighting for the survival of democracies. "The king of the south" suffers complete defeat so far as its announced purpose is concerned, and that defeat is not in battle with "the king of the north" by force of arms, but in this: All nations forming "the king of the south" become arbitrary and totalitarian; and the facts show that that is now practically accomplished. All these nations becoming totalitarian, the liberties of the people completely disappear, and the people are regimented and controlled in all matters. The nations composing "the king of the south" manifestly have reasoned that they must adopt the totalitarian system in order to successfully fight against the "Axis powers". All admit that regardless of the result of the present war the nations will never return to the former method of rule. Thus it will be seen that Satan accomplishes his purpose to drive all nations into the dictatorial camp. As the visible world power began with Nimrod, the dictator of Babylon, which name stands for Satan's "woman" or organization (Rev. 17:1-5), so in these last days the visible world powers have all become dictatorial under Satan's organization, and hence all are properly called "Babylon the great"; that is, nations composing the entire earthly organization. "And he cried mightily with a strong voice, saying, Babylon the great is fallen, is fallen, and is become the habitation of devils, and the hold of every foul spirit, and a cage of every unclean and hateful bird. For all nations have drunk of the wine of the wrath of her fornication, and the kings of the earth have committed fornication with her, and the merchants of the earth are waxed rich through the abundance of her delicacies." (Rev. 18:2, 3) Thus the Lord identifies those who are of "Babylon".

"PEACE"

⁶ Will the present world conflict between the "Axis powers" and the so-called "democracies", the opposers, end in a decisive victory for either side? The prophecy indicates the contrary result; and since we have no way of determining the future save by the prophecy of God, as set forth in the Bible, we know that that way is correct. All the prophecies and the present-day facts indicate that the contending nations will before long enter into some sort of peace treaty. It is quite manifest that the religious element of these belligerent nations now plays a double role, with the expectation of being the leader or chief element sitting at the peace conference or peace table. On September 4, 1941, while this was being written, the New York *Journal-American* and other papers published the following pertinent statements, to wit: "Pope ready to sit at peace parley." "Pope will seek a peace to last through the ages." 'It is the constant

The Watchtower, Dec. 15, 1941, p. 372.

forces of THE KING OF THE THEOCRACY: "For the Egyptians shall help in vain, and to no purpose; therefore have I cried concerning this, Their strength is to sit still." (Isa. 30:7) "Now the Egyptians are men, and not God; and their horses flesh, and not spirit. When the LORD shall stretch out his hand, both he that helpeth shall fall, and he that is holpen shall fall down, and they all shall fail together." (Isa. 31:3) "And they shall know that I am the LORD, when I have set a fire in Egypt, and when all her helpers shall be destroyed."—Ezek. 30:8.

[33] The Devil, the chief of demons, and all of his demon forces shall be of no help in that great fight. It is the time when JEHOVAH shows his supreme power, as he promised (Ex. 9:16); and that power nothing can resist. Thus the end for ever of Nazi-Fascist-Hierarchy rule will come, and that will mark the end for ever of demon rule.

[34] It is in the days of these dictatorial powers that oppress the people and persecute all who serve THE THEOCRACY, all of these kings of the earth described by Daniel's prophecy, that the God of heaven will bring into action his kingdom, which he has builded up, that blessed kingdom, THE THEOCRACY. All who serve under that kingdom must be righteous; therefore none of the worldly crowd now known shall have any part in it. THE THEOCRACY is the everlasting kingdom. Christ Jesus the King is pictured in Daniel's prophecy (chapter two) as a "stone . . . cut out" of Jehovah's universal organization, which destroys all demon rule and every vestige thereof. That glorious THEOCRACY shall "break in pieces and consume all these [demonized] kingdoms, and it shall stand for ever".—Dan. 2:44, 45.

OTHER PICTURES

[35] Further confirming the conclusion that neither "the king of the north" nor "the king of the south" will win a decisive victory in the conflict now raging between them for world domination, take note of the prophetic picture set forth at Revelation 19:19, to wit: "And I saw the beast, and the kings of the earth, and their armies, gathered together to make war against him that sat on the horse, and against his army."

[36] This pictures all the forces of demon rule in battle array against the King of THE THEOCRACY. The "beast" there mentioned symbolizes the demonized rule of the earth, represented particularly in the "Axis powers", and which will include all the kings and nations of the earth finally. The "false prophet" there mentioned particularly pictures the nations that claim to be fighting for democracy in proclaiming the rights of the people, but which in fact contend for world domination for selfish reasons. Therefore it appears that at the battle of Armageddon both "the king of the north" and "the king of the south" will be living, going concerns, and active and, while thus living, will be destroyed by THE KING OF THE THEOCRACY, as stated, to wit: "And the beast was taken, and with him the false prophet that wrought miracles before him, with which he deceived them that had received the mark of the beast, and them that worshipped his image. These both were cast alive into a lake of fire burning with brimstone." (Rev. 19:20) This is another picture marking the end of demonized rule.

[37] All prophecies of God set down in the Scriptures are in exact harmony and entirely consistent. Each one makes known the development of some part of Jehovah's purpose. The meaning of these prophecies the Lord reveals to his faithful people in his own due time and for their aid and comfort. Another prophecy disclosing the end of demon rule is that set down at 2 Chronicles 20th chapter. That prophecy is considered in detail in *The Watchtower* of July 1 and 15, 1938. Briefly attention is here directed to it.

[38] Jehoshaphat, whose name means "Jehovah Vindicated", was the king of Israel, the typical covenant people of Jehovah. As king he prefigured Christ Jesus, the King of THE THEOCRACY, who is the vindicator of Jehovah's name. The nations Ammon, Moab and Mount Seir, in the order named, pictured the political, commercial and religious elements that form the visible governing powers of the dictatorial or totalitarian state. Those three nations conspired together to bring about the destruction of Jehovah's typical people, and with that malicious purpose they marched into the land of Palestine to make their destructive attack. The Israelites were entirely unable to repel that attack alone, even as the representatives of THE THEOCRACY now on earth could not possibly repel the attack of the totalitarian powers. God, through his prophet, sent a message to the Israelites, to wit: 'Be not afraid by reason of this great multitude; the battle is not yours, but God's.' A like situation obtains at Armageddon. The Israelites marched in force to meet the enemy, singing as they went the praises of JEHOVAH. Then the Lord set an ambushment against the enemy, and they were smitten. Ammon and Moab destroyed first those of Mount Seir, and then destroyed each other. The Israelites struck not a blow, but they saw the work of the Lord, and returned with songs of praise to his name.

[39] The antitypical monstrosity pictured by Ammon, Moab and Mount Seir is the totalitarian combine now insisting upon world domination. As to the time of the complete fulfillment of this part of the prophecy, it appears that all the nations, which will have gone totalitarian, will at the time be at peace, apparently. They will all be engaged in the same thing. The cry by them, "Peace and safety!" will be made. As Daniel

The Watchtower, Dec. 15, 1941, p. 377.

the result. Based upon this authority, I stated in a public address in Paris more than three years ago that the Nazis and Fascists would overrun France. That has been accomplished. I stated in a public address in Berne, Switzerland, that the Nazis and Fascists would in time grab Switzerland. Watch for that to be accomplished in the near future. At a public address in London, which was transmitted throughout the British Empire, and was delivered in 1938, I stated that the Nazis and Fascists were bent upon destroying the British Empire, and that that would be accomplished. The Nazis have planted their agents throughout the earth. The Roman Catholic Hierarchy have planted their men in every big newspaper office in America, and their men in every department of the government of the United States. Their purpose is to seize the government of the United States, as Holland and other countries have been seized. I ask you now to refer to the booklet *Fascism or Freedom,* page 14, under the subtitle of "America", and read there what Catholic priest O'Brien has to say about grabbing America in 1940, and mark at the same time how these are coming to pass, showing that O'Brien, in a measure, announced the purpose of the Hierarchy. That booklet, together with *Face the Facts* and *Government and Peace,* contains considerable information on this point.

You may expect totalitarian dictators, acting with the Roman Catholic Hierarchy, to overrun the earth, seize control of almost all the nations,

Judge Rutherford Uncovers Fifth Column, 1940, p. 15.

be able to give you girls proper advice, you girls who are looking for a husband. When you see Daniel, David, Moses and all the prophets, listen to what they have to say, and they will properly advise you boys and girls. I am going to have handed to every one of you 15,000 children one of these books as a gracious gift. I ask that you first study it faithfully. Ask someone else to sit with you under the shade of a tree and study that which leads to life and endless blessings. . . . It is your privilege between now and before the day school opens to spend six hours a day in taking the book *Children* to others." The parents should encourage their children to do this very thing, if they would have them live.

Cartons of *Children* that had been deposited in The Arena were now opened, and Judge Rutherford instructed the children how to come and each get a copy thereof, those in the rear half of The Arena marching in two columns out through a side exit, and those in the front half of The Arena marching up over the platform and out through a rear exit. As the march began, the orchestra (minus all its children instrumentalists) struck up and rendered songs, "Children of the Heavenly King," "The Sword of the Lord and of Gideon," and "Who Is on the Lord's Side?" while the vast audience sang. Never was there a more moving sight in these "last days". Many, including strong men, wept at the demonstration. Receiving the gift, the marching children clasped it to them, not a toy or plaything for idle pleasure, but the Lord's provided instrument for most effective work in the remaining months before Armageddon. What a gift! and to so many! The manner of releasing the new book *Children* was an outright surprise to all, but the almighty hand of the All-wise One, Jehovah, was in it, and the maneuver was most blessed indeed. Thereafter *Children*, the author's edition, was disposed of to adult conventioners, on a contribution.

The blessings of the Assembly were further enhanced by the afternoon session, which provided a delightful anticlimax to "Children's Day". The Arena was again packed out to hear about "Your New Work" and the president's parting words. For weeks the question had been upon many consecrated minds, and at 3 p.m. the first speaker, the factory and office servant at Brooklyn, disclosed the "new work", to wit, the placing of *Children*, and thereafter, over a period of three weeks, sending each obtainer, at no extra cost to him, the "*Children* Study Course", to wit, three attractive, illuminated question-and-answer folders, these to be followed the fourth week by a back-call service by the one placing *Children*. Another speaker, on "Solving the Problem", showed how the new book, together with the "*Children* Study Course", provided the solution for the problem of company publishers to reach their individual quota of twelve back-calls monthly and one model study weekly, as suggested in the recent communication of the president of the Society. Three speakers then spoke, each briefly on "When to Begin", and were in concert as to the answer, that NOW is the time.

When, next, Judge Rutherford came on the platform, he talked extemporaneously, but the unspeakable blessing the Lord bestowed in the morning appeared to have put him in the best of condition and filled his heart and mouth full of words "in season" and "fitly spoken". For forty-five minutes the audience spent a most delightful time listening. Said Judge Rutherford: "It is not exactly a new work, but it is putting on a little more steam for the final roundup." Then concerning the book just released, he added: "We had on the grounds this morning only 40,000 of the autographed edition. . . . But I am glad to tell you that, while that 40,000 are gone, there is another 150,000 copies on the grounds ready for use. [Applause] So you will have 150,000 on the grounds here to start with NOW, and I think it might be well for two or three thousand first-class workers to go into the St. Louis field and get those in the hands of the people here who want to know something about it before you go away." (It developed that more than 3,000 persons of good-will turned in their names at the public meetings, requesting calls by Jehovah's witnesses and further information.)

Then in most interesting fashion he told of his visit to the trailer camp Saturday, and also of the opposition and the difficulties caused by the public service bodies, such as the Chamber of Commerce and the Convention Bureau, all due to their subservience to the religious organization, whom he symbolized under the figure of one distressed "Fayther O'Hooligan". The description of the actions and the bossy orders of this "Fayther O'Hooligan" in his own brogue to local businessmen and Catholic population caused great amusement, and the assembly laughed again and again. (Pss. 2:4; 37:12,13; 52:6) Then he told of the good people of St. Louis and showed how the parable of the "sheep" and "goats" had thus had local fulfillment.—Matthew 25.

The city editor of the *Globe Democrat* sent him a question, "Do you not think it discourteous to criticize another person's religion in his own community?" but, due to "Father O'Hooligan", they refused to publish the answer submitted, though it was of great public interest. The Roman Catholic Hierarchy in America have treated in like manner all proposals, challenges and petitions to public discussion in debate over radio. They have all been warned, and now "we are going to spend our energy and time and strength in going to the people of good-will toward God and his Theocratic kingdom, carrying to them the message". Hope-rousing and stirring was his statement: "I feel absolutely certain that from henceforth . . . those who will form the great multitude will grow by leaps and bounds." The arising of 15,000 children this morning was a decisive answer and reproof to the "evil servant" class who say, "Humph! where's the great multitude?"

For ever to disprove all published false charges and slurs that he is the leader of Jehovah's witnesses, he said: "I want to let any strangers here know what you think about a man being your LEADER, so they won't be forgetting. Every time something rises up and starts to grow, they say there is some man a leader who has a great following. If there is any person in this audience who thinks that I, this man standing here, is the leader of Jehovah's witnesses, say Yes." But there was a unanimous "No"! emphatically. "If you who are here believe that I am just one of the servants of the Lord, and we are working shoulder to shoulder in unity, serving God and serving Christ, say Yes." The unanimous "Yes!" was strong and unequivocal. "Well, you don't have to need me as an earthly leader to get a crowd like that to work." He now asked them to return to their respective parts and "put on more steam . . . put in all the time you can". Then he offered words of benediction.

Briefly referring to the coming convention in Britain in September he asked them to join with him in a cablegram, as follows: "To the Leicester Assembly: Your fellow servants, assembled 115,000 strong at St. Louis, bid our British brethren be very courageous and hold fast your integrity. Theocratic victory is certain. [Signed] Jehovah's witnesses in America." This was adopted with a unanimous "Aye".

His final words were, "Well, my dear brethren, the Lord bless you. Now I won't say Good-bye, because I expect to see you at some time again." By this the brethren were greatly encouraged, and their hearts and minds were turned to the still greater and grander event, "the general assembly" spoken of at Hebrews 12:23. Till then they would keep covenant and maintain integrity toward Jehovah God, and endure hardness as good soldiers of Jesus Christ, and continue on in God's "strange work" as his faithful and true witnesses, till done.

[A more detailed report of the convention will appear in *Consolation*.]

(*Continued from page 274*)

in support of Jehovah's witnesses and in defense of their rights and liberties in His service. The 32 pages of this important documentary matter are enclosed in a neat and strong cover. It is 5c a copy, mailed postage prepaid.

The Watchtower, Sept. 15, 1941, p. 288.

councilman, claiming to reside in Kensington Heights, who based his entire testimony on admitted prejudice against Jehovah's witnesses and who became so angered at the truth that the judge had to rebuke him for his uncouth language, used in open court.

The San Diego city planning engineer, Mr. Rick, summed up their real position as follows: If it were an ordinary man there could be no objection to this burial.

The undisputed facts showed that plaintiffs Heath, Knorr and WATCHTOWER were entitled to have the permit for the burial of Judge Rutherford issued as requested.

The Board of Supervisors and County Planning Commission questioned the validity of the trust in the deed covering the property where the proposed burial was to take place. The plaintiffs hold the property in trust for the ancient witnesses of Jehovah God described in Hebrews 11, who died in faith of THE THEOCRACY and whom Jehovah has promised to resurrect and bring back to earth as the visible governors of all people under The THEOCRATIC GOVERNMENT. The Planning Commission and Board of Supervisors contended that the property could be conveyed and subdivided. Under the law and the deed it cannot. It therefore became necessary to show that the deed contained a reasonable and legal trust.

The plaintiff Wm. P. Heath, Jr., one of the creators of the trust in question, testified as a witness and explained to the court that the trust was for real men and was altogether reasonable and certain of performance. In this connection he told the court, among other things, as follows:

Awaiting New Earth's Princes

Jesus bought all the obedient of mankind, including those who will be the princes. (Romans 5:12; 6:23; 1 Corinthians 15:22) At present these men, who died long ago, are in "hell", which means the grave. Jesus testified to the fact that no one had ascended to heaven before His resurrection and therefore the conclusion is inescapable that these men are resting in death. Explaining their certainty of resurrection Jesus showed that when God told Moses that He was the God of Abraham, Isaac and Jacob He was not the God of the dead but the God of these men who would receive the promise of life in due time.—Psalm 89:48; John 3:13; Acts 2:34; Matthew 11:11; 22:31, 32; Exodus 3:4-6.

A "prince" is a sovereign ruler appointed by and acting under the direct command of the supreme or higher powers. Jehovah and Christ Jesus are the Higher Powers. (Romans 13:1) The chief ruler amongst men appointed by Jehovah is a "prince".—Book *Children*, pages 180-181; Genesis 32:28; 1 Kings 14:7.

The faithful acts of the men who were known as "fathers in Israel" are recounted in the eleventh chapter of Hebrews.—Genesis 12:1-3; 28:13, 14; Acts 7:2-5.

As previously pointed out these men will receive their life as all other human creatures through the King Christ Jesus; therefore it is written, "Instead of thy fathers shall be thy children, whom thou mayest make princes in all the earth." (Psalm 45:16) "Behold, a king [Christ Jesus] shall reign in righteousness, and princes [Abraham and the others] shall rule in judgment." (Isaiah 32:1) The Lord further declares, "I have purposed it, I will also do it" (Isaiah 46:11); and, 'My word shall not return unto me void.' (Isaiah 55:11) Therefore we have it upon the highest authority, the Word of God, that these men shall be resurrected as princes. We know that they will be.

These men will be the visible representatives of The THEOCRACY, which is the government created and built up by the Almighty God as His capital organization and which shall rule the world. Further proof that these princes will *shortly* take office upon earth as perfect men is found in the prophecy of Daniel. "But go thou thy way till the end be; for thou shalt rest, and stand in thy lot at the end of the days." (Daniel 12:13) Daniel's "lot" is that of these princes. Proof is now submitted that we are now living at "the end of the days", and we may expect to see Daniel and the other mentioned princes any day now!

Consolation, May 27, 1942, p. 13.

ed to be October 5 (Julian) or September 29 (Gregorian) 537 B.C.E.—Ezra 1:1-4; 3:1-6.

[24] Here, then, very definitely established, is another milestone—the time when the seventy years of desolation of the land of Judah came to an end—about October 1, 537. (Jer. 25:11, 12; 29:10) It is now a simple formula to determine when the seventy years began. One has only to add 70 to 537 to get 607. So about October 1, 607 B.C.E., the desolating of the land of Judah and the complete emptying out of its inhabitants was fully accomplished.

[25] The importance of the year 607 B.C.E. in this Biblical chronology will become more apparent in the following article, as we seek an answer to the provocative question, When was Adam created?

24. So when did the seventy years of desolation begin, and when did they end?

25. The answer to what question is related to the year 607 B.C.E.?

WHY ARE YOU LOOKING FORWARD TO 1975?

WHAT about all this talk concerning the year 1975? Lively discussions, some based on speculation, have burst into flame during recent months among serious students of the Bible. Their interest has been kindled by the belief that 1975 will mark the end of 6,000 years of human history since Adam's creation. The nearness of such an important date indeed fires the imagination and presents unlimited possibilities for discussion.

[2] But wait! How do we know their calculations are correct? What basis is there for saying Adam was created nearly 5,993 years ago? Does the one Book that can be implicitly trusted for its truthful historical accuracy, namely, the Inspired Word of Jehovah, the Holy Bible, give support and credence to such a conclusion?

[3] In the marginal references of the Protestant *Authorized* or *King James Version*, and in the footnotes of certain editions of the Catholic *Douay* version, the date of man's creation is said to be 4004 B.C.E. This marginal date, however, is no part of the inspired text of the Holy Scriptures, since it was first suggested more than fifteen centuries after the last Bible writer died, and was not added to any edition of the Bible until 1701 C.E. It is an insertion based upon the conclusions of an Irish prelate, the Anglican Archbishop James Ussher (1581-1656). Ussher's chronology was only one of the many sincere efforts made during the past centuries to determine the time of Adam's creation. A hundred years ago when a count was taken, no less than 140 different timetables had been published by se-

1, 2. (a) What has sparked special interest in the year 1975, and with what results? (b) But what questions are raised?

3. Is the date for Adam's creation as found in many copies of the Bible part of the inspired Scriptures, and do all agree on the date?

The Watchtower, August 15, 1968, p. 494.

FULL-TIME SERVICE—YOUTH'S SPLENDID OPPORTUNITY

"JEHOVAH is taking pleasure in his people." (Ps. 149:4) Just think of that, brothers! Our great God, Jehovah, takes pleasure in us, even though we are only tiny dust particles on this small earth in his vast universe. Though we are living scattered "in among a crooked and twisted generation," still he notices us and rejoices. (Phil. 2:15) Why? Because we are the ones he has seen to be righteous, the ones who are doing his will, among this generation. (Gen. 7:1) Yes, we have offered ourselves willingly in this day when he will take military action against this wicked system of things.—Ps. 110:3.

Among Jehovah's people there are many dedicated youths. Are you one of these? If you are, rejoice that you too have a share in making Jehovah's heart happy! (Prov. 27:11) Will you be finishing school soon? If so, what have you decided to do after you graduate? Or, are you one who has already finished school? What course of activity are you pursuing?

Of course, there may be a tempting offer of higher education or of going into some field of work that promises material rewards. However, Jehovah God holds out to you young folks many marvelous privileges of service in his organization. Which will you decide to take up? In view of the short time left, a decision to pursue a career in this system of things is not only unwise but extremely dangerous. On the other hand, a decision to take advantage of what God offers through his organization opens up excellent opportunities for advancement as well as a rich, meaningful life that will never end.

If you are out of school, can you take advantage of the many grand privileges open to you in the service of Jehovah God? One way you can do this is by deciding to enter the ranks of full-time service as a pioneer. There is a great need for full-time preachers and teachers today. It is a field of activity with a marvelous future.

Think of Jehovah's Christian ministry as a delightful corridor down which we are walking. Along this corridor is a large glass door, and, peering through it, we see another corridor with other doors leading to various privileges of service. We notice that one glass door is marked Pioneer Service and the other doors beyond it are marked Special Pioneer Service, Bethel Service, Gilead Training and Missionary Service. Going through these doors offers you the splendid opportunity to use your life to the full in Jehovah's service. Will you put yourself in a position to do so by walking through the door marked Pioneer Service?—1 Cor. 16:9.

Yes, will you make yourself available for greater privileges of service in the organization that Jehovah has purposed to preserve forever? Or will you pursue a career in this unhappy, dying system of things? Consider what other youths decided when they were faced with the decision that you must now make.

TURNING DOWN WORLDLY OPPORTUNITIES IN ORDER TO PIONEER

Many young brothers and sisters were offered scholarships or employment that promised fine pay. However, they turned them down and put spiritual interests first. In some cases this was not easy, because of pressure from the world to take up its offers. For example, one young brother in Florida was offered a four-year scholarship in engineering at the University of Miami. One of his teachers did all he could to convince this young man to go to college. He even took him to visit some of these institutions to let him see what they were like, thereby hoping to get him to take advantage of the offer.

What did this brother decide to do? He went into the full-time pioneer service. Did he make the right decision? Well, think about this: During his pioneering he helped a family of five to take up Jehovah's pure worship. The father of the family was baptized in six months' time and later became a servant in the congregation. Also this pioneer helped two teen-agers to get on the road leading to life. Is it likely that he would have

Kingdom Ministry, June 1969, p. 3.

HOW ARE YOU USING YOUR LIFE?

IS IT not apparent that most of mankind are living their lives for themselves? They are using their lives as *they* see fit, without concern for others. But what about us? The apostle Paul wrote to fellow servants of Jehovah, saying: "None of us, in fact, lives with regard to himself only, and no one dies with regard to himself only; for both if we live, we live to Jehovah, and if we die, we die to Jehovah. Therefore both if we live and if we die, we belong to Jehovah."—Rom. 14:7, 8.

This is something for all of us to give serious thought to: It would be entirely inappropriate for us, while professing to be Jehovah's people, to try to live our lives with regard to ourselves only. As the apostle Paul wrote: "You do not belong to yourselves, for you were bought with a price. By all means, glorify God."—1 Cor. 6:19, 20.

Are we not thankful that Jehovah God has purchased us and that we now belong to Him? He has bought us with the life of his own dear Son so that eternal death does not have to be our lot, but we have before us the opportunity to enjoy everlasting life. (John 3:16, 36) How are you affected by this loving provision of God? Does it not cause you to want to show Jehovah your deep appreciation? The apostle Peter noted that if we have the proper mental disposition we will be moved to "live the remainder of [our] time in the flesh, no more for the desires of men, *but for God's will.*"—1 Pet. 4:2.

Is that what you are doing? Are you living no longer simply to satisfy personal ambitions or desires, but to do God's will? Are there ways in which you could share more fully in doing the will of God?

God's Will for Us

Jehovah makes clear in his Word that his will for us today includes accomplishing a great work of Kingdom-preaching before the end of this system comes. (Matt. 24:14) Jesus Christ did a similar work. He said: "Also to other cities I must declare the good news of the kingdom of God, *because for this I was sent forth.*"—Luke 4:43.

Jesus did not hold back, but was whole-souled in his service to God. When we read the historical accounts of his ministry in the Gospels, how impressed we are with his energy and zeal in doing the Kingdom-preaching! Jesus knew that he had only a short time, and he did not spare himself in finishing his assignment. Should we not today be imitating his example, especially since we have such a short time left now in which to complete the Kingdom-preaching?

Yes, the end of this system is so very near! Is that not reason to increase our activity? In this regard we can learn something from a runner who puts on a final burst of speed near the finish of a race. Look at Jesus, who apparently stepped up his activity during his final days on earth. In fact, over 27 percent of the material in the Gospels is devoted to just the last week of Jesus' earthly ministry!—Matt. 21:1–27:50; Mark 11:1–15:37; Luke 19:29–23:46; John 11:55–19:30.

By carefully and prayerfully examining our own circumstances, we also may find that we can spend more time and energy in preaching during this final period before the present system ends. Many of our brothers and sisters are doing just that. This is evident from the rapidly increasing number of pioneers.

Yes, since the summer of 1973 there have been new peaks in pioneers every month. Now there are 20,394 regular and special pioneers in the United States, an all-time peak. That is 5,190 more than there were in February 1973! A 34-percent increase! Does that not warm our hearts? Reports are heard of brothers selling their homes and property and planning to finish out the rest of their days in this old system in the pioneer service. Certainly this is a fine way to spend the short time remaining before the wicked world's end.—1 John 2:17.

Circumstances such as poor health or responsibilities in connection with your family may limit what you can do in the field ministry. And yet, the pioneer ranks include many who have health limitations, as well as some persons with families. But these broth-

Kingdom Ministry, May 1974, p.3.

SECTION TWO

MAJOR DOCTRINE

INTRODUCTION

> The Word (God's message in Christ) is near you, on your lips and in your heart; that is, the Word—the message, the basic and object—of faith, which we preach.
>
> Because if you acknowledge and confess with your lips that Jesus is Lord and in your heart believe (adhere to, trust in and rely on the truth) that God raised Him from the dead, you will be saved. (Rom. 10:8–9, Amp.)

As Christians, we accept Paul's statement of faith as basic and essential to one's salvation. Here are two fundamental truths that one cannot deny and be a Christian. These two truths touch not only the nature of Christ's resurrection and deity, but also the nature of the Godhead, and result in the assurance of one's eternal destiny.

While professing to be a Christian organization, the Watchtower Society teaches Jehovah's Witnesses that the doctrine of the Trinity is of the devil; that Jesus is not God; that the Holy Spirit is not a person; and that Jesus did not physically rise from the grave. Many of the things that the Jehovah's Witness and the Christian believes regarding these subjects will come to light in this chapter. A systematic approach toward a dialogue through the resurrection and deity of Christ can also be found in *From Kingdom Hall to Kingdom Come* (Witness, Inc.).

Chapter Nine

THE RESURRECTION OF CHRIST—ANALYSIS

When the Apostle Paul spoke of the gospel he preached to the Corinthians, he said he delivered to them "as of first importance" the *death, burial* and *resurrection* of Jesus Christ (1 Cor. 15:1–4).

As Paul addressed the men of Athens, they scoffed when he declared the resurrection of the body of Christ because they viewed the flesh as an evil thing (Acts 17:31, 32).

When Ignatius, the bishop of Antioch, was being transported to Rome for his execution (A.D. 110–115), he wrote these words regarding our Lord's resurrection: "For I know that after His resurrection also He was still possessed of flesh and I believe He is so now. . . . And thus was He, with the flesh, received up in their sight unto Him that sent Him, being with that same flesh to come again, accompanied by glory and power" (see p. 104).

The conclusion of "The Old Roman Creed," referred to today as the "Apostles' Creed," affirms the "resurrection of the flesh" (*sarkos anastasin*) and the "life everlasting."

When the Watchtower comes to the resurrection of Christ they say:

> The religious leaders could not stop God's Son from coming out of the tomb. . . . There can be no doubt that Christ was raised from the dead. . . . (See p. 105.)

But does this mean they teach the resurrection of the flesh—a physical resurrection of Christ? No. Rather, they say:

> Having given up his flesh for the life of the world, Christ could never take it again and become a man once more. (See p. 106.)

Yet, what is a resurrection if that which dies is not also that which is raised up? Moreover, it is taught that Jesus' body was removed, not raised, by Jehovah, lest the disciples fail to see that Jesus had been resurrected:

> Also, if the body had been left in the tomb, Jesus' disciples could not have understood that he had been raised from the dead, since at that time they did not fully appreciate spiritual things. (See p. 107.)

What, then, does the Watchtower say concerning the nature of Christ's resurrection if they deny the resurrection of the flesh? They teach that Jesus was "raised" not in a glorified human body but as an invisible, immaterial spirit person:

> Jesus Christ is spoken of as "the first to be resurrected from the dead." (Acts 26:23) This means that he was the first to be resurrected of those who would not have to die again. Also, he was the first to be raised as a spirit person. (See p. 108.)

How sad is the diligent proselytizing of the Jehovah's Witness and his earnest zeal for God when he denies the reality of Christ's resurrection!

> If Christ has not risen, then our preaching is in vain (amounts to nothing) and your faith is devoid of truth *and* is fruitless—without effect, empty, imaginary and unfounded. (1 Cor. 15:14, Amp.)

CHAP. II. — CHRIST'S TRUE PASSION.

Now, He suffered all these things for our sakes, that we might be saved. And He suffered truly, even as also He truly raised up Himself, not, as certain unbelievers maintain, that He only seemed to suffer, as they themselves only seem to be [Christians]. And as they believe, so shall it happen unto them, when they shall be divested of their bodies, and be mere evil spirits.[3]

Now, He suffered all these things for us; and He suffered them really, and not in appearance only, even as also He truly rose again. But not, as some of the unbelievers, who are ashamed of the formation of man, and the cross, and death itself, affirm, that in appearance only, and not in truth, He took a body of the Virgin, and suffered only in appearance, forgetting, as they do, Him who said, "The Word was made flesh;"[1] and again, "Destroy this temple, and in three days I will raise it up;"[2] and once more, "If I be lifted up from the earth, I will draw all men unto Me."[4] The Word therefore did dwell in flesh, for "Wisdom built herself an house."[5] The Word raised up again His own temple on the third day, when it had been destroyed by the Jews fighting against Christ. The Word, when His flesh was lifted up, after the manner of the brazen serpent in the wilderness, drew all men to Himself for their eternal salvation.[6]

CHAP. III. — CHRIST WAS POSSESSED OF A BODY AFTER HIS RESURRECTION.

For I know that after His resurrection also He was still possessed of flesh,[7] and I believe that He is so now. When, for instance, He came to those who were with Peter, He said to them, "Lay hold, handle Me, and see that I am not an incorporeal spirit."[8] And immediately they touched Him, and believed, being convinced both by His flesh and spirit. For this cause also they despised death, and were found its conquerors.[12] And after his resurrection He did eat and drink with them, as being possessed of flesh, although spiritually He was united to the Father.

And I know that He was possessed of a body not only in His being born and crucified, but I also know that He was so after His resurrection, and believe that He is so now. When, for instance, He came to those who were with Peter, He said to them, "Lay hold, handle Me, and see that I am not an incorporeal spirit."[8] "For a spirit hath not flesh and bones, as ye see Me have."[9] And He says to Thomas, "Reach hither thy finger into the print of the nails, and reach hither thy hand, and thrust it into My side;"[10] and immediately they believed that He was Christ. Wherefore Thomas also says to Him, "My Lord, and my God."[11] And on this account also did they despise death, for it were too little to say, indignities and stripes. Nor was this all; but also after He had shown Himself to them, that He had risen indeed, and not in appearance only, He both ate and drank with them during forty entire days. And thus was He, with the flesh, received up in their sight unto Him that sent Him, being with that same flesh to come again, accompanied by glory and power. For, say the [holy] oracles, "This same Jesus, who is taken up from you into heaven, shall so come, in like manner as ye have seen Him go unto heaven."[13] But if they say that He will come at the end of the world without a body, how shall those "see Him that pierced Him,"[14] and when they recognise Him, "mourn for themselves?"[15] For incorporeal beings have neither form nor figure, nor the aspect[16] of an animal possessed of shape, because their nature is in itself simple.

CHAP. IV. — BEWARE OF THESE HERETICS.

I give you these instructions, beloved, assured that ye also hold the same opinions [as I do]. But I

I give you these instructions, beloved, assured that ye also hold the same opinions [as I do]. But I guard you beforehand from these beasts in the shape of men, from

[1] John i. 14. [2] John ii. 19. [3] Or, "seeing that they are phantasmal and diabolical," as some render, but the above is preferable. [4] John xii. 32. [5] Prov. ix. 1. [6] Num. xxi. 9; John iii. 14. [7] Literally, "in the flesh." [8] Literally, "demon." According to Jerome, this quotation is from the Gospel of the Nazarenes. Comp. Luke xxiv. 39. [9] Luke xxiv. 39. [10] John xx. 27. [11] John xx. 28. [12] Literally, "above death." [13] Acts i. 11. [14] Rev. i. 7. [15] Zech. xii. 10. [16] Or, "mark."

The Ante-Nicene Fathers, Alexander Roberts and James Donaldson, Eerdmans Publishing Company, 1969, p. 87.

[8] A few weeks later Jesus himself was killed and placed in a tomb. But he was there only parts of three days. The apostle Peter explains why, saying: "This Jesus God resurrected, of which fact we are all witnesses." The religious leaders could not stop God's Son from coming out of the tomb. (Acts 2:32; Matthew 27:62-66; 28:1-7) There can be no doubt that Christ was raised from the dead, for afterward he showed himself alive to many of his disciples, once to some 500 of them. (1 Corinthians 15:3-8) So strongly did Jesus' disciples believe in the resurrection that they were willing to face even death to serve God.

[9] Further proof that the dead can be raised was given later through the apostles Peter and Paul. First, Peter resurrected Tabitha, also called Dorcas, of the city of Joppa. (Acts 9:36-42) And then Paul brought back to life young Eutychus, who had died when he fell from a third-floor window while Paul was speaking. (Acts 20:7-12) Surely these nine resurrections recorded in the Bible give certain proof that the dead can be brought back to life!

8. What evidence is there that Jesus was resurrected?
9. What nine persons does the Bible say were resurrected?

You Can Live Forever in Paradise on Earth, 1982, p. 169.

The "world" refers to humankind. So Jesus here plainly said that people on earth would not see him again after his death. The apostle Paul wrote: "Even if we have known Christ according to the flesh, certainly we now know him so no more." —2 Corinthians 5:16.

4 Yet many persons believe that Christ will return in the same human body in which he was put to death, and that all those living on earth will see him. The Bible, however, says that Christ returns in glory with all the angels, and that he sits "down on his glorious throne." (Matthew 25:31) If Jesus were to come and sit as a man on an earthly throne, he would be lower in station than the angels. But he comes as the mightiest and most glorious of all these spirit sons of God and is therefore invisible, just as they are.—Philippians 2:8-11.

5 On the other hand, over 1,900 years ago it was necessary for Jesus to lower himself and become a man. He needed to give his perfect human life as a ransom for us. Jesus once explained it this way: "The bread that I shall give is my flesh in behalf of the life of the world." (John 6:51) Jesus thus gave up his fleshly body in sacrifice for humankind. For how long was that sacrifice to be in effect? The apostle Paul answers: "We have been sanctified through the offering of the body of Jesus Christ *once for all time*." (Hebrews 10:10) Having given up his flesh for the life of the world, Christ could never take it again and become a man once more. For that basic reason his return could never be in the human body that he sacrificed once for all time.

FLESHLY BODY NOT TAKEN TO HEAVEN

6 However, many persons believe that Christ took his fleshly body to heaven. They point to the fact that when Christ was raised from the dead, his fleshly body was no longer in the tomb. (Mark 16:5-7) Also, after his death Jesus appeared to his disciples in a fleshly body to show them that he was alive. Once He even had the apostle Thomas put his hand into

4. What shows that Christ returns as a mighty invisible spirit person?
5. Why could Christ not return in a human body?
6. Why do many persons believe that Christ took his fleshly body to heaven?

You Can Live Forever in Paradise on Earth, 1982, p. 143.

the hole in His side so that Thomas would believe that He had actually been resurrected. (John 20:24-27) Does this not prove that Christ was raised alive in the same body in which he was put to death?

[7] No, it does not. The Bible is very clear when it says: "Christ died once for all time concerning sins . . . , *he being put to death in the flesh, but being made alive in the spirit.*" (1 Peter 3:18) Humans with flesh-and-blood bodies cannot live in heaven. Of the resurrection to heavenly life, the Bible says: "It is sown a physical body, it is raised up a spiritual body. . . . *flesh and blood cannot inherit God's kingdom.*" (1 Corinthians 15:44-50) Only spirit persons with spiritual bodies can live in heaven.

Why did Mary Magdalene mistake Jesus for a gardener after his resurrection?

[8] Well, then, what happened to Jesus' fleshly body? Did not the disciples find his tomb empty? They did, because God removed Jesus' body. Why did God do this? It fulfilled what had been written in the Bible. (Psalm 16:10; Acts 2:31) Thus Jehovah saw fit to remove Jesus' body, even as he had done before with Moses' body. (Deuteronomy 34:5, 6) Also, if the body had been left in the tomb, Jesus' disciples could not have understood that he had been raised from the dead, since at that time they did not fully appreciate spiritual things.

[9] But since the apostle Thomas was able to put his hand into the hole in Jesus' side, does that not show that Jesus was raised from the dead in the same body that was nailed to the stake? No, for Jesus simply materialized or took on a fleshly body, as

---

7. What proves that Christ went to heaven as a spirit person?
8. What happened to Christ's human body?
9. How was it possible for Thomas to put his hand into a wound in the materialized body of the resurrected Jesus?

You Can Live Forever in Paradise on Earth, 1982, p. 144.

172 YOU CAN LIVE FOREVER IN PARADISE ON EARTH

[17] The fact is that not all who receive everlasting life will need to be resurrected. Many servants of God now living in these "last days" of this system of things will live through Armageddon. And then, as part of the righteous "new earth," they will never need to die. What Jesus said to Martha can in a literal way be true of them: "And everyone that is living and exercises faith in me will never die at all."—John 11:26; 2 Timothy 3:1.

[18] Who are the "righteous" that are to be resurrected? These will include faithful servants of God who lived before Jesus Christ came to earth. Many of these persons are mentioned by name in Hebrews chapter 11. They did not hope to go to heaven, but hoped to live again on earth. Also among the "righteous" to be resurrected are faithful servants of God who have died in recent years. God will see to it that their hope of living forever on earth is realized by raising them from the dead.

WHEN AND WHERE RESURRECTED

[19] Jesus Christ is spoken of as "the first to be resurrected from the dead." (Acts 26:23) This means that he was the first to be resurrected of those who would not have to die again. Also, he was the first to be raised as a spirit person. (1 Peter 3:18) But the Bible tells us that there would be others, saying: "Each one in his own rank: Christ the firstfruits, afterward those who belong to the Christ during his presence." (1 Corinthians 15:20-23) So in the resurrection some would be raised up before certain others.

[20] "Those who belong to the Christ" are the 144,000 faithful disciples chosen to rule with him in the Kingdom. Of their heavenly resurrection, the Bible says: "Happy and holy is anyone having part in *the first resurrection;* over these the second death has no authority, but they will . . . rule as kings with him for the thousand years."—Revelation 20:6; 14:1, 3.

17. Who will not need to be resurrected to enjoy everlasting life?
18. Who are the "righteous" that will be resurrected?
19. (a) In what sense was Jesus the first to be resurrected? (b) Who are resurrected next?
20. (a) Who are "those who belong to the Christ"? (b) What resurrection do they have?

You Can Live Forever in Paradise on Earth, 1982, p. 172.

Jesus—Spirit or Man?

One of the most important beliefs of historical Christianity is the resurrection of Jesus Christ. The Apostle Paul says, "If Christ has not been raised, your faith is worthless; you are still in your sins" (1 Cor. 15:17). The Watchtower Society claims that the man Jesus did not rise from the dead. They say, "The *man* Jesus is dead, forever dead" (see p. 110). They claim that Jesus was not a spirit on earth, but was a man. So, what is the Watchtower really teaching? They are claiming that the one who died for our sins, the man Jesus, did not rise from the dead!

The word "resurrection" means to raise up what died. The Bible says that the one who died was the *man* Jesus—the *same* one who rose form the dead—the man Jesus. Now, since we all know that a "spirit" did *not* die for anybody, then obviously a "spirit" could not have risen from the dead! Yet, they teach that there now is an invisible spirit in heaven by the name of "Jesus." It is clear that the Watchtower does not teach the resurrection of Jesus but instead teaches His annihilation, and this *brand new* spirit creature, who did *not* die for us, took His place. This spirit creature is the Jesus of the Watchtower, but not the Jesus of the Bible!

Let's compare this Watchtower teaching with the words of Jesus himself, shortly after His resurrection. In Luke, the 24th chapter, beginning with verse 36, Jesus appears to His disciples. They were frightened and thought that He was a materialized spirit. Remember, the Watchtower teaches that Jesus at this point after His resurrection was a materialized spirit (see p. 111). Yet, in verse 39, Jesus comforts His disciples and says, "See My hands and My feet, that it is I Myself; touch Me and see, for a spirit does not have flesh and bones as you see that I have." Jesus said it in the strongest way He could; He was risen from the dead. He presented physical proof—His human body!

The Watchtower says the man Jesus is dead, and that a *spirit* named Jesus is in heaven. But the Bible says these words in 1 Timothy 2:5, "For there is one God, and one mediator between God and men, the *man* Christ Jesus" (KJV).

Nor could our Lord have been raised from the dead *a man*, and yet have left with Justice our *ransom-price:* in order to the release of Adam (and his condemned race) from the sentence and prison-house of death, it was necessary, not only that the *man* Christ Jesus should die, but just as necessary that the *man* Christ Jesus should never live again, should remain dead, should remain our ransom-price to all eternity.

For our Lord Jesus to have been raised a man would have implied two evils: (1) It would have implied the taking back of our ransom, which would have left us as much under sentence of death as before. (2) It would have implied to him an everlasting loss of the higher nature which he had left in order to become a man, and to be our Redeemer; and thus it would have implied that faithfulness to God on his part had resulted in his everlasting degradation to a lower nature. But no such absurdities and inconsistencies are involved in the divine arrangement. Our Lord humbled himself, and became a man, and as a man he gave up his life, the *ransom-price* for the fallen man; and as a reward for this faithfulness, the Heavenly Father not only restored him to conscious being, but gave him a nature not only higher than the human, but higher also than his own previous nature, making him partaker of the divine nature, with its superlative qualities and honors. In his present exalted condition death would be *impossible*,—he is now immortal.

Since the man Jesus was the ransom-price, given for the purchase of Adam and his race, it could not be that the man Jesus is the Second Adam, the *new* father of the race instead of Adam; for the *man* Jesus is dead, forever dead, and could not be a father or life-giver to the world.

He who now owns, by purchase, the title of father to the human family, is the risen and glorified Jesus, partaker of the divine nature—this is the Second Adam

The Atonement Between God and Man, Studies in the Scriptures, Vol. 5, 1899, p. 454.

And he further said: "The bread that I shall give is my flesh in behalf of the life of the world." (John 6:51) So, if Jesus gave his human life, including his fleshly body, as a ransom for mankind, he could not have been raised from the dead as a human, with his flesh-and-blood body. Had he taken back the human life that he sacrificed, mankind would no longer be ransomed.

Moreover, Jesus could not have ascended to heaven forty days after his resurrection had he been raised as a human of flesh and blood. Why not? The Bible answers: "Flesh and blood cannot inherit God's kingdom." (1 Cor. 15:50) How, then, was Jesus raised from the dead? He was "made alive in the spirit."—1 Pet. 3:18.

As to Jesus' condition since his resurrection and ascension to heaven, God's Word says: "He is the reflection of [God's] glory and the exact representation of his very being." (Heb. 1:3) So he must be a spirit being, just as "God is a Spirit."—John 4:24.

That is why when Saul of Tarsus (on his way to persecute Christians in Damascus) met Jesus Christ, he saw no form or body but only such a bright light that it blinded him. (Acts 9:3-9) It was quite fitting that Jesus should have appeared to Saul in this manner, for the glorified Jesus is the "exact representation" of the person of his Father and God. (Heb. 1:3; John 20:17) And God is spoken of as the "Father of the celestial lights." (Jas. 1:17) No man could see the glorious face of God and yet live. (Ex. 33:20) So, can humans on earth see the glorified Lord Jesus Christ? The Bible's answer is, No. Of the glorified, immortal Lord Jesus Christ, 1 Timothy 6:16 says that he is one who "dwells in unapproachable light, whom not one of men has seen or can see."

This being the case, will Jesus ever again take on a corruptible body of flesh in order to be seen by humans who are too frail to endure the sight of his glorified spirit body? That is not God's purpose respecting his Son. As the inspired apostle Paul said on one occasion: "[God] resurrected him from the dead destined *no more to return to corruption.*"—Acts 13:34.

Accordingly, when the Scriptures speak of "every eye" as seeing Jesus, this is manifestly to be understood in a figurative sense. As a result of what humans see and hear on earth, they will perceive that the events taking place are because Jesus Christ is taking a personal hand in the affairs of mankind.—Rev. 11:15; 12:10-12.

Objections Considered

But someone may object: 'Did not the apostles see Jesus in human form after his resurrection?' True, but he had not yet ascended to heaven and assumed his place at the right hand of God, thereafter dwelling in "unapproachable light." Therefore he was in position to assume a human form, even as angels had materialized on other occasions. For example, an angel appeared in human form to the parents of Samson and, after accomplishing his mission, ascended in a flame out of their sight. (Judg. 13:3-21) The fact that Jesus simply materialized bodies explains why on various occasions after his resurrection he was not always immediately recognized. Also, Jesus was able to appear suddenly in the midst of his apostles even though they were in a room with the door bolted due to their fear of the Jews. That there might be no doubt that he had truly been resurrected, Jesus appeared in human form, yes, even assuming a body with visible wounds so as to convince doubting Thomas.—John 20:19-29.

But do we not read at Acts 1:11, "This Jesus who was received up from you into the sky will come thus in the same man-

Awake!, July 22, 1973, p. 4.

Who Rose from the Dead?

Few people realize that Jehovah's Witnesses are taught that the *man* Jesus did not rise from the dead. The Watchtower teaches that Jesus is an invisible spirit, and it denies the bodily resurrection of Christ. Is that really what God's Word reveals?[1] Let's compare their view with the biblical account found in John 2:18–22.

Here we find that Jesus has just thrown the moneychangers out of the temple. The Jews have said to him, " 'What sign have you to show us, since you are doing these things?' In answer Jesus said to them, 'Break down this temple, and in three days I will raise it up.' " In verse 21 we read, "But he was talking about the temple of his body." Verse 22 reads, "When, though, he was raised up from the dead, his disciples called to mind that he used to say this; and they believed the Scripture and the saying that Jesus said."

Notice, in verse 19, Jesus responded that the sign for these Jews would be the destruction of a temple and this *same* temple would be resurrected in three days. What was this temple that Jesus was going to raise? We have the answer in verse 21 which reads, "the temple of his body"!—His own physical body that was present when He spoke to these Jews. Then, in verse 22, Christ's disciples remembered His words when they saw the temple of *Jesus' body* was resurrected from the dead. They believed the physical proof!

The faith of every Christian is based on a firm foundation—the resurrection of Jesus Christ. Do you believe that *right now* there is in heaven a mediator between God and men, the man Christ Jesus who was raised from the dead? If you do, then your belief is contrary to the teachings of the Watchtower Society which claims He was raised a spirit creature and *not* a man! Now is the time to decide whether you believe the Watchtower or the Bible, for God's Word says in 1 Timothy 2:5, "For there is one God, and one mediator between God and men, the man Christ Jesus." Do you want Him to be your mediator?

Was Thomas Deceived?

Paul said, "If Christ has not been raised, your faith is worthless" (1 Cor. 15:17). But the Watchtower Society teaches Jehovah's Witnesses that the man Jesus never rose from the dead. They say, "We deny that He was raised in the flesh, and challenge any statement

[1]Scriptures are taken from the Jehovah's Witness Bible, *New World Translation of the Holy Scriptures*, 1981 edition.

to that effect as being unscriptural" (see p. 114).

Let's drop in now on a conversation between Jay, a Jehovah's Witness, and Chris, a Christian, as they discuss this subject.

Chris: I know you find it hard to believe that Jesus was really raised from the dead, Jay, but that *is* what the Bible teaches.

Jay: But I do believe Jesus was raised, Chris. It's just that I don't think His *body* was raised.

Chris: Do you remember the Apostle Thomas? Even he found it hard to believe that Jesus had been raised. But the Lord came to him and said, "Reach here your finger and see My hands; and reach here your hand, and put it into My side; and be not unbelieving, but believing" (John 20:27).

Jay: Yes, I've read that before, but I have to agree with the Society—and they say "the bodies in which Jesus manifested himself to his disciples after his return to life were not the body in which he was nailed to the tree." (See p. 115.)

Chris: But, Jay, do you think Jesus would purposely *deceive* Thomas?

Jay: Of course not.

Chris: Then have you ever really noticed what Jesus said to Thomas? Let's read John 20:27 together once more. "Reach here your finger and see My hands; and reach here your hand, and put it into My side." Notice that Thomas is encouraged to touch that he may *know* that the man Jesus whom he could see with his eyes was actually, *physically* present.

Jay: It's true, Jesus does say "My hands" and "My side." Well, maybe it's different in my Bible.

Chris: No, it's the same in your Bible.

Jay: Well, I guess Jesus really did want Thomas to believe it was Him—in the flesh!

Chris: You're right, Jay, the hands were not the hands of some body that had just been created, the body was of our Savior—risen from the dead!

Jesus did not deceive Thomas and He will not deceive you. We believe Jesus; how about you?

humanity of Jesus, we equally affirm the Divinity of Christ—'God also hath highly exalted Him, and given Him a name above every name.' (Heb. 7:26; Phil. 2:9.)

"We acknowledge that the personality of the Holy Spirit is the Father and the Son; that the Holy Spirit proceeds from both, and is manifested in all who receive the begetting of the Holy Spirit and thereby become sons of God. (John 1:12; 1 Pet. 1:3.) We affirm the resurrection of Christ—that He was put to death in flesh but quickened in Spirit. We deny that He was raised in the flesh, and challenge any statement to that effect as being unscriptural. (1 Pet. 3:18; 2 Cor. 3:17; 1 Cor. 15:8; Acts 26:13-15.) That the basis of Hope, for the Church and the World, lies in the fact that 'Jesus Christ, by the grace of God, tasted death for every man,' 'a Ransom for all,' and will be 'the true Light which lighteth every man that cometh into the world,' 'in due time.' (Heb. 2:9; John 1:9; 1 Tim. 2:5, 6.) That the Hope of the Church is that she may be like her Lord, 'see Him as He is,' be 'partaker of the Divine nature,' and share His glory as His joint-heir. (1 John 3:2; John 17:24; Rom. 8:17; 2 Pet. 1:4.) That the present mission of the Church is the perfecting of the saints for the future work of service; to develop in herself every grace; to be God's witness to the world; and to prepare to be kings and priests in the next Age. (Eph. 4:12; Matt. 24:14; Rev. 1:6; 20:6.) That the Hope for the World lies in the blessings of knowledge and opportunity to be brought to all by Christ's Millennial Kingdom—the Restitution of all that was lost in Adam, to all the willing and obedient, at the hands of their Redeemer and His glorified Church—when all the wilfully wicked shall be destroyed. (Acts 3:19-23; Isa. 35.)"—B. S. M.

The amount of work that Pastor Russell performed *is incredible*, and it is doubtful whether it was ever equalled by any other human being. When he was in his twenties he was refused the lease of a property because the owner thought he would surely die before the lease had expired. For fifty years he suffered constantly with sick headaches, due to a fall in his youth, and for twenty-five years had such distressing hemorrhoids that it was impossible for him to rest in the easiest chair; yet in the past forty years he traveled a million miles, delivered 30,000 sermons and table talks—many of them 2½ hours long—wrote over 50,000 pages (of this size) of advanced Biblical exposition, often dictated 1,000 letters per month, managed every department of a world-wide evangelistic campaign employing 700 speakers, per-

The Finished Mystery, 1917, p. 57.

natural body; it is raised a spiritual body." (1 Corinthians 15:44) Jesus was raised to immortality, beyond the power of death to touch him again, and never can die for sins again. —Romans 6:9, 10.

Therefore the bodies in which Jesus manifested himself to his disciples after his return to life were not the body in which he was nailed to the tree. They were merely materialized for the occasion, resembling on one or two occasions the body in which he died, but on the majority of occasions being unrecognizable by his most intimate disciples. The body which was put in the sepulcher was disposed of without corruption according to God's prophecy and by his almighty power. Years after, when the resurrected Jesus appeared to Saul of Tarsus without a body of flesh to veil his heavenly glory, that future apostle Paul was smitten blind. His sight was restored three days later by a miracle.—Acts 9:3-18.

When Jehovah raised his beloved Son from death to life immortal, then in the completest sense He begot him by His spirit by means of which spirit he resurrected him. Says the apostle Paul: "We declare unto you glad tidings, how that the promise which was made unto the fathers, God hath fulfilled the same unto us their children, in that he hath raised up Jesus again; as it is also written in the second psalm, *Thou art my Son, this day have I begotten thee.* And as concerning that he raised him up from the dead, now no more to return to corruption,

The Kingdom Is at Hand, 1944, p. 259.

What Happened to the Body?

As a Christian, one's hope resides in the fact that Jesus has been raised from the dead. If Christ has not been raised, our faith is worthless. Jehovah's Witnesses around the world claim to believe in the resurrection of Jesus. However, is this a valid claim, when they believe that Jesus' *body* was never raised? As a Jehovah's Witness, one is taught that Jesus was raised as an invisible spirit. But if Jesus became a spirit, one wonders what happened to the body that died at Calvary.

The Watchtower claims the body was disposed of (see p. 117). For most, this would seem too wild an assumption. But the Watchtower stands firm in its own guesswork—even though a disposal of Christ's body is not taught anywhere in the Bible! The truth is, the Watchtower's teaching is hostile to the King, Christ Jesus, who did not believe His body would be disposed of, but instead prophesied it would be raised from the dead!

In John 2, Jesus is confronted by the Jewish leaders who were seeking a sign, to whom Jesus replies (v. 19), "Destroy this temple and in three days I will raise it up" (KJV). Then just two verses later, the beloved Apostle John tells us the temple to which Jesus was referring "was the temple of his body"! Here we have Jesus' promised sign, confirmed and clarified by John, and recorded forever in God's perfect word—Jesus' body was without a doubt to be raised from the dead! (John 2:21).

Our hope and the purpose of this message is that you will see through the Watchtower's fantasy, that you will trust and obey Jesus, and receive Him as your personal Lord and Savior. Through your decision to receive Christ, you can be assured of God's favor and His promise of life. The Bible is your written guarantee. It tells us, "He who believes in the Son has eternal life." But it also guarantees that "he who does not obey the Son shall not see life, but the wrath of God abides on him" (John 3:36).

the Hebrew word Sheol by the Greek word Ha′des. The two words, Sheol and Ha′des, are thereby seen to mean the same thing, namely, the common grave of dead mankind in the ground.

[20] The cases of Jesus Christ and his congregation are actual illustrations of the fact that it is not the physical body with which a person dies that is raised from the dead or freed from Ha′des. What is raised is the personality that the person has developed by the time of his death and that identifies him and that helps us to remember his personal history. It is this personality that is brought back into existence by being clothed upon with a suitable live body at the resurrection time. In this way the soul that once died because of sin or as a sacrifice is re-created. As it is stated, in Psalm 104:29, 30, in an address to God: "If you take away their spirit, they expire, and back to their dust they go. If you send forth your spirit, they are created; and you make the face of the ground new."

[21] Correctly, then, the apostle Peter applied to Jesus Christ the words of Psalm 16:10: "You will not leave my soul [not, my human body] in Ha′des." (Acts 2:27-31) The human body of flesh, which Jesus Christ laid down forever as a ransom sacrifice, was disposed of by God's power, but not by fire on the altar of the temple in Jerusalem. The flesh of a sacrifice is always disposed of and put out of existence, so not corrupting. But the value of the fleshly sacrifice remains and counts in behalf of the one offering the sacrifice.

[22] So, if the patriarch Abraham had been allowed to go through with the actual sacrifice of

20. How do the cases of Jesus and his congregation help us to understand just what is resurrected?
21. (a) As shown by Peter's quotation from Psalm 16:10, what was raised from Hades in the case of Jesus? (b) What happened to the human body that Jesus had laid down in sacrifice?
22. Who was pictured by both Isaac and the ram that Abraham offered on Mount Moriah, and what was done with the body of the ram?

Things in Which It Is Impossible for God to Lie, 1965, p. 354.

Chapter Ten

THE GODHEAD (THE TRINITY)—ANALYSIS

> Being then the offspring of God, we ought not to think that the Divine Nature is like gold or silver or stone, an image formed by the art and thought of man. (Acts 17:29)

The three persons of the Godhead, known as the TRINITY, and exactly how they are co-related and co-existent, has long been a topic of discussion in the Christian Church. The Scriptures speak of the Father, the Son, and the Holy Spirit as the one God. This is not so unintelligible to the Christian as is the question as *how* they are the one God. Bible believers know:

> There are certainly things God asks us to believe concerning Himself which we do not fully comprehend, "So are My ways higher than your ways, and My thoughts than your thoughts" (Isa. 55:9). The Lord reveals only so much, and that He asks us to believe. "The secret things belong to the Lord our God, but the things revealed belong to us. . ." (Dt. 29:29). Beyond what the Lord has revealed is idle speculation.[1]

The Christian accepts the fact that the Father, Son and Holy Spirit—three eternal persons—are existing as the one God, who is revealed in the Old Testament as Jehovah. This is not without reason or question, but is based upon the totality of the revealed Word of God. The more one considers the mystery of God's very being, the more he must acknowledge that even the *concept* of an eternal being is beyond our ability to comprehend; and apart from His revelation of himself to mankind, we can truly know nothing of His personal nature.

The Watchtower teaches that the doctrine of the Trinity is a product of Satan himself:

---

[1] *From Kingdom Hall to Kingdom Come*, Witness, Inc., 1982 ed, p. 75.

> Never was there a more deceptive doctrine advanced than that of the trinity. It could have originated only in one mind, and that the mind of Satan the Devil. (See p. 121.)

The Christian believes that in the nature of the *one* God, there are three eternal persons. The Jehovah's Witness is often told something quite different by the Watchtower. The Society's 1982 publication *You Can Live Forever in Paradise on Earth,* on page 39, offers the Witness a rarely seen, realistic definition of the Trinity:

> According to the teaching of the Trinity, there are three persons in one God, that is, there is one God, Father, Son, and Holy Spirit. (See p. 122.)

Yet, even where the concept of the Trinity may be most correctly stated, the Society continues on the same page to distort its true meaning by saying the Trinity doctrine teaches that Jesus and God are the same *person*:

> Since Jesus prayed to God, asking that God's will, not his, be done, the two could not be the same person.

Jesus praying to the Father, or referring to God as His God, is not surprising, or something so obscure that trinitarian believers have failed to consider it. Rather, such passages are considered in the context in which they were spoken as outlined by Paul in Philippians 2:4–8:

> Do not merely look out for your own personal interests, but also for the interests of others. Have this attitude in yourselves which was also in Christ Jesus, who, although He existed in the form of God, did not regard equality with God a thing to be grasped, but emptied Himself, taking the form of a bond-servant, and being made in the likeness of men. And being found in appearance as a man, He humbled Himself by becoming obedient to the point of death, even death on a cross.

This is a passage distorted almost beyond recognition in the Watchtower's *New World Translation*. Here we realize that Jesus, having the nature of God and being equal with God, emptied himself and took on another nature, an additional nature, the nature of a slave and was made a man.[2]

---

[2]"This additional nature was expressed by a new form—human. 'Form' is an inadequate rendering of *morphe*, but our language affords no better word. By 'form' is commonly understood 'shape', 'sensible appearance.' So of Christ's human form (Mark 16:12). But the word in this sense cannot be applied to God. *Morphe* here means that expression of being which is identified with the essential nature and character of God which reveals it" (Marvin Vincent, *The Epistles to the Philippians and to Philemon*, The International Critical Commentary, Edinburgh: T & T Clark, first printed 1897, pp. 57, 58).

Jesus humbled himself and became obedient to the Father until death. Speaking as a *man*, Jesus indeed has a God whom He called Father.

While Philippians 2 assists the Christian in understanding the incarnation, at the same time it throws a "monkey wrench" into the Watchtower idea that Jesus was a created being, a creature brought into existence by Jehovah. How? The scripture said Jesus took on the form of a slave, and *became* obedient. He became obedient *when He became a man*. But if the Watchtower was right, He would have been a creature, and as such would already have been a servant.

The Watchtower habitually misrepresents the biblical doctrine of Trinity, as will be seen in the dialogues between Chris and Jay.

A council of the clergy was held at Nice, in 325 A. D., which council confirmed the doctrine of the trinity; and later a similar council at Constantinople, by confirming the divinity of the Holy Ghost and the unity of God, declared the doctrine of the trinity in unity to be the doctrine of the church. The clergy have ever held to this senseless, God-dishonoring doctrine. To aid his agents to keep this doctrine before their mind the Devil must have some visible object symbolizing it. The mystic triangle was adopted as a symbol, which may be found in the tombs of those who were buried contemporaneously therewith. Also there was an attempt to prove it by three heads or faces on one neck, the eyes becoming a part of each individual face. Also a combination of the triangle and circle and sometimes the trefoil was used for the same purpose. If you ask a clergyman what is meant by the trinity he says: "That is a mystery." He does not know, and no one else knows, because it is false.

Never was there a more deceptive doctrine advanced than that of the trinity. It could have originated only in one mind, and that the mind of Satan the Devil. The purpose was and is to produce confusion in the mind of man and to destroy the true philosophy of the great ransom sacrifice. If Jesus when on earth was God he was more than a perfect man and therefore could not become an exact corresponding price for the redemption of men. Therefore it logically follows that the shed blood of Jesus would form no basis for the reconciliation of man to God. If Jesus was one part of the trinity, then it would be impossible for the trinity or any part of it to have furnished the

Reconciliation, 1928, p. 101.

GOD—WHO IS HE? 39

to his laws, God rejoices. (Proverbs 27:11) Also, God describes how he feels when his servants are made to suffer by enemies: "He that is touching you is touching my eyeball." (Zechariah 2:8) Are you not moved to love a God who has such affection for lowly, insignificant humans of all races and peoples?—Isaiah 40:22; John 3:16.

IS GOD JESUS OR A TRINITY?

[14] Who is this wonderful God? Some persons say his name is Jesus. Others say he is a Trinity, although the word "trinity" does not appear in the Bible. According to the teaching of the Trinity, there are three persons in one God, that is, there is "one God, Father, Son and Holy Spirit." Many religious organizations teach this, even though they admit it is "a mystery." Are such views of God correct?

[15] Well, did Jesus ever say that he was God? No, he never did. Rather, in the Bible he is called "God's Son." And he said: "The Father is greater than I am." (John 10:34-36; 14:28) Also, Jesus explained that there were some things that neither he nor the angels knew but that only God knew. (Mark 13:32) Further, on one occasion Jesus prayed to God, saying: "Let, not *my* will, but *yours* take place." (Luke 22:42) If Jesus were the Almighty God, he would not have prayed to himself, would he? In fact, following Jesus' death, the Scripture says: "This Jesus God resurrected." (Acts 2:32) Thus the Almighty God and Jesus are clearly two separate persons. Even after his

Since Jesus prayed to God, asking that God's will, not his, be done, the two could not be the same person

14. What is the Trinity teaching?
15. How does the Bible show that God and Jesus are two separate persons who are not equal?

You Can Live Forever in Paradise on Earth, 1982, p. 39.

One God or Many?

"Hear, O Israel: The Lord our God is one Lord" (Deut. 6:4, KJV). This expression of the unity of God is the central confession of the Jewish faith. Heathen religions worshiped many gods. Yet Jehovah revealed himself to the descendants of Abraham, saying, "You shall be My people, and I will be your God" (Jer. 30:22). Early Hebrews believed that while there were indeed many gods, they were to recognize only Jehovah as God.

This understanding is very similar to the teachings of many pseudo-Christian religions today. Such groups say there are indeed many gods, calling Jesus "a mighty god," but also saying that Satan himself is a god. Such so-called Christian religions acknowledge the existence of many gods. They too say, for us there is only one God, the Father: He is the only one we *recognize* in our worship.

Monotheism v. Polytheism

These pseudo-Christian groups claim to have found polytheism (belief in more than one god) in the Bible, yet their revelation has stopped short of the whole revelation by God. Jehovah continued to reveal himself to the Jewish nation. Jehovah revealed that there are absolutely no other Gods. He is the only real God. He showed them that the so-called gods of the other nations are only idols, that is, things having no existence as a real God (Ps. 96:4). Jehovah repeatedly revealed himself as the only true God. "Before Me there was no God formed, and there will be none after Me" (Isa. 43:10). He declared, "Besides Me there is no God" (Isa. 45:5). The Jews believed what God said. The Jews are therefore monotheists—people believing in the existence of only one God. All other "gods" are not gods at all, they are false gods. Monotheism is the understanding true to the whole revelation by God. This is what the Bible teaches.

Monotheism was however a belief not shared by the pagan world. The common pagan opinion was that the world is populated by many gods. Such people who believe in the existence of more than one god are called polytheists. Unfortunately, polytheism did not die off with the rest of ancient culture. It is alive and well among many pseudo-Christian religions.

Although Jehovah clearly said, "Before Me there was no God formed, and there will be none after Me" (Isa. 43:10), some pseudo-Christian groups, like the Mormons and Jehovah's Witnesses, will not believe Him. Mormons and Jehovah's Witnesses are polytheists. Mormons themselves hope to become gods. Jehovah's Witnesses translate John 1:1, "In the beginning the Word was, and the Word was with God, and the Word was *a* god." Jehovah's Witnesses do not believe Jesus (the Word) is *the* God, but *another* god! There is no way John could have meant that Jesus was *a* god. John was a Jewish Christian, a monotheist! He did not believe there were any other gods! That is why most recognized translations will read "and the Word was God."

New Testament Monotheists

Just as God's people in the Old Testament were monotheists, so too were the New Testament believers. The Apostle Paul claims that God's existence is obvious to everyone. He says, "That which is known about God is evident within them; for God made it evident to them" (Rom. 1:19). Notice, he does not say that which is known about the *Gods*. He does not say the Gods made it evident to them. In Paul's mind there is only one God. This God alone has made it evident that He is God. Is this not what Jehovah revealed to the Old Testament believers? Is this not what seems evident to you as you scan the creation? Paul continues, in Romans 1:20, "Since the creation of the world His [not their] invisible attributes [again, not theirs, but], His eternal power and divine nature, have been clearly seen, being understood through what has been made, so that they are without excuse."

Futile Speculations

What happens to people or religious groups when they have not believed what God has made evident? When they believe there are other gods? When they have not believed what God has said? When they have not honored God as God? God's Word says, "They became futile in their speculations, and their foolish heart was darkened. Professing to be wise, they became fools" (Rom. 1:21, 22).

That one God does exist has been evident since the creation of the world—not that there are many gods! Saying there is more than one true God is futile speculation. It is contrary to God's Word.

What Is the Basis for Their Speculation?

Jehovah said, "There is no other God besides Me, a righteous

God and a Savior; there is none except Me" (Isa. 45:21). But occasionally a group like the Jehovah's Witnesses or the Mormons will cite 1 Corinthians 8:5, "Indeed there are many gods and many lords," hoping to prove there is more than one true God. But notice the context (from v. 4) shows that idols are Paul's subject. He first shows that idols have no real existence as gods, and "there is no God but one" (1 Cor. 8:4). Then he continues:

> For even if there are so-called gods whether in heaven or on earth, as indeed there are many gods and many lords, yet for us there is but one God, the Father, from whom are all things, and we exist for Him; and one Lord, Jesus Christ, through whom are all things, and we exist through Him. (1 Cor. 8:5, 6)

What is Paul teaching? Does he mean there are many true gods? That Christians only worship one of them? Is he contradicting what he just said in verse 4, there is no God but one? No, these idols are not true gods. In verse 4 he said there is no God but one, and in verse 7 he regretfully says, "However not all men have this knowledge." Why don't they know? Paul tells us in Romans, they became futile in their speculations. Professing to be wise, they became fools.

The pseudo-Christian polytheist may cite 2 Corinthians 4:4, and ignoring what Jehovah says, hope to prove that even Satan is one of the gods. It is true, many people do worship Satan and his cohorts, some without even knowing it! Again referring to idols, Paul says, "The things which the Gentiles sacrifice, they sacrifice to demons, and not to God" (1 Cor. 10:20). Although people may worship Satan and make him their "god," he is not a god by nature. He is only a so-called god; by nature he is only a creature. He is a so-called god of this age, because men allow him to rule in their lives. Thus to them he has become a god, but he is not a true god.

One True God by Nature

Monotheists believe in the existence of only one God. If you believe there is more than one true God, you are not a monotheist; you are a polytheist. Monotheists side with God, believing there is by nature only one true God. No matter what men call god, or worship, if it is not the one true God, Jehovah, it is a false god whom they serve. Paul writes the Galatians about the time "when you did not know God," and explains, "You were slaves to those which by nature are no gods" (Gal. 4:8). No man, not even Satan, is a God by nature. There is only one true God by nature. "Hear,

O Israel: The Lord our God is one Lord" (Deut. 6:4, KJV). All others are false gods, "For I am God, and there is no other" (Isa. 45:22).

Who Is Jesus?

The Bible says Jesus is God! Yet that does not mean the Son is the Father, but that He shares the Father's very nature. Since Jesus is a true God, He *must* be Jehovah, for Jehovah is the only true God. If the Bible shows Jesus and the Father are God, they must be Jehovah! Since Jehovah is the only true God, all others must be false gods.

If your religion teaches that Jesus is a god, you have a decision to make: Is Jesus the one true God or is He a false god?[3]

> And we know that the Son of God has come, and has given us understanding, in order that we might know Him who is true, and we are in Him who is true, in His Son Jesus Christ. This is the true God and eternal life. (1 John 5:20)

The Trinity—Misrepresented

While the Watchtower Society realizes that particular doctrines separate the various Christian denominations, they also recognize that there are certain doctrines that are considered essential and held in common. One of these central doctrines is that of the Trinity (see p. 131). As most people know, the Watchtower denies this doctrine is a biblical teaching. Moreover, they often misrepresent what Christians believe concerning the nature of God as expressed by the doctrine of the Trinity. We find Jay and Chris discussing this now.

Chris: Jay, as a Jehovah's Witness, you don't believe in the Trinity, right?

Jay: That's right, Chris. That pagan doctrine has been "exposed by *The Watchtower* for over 100 years." (See p. 132.)

Chris: I know the Watchtower has claimed that the Trinity is unscriptural for a long time. But did you know they have misrepresented what trinitarians believe for just as long?

Jay: How is that?

Chris: Christians believe there is only one God, not three gods; that there are three persons who exist as the one God, not

[3]John 1:1; 20:28; Titus 2:13; 2 Pet. 1:1.

one person revealing himself as three persons. In other words, the three persons, Father, Son and Holy Spirit, are the one God. We believe there are three distinct personalities; therefore, we do not teach Jesus is the Father, or the Holy Spirit is Jesus. But when the Watchtower speaks of the Trinity, this doctrine is often presented in an inaccurate and confusing manner.

Jay: Like what?

Chris: In a recent Watchtower book, they describe the concept of the Trinity rather plainly. But on the same page they proceed to prove that the Almighty God (the Father only, to Witnesses) and Jesus are not the same person, as though this was *inconsistent* with trinitarian thought. (See p. 133.)

Jay: Well, isn't it?

Chris: No. As I just explained, Jesus is not the Father; they are two separate persons. While Jesus walked as a man, the Father was greater than Jesus. But that is nowhere in the Scriptures shown to be true before Jesus humbled himself and took on the nature of a man!

Jay: I see. I don't think I really understood what you believed before.

Chris: Glad I could help. You see, the Watchtower proves nothing against trinitarians. What the Society prints only confuses what Christians believe. For example:

> Since Jesus prayed to God, asking that God's will, not his, be done, the two could not be the same person. (See p. 133.)

Jay: Hmm. But that is just one time.

Chris: They have done similar things all along. In 1882 the Society misrepresented the Trinity this way:

> Our readers are aware that while we believe in Jehovah and Jesus, and the holy Spirit, we reject as totally unscriptural, the teaching that these are *three* Gods in *one person*, or as some put it, *one* God in *three* persons. (See p. 134.)

In 1952, a book that was long the major doctrinal book for the Witnesses misrepresented the Trinity, saying:

> The doctrine, in brief, is that there are three gods in one: "God the Father, God the Son, and God the Holy Ghost," all three equal in power, substance and eternity. (See p. 135.)

They said this, Jay, even though on the same page, they quote the Athanasian Creed, which *correctly* states the Trinity:

> Thus, in the words of the Athanasian Creed: "The Father is God, the Son is God, and the Holy Spirit is God, and yet there are not three Gods, but one God."

Jay: I can see how that kind of representation could mislead people concerning what you might really believe. But I don't think it's any big deal; it's not that far off.

Chris: I think it's a big deal, and I think it is done to make trinitarianism appear both confused and unreasonable. It is done often and it's a long way off. (See pp. 136–142.)

Jay: Well, sometimes the Watchtower doesn't misrepresent the doctrine of the Trinity. Doesn't that count for anything?

Chris: Sure, it counts for something, Jay; but how would you feel if I printed a paper where I occasionally told the truth about what the Watchtower teaches?

Jay: I get the point.

Chris: Besides, the Watchtower tells its followers to speak the truth in every detail, even when they represent others.

> Jehovah's witnesses are an organization of truth. We should want to speak the truth and be absolutely accurate in every detail at all times. This should be so not only as regards doctrine but also in our quotations, what we say about others or how we represent them. (See p. 143.)

Jay: Okay, okay. I concede that point, but still they weren't actually quoting anybody.

Chris: I doubt that any group that would intentionally misrepresent what people think would balk at misrepresenting what someone writes.

Jay: That seems stupid to me. If it was in print, people could easily check it out.

Chris: Sure they could. But the facts are, they usually don't, especially if they don't have the books or if they have no reason to assume the Watchtower is not telling the truth.

Jay: Evidence, evidence!

Chris: You have read the Watchtower's *Truth* book, right?

Jay: You bet, many Bible studies were centered around that book.

Chris: On page 22, it discusses the Trinity and says:

> This doctrine was unknown to the Hebrew prophets and Christian apostles. The *New Catholic Encyclopedia* (1967 edi-

> tion, Vol. XIV, p. 306) admits that "the doctrine of the Holy Trinity is not taught in the OT [Old Testament]." It also admits that the doctrine must be dated as from about three hundred and fifty years after the death of Jesus Christ. So the early Christians who were taught directly by Jesus Christ did not believe that God is a "Trinity." (See p. 144.)

Did you look up what the Catholic Encyclopedia actually said, or did you just believe the Watchtower?

Jay: Well, I didn't look it up. . . . Why, isn't that what it says?

Chris: Again we find the Watchtower practices what it actually believes—it's all right to misrepresent what others believe and teach in order to make what it teaches look better. The actual quote says:

> The doctrine of the Holy Trinity is not taught in the OT. In the NT the oldest evidence is in the Pauline epistles, especially 2 Cor. 13.3, and 1 Cor 12.4–6. In the Gospels evidence of the Trinity is found explicitly only in the baptismal formula of Mt 28.19.[4] (See p. 145.)

What the Catholic Encyclopedia *actually* said is quite different from the impression one gets by reading the Watchtower's book about what is said.

Jay: Quite different.

Chris: In fact, the Encyclopedia, on the same page, shows there is evidence in the Old Testament that to them indicates that

> . . . the minds of God's people were being prepared for the concepts that would be involved in the forthcoming revelation of the doctrine of the Trinity.

The same page shows that the author did not believe what the *Truth* book said, that the doctrine was unknown to the Christian apostles, but the very opposite. Concerning the trinitarian formulas found in the Gospels, the article says:

> . . . they testify, under divine inspiration, to the belief of the Apostolic Church in a doctrine of three Persons in one God.

The article concludes with a rebuttal of the modern scholars who see something less than a trinitarian expression in the baptismal formulas:

---

[4]Probably 2 Cor. 13:14 is to be read for 2 Cor. 13:13 in the quotation.

> Yet in the light of the fullness of revelation, the possibility is not to be excluded that the Evangelists had the doctrine of the Trinity in mind when they described this event.

It should be rather clear that the Watchtower takes a free hand in misrepresenting what trinitarians believe regarding the doctrine of the Trinity. The word "trinity" is a description of the *nature* of the one God as He has revealed himself in the Scriptures. Christians do not believe there are three gods and ought not to be confused or confounded by the Watchtower's deceptive tactics.

Does Christianity Require Belief IN A TRINITY?

ALL major religions of Christendom accept the Trinity doctrine as an article of faith. The more than 250 churches belonging to the World Council of Churches confess "the Lord Jesus Christ as God and Savior according to the Scriptures and therefore seek to fulfill together their common calling to the glory of the one God, Father, Son and Holy Spirit."

While the views of the various religious bodies belonging to this fellowship vary radically, all are required to be in agreement that the "Father, Son and Holy Spirit" are but "one God." Hence, rejection of the Trinity doctrine is, in effect, regarded as a rejection of Christianity.

Though not belonging to the World Council of Churches, the Roman Catholic Church likewise adheres to belief in the Trinity. Of this teaching, Catholic theologian Walter Farrell noted:

> "The mystery of the Trinity, as God has told it to us, is the mystery of three divine persons, really distinct, in one and the same divine nature: coequal, coeternal, consubstantial, one God. Of these persons, the Second proceeds from the First by an eternal generation; the Third proceeds from the First and the Second by an eternal spiration. . . .
>
> "The Trinity is a mystery; no doubt about it. Unless we had been told of its existence, we would never have suspected such a thing. Moreover, now that we know that there is a Trinity, we cannot understand it. The man who attempts to unravel the mystery is in the position of a near-sighted man straining his eyes from the Eastern Shore of Maryland for a glimpse of Spain."

The words of this theologian imply that it is impossible to know the God whom one worships. But that is not in agreement with Jesus' words to a Samaritan woman: "You worship what you do not know; we [Jews] worship what we know." (John 4:22) Though the Jews never viewed God as a trinity, Jesus Christ could still say that they knew what they were worshiping. Those accepting the Trinity doctrine, however, cannot explain or understand whom they are venerating. God is a great mystery to them. Does this not suggest that something is amiss in trying to speak of God in terms of a mysterious Trinity?

The previously quoted Catholic theologian indicated that it would be impossible to have come up with the idea of the Trinity apart from divine revelation. If that were so, why do even non-Christian religions teach a trinity concept? On the basis of his studies, Professor E. Washburn Hopkins said of the trinities of Hinduism, Buddhism and Christendom: "The three trinities *as religious expressions* are identical. . . . One may say: I believe in God as godhead, and in the divine incarnation, and in the creative Holy Spirit, as a Christian, a Vishnuite, or a Buddhist."

Noteworthy, too, is the fact that the trinity of Chinese Buddhism is defined in a way that is practically identical to what professed Christians say. We read:

The Watchtower, Feb. 1, 1974, p. 75.

TRIALS 236

elm: g80 11/8 30; g79 7/22 21-3; g76 2/8 30
eucalyptus: g77 9/22 26
fig: w79 9/15 16-18
fig-mulberry: w76 3/15 192
flamboyant: g77 8/22 20-1
frangipani: g77 8/22 21
mangrove: g80 9/22 22-4
Montezuma cypress: g77 9/22 26
olive: g79 3/8 13-15; g76 9/22 10
palm: w76 10/1 581; g76 12/22 24
papaya: g78 8/8 14-15
redwood: g77 9/22 26
rubber: g77 4/8 24-6
sequoia:
 tallest: go 73
sycamore: w76 3/15 192
(SEE ALSO PLANTS)

TRIALS

Christians subjected to: cj 14-16
 benefits resulting: cj 26-7; g78 3/22 27-8
enduring: w79 3/1 25-6; w78 7/15 25-9
 purpose: w78 7/15 26-7
Jesus' trial: cj 30; my 101
not from God: cj 27-30
prayer for wisdom to face: cj 17-21

TRIBE

Amis: w79 9/1 10-11
Aucaner (Suriname): w80 7/15 11-16
Bagobo tribe of Philippine Republic: g78 7/22 21-4
Central African Republic:
 tribalism in Protestantism: w80 8/1 7
decline of African tribe because of gonorrhea-caused infertility: g77 1/8 30
Hunza: g79 5/22 30
Negritos (pygmies): g80 8/8 23-5
newfound Niawa Indian tribe: g78 1/8 30
Onges tribe:
 fertility reduced by eating certain tuberous plants: g78 11/22 30
Papua New Guinea:
 discovery of unknown tribe: g80 4/22 30
Tasaday tribe of Philippine Republic: g79 1/8 14; g77 8/22 12-15
tribalism:
 cause of conflict: g79 5/8 22
Tswana:
 absence of coronary heart disease: g79 5/22 30
Yungnara (Australia): g80 11/22 30
Zulus:
 "virginity tests": g79 6/8 31

TRIBULATION

"great tribulation" (Mt 24:21):
 at proper time: w77 4/15 235-6
 attack on God's people: w80 11/15 27; w80 10/15 23; w80 7/1 17-18; w80 5/15 27; w80 3/1 23
 collapse of world's systems not necessary as a prelude to: w76 7/15 442
 comes at an 'unlikely' time: w76 7/15 441
 cry of "peace and security" before: w78 4/1 5; w76 7/15 442
 "day and hour": go 157-9
 discussion: w80 10/15 11-16; w77 4/15 232-6; w77 1/15 40-9; go 175-82
 global aspect: w78 8/15 31; w77 4/15 232-6
 "goats" destroyed: go 171
 "great crowd" come out of (Re 7:14): w80 8/15 19-20; w78 9/1 30; go 172-4
 Jerusalem (70 C.E.): w78 10/1 31; w78 8/15 31; w77 1/15 41-2, 44; go 148-50; w76 7/15 435
 material possessions: w77 4/1 200-2; w77 1/15 49
 modern-day fulfillment: w78 10/1 31; w78 8/15 31; w76 7/15 435-6
 no mourning for those destroyed: w77 6/1 345
 outbreak ends opportunity for salvation: w79 10/1 28-9
 premature expectations concerning: w79 7/1 29
 proper view of setting dates for: w76 7/15 440-1
 protection during: w78 1/15 23-4; w77 1/15 49
 reasons for facing, with confidence: w77 1/15 40-9
 rulers to drink from the "cup of the wine of rage" of God (Jer 25:15): w79 9/15 21-9
 sequence of events following outbreak of: w80 3/1 18-19, 23-4
 spirit of self-sacrifice needed during: w78 8/1 20
 survivors: w80 2/1 27-8; w79 8/1 7-8; w78 9/1 23-4, 30-1; w77 4/15 237-42; w77 1/15 49; lp 140-2; go 181-2
 "this generation": w78 10/1 31; go 152, 155-6
 time of, a surprise to God's people: w76 11/15 689
 "time of distress" (Da 12:1): go 122-3, 178-9; w76 2/1 95
 when it begins: w80 10/15 23; w80 10/1 25; w79 2/1 26; w77 1/15 42; go 177
 why date not given: go 158-9; w76 7/15 442
 worshipers of wild beast destroyed: w79 8/1 31-2
(SEE ALSO ARMAGEDDON)

TRIER

discussion: g80 4/22 21-3

TRIFLES

avoiding issues over: g78 2/8 3

TRINIDAD

automobile tire-making: g78 11/8 13-15
island reporting under: yb79 23
Jehovah's Witnesses: yb81 28-9; yb80 30-1; yb79 30-1, 190; yb78 30-1; yb77 30-1; w76 9/15 553-5
 service experiences: w80 4/1 32; yb78 17-18
leprosy: g77 12/8 14-15
population: yb81 28

TRINITY

Athanasian Creed: g76 8/22 23-4
Babylon: g80 10/8 19
clergy disbelief: w79 7/1 15-16
 book *The Myth of God Incarnate:* w77 11/15 687
confusion caused by removal of divine name from Greek Scriptures: w78 5/1 12
Constantine's role: g80 4/22 20, 22
discussion: g80 4/22 20; g76 8/22 23-6
Egyptian: g78 6/22 10
Elohim: g78 11/22 27
exposed by *The Watchtower* for 100 years: w79 7/1 15
Gallup poll:
 Jesus Christ a man or both fully God and fully man?: w80 8/15 11
Hinduism: gh 48
Jesus had a beginning: g76 8/22 25-6
Jesus inferior to Jehovah: w79 7/1 16; w79 5/15 31; g79 2/22 27-8; g76 8/22 26
"one Jehovah" (De 6:4): g78 11/22 27-8
origin: g80 4/22 20; w78 10/15 32; g76 8/22 23-6
pagan belief in: g80 4/22 20; g78 7/22 15
penalty for denying: w77 4/15 245
scriptures misapplied to support:
 John 1:1: w77 5/15 319-20
 1 Timothy 3:16: w77 4/15 245
 1 John 5:7: g79 10/8 16; w77 4/15 244-6; g77 3/8 25
symbols of—
 fleur-de-lis: g76 12/22 13
 shamrock: g76 12/22 13-14
view of Isaac Newton: w77 4/15 244-7
view of Michael Servetus: gh 100

Quotations

did not form part of the apostles' preaching: w79 7/1 15
doctrine has not much future: w79 7/1 16
Jesus did not teach the doctrine of the Trinity: w77 11/15 687
neither the word nor doctrine appears in Bible: g80 4/22 20
no New Testament writings supply explicit assurance of a triune God: w79 7/1 15
not directly the word of God: g80 4/22 20
source foreign from that of Jewish and Christian Scriptures: w78 10/15 32
that Jesus did not present himself as God incarnate is accepted by all theologians: w77 11/15 687

TRIUMPHAL PROCESSIONS

Roman: w77 9/15 576
significance for Christians: w80 6/1 27

bq, Witnesses and the Question of Blood; **bw**, Choosing the Best Way of Life; **cj**, Commentary on James; **dt**, Path of Divine Truth; **fl**, Making Your Family Life Happy; **g**, Awake!; **gh**, Good News—to Make You Happy; **go**, Our Incoming World Government; **hp**, Happiness—How to Find It; **hs**, Holy Spirit; **km**, Our Kingdom Service; **lp**, Life Does Have a Purpose; **my**, Bible Stories; **us**, Unseen Spirits; **w**, Watchtower; **yb**, Yearbook; **yy**, Your Youth. **Full titles on page 6.**

Watch Tower Publications Index 1976–1980, 1981, p. 236.

to his laws, God rejoices. (Proverbs 27:11) Also, God describes how he feels when his servants are made to suffer by enemies: "He that is touching you is touching my eyeball." (Zechariah 2:8) Are you not moved to love a God who has such affection for lowly, insignificant humans of all races and peoples?—Isaiah 40:22; John 3:16.

IS GOD JESUS OR A TRINITY?

14 Who is this wonderful God? Some persons say his name is Jesus. Others say he is a Trinity, although the word "trinity" does not appear in the Bible. According to the teaching of the Trinity, there are three persons in one God, that is, there is "one God, Father, Son and Holy Spirit." Many religious organizations teach this, even though they admit it is "a mystery." Are such views of God correct?

15 Well, did Jesus ever say that he was God? No, he never did. Rather, in the Bible he is called "God's Son." And he said: "The Father is greater than I am." (John 10:34-36; 14:28) Also, Jesus explained that there were some things that neither he nor the angels knew but that only God knew. (Mark 13:32) Further, on one occasion Jesus prayed to God, saying: "Let, not *my* will, but *yours* take place." (Luke 22:42) If Jesus were the Almighty God, he would not have prayed to himself, would he? In fact, following Jesus' death, the Scripture says: "This Jesus God resurrected." (Acts 2:32) Thus the Almighty God and Jesus are clearly two separate persons. Even after his

Since Jesus prayed to God, asking that God's will, not his, be done, the two could not be the same person

14. What is the Trinity teaching?
15. How does the Bible show that God and Jesus are two separate persons who are not equal?

You Can Live Forever in Paradise on Earth, 1982, p. 39.

Very shortly now, this mystery of God, this company of divinely-begotten sons, will be FINISHED—completed: "The church of the first born," of which Jesus is the head, will soon cease to be, God manifest in the *flesh*. The entire company shall be glorified together, and "shall shine forth as the sun in the kingdom of their Father." (Matt. 13:43.) They shall arise in power and strength to bless all the families of the earth. "The Sun of Righteousness shall arise with *healing* in his wings"—for the Jew first, and also for the Gentile.

It is for the completion of this church that we ourselves groan within ourselves, waiting for the adoption, to-wit, the redemption of the body of Christ; the ending of the mystery part of God's plan, in the full glory of Millennial brightness and joy. It is for this event also that the world's release from pain and death waits. The whole creation groaneth and travaileth in pain together until now, waiting for the manifestation of the Sons of God. Rom. 8:19-24.

The necessity of the vailing of God's mysterious purpose with reference to the church is very evident. If the religious rulers of the Jews had *known* that Jesus was really the anointed of God, they would not have crucified the Lord of glory. (1 Cor. 2; 7, 8.) And had the rulers of the world and of the nominal church, recognized the Lord's anointed body during this age, they would not have had the privilege of suffering with their Head.

Again, Paul tells us that God gave him wonderful revelations concerning the mystery, "To make all see what [are the conditions of] fellowship of the mystery." (Eph. 3:3-6, 9.) And it is to Paul as our Lord's instrument that we are indebted more than to any other Apostle, for a clear record of the conditions on which we may become members of this *mystery* band, and as such be in due time revealed in glory of power. He tells us that we must have fellowship in the sufferings of Christ, if we would have share in His coming glory. We must with our Head become *dead* to the world, its ambitions, its prizes, if we would become heirs of the glory which God hath in preparation and reservation for this mystery church of which Jesus is the Head.

We believe that we are just on the eve of the finishing of this church, or mystery. You and I, my brother, are, by our covenants, *candidates* for a crown of life and a position in the throne of the coming kingdom. Let us make our calling and election to that high position sure, by so running our race as to be approved of God, as living sacrifices for the gospel of truth. We have full little enough time to fulfill all our covenant; let us lay aside every weight and all besetting sins, and run, with patience, the race for the prize of our high calling, that when the church is complete—the mystery finished—we may be among the glorified members. Then no longer the mystery, we shall be Jehovah's agents in blessing all the families of the earth.

Up, then, and linger not, thou saint of God,
Fling from thy shoulders each impeding load;
Be brave and wise, shake off earth's soil and sin,
That with the Bridegroom thou mayest enter in—
Oh. watch and pray!

Clear hath the voice been heard, Behold, I've come—
That voice that calls thee to thy glorious home,
That bids thee leave these vales and take swift wing,
To meet the hosts of thy descending King;—
And thou may'st rise!

'Tis a thick throng of foes, afar and near;
The grave in front, a hating world in rear;
Yet flee thou canst not, victory must be won,
Ere fall the shadows of thy setting sun:—
And thou must fight.

Gird on thy armor; face each weaponed foe;
Deal with the sword of heaven the deadly blow;
Forward, still forward, till the prize divine
Rewards thy zeal, and victory is thine.
Win thou the crown.

—Selected.

"HEAR, O ISRAEL! JEHOVAH OUR GOD IS ONE—JEHOVAH"

Our readers are aware that while we believe in Jehovah and Jesus, and the holy Spirit, we reject as totally unscriptural, the teaching that these are *three* Gods in *one person*, or as some put it, *one* God in *three persons*. The doctrine of the Trinity had its rise in the third century, and has a very close resemblance to the heathen doctrines prevalent at that time, particularly Hindooism.* The only text in Scripture which was ever claimed to prove, or affirm, that the Father, Son and Spirit are one, is a portion of 1 John 5:7, 8. This appears only in Manuscripts written since the fifth century, and is acknowledged by all Trinitarians to be a *"forgery."* So undisputable is this, that the translators of the "Revised Version" recently published omit the clause without note of comment, though those Revisors were themselves believers in *Trinity*.

Like some other doctrines received by Protestants through Papacy, this one is received and fully endorsed, though its adherents are aware that not a word of Scripture can be adduced in its support. Nay more, any one who will not affirm this unscriptural doctrine as his faith, is declared by the action of the *Evangelical Alliance* to be nonorthodox—a heretic.

However, it behooves us as truth seekers, to deal honestly with ourselves and with our Father's Word, which is able to make us truly wise. Therefore, ignoring the traditions and creeds of uninspired men and corrupt systems, let us hold fast the form of sound words received from our Lord and the Apostles. (2 Tim. 1:13.)

Let us inquire of these "standards" and "authorities" of the true church, what is truth on this subject. Paul answers clearly and forcibly—There is *"one* God and Father of all." (Eph. 4:6.) And again he says, (1 Cor. 8:5-6.) "There be gods many and lords many, but to US there is but *one* God, the Father, of whom are [or who created] all things, and we in him: and one Lord Jesus Christ by whom are all things, and we by Him." We believe this exactly: All things are of our Father; he is the first cause of all things; and all things are by our Lord Jesus. He *"the beginning of the* CREATION *of God,"* (Rev. 3:14.) has been the agent of Jehovah in all that has since been done—"Without him was not anything made that was made." (John 1:3.) Jesus' testimony is the same; his claim was that he was "a Son," an obedient son, who did not do his own will, but the Father's who sent him—"Not my will but thine be done." Again Jesus said he could do nothing of himself—"The Father that dwelleth in me, *He doeth the works."* (John 5:19 and 14:10.) True he said, I and my Father are *one*, but he shows in what sense he meant they were one, by praying that just so His disciples all might be *one*. (John 10:30 and 17; 11.) It is a oneness which results from having the same *mind* or *spirit;* it is the same oneness that should exist between a heart union of man and wife; they twain are *one*.

It is far from honoring the Master, as many appear to think they do, when they contradict his direct teachings, affirming that Father and Son are *one and the same being*, equal in all respects. No, says Jesus, "My Father is greater than I." (John 14:28.) And he also says, God is not only his Father but ours:—"I ascend to *my Father* and *your Father*, to my God and your God." (John 20:17.) A more correct translation of Phil. 2:6. settles the question of the Father's supremacy, in harmony with other scriptures, such as 1 Cor. 15:28 and John 14:28. The Emphatic Diaglott translation is, "Who though being in a form of God, yet did not meditate a usurpation, to be like God." The idea here, is the very opposite of equality, as conveyed in the King James translation: Jesus did not claim equality, nor aspire to a usurpation of God's authority. That was Satan's claim and effort. Isa. 14:12-14. He said, "I will exalt my throne above the stars of God . . . . I will be like the Most High."

Jesus said: Ye call me Lord and Master and ye do well, for so I am, but call no man on earth Father, for *one is your Father*, which is in heaven. (Matt. 23:9.) Peter also carries the same thought, saying, "The God and Father of our Lord Jesus Christ hath *begotten us*." (1 Pet. 1:3 and Eph. 3:9-11, Gal. 1:3, 4, Rom. 16:25-27.) How clear and harmonious are these words of our standards, and we could quote much more in perfect harmony.

Briefly stated then, we find the Scriptures to teach that there is but *one* Eternal God and Father—who is "from everlasting to everlasting" (Psa. 90:2 and Rom. 16:26, 27.)—that

* It was not until the beginning of the fourth century that the Trinitarian views began to be elaborated and formulated into a doctrine and an endeavor made to reconcile it *"with the belief of the church in one* GOD." *"Out of the attempt to solve this problem sprang the doctrine of the Trinity."* . . . Trinity "is a very marked feature in Hindooism, and is discernible in Persian, Egyptian, Roman, Japanese, Indian and the most ancient Grecian *Mythologies."—Abbott & Conant's Religious Dictionary, page 944.*

The Watchtower, July 1882, Reprints, p. 369.

CHAPTER IX

IS THERE A TRINITY?

A FUNDAMENTAL doctrine of so-called "Christendom" is that known as the "Holy Trinity". It is accepted as Scriptural truth and held sacred by millions of persons. The doctrine, in brief, is that there are three gods in one: "God the Father, God the Son, and God the Holy Ghost," all three equal in power, substance and eternity. As defined by the *Catholic Encyclopedia* under the heading "Trinity, The Blessed", "The Trinity is the term employed to signify the central doctrine of the Christian religion— . . . in the unity of the Godhead there are Three Persons, the Father, the Son, and the Holy Spirit, these Three Persons being truly distinct one from another. Thus, in the words of the Athanasian Creed: 'The Father is God, the Son is God, and the Holy Spirit is God, and yet there are not three Gods, but one God.' "

2 Such a doctrine, with its attempted explanation, is very confusing. To excuse it with the word "Mystery!" is not satisfying. If one has in mind the apostle's words, "God is not the author of confusion" (1 Corinthians 14:33), it is at once seen that such doctrine is not of God. Well, one might ask, if God is not the author of this confusing doctrine, who is?

---

1. How is the "trinity" doctrine defined?
2. What points are raised that are cause for doubt as to God's being the author of the doctrine?

Let God Be True, 1952 ed., p. 100.

enant; together with the repeated declarations of the New Testament Scriptures, that he is the Mediator of the New Covenant,—the one Mediator *between* God and men, the man Christ Jesus, who gave himself a ransom for all." These various Scriptures all consistently and harmoniously teach a distinction of person and glory and power as between the heavenly Father and the heavenly Son; but a most absolute and profound unity of plan, will, purpose: for the Son was *worthy* to be the executor of the great plan of Jehovah, *because* he had no will of his own, but renounced his own will that he might be filled with the Father's spirit and do his will in every particular.—John 6:38, 39.

Moreover, the very words "Father" and "Son" imply a difference, and contradict the thoughts of the Trinity and oneness of person, because the word "father" signifies *lifegiver*, while the word "son" signifies the *one who has received life* from another. The heavenly Father received life from no one; he is the fountain, the source of life, not only to our Lord Jesus, his *only begotten* Son, but through him the source of life to all others of his creatures. And all this is fully in accord with the Scripture which stands at the head of this chapter, in which the Apostle plainly denies that the Father and the Son are one in person or in power, saying, "To us there is one God, the Father, *of* whom are all things . . . and one Lord, Jesus Christ, *by* whom are all things."

The thoughtful reader will at once recognize the Scriptural harmony and simplicity of the view herein presented, while all will admit that the doctrine of the Trinity is impossible of reasonable understanding or explanation. Its most earnest advocates admit this, and instead of endeavoring to do the impossible thing of explaining it, they avoid discussion, claiming that it's "a great mystery," unexplainable. But, strange to say, this doctrine of three Gods in one God, which not only has no Scriptural support, but is opposed by the Scriptures from Genesis to Revelation, both directly and indirectly, and which is so opposed to reason as to be unreasonable, is nevertheless a

The Atonement Between God and Man, Studies in the Scriptures, Series V, 1906 ed., p. 60.

perfect harmony with the Father, and with the Son, by doing not their own wills, but by setting aside their own wills and accepting the *will of Christ*, which is the *will of the Father*. Thus, and thus only, will the Church ever come into the *oneness* for which our Lord here prayed, and which he refers to as of the same kind as the *oneness* between the Father and himself. How strange that any should attempt to misuse and pervert these our Lord's words, to make them support the unreasonable and unscriptural doctrine of a Trinity,—three Gods in *one person*. On the contrary, how beautiful and reasonable is the Scriptural *oneness* of the spirit of the Father and Son and Church.

"HE THAT HATH SEEN ME HATH SEEN THE FATHER."

After our Lord had declared himself to be the Way, the Truth and the Life, and that no man could come to the Father but by him, and that whoever knew him would know the Father also, Philip said to our Lord Jesus, "Lord, show us the Father, and it sufficeth us." Jesus answered him, "Have I been so long time with you, and yet hast thou not known me, Philip? He that hath seen me hath seen the Father; and how sayest thou then, Show us the Father? Believest thou not that I am in the Father and the Father in me? The words that I speak unto you I speak not of myself: but the Father that dwelleth in me, he doeth the works."—John 14:7-10.

We are asked to accept this statement by our Lord Jesus as proof that he is Jehovah (and not Jehovah's Son), and that as such the name Jehovah is properly applicable to him. But all should notice that the entire context shows a distinction between the Father and the Son, such as no reasonable person would use if he desired to give the impression which Trinitarians seek to draw from it. The whole question, therefore, is, What did our Lord wish us to understand by his words, "He that hath seen me hath seen the Father?" We answer, he meant us to under-

The Atonement Between God and Man, Studies in the Scriptures, Series V, 1906 ed., p. 76.

shown by the Scripture which says, "Both he that sanctifieth and they who are sanctified are all of one [of one spirit, of one mind, begotten of the Spirit of Truth], for which cause he is not ashamed to call them brethren." (Heb. 2:11.) Thus it is that we are "washed, sanctified, justified, in the name of our Lord Jesus and by the Spirit of our God"—the Spirit of Truth.

BE YE FILLED WITH THE SPIRIT.

"Be filled with the Spirit; speaking to yourselves in psalms and hymns and spiritual songs, singing and making melody in your heart to the Lord; giving thanks always."—Eph. 5:18-20.

The intimation of this Scripture is that the Lord's people may have a greater or less degree or fulness of his Spirit. To be his they must have some of his Spirit for "if any man *have not* the Spirit of Christ he is none of his." (Rom. 8:9.) It rests with ourselves largely with our use of the means which God had provided, how fully we may be filled with his Spirit and disposition, his influence,—the Spirit or influence of his Truth, which he has revealed for the very purpose of sanctifying our hearts and lives, and separating us from those who have the spirit of the world.

Nothing in this and similar texts involves the thought of a personal holy Spirit: quite the contrary. If a person were meant, it would be inconsistent to urge the recipient to a greater or less filling. The person who could enter could alone have to do with the filling; if he is great, he will fill the more, if small, he will fill the less. The holy Spirit conceived of as a person, one of a trinity of Gods, equal with the Highest, could not be supposed to get into the small compass of an imperfect man, and then not even fill that little heart. But when the correct thought of the divine power and influence is understood the Apostle's exhortation is thoroughly reasonable. We should continue seeking to be filled with the holy

The Atonement Between God and Man, Studies in the Scriptures, Series V, 1906 ed., p. 244.

THE REVELATION

OF [ST.] JOHN [THE DIVINE]*

REVELATION 1

THE MESSAGE FOR THIS DAY

The Revelation of Jesus Christ.—John the Revelator and the Prophet Habakkuk have foretold that the understanding of this revelation, given in 96 A. D., is set for an appointed time, the end of the age; and that, at this time, now, when the predicted "Faithful and wise servant" would be present with God's people, the vision would be made plain.—Rev. 1:10; Matt. 24:45; Hab. 2:1-3; 1 Pet. 1:13.

Which God gave unto Him.—"The declaration that 'the Son can do nothing of Himself,' if it were not backed up as it is by a score of other testimonies from the same interested and inspired Teacher, is <u>a contradiction to the common thought of Trinitarians, that the Son is the Father.</u>"—Z.'99-45; John 5:20; 12:49; 17:7, 8.

To shew unto His [servants] SAINTS.†—"Our Lord Jesus has promised us that, as the Elder Brother (of the Gospel House of Sons), whatsoever the Father shall make known to Him He in turn will make known to us."—Z.'99-45.

The things.—The shifting scenes of Church and State, the history of the Gospel and Millennial Ages.

Which must shortly come to pass.—Which began at once, in St. John's day, and will continue until the completion of all that he foresaw.

And He sent.—He did not come Himself, but acted with the dignity becoming Him who is now the express Image of the Father's person. "Dwelling in the light which no man can approach unto, whom no man hath seen, nor can see."—Heb. 1:3; 1 Tim. 6:16.

---

*Words not in Sinaitic MS. are enclosed in brackets. The Sinaitic MS. is the oldest known copy of the Scriptures, having been written, it is believed, in A. D. 331. The "Authorized" Version was made from MSS. none of which were older than the tenth century.

†Words in Sinaitic MS. which do not appear in "Authorized" Version are printed in capitals.

The Finished Mystery, Studies in the Scriptures, Series VII, 1917, p. 11.

TRINITY

Another lie made and told by Satan for the purpose of reproaching God's name and turning men away from God is that of the "trinity". That doctrine is taught by the religionists of "Christendom" and is in substance this: 'That there are three gods in one; God the Father, God the Son, and God the Holy Ghost, all equal in power, substance and eternity.' No man can explain that doctrine, because it is false. That false doctrine was prominent in the religions of ancient Babylon and Egypt and among other mythologists, all of which are Devil religions.

If you ask a teacher of the trinity doctrine to explain it, he invariably answers: "That is a mystery which you cannot understand." The doctrine was first introduced into "organized Christianity" by a Greek clergyman in the fourth century. To aid the gullible people to keep the thing somewhat fixed in mind an image was introduced, a triangle, a circle, a trefoil or three-pointed thing that was used as an object lesson. Men desiring to appear wise before others fell easy victims to Satan's subtility and were induced to turn away from the truth of God's Word and to make images to be employed in their worship and thus to induce others to believe that there is not one Almighty God, but three. Concerning such foolish persons the Scriptures say, "They . . . became vain in their imaginations, and their foolish heart was darkened: professing themselves to be wise, they became fools, and changed the glory of the uncorruptible God into an image made like to corruptible man." (Romans 1:21-23) The fraud and deceit of Satan's agents appears in connection with the so-

Riches, 1936, p. 185.

tions to see if he understands what it means to be "peaceable." A peaceable person is not pugnacious, not quarrelsome, faultfinding, bickering, nagging or gossiping. He is peaceable. Help the householder to see that this applies in the family, with sons and daughters, husbands and wives. Help them to feel the power of God's Word. "For the word of God is alive and exerts power." (Heb. 4:12) Through your method of studying, you have to see whether he is a reasonable person or not, whether he is moderate in habits, acceptable, sensible, not overly demanding, as a reasonable person should be. Is he ready to obey the commandments of God? This applies both inside the congregation and outside, and to children as well as adults.

8 Further, we are told that heavenly wisdom is also "full of mercy and good fruits," without "partial distinctions, not hypocritical." Dwell on such points that strike the heart. Have the home Bible student examine himself to see if he is full of mercy and whether he has good fruits to show for the days he has lived upon the earth. Partial distinctions divide, and hypocrisy is distasteful. Allow the power of God to examine the heart and to cut it if necessary. This probing action gives the learner a chance to see himself as God sees him. Take one point at a time, however. And take time to see that he understands what the Bible is saying. In this way we will be building in disciples an appreciation for the godly qualities of heavenly wisdom.—Rom. 2:6, 11.

BUILDING TO DEVELOP ENDURANCE

9 Implanting spiritual discernment in others, getting them to understand and teaching them to think on their own is by no means a simple task. As a rule, people today are just not spiritually minded. They do not discern things spiritually. Still a key to developing endurance is spiritual discernment, understanding and thinking ability. Here, too, the heart of the disciple must be reached by stressing the lasting appreciation one should have for these qualities and their worth to us individually. This is what Jesus did. To stimulate and maintain appreciation for these qualities Jesus drank regularly from the Word of God. Thus he was able to understand Jehovah's principles completely as they related to him. He was also able to discern clearly the course that should be followed to the praise of Jehovah and to the eternal good of mankind.

10 It may be necessary for us to teach those with whom we study the Bible how to reason on Scripture texts. For example, Mark 12:29 might be read: "Hear, O Israel, Jehovah our God is one Jehovah." Ask the student, "How many Jehovahs are there?" Let him answer. The answer is obvious that there is only one Jehovah. When he discerns this, you have caused him to register an important fact in his mind that he might otherwise have missed. Help him to appreciate further what this means to him. Reason with him, perhaps in this way: "If he is one Jehovah, then could he be three gods, God the Father, God the Son and God the Holy Ghost, as the Trinitarians teach?" Again, let him answer. "No, Jehovah could not be three gods, for the Bible plainly says he is one God." Now, you have caused the student to think on a basic Scriptural truth and to understand that Jehovah is but one God. You have also exposed a basic false doctrine—the doctrine of the Trinity. With almost everything we teach, it is profitable to the

8. What other aspects of heavenly wisdom should the student be taught, and how can these be inculcated?
9. (a) As a rule, why is spirituality difficult to inculcate? (b) What is the key to endurance, and how may this be communicated to interested persons?

10. (a) What else may be necessary for us to do in our teaching work? Give an example of how this may be done. (b) What is accomplished by instructing in this manner?

The Watchtower, April 1, 1970, p. 210.

WHAT IS GOD'S PERSONAL NAME?

How many people today know? Do you?

God's name is Jehovah. Is that just our idea? No.

The Protestant King James Version Bible says: "Thou, whose name alone is Jehovah, art the most high." —Psalm 83:18.

The Catholic Encyclopedia (1910, Vol. VIII, p. 329) says: "Jehovah [is] the proper name of God in the Old Testament." And according to a new Catholic translation, God says: "Yahweh [Hebrew form of Jehovah] . . . is my name for all time."—Exodus 3:15, The Jerusalem Bible.

Do you use that name?

WHO IS GOD?

Is he three Gods in one—a trinity? No, the Bible says 'there is actually one God the Father.'—1 Corinthians 8:6.

Is he the same as Jesus Christ? No, for Jesus himself said: "The Father is greater than I am." And Jesus also said that his Father in heaven is "the only true God." —John 14:28; 17:3.

Did you realize this? Have you been worshiping the true God?

WHAT DOES IT MEAN TO KNOW GOD?

Many believe that God exists and has great power. Some also know his name. Does that prove that they really know God? No, far from it.

To know God means to know what kind of person he is.

He is a wise and loving God. You have evidence of this all around you—in the sun, air, rain, food and beauty of this earth.

He is also a God of power and justice—a fact that some persons do not like. Yet because he is, he will soon put an end to all injustice, all crime and corruption, all oppression.

Really, how well do you know God?

What Do You Really Know About God?, 1971, p. 2.

selves, Is the material adapted to the particular audience involved in the presentation? Will the audience be informed and instructed by it?

6 In preparation ask yourself, What do I want to accomplish in this talk? How much of what I want to say does this person or group already know? What foundation must I lay before these points can be made clear? How would I say it differently to an altogether different group? Comparisons often clarify our viewpoints. Try different approaches to different groups in your preparation just to get the feel of the difference in considering the audience and making the material informative to the particular audience you are going to address.

7 **Material of practical value.** There is much to be learned, but not all of it is practical. To us, informative material concerns those things we need to know for Christian living, for our ministry. We want to know how to use this information that we have acquired.

8 The student, in preparation, and the school servant, in counseling, might consider this point by asking: What guiding principles are to be found in the talk? Could the material be used in making decisions? Can the information presented be adapted to the field ministry? Does it magnify God's Word and point to his purpose? Few talks can contribute all this information, but to be practical, material presented should be usable in some way by the audience.

9 **Accuracy of statement.** Jehovah's witnesses are an organization of truth. We should want to speak the truth and be absolutely accurate in every detail at all times. This should be so not only as regards doctrine but also in our quotations, what we say about others or how we represent them, also in matters involving scientific data or news events.

10 Wrong statements delivered to an audience may be repeated and the error magnified. Inaccuracies that are recognized by an audience raise questions as to the authority of the speaker on other points, perhaps even calling in question the truth of the message itself. A newly interested person hearing such statements, and having heard a different view expressed on another occasion, might come to the conclusion there

Theocratic Ministry School Guidebook, 1971, p. 110.

IS GOD A "TRINITY"?

12 Many religions of Christendom teach that God is a "Trinity," although the word "Trinity" does not appear in the Bible. The World Council of Churches recently said that all religions that are part of that Council should advocate the belief that there is "one God, Father, Son and Holy Spirit," that is, three persons in one God. Those teaching this doctrine admit that it is "a mystery." The Athanasian Creed, of about the eighth century of the Common Era, says that the Father, the Son and the Holy Ghost (Spirit) are all three of the same substance, all three are eternal (and hence had no beginning), and all three are almighty. So the creed reads that in the "Trinity none is afore or after other; none is greater or less than another."* Is that reasonable? More importantly, is it in agreement with the Bible?

13 This doctrine was unknown to the Hebrew prophets and Christian apostles. The *New Catholic Encyclopedia* (1967 edition, Vol. XIV, p. 306) admits that "the doctrine of the Holy Trinity is not taught in the OT [Old Testament]." It also admits that the doctrine must be dated as from about three hundred and fifty years after the death of Jesus Christ. So the early Christians who were taught directly by Jesus Christ did not believe that God is a "Trinity."

14 When Jesus was on earth he certainly was *not* equal to his Father, for he said there were

---

* *Cyclopædia of Biblical, Theological, and Ecclesiastical Literature,* by J. M'Clintock and J. Strong, Vol. II, p. 561.

---

12. (a) What do church creeds, such as the Athanasian Creed, teach about God? (b) What questions should we ask about this teaching?
13. According to the *New Catholic Encyclopedia,* did the Hebrew prophets and the first Christians believe in a "Trinity"?
14. How did Jesus show that he was not equal with his Father?

The Truth That Leads to Eternal Life, 1968, p. 22.

the Holy Spirit are significant in this context. H. MÜHLEN, *Der Heilige Geist als Person* (Münster 1963). I. HERMANN, *Kyrios und Pneuma* (Munich 1961), raises a serious exegetical question in Paul. C. DAVIS, *Theology for Today* (New York 1962), ch. 9 and 2 taken together help to pinpoint the present-day problem of exegesis and doctrine in Trinitarianism.

Illustration credits: Fig. 1, Leonard Von Matt. Fig. 2, Widener Collection, National Gallery of Art, Washington, D.C. Fig. 3, H. P. Kraus, New York. Fig. 4, Rare Book Department, Free Library of Philadelphia.

[R. L. RICHARD]

TRINITY, HOLY (IN THE BIBLE)

The doctrine of the Holy Trinity is not taught in the OT. In the NT the oldest evidence is in the Pauline epistles, especially 2 Cor 13.13, and 1 Cor 12.4–6. In the Gospels evidence of the Trinity is found explicitly only in the baptismal formula of Mt 28.19.

In the Old Testament. The mystery of the Holy Trinity was not revealed to the Chosen People of the OT. On account of the polytheistic religions of Israel's pagan neighbors it was necessary for the teachers of Israel to stress the oneness of God. In many places of the OT, however, expressions are used in which some of the Fathers of the Church saw references or foreshadowings of the Trinity. The personified use of such terms as the *Word of God [Ps 32(33).6] and the *Spirit of God (Is 63.14) is merely by way of poetic license, though it shows that the minds of God's people were being prepared for the concepts that would be involved in the forthcoming revelation of the doctrine of the Trinity.

In the New Testament. The revelation of the truth of the triune life of God was first made in the NT, where the earliest references to it are in the Pauline epistles. The doctrine is most easily seen in St. Paul's recurrent use of the terms God, Lord, and Spirit. What makes his use of these terms so significant is that they appear against a strictly monotheistic background.

In Pauline Epistles. The clearest instance of this usage is found in 2 Cor 13.13, "The grace of our Lord Jesus Christ, and the charity of God, and the fellowship of the Holy Spirit be with you all." This blessing is perhaps a quotation from the early Christian liturgy. The grammatical usage in this blessing, especially the subjective genetives *τοῦ κυρίου Ἰησοῦ Χριστοῦ . . . τοῦ θεοῦ . . . τοῦ ἁγίου πνεύματος* gives us a basis not only for the distinction of persons, but also for their equality inasmuch as all the benefits are to flow from the one Godhead.

Another example of Paul's probable reference to the Trinity by his use of the triad, Spirit, Lord, God, can be seen in 1 Cor 12.4–6. Here, in speaking of the spiritual gifts or *charisms that are bestowed upon Christians, he says, "Now there are varieties of gifts, but the same Spirit; and there are varieties of ministries, but the same Lord; and there are varieties of workings, but the same God, who works all things in all." This passage witnesses to the doctrine of the Trinity by ascribing the various charisms, viz, gifts, ministries, and workings, to the Spirit, the Lord (the Son), and God (the Father), respectively. Since all these charisms of their very nature demand a divine source, the three Persons are put on a par, thus clearly indicating their divine nature while at the same time maintaining the distinction of persons.

In the Gospels. The only place in the gospels where the three divine Persons are explicitly mentioned together is in St. Matthew's account of Christ's last command to His Apostles, "Go, therefore, and make disciples of all nations, baptizing them in the name of the Father, and of the Son, and of the Holy Spirit" (Mt 28.19). In this commission Christ commands the Apostles to baptize all men "in the name of" the Father, Son, and Holy Spirit. The expression "in the name of" (*εἰς τὸ ὄνομα*, literally, "into the name") indicates a dedication or consecration to the one named. Thus Christian Baptism is a dedication or consecration to God—Father, Son, and Holy Spirit. Since the Son and the Holy Spirit are mentioned here on a par with the Father, the passage clearly teaches that they are equally divine with the Father, who is obviously God. Whether these are the very words of Our Lord (*see* JESUS CHRIST, IPSISSIMA VERBA OF) or whether they come from an early baptismal formula based on the general teaching of Christ, they testify, under divine inspiration, to the belief of the Apostolic Church in a doctrine of three Persons in one God.

The accounts of the *Baptism of Christ as described in Mt 3.13–17; Mk 1.9–11; Lk 3.21–22; Jn 1.32–34 have been understood by older scholars as indications of the doctrine of the Trinity. Modern scholars, however, see rather in these accounts references to the authoritative anointing of Jesus as the Messiah. Yet in the light of the fullness of revelation, the possibility is not to be excluded that the Evangelists had the doctrine of the Trinity in mind when they described this event.

See also JOHANNINE COMMA.

Bibliography: EncDictBibl 2493–96. H. DE LAVALETTE, LexThK[2] 3:546–548. P. PARENTE, EncCatt 12:530–531. J. LEBRETON, "La Révélation de la Sainte Trinité," VieSpirit 74 (1946) 225–240. E. B. ALLO, *Saint Paul: Première epître aux Corinthiens* (ÉtBibl, 2d ed. Paris 1956) 323. J. SCHMID, *Das Evangelium nach Matthäus* (Regensburg 1956). For fuller bibliography see LumetVie 29 (1956) 579–584.

[C. DRAINA]

TRINITY, HOLY, DEVOTION TO. There are few signs of devotion to the Trinity in the early Church, aside from the ritual use of the Trinitarian formula in the administration of the Sacraments. Doxologies of praise are found in the writings of St. Justin (d. 166) and Clement of Alexandria (d. 199). St. Basil (d. 397) cites a prayer used by Christians when lighting the evening lamps, "We praise the Father, the Son, and the Holy Spirit" (*De Spir. Sancto* 290.72). A number of early carvings, representing the Trinity or praising it, are dated as of the 4th century (cf. DACL 15: 2787).

Devotion to the Trinity as it is known today seems to have begun in monasteries at Aniane and Tours, in the 8th century. St. Benedict of Aniane, who spread the devotion through his monastic reform, dedicated his abbey church to the Trinity in 872. And there are references to Masses in honor of the Trinity, at Tours and at Fulda in 796 and 804. A feast of the Trinity was introduced at Cluny in 1091, and at Canterbury by Thomas Becket in 1162. Rome resisted this observance, and it was not until 1331 that the Feast of the Trinity was approved by John XXII for the whole Church.

The revitalization by the early scholastics of the doctrine on the divine indwelling led to many works on the subject and to a devotion to the divine Persons that continues to modern times. SS. Thomas Aquinas and Bonaventure brought to light and refined the ancient teachings of the Fathers, especially of St. Augustine, on

The New Catholic Encyclopedia, Catholic University of America 1967 ed., Vol. XIV, p. 306.

"Trinity"—That's not in the Bible!

Jehovah's Witnesses are taught that the doctrine of the Trinity is unscriptural. One of the reasons frequently given is that the *word* "trinity" is not found in the Bible. We find Chris and Jay discussing the origin of the Trinity and the relevance of the word "trinity" not being found in the Bible as we read on.

Chris: Jay, why don't you believe in the Trinity?

Jay: Because the doctrine of the Holy Trinity is of pagan origin and inspired by the devil himself. One of the past presidents of the Watchtower said:

> Never was there a more deceptive doctrine advanced than that of the trinity. It could have originated only in one mind, and that the mind of Satan the Devil. (See p. 150.)

Chris: I have no doubt that many Jehovah's Witnesses share that opinion, but why do you say the Trinity is of pagan origin?

Jay: Among Jehovah's Witnesses, a book by Alexander Hislop, *The Two Babylons*, is popularly referred to and quoted by the Watchtower.[5] Our older edition of *Make Sure of All Things* refers the reader to read McClintock and Strong's *Cyclopaedia*, under the entry "Trinity"; and *The Two Babylons*, pp. 16, 17, to show the origin of the Trinity doctrine in "ancient Babylonish paganism." (See p. 151.)

Chris: You mean these books show that the Christian doctrine of the Trinity had its origins in paganism?

Jay: That's right!

Chris: Have you checked these references for yourself?

Jay: Well, not specifically.

Chris: I know we already talked about the Watchtower misrepresenting what people say and believe [see previous dialogue], but if we check the references in these books, we again find the Watchtower is not being honest.

Jay: Okay, let's see.

Chris: The book *Apostles of Denial* points out the Watchtower's error on both accounts. Referring to the *Make Sure* book, Edmund Gruss, the author, says:

> This writer would strongly urge the reader to read the "Trinity" article [re: McClintock and Strong's] which completely refutes the position set forth in both *Let God Be True*

---

[5]A sampling can be found in *Babylon the Great Has Fallen*, 1963, pp. 20, 33, 35, 145.

> and *Make Sure of All Things*. Possibly the compilers of *Make Sure of All Things* actually wished to refer the reader to the article "Trinity, Heathen Notions of," which follows the "Trinity" article.[6]

Jay: You mean the Watchtower referred readers to the wrong article?

Jay: Right. But even when we go to the article the Society probably wanted to refer to, "Trinity, Heathen Notions of," we find they have clearly misrepresented the work they refer to as Gruss points out. The article begins:

> In examining the various heathen philosophies and mythologies, we find clear evidence of a belief in a certain sort of trinity, and yet something very different from the Trinity of the Bible.[7]

Jay: This *Cyclopaedia* makes a difference between the mythological trinities and the Christian Trinity?

Chris: That's right.

Jay: In other words, it doesn't show that the Trinity shares the pagan origins of the false trinities?

Chris: No, it doesn't. As a matter of fact, the same thing is true of the other book the Watchtower referred to, *The Two Babylons*.

Jay: Now *that* book I've seen; some of the brothers have copies.

Chris: Well, if you read through it, you must have overlooked a few essential points Mr. Hislop's book is demonstrating.

Jay: I guess you're going to say it doesn't trace the Trinity to pagan origins either—but *that* I'll have to see.

Chris: I'll not only say that, but I'll be happy to show you. First, Hislop points out that the images of the "Triune God, with three heads on one body" found in some of the papacy's churches, "utterly debase the conceptions of those, among whom such images prevail, in regard to that sublime mystery of our faith." (See p. 152.)

Jay: "Our faith?" You mean Hislop was a trinitarian?

Chris: That's correct. Hislop's book doesn't show that the Trinity is of pagan origin. Rather, it shows how the Christian doctrine of the Trinity has been corrupted, especially by the papacy.

---

[6]Edmund Gruss, *Apostles of Denial* (Presbyterian and Reformed Publ. Co., 1970), p. 107.

[7]John McClintock and James Strong, "Trinity, Heathen Notions of," *Cyclopaedia of Biblical, Theological, Ecclesiastical Literature* (New York: Harper & Brothers, 1881), X., p. 556.

Jay: Wow!

Chris: If you will let me go on, I'll show you more. The footnote on page 17 illustrates the belief that the plurality of the Godhead even has a basis in Genesis.

> Some have said that the *plural* form of the name of God, in the Hebrew of Genesis, affords no argument for the doctrine of plurality of persons in the Godhead, because the same word in the plural is applied to heathen divinities. But if the supreme divinity in almost all ancient heathen nations was triune, the futility of this objection must be manifest. (See p. 152.)

On the next page Hislop continues, and here the misrepresentation by the Watchtower becomes obvious:

> All these have existed from ancient times. While overlaid with idolatry, the recognition of a Trinity was universal in all the ancient nations of the world, proving how deep-rooted in the human race was the primeval doctrine on this subject, which comes out so distinctly in Genesis. (See pp. 153, 154.)

Jay: That really lets the wind out of that sail. Hislop doesn't see the Trinity of Christians as sharing the same origin as the heathen trinities. But still you have to admit the word "trinity" isn't found in the Bible.

Chris: You're right, Jay, and I'd be the first to admit that "trinity" is not found in the Bible. But neither are so many of the words the Watchtower is so fond of.

Jay: Like what?

Chris: Take "theocracy" for instance. While the word is not found in the Bible, the Roman Empire had theocracy of a sort wherein the emperor was considered a god himself, a deified king. This is true again in Egypt, where the pharaoh was a god ruling the nation. This is very similar to the Watchtower structure.

Jay: How's that?

Chris: The Society claims to be a theocracy, governed from the "Divine Ruler" down, across the whole of God's people [all the Jehovah's Witnesses], right? (See p. 155.)

Jay: Oh, yes, the Watchtower Society is a theocratic organization.

Chris: Well, the fact that a "theocracy" is found in pagan structures, and that the word is not found in the Bible, doesn't rule out the fact that the concept might be biblical, does it?

Jay: I guess not . . . even the children of Israel in the Old Testament were ruled by a theocracy.

Chris: That's right. The same holds true for the concept of the Trinity. The word is not found in the Bible, and a corrupted understanding of the nature of God is found in pagan religions, but that doesn't mean the concept is unbiblical. That would be like saying there is no God because gods are worshiped in heathen religions.

Jay: I understand what you're saying now.

Chris: What is found in the Bible are formulas like that in Matthew 28:19 where the three persons are so closely linked.

> Go therefore and make disciples of all the nations, baptizing them in the name of the Father and the Son and the Holy Spirit.

As well as passages that say there is no God but one:

> Now to the King eternal, immortal, invisible, the only God, be honor and glory forever and ever. Amen. (1 Tim. 1:17)

Far from being pagan in origin, the concept of the Trinity is firmly founded within the Scriptures themselves. While the word itself is not found in the Bible, it describes the God of the Bible as He has chosen to reveal himself to us. We must choose either to accept what He has revealed, or become like those the apostle describes in Romans 1:21:

> For even though they knew God, they did not honor Him as God, or give thanks; but they became futile in their speculations, and their foolish heart was darkened.

A council of the clergy was held at Nice, in 325 A. D., which council confirmed the doctrine of the trinity; and later a similar council at Constantinople, by confirming the divinity of the Holy Ghost and the unity of God, declared the doctrine of the trinity in unity to be the doctrine of the church. The clergy have ever held to this senseless, God-dishonoring doctrine. To aid his agents to keep this doctrine before their mind the Devil must have some visible object symbolizing it. The mystic triangle was adopted as a symbol, which may be found in the tombs of those who were buried contemporaneously therewith. Also there was an attempt to prove it by three heads or faces on one neck, the eyes becoming a part of each individual face. Also a combination of the triangle and circle and sometimes the trefoil was used for the same purpose. If you ask a clergyman what is meant by the trinity he says: "That is a mystery." He does not know, and no one else knows, because it is false.

Never was there a more deceptive doctrine advanced than that of the trinity. It could have originated only in one mind, and that the mind of Satan the Devil. The purpose was and is to produce confusion in the mind of man and to destroy the true philosophy of the great ransom sacrifice. If Jesus when on earth was God he was more than a perfect man and therefore could not become an exact corresponding price for the redemption of men. Therefore it logically follows that the shed blood of Jesus would form no basis for the reconciliation of man to God. If Jesus was one part of the trinity, then it would be impossible for the trinity or any part of it to have furnished the

Reconciliation, 1928, p. 101.

Trinity

DEFINITION

"The Trinity is the term employed to signify the central doctrine of the Christian religion—the truth that in the unity of the Godhead there are Three Persons, the Father, the Son, and the Holy Spirit, these Three Persons being truly distinct one from another."—*Catholic Encyclopedia,* Vol. XV, p. 47.

"In this one God there are three distinct Persons, the Father, the Son, and the Holy Ghost, who are perfectly equal to each other. We believe that Jesus Christ . . . He is God of the substance of the Father."—*The Faith of Our Fathers,* by Cardinal Gibbons, p. 1.

A false, unbiblical doctrine.

ORIGIN

Ancient Babylonish paganism c.2200 B. C. Brought into the deflected "Christian church" about the second century, being especially established in the Nicene Creed, A. D. 325. (See McClintock and Strong's *Cyclopædia,* under "Trinity"; *The Two Babylons,* pp. 16, 17.)

Texts Misapplied

[1]Heb. 1:8; [2]John 14:9, 10; Rom. 9:5; Titus 2:13; 1 John 5:7; [3]John 1:1; Rev. 3:14; [4]John 20:28; [5]John 8:58; Rev. 1:8, 11; 21:6; 22:13; [6]Col. 2:9; [7]John 10:30; [8]Acts 20:28; [9]John 10:18; 1 Tim. 3:16; [10]John 2:19; [11]Matt. 1:23; [12]John 15:26; 16:13-15, *AV, Dy*.

Jehovah One God, Greatest Person[1]

Deut. 6:4 "Jehovah our God is one Jehovah."

John 14:28 "The Father is greater than I am."

John 10:29 ***(footnote)*** "My Father . . . is greater than all others."

Ps. 83:18 "Jehovah . . . [is] the Most High over all the earth."

1 Cor. 15:28 "That God may be all things to everyone."

Phil. 2:11 "Every tongue should openly confess that Jesus Christ is Lord to the glory of God the Father."

Isa. 42:8 "I am Jehovah, that is my name; and my glory will I not give to another."

Heb. 1:8 "With reference to the Son: 'God is your throne forever.' "

Jehovah and Jesus Different Persons[2]

John 8:17, 18 " 'The witness of two men is true.' I am one that bears witness about myself and the Father who sent me bears witness about me."

1 John 5:7, *AV* "For there are three that bear record in heaven, the Father, the Word, and the Holy Ghost: and these three are one."—This text spurious.

See Appendix on 1 John 5:7, *NW*.

Rom. 9:5 "God who is over all be blest forever. Amen."

See Appendix, Romans 9:5, *NW*.

Titus 2:13 "The . . . glorious manifestation of the great God and of our Savior Christ Jesus."

See Appendix, Titus 2:13, ***NW***.

The Son Created by God[3]

John 1:1 "Originally the Word was, and the Word was with God, and the Word was a god."

See Appendix, John 1:1, ***NW***.

Make Sure of All Things, 1953, p. 386.

such a comparison is most degrading to the King Eternal, and is fitted utterly to pervert the minds of those who contemplate it, as if there was or could be any similitude between such a figure and Him who hath said, "To whom will ye liken God, and what likeness will ye compare unto Him?"

The Papacy has in some of its churches, as, for instance, in the monastery of the so-called Trinitarians of Madrid, an image of the Triune God, with three heads on one body.* The Babylonians had something of the same. Mr. Layard, in his last work, has given a specimen of such a triune divinity, worshipped in ancient Assyria † (Fig. 3). The accompanying cut (Fig. 4) of such another divinity, worshipped among the Pagans of Siberia, is taken from a medal in the Imperial Cabinet of St. Petersburg, and given in Parson's "Japhet." ‡ The three heads are differently arranged in Layard's specimen, but both alike are evidently intended to symbolise the same great truth, although all such representations of the Trinity

Fig. 3. Fig. 4.

necessarily and utterly debase the conceptions of those, among whom such images prevail, in regard to that sublime mystery of our faith. In India, the supreme divinity, in like manner, in one of the most

* PARKHURST's *Hebrew Lexicon, sub voce,* "Cherubim." From the following extract from the *Dublin Catholic Layman,* a very able Protestant paper, describing a Popish picture of the Trinity, recently published in that city, it will be seen that something akin to this mode of representing the Godhead is appearing nearer home:—"At the top of the picture is a representation of the Holy Trinity. We beg to speak of it with due reverence. God the Father and God the Son are represented as a MAN with *two heads,* one body, and two arms. One of the heads is like the ordinary pictures of our Saviour. The other is the head of an old man, surmounted by a triangle. Out of the middle of this figure is proceeding the Holy Ghost in the form of a dove. We think it must be painful to any Christian mind, and repugnant to Christian feeling, to look at this figure."—*Catholic Layman,* 17th July, 1856.

† *Babylon and Nineveh,* p. 160. Some have said that the *plural* form of the name of God, in the Hebrew of Genesis, affords no argument for the doctrine of plurality of persons in the Godhead, because the same word in the plural is applied to heathen divinities. But if the supreme divinity in almost all ancient heathen nations was triune, the futility of this objection must be manifest.

‡ *Japhet,* p. 184.

A. Hislop, *The Two Babylons,* Loizeaux Brothers, Neptune, New York, 1959 ed., p. 17.

ancient cave-temples, is represented with three heads on one body, under the name of "Eko Deva Trimurtti," "One God, three forms." * In Japan, the Buddhists worship their great divinity, Buddha, with three heads, in the very same form, under the name of "San Pao Fuh." † All these have existed from ancient times. While overlaid with idolatry, the recognition of a Trinity was universal in all the ancient nations of the world, proving how deep-rooted in the human race was the primeval doctrine on this subject, which comes out so distinctly in Genesis.‡ When we look at the symbols in the triune figure of Layard, already referred to, and minutely examine them, they are very instructive. Layard regards the circle in that figure as signifying "Time without bounds." But the hieroglyphic meaning of the circle is evidently different. A circle in Chaldea was zero; § and zero also signified "the seed." Therefore, according to the genius of the mystic system of Chaldea, which was to a large extent founded on double meanings, that which, to the eyes of men in general, was only zero, "a circle," was understood by the initiated to signify zero, "the seed." Now, viewed in this light, the triune emblem of the supreme Assyrian divinity shows clearly what had been the original patriarchal faith. First, there is the head of the old man; next, there is the zero, or circle, for "the seed;" and lastly, the wings and tail of the bird or dove; ‖ showing, though blasphemously, the unity of Father, Seed, or Son, and

* Col. KENNEDY's *Hindoo Mythology*, p. 211. Col. Kennedy objects to the application of the name "Eko Deva" to the triform image in the cave-temple at Elephanta, on the ground that that name belongs only to the supreme Brahm. But in so doing he is entirely inconsistent, for he admits that Brahmà, the first person in that triform image, is *identified* with the supreme Brahm; and further, that a curse is pronounced upon all who distinguish between Brahmà, Vishnu, and Seva, the three divinities represented by that image.

† GILLESPIE's *Sinim*, p. 60.

‡ The threefold invocation of the sacred name in the blessing of Jacob bestowed on the sons of Joseph is very striking: "And he blessed Joseph, and said, God, before whom my fathers Abraham and Isaac did walk, the God which fed me all my life long unto this day, the Angel which redeemed me from all evil, bless the lads" (Gen. xlviii. 15, 16). If the angel here referred to had not been God, Jacob could never have invoked him as on an equality with God. In Hosea xii. 3-5, "The Angel who redeemed" Jacob is expressly called God: "He (Jacob) had power with God: yea, he had power over the Angel, and prevailed; he wept and made supplication unto him: he found him in Bethel, and there he spake with us; even the Lord God of Hosts; The Lord is his memorial."

§ In our own language we have evidence that Zero had signified a circle among the Chaldeans; for what is Zero, the name of the cypher, but just a circle? And whence can we have derived this term but from the Arabians, as they, without doubt, had themselves derived it from the Chaldees, the grand original cultivators at once of arithmetic, geometry, and idolatry? Zero, in this sense, had evidently come from the Chaldee, *zer*, "to encompass," from which, also, no doubt, was derived the Babylonian name for a great cycle of time, called a "*saros*."—(BUNSEN, vol. i. pp. 711, 712.) As he, who by the Chaldeans was regarded as the great "Seed," was looked upon as the *sun* incarnate (see chap. iii. sect. i.), and as the emblem of the sun was a *circle* (BUNSEN, vol. i. p. 335, and p. 537, No. 4), the hieroglyphical relation between zero, "the circle," and zero, "the seed," was easily established.

‖ From the statement in Gen. i. 2, that "the Spirit of God *fluttered* on the face of the deep" (for that is the expression in the original), it is evident that the *dove* had very early been a Divine emblem for the Holy Spirit.

A. Hislop, *The Two Babylons,* Loizeaux Brothers, Neptune, New York, 1959 ed., p. 18.

of Dublin. Will any one after this say that the Roman Catholic Church must still be called Christian, because it holds the doctrine of the Trinity? So did the Pagan Babylonians, so did the Egyptians, so do the Hindoos at this hour, in the very same sense in which Rome does. They all admitted A trinity, but did they worship THE Triune Jehovah, the King Eternal, Immortal, and Invisible? And will any one say with such evidence before him, that Rome does so? Away then, with the deadly delusion that Rome is Christian! There might once have been some palliation for entertaining such a supposition; but every day the "Grand Mystery" is revealing itself more and more in its true character. There is not, and there cannot be, any safety for the souls of men in "Babylon." "Come out of her, my people," is the loud and express command of God. Those who disobey that command, do it at their peril.

A. Hislop, *The Two Babylons*, Loizeaux Brothers, Neptune, New York, 1959 ed., p. 90.

ernment at Jerusalem or by the Senate of the Roman Empire, with officers to be appointed according to Caesar's specifications. No, but it was a theocratic organization with officers and assistants that were theocratically appointed by the governing body and Jesus Christ, the "head of the congregation." The "gifts in men" that had been given to it were, not from the Roman Emperor Caesar, but from the great Theocrat, Jehovah God, through Jesus Christ. For what purpose? "With a view to the readjustment of the holy ones, for ministerial work." (Eph. 4:11, 12) The whole congregation was a service body, all members rendering sacred service to the great Theocrat Jehovah. They were one composite "servant" of their Divine Ruler, whose witnesses they were. They were bearing witness that He had sent the promised Messiah in the person of Jesus Christ his Son. To them as spiritual Israelites the words applied:

5 " 'You are my witnesses,' is the utterance of Jehovah, 'even my servant whom I have chosen.' "—Isa. 43:10.

6 Thus the many witnesses form one "servant," whom Jehovah calls "my servant whom I have chosen." This composite "servant" is the one whom Jesus Christ had in mind when he spoke of his going away and his returning, saying: "Who really is the faithful steward, the discreet one, whom his master will appoint

6. Who, then, is that "steward" and "slave" mentioned by Jesus in Luke 12:42-44?

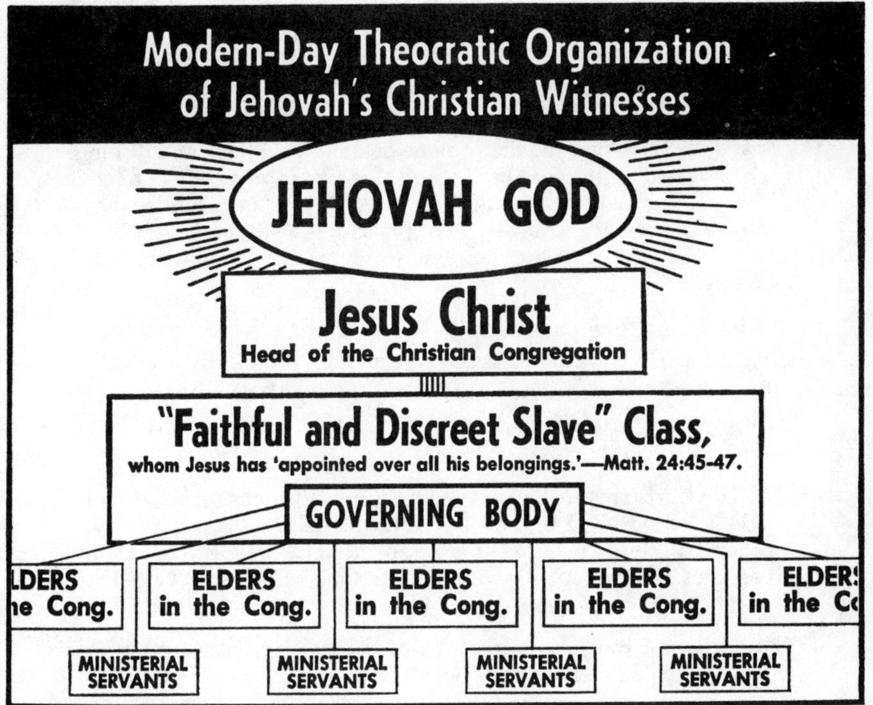

The Watchtower, Dec. 15, 1971, p. 749.

Chapter Eleven

THE DEITY OF CHRIST—ANALYSIS

In the first centuries many Christians were put to death because they could not confess "Caesar is Lord." Why? They believed and confessed "Jesus is Lord" and preferred death to confessing another as their Lord. The term "Lord" in such contexts certainly refers to something more than a polite term of respect such as "sir." Indeed, the Roman Emperor came to be considered a living deity, a *god*, and as such he was to be called "Lord." For the Christian there was one Lord, Jesus.

The confession that Jesus is Lord also means something more than ruler. In the Greek Old Testament, Lord (*Kyrios*) was the usual name for Jehovah (translated *Adonai*). As Michael Green says:

> There could be no mistake about the matter. Jesus himself, followed by the early Christians, made great play with Psalm 110:1 in which David addresses "my Lord." This was interpreted as referring to Jesus, who was thus David's Lord. Is it any wonder that the Jews thought Christians were preaching a second God? How could they, in their pure monotheism, have any truck with such blasphemy?[1]

While many Jews saw blasphemy, as do the Jehovah's Witnesses today, the early Christians saw a plurality in the Godhead that was confirmed by the trinitarian formulas linking the Father, Son, and Holy Spirit so closely together (Matt. 28:19). To the question "Was Christ really God?", history reveals:

> The Christians took over the Jews' uncompromising belief that "The Lord our God is one God." But they also soon came to the belief that "Jesus is Lord." They applied to Christ Old Testament passages referring to *Yahweh*, the Lord; they worshipped Christ as God.[2]

But what of the Jehovah's Witness? Does he worship Christ as

---

[1]Michael Green, *Evangelism in the Early Church* (Grand Rapids: Eerdmans, 1970), p. 31.

[2]*The History of Christianity*, Gen. ed., Tim Dowley (Grand Rapids: Eerdmans, 1977), p. 110.

God? No. Jehovah's Witnesses are taught that Jesus is Michael the Archangel:

> He [Jesus] resumed his prehuman name, Michael, so that again there was a "Michael the archangel" in heaven. (See p. 158.)

Rather than being taught that Jesus is God, they are made to believe that Jesus is *a god*, even as Satan is a god:

> 'But isn't Jesus called a god in the Bible?' someone may ask. This is true. Yet Satan is also called a god. (See p. 159.)

While the Watchtower professes to be monotheistic, they practice polytheism. Although they claim purity in denying the deity of Christ, they have taught not only that Jesus and Satan are gods, but so are each of 144,000 members of the Church!

> When we claim on the scriptural warrant, that we are begotten of a divine nature and that Jehovah is thus our father, it is claiming that we are divine beings—hence all such are Gods. Thus we have a family of God, Jehovah being our father, and all his sons being brethren and joint-heirs: Jesus being the chief, or first-born. (See p. 160.)

Most Holy for sin were disposed of, so God accepted the sacrifice of Jesus' human nature and disposed of Jesus' human body. How? We do not know. (Hebrews 13:10-13; Leviticus, chapter sixteen) Although Almighty God did not resurrect his Son Jesus Christ in a human body, the resurrected Son of God did retain the value or merit of his human sacrifice, which was like the sacrificial blood that the Jewish high priest carried into the Most Holy of the temple so as to make atonement for sin.

22 As a spirit Son of God, Jesus Christ was able to ascend back to heaven on the fortieth day from his resurrection from the dead. A number of his faithful disciples were witnesses to that ascension. (Acts 1:1-11) Just as the Jewish high priest in the Most Holy sprinkled the Atonement blood toward the golden Ark of the Covenant, so Jesus entered into God's heavenly presence and presented the value or merit of his perfect human sacrifice. (Hebrews 9:11-14, 24-26) Then the Most High God seated him at His own right hand as the "priest to time indefinite according to the manner of Melchizedek."—Psalm 110:1-4; Acts 2:31-36; Hebrews 5:10; 10:11-13.

23 In this way the Son of God was rewarded with a heavenly position higher than the one he held before becoming a perfect man and being bruised "in the heel" by the Great Serpent. He resumed his prehuman name, Michael, so that again there was a "Michael the archangel" in heaven. (Jude 9; Revelation 12:7) The glorified "seed" of God's "woman" was now in a far stronger position to bruise the Serpent's head in God's due time.—Genesis 3:15.

24 How thankful and glad all humanity, natural Jews and Gentiles alike, should be that God's promised Messiah will be a deathless heavenly Messiah, and not a mere earthly human "anointed one" like King David! Under prophetic inspiration, David humbly acknowledged this highly exalted one as his Lord, and this should be our attitude also. We are exhorted to have

---

22, 23. (a) As a spirit person by resurrection, what was Jesus now able to do as prefigured by the high priest on Atonement Day? (b) How was Jesus now in a stronger position for bruising the Serpent "in the head"?

24, 25. (a) Jews and Gentiles can alike be glad that God's Son is not what kind of a Messiah? (b) In Philippians 2:5-11, what mental attitude are we exhorted to have?

God's Eternal Purpose Now Triumphing, 1974, p. 155.

death and resurrection and ascension to heaven, Jesus was still not equal to his Father.—1 Corinthians 11:3; 15:28.

16 'But isn't Jesus called a god in the Bible?' someone may ask. This is true. Yet Satan is also called a god. (2 Corinthians 4:4) At John 1:1, which refers to Jesus as "the Word," some Bible translations say: "In the beginning was the Word, and the Word was with God, and the Word was God." But notice, verse 2 says that the Word was "in the beginning *with* God." And while men have seen Jesus, verse 18 says that "no man hath seen God at any time." (*Authorized* or *King James Version*) So we find that some translations of verse 1 give the correct idea of the original language when they read: "The Word was with God, and the Word was divine," or was "a god," that is, the Word was a powerful godlike one. (*An American Translation*) Clearly, Jesus is not Almighty God. In fact, Jesus spoke of his Father as "my God" and as "the only true God."—John 20:17; 17:3.

17 As for the "Holy Spirit," the so-called third Person of the Trinity, we have already seen that this is not a person but God's active force. John the Baptizer said that Jesus would baptize with holy spirit, even as John had been baptizing with water. Hence, in the same way that water is not a person, holy spirit is not a person. (Matthew 3:11) What John foretold was fulfilled when, following the death and resurrection of Jesus, holy spirit was poured out on his followers gathered in Jerusalem. The Bible says: "They all became filled with holy spirit." (Acts 2:4) Were they "filled" with a person? No, but they were filled with God's active force. Thus the facts make clear that the Trinity is not a Bible teaching. Actually, long before Jesus walked the earth

16. Even though Jesus is referred to as "God," what shows that he is not Almighty God?

17. How does the pouring out of holy spirit on Jesus' followers prove that it is not a person?

You Can Live Forever in Paradise on Earth, 1982, p. 40.

NOTTINGHAM, ENGLAND,
November 8th, 1881.

MY DEAR SIR—Permit me though a stranger to assure you, that I can never feel sufficiently thankful that out of the thousands of copies of your book, *"Food for Thinking Christians"* distributed in this town—a copy fell into my hands: apparently it was the merest accident; but really I regard it as a direct providence. It has thrown light upon subjects which have perplexed me for years; and has made me feel more than ever, what a glorious book the Bible is, how worthy of our profoundest study. At the same time, I came from the study of your book with the conviction that a very large proportion of the Theology of our Churches and Schools, is the merest scraps of human notions, and that our huge *systems of Theology* upon the study of which, some of us have spent so many laborious years—only to be the worse confused and perplexed—are infinitely more the work of mistaken men, than the inspiration of the allwise God.

However I may differ from the book in a few minor details, I found the main argument to be resistless, commending itself to both my head and my heart. Again let me thank you on my own behalf, for the good I have received.

I find at the close of it, you make an offer to send copies to any who have reason to believe they can make a good use of them. In my church and congregation, there is a number of intelligent persons who are interested in the second coming, and who would be only too glad to read your book, I could distribute 60 or 70 copies with advantage, you say, "ask and ye shall receive"—I have faith in your generosity. Believe me to remain yours, Most faithfully ———.

LOUISVILLE, KENTUCKY,
November 22, 1881.

GENTLEMEN—Having read with the most profound interest your publication entitled; "Food for Thinking Christians," and being fairly dazzled by the wonderful light it reveals on the great "subject," I find myself thirsting for more knowledge from this seemingly inspired pen.

Therefore in accordance with the invitation extended by you on the cover of this little work I ask that you send me a few copies of "The Tabernacle and its Teachings," if in print.

With reference to the first named book, permit me to say, that I have never yet read or heard anything equal to that little volume in its influence upon my heart and life; and to my mind, it answers most grandly and conclusively the great question, "Is life worth living." Such views as it sets forth, are bound to find response in the minds and hearts of all unbiased thinking christians, for they bear the stamp of something greater than mere human conception. I only wish we could hear it from the pulpits; but I think this must shortly follow. It is good seed and in its *"due time"* will come forth.

Believe me, I am
Very Truly Yours ———

"A LITTLE WHILE"

A little while, our fightings shall be over;
A little while, our tears be wiped away;
A little while, the presence of Jehovah
Shall turn our darkness into Heaven's bright day.

A little while, the fears that oft surround us
Shall to the memories of the past belong;
A little while, the love that sought and found us
Shall change our weeping into Heaven's glad song

A little while! His presence goes before us,
A fire by night, a shadowy cloud by day;
His banner, love-inscribed, is floating o'er us;
His arm almighty is our strength and stay.

A little while! 'Tis ever drawing nearer—
The brighter dawning of that glorious day,
Blest Saviour, make our spirits' vision clearer,
And guide, oh, guide us in the shining way.

A little while! Oh, blessed expectation!
For strength to run with patience, Lord we cry;
Our hearts up-leap in fond anticipation.
Our union with the Bridegroom draweth nigh.

—*Selected.*

"YE ARE GODS"

"I have said, Ye are Gods; and all of you are children of the Most High. But ye shall die like men, and fall like one of the princes" [literally heads]. Psa. 82:6.

Our high calling is so great, so much above the comprehension of *men*, that they feel that we are guilty of blasphemy when we speak of being *"new* creatures"—not any longer human, but "partakers of the *divine nature."* When we claim on the scriptural warrant, that we are begotten of a divine nature and that Jehovah is thus our father, it is claiming that we are divine beings—hence all such are Gods. Thus we have a family of God, Jehovah being our father, and all his sons being brethren and joint-heirs: Jesus being the chief, or first-born.

Nor should we wonder that so few discern this grand relationship, into the full membership of which, we so soon hope to come. The apostle tells us that "the *natural* man receiveth not the things of the Spirit of God .... *neither can he know them* because they are spiritually discerned." (1 Cor. 2:14). Just so it was, when our great Head and Lord was among men: He, having consecrated the human at 30 years of age was baptized of the spirit, and became a part-taker of the divine nature. When Jesus said he was *a son of God* the Jews were about to stone him, reasoning thus, that if a son of God, he was making himself to be also a God, or of the God family. [Just what we claim. "Beloved, now are we the sons of God"—"The God and Father of our Lord Jesus hath begotten us."] (1 John 3:2 and 1 Pet. 1:3).

Jesus does not deny that when he said he was a son, it implied that he was of the divine nature, but he quotes to them the above passage from the Psalms as being good authority and it seems as though it satisfied them, for they did not stone him. Jesus said, "Is it not written in your law, I said, Ye are Gods"? Then he proceeds to show that the "Gods" there mentioned, are the ones who receive obediently his words and example, and concludes his argument by asking whether if God calls such ones as receive his (Jesus,) teachings, Gods, whether they think that he the teacher, whom the Father had specially set apart as the head of *those Gods* could be properly said to blaspheme, when he claimed the *same* relationship as a son of God. (John 10:35).

These sons of God, like him from whom they heard the word of truth by which they are begotten, are yet in disguise; the world knoweth us not for the same reason that it knew him not. Our Father puts no outward badge or mark of our high relationship, but leaves each to walk by faith and not by sight all through the earthly pilgrimage—*down into* death. His favor and love and the Glory and Honor which belong to our station, we can now see by the eye of faith, but soon it will be realized in fact. Now we appear like *men*, and all die naturally like *men*, but in the resurrection we will rise in our true character as Gods.

"It doth not yet appear
How great we must be made;
But when we see him as he is,
We shall be like our Head."

How forcibly this is expressed by the prophet and how sure it is too, Jesus says—It cannot be broken: "I have said ye are Gods, all of you sons of the Most High. But *ye shall die like men*, and fall like one of the princes." [lit. *heads*—Adam and Jesus are the two heads.]

Then the whole family—head and body are addressed as *one*, as they will be under Christ their head, saying—"Arise O God, judge [rule, bless] the earth: for thou shalt inherit all nations." The Mighty God, and everlasting Father of the nations, is Christ whose members in particular we are. He it is that shall inherit all things and He it is that promised his body that they too should have power over the nations, and of whom Paul says "Know ye not that the saints shall judge the world?"

How forcible this scripture in connection with the thought that *all* must die like men—like the (last) one of the heads. [See article "Who Can Hear It."—*November Number, 1881, Z. W. T.*]

The Watchtower, Dec. 1881, reprints, p. 301.

Is Jesus Christ Worthy of Worship?

The Watchtower Society teaches that only Jehovah God deserves worship. They claim that Jesus is not Jehovah, but only an angel. They say it would be idolatry to worship angels (see p. 162). But, is this what they have *always* taught Jehovah's Witnesses? At one time they claimed, "Was he *really* worshiped, or is the translation faulty? Yes, we believe our Lord Jesus while on earth was really worshiped, and properly so" (see p. 163). Regarding the worship of Jehovah, they also said, " . . . whosoever would worship Him must also worship and bow down to Jehovah's Chief One . . . namely, Christ Jesus. . ." (see p. 164). So here the Watchtower directed Jehovah's Witnesses to also worship Jesus Christ.

One way that worship is performed is through prayer. Can Jesus be prayed to? It is taught by the Society that the Christian martyr Stephen properly prayed to Jesus Christ (see p. 165.). Let's look at this biblical account in Acts 7:59 in the Watchtower's own Bible:

> And they went on casting stones at Stephen as he made appeal and said: "Lord Jesus, receive my spirit."

Here the Watchtower Bible, in a footnote, admits Stephen prayed to Jesus. Stephen is certainly a good example for the rest of us.[3]

Yet, today, the Watchtower has changed its teaching. Now they claim that Jesus doesn't deserve worship but only "obeisance." They say "obeisance" is merely a form of respect. Let us now read from their own Bible an example of "obeisance." In Acts 10:25 we find Cornelius bowing down to do obeisance to the Apostle Peter. Does Peter accept this "bowing down" merely as respect or as worship? In verse 26 he says: "Stand up; I myself also am a man" (KJV). He refused this act of obeisance, for he was only a man. Elsewhere in Scripture, angels refuse to be bowed down to in worship, as in Revelation 19 and 22. Unlike Peter and the angels, Jesus Christ *never* refused worship but always freely accepted it. One example is Matthew 28:9, "They came and held him by the feet, and worshipped him" (KJV).

We have seen how the Watchtower Society had formerly acknowledged that Christ is to be worshiped the *same* as the Father. Yet, now they have changed this doctrine. Based on what the Bible teaches, why do you think they have done this?

---

[3]*New World Translation of the Christian Greek Scriptures,* Watchtower Bible and Tract Society, 1951 ed., p. 377.

"Relative" Worship, Using Physical 'Aids to Devotion,' Contrary to Christian Principle of Worship

John 4:24 "God is a Spirit, and those worshiping him must worship with spirit and truth."

2 Cor. 5:7 "We are walking by faith, not by sight."

2 Cor. 4:18 "We keep our eyes, not on the things seen, but on the things unseen."

Jehovah refuses to share his glory with graven images

Isa. 42:8 "I am Jehovah. That is my name; and to no one else shall I give my own glory, neither my praise to graven images." (See also Isa. 48:11.)

Prayer to be offered to Jehovah in Jesus' name; no images needed

John 14:13 "Whatever it is that you ask in my name, I will do this, in order that the Father may be glorified in connection with the Son."

John 15:16 "I chose you, and I appointed you to go on and keep bearing fruit and that your fruit should remain; in order that no matter what you ask the Father in my name he might give it to you."

Only one mediator; images of "saints" of no value

1 Tim. 2:5 "There is one God, and one mediator between God and men, a man Christ Jesus."

John 14:6, 14 "Jesus said to him: 'I am the way and the truth and the life. No one comes to the Father except through me. If you ask anything in my name, I will do it.'"

Bowing in worship before men or even angels as representatives of God forbidden

Acts 10:25, 26 "As Peter entered, Cornelius met him, fell down at his feet and did obeisance to him. But Peter lifted him up, saying: 'Rise; I myself am also a man.'"

Rev. 22:8, 9 "Well, I John was the one hearing and seeing these things. And when I had heard and seen, I fell down to worship before the feet of the angel that had been showing me these things. But he tells me: 'Be careful! Do not do that! All I am is a fellow slave of you and of your brothers who are prophets and of those who are observing the words of this scroll. Worship God.'" (See also Rev. 19:10.)

Idolatrous Practices Cannot Properly Be Mixed with True Worship

2 Cor. 6:16, 17 "What agreement does God's temple have with idols? For we are a temple of a living God; just as God said: 'I shall reside among them and walk among them, and I shall be their God, and they will be my people.' '"Therefore get out from among them, and separate yourselves," says Jehovah, "and quit touching the unclean thing"'; '"and I will take you in."'"

Ex. 32:4-10 "He took the gold from their hands, and he formed it with a graving tool and proceeded to make it into a molten statue of a calf. And they began to say: 'This is your God, O Israel, who led you up out of the land of Egypt.' When Aaron got to see this, he went to building an altar before it. Finally Aaron called out and said: 'There is a festival to Jehovah tomorrow.' . . . Jehovah now said to Moses: 'Go, descend, because your people whom you led up out of the land of Egypt have acted ruinously. They have turned aside in a hurry from the way I have commanded them to go. They have made a molten statue of a calf for themselves and keep bowing down to it and sacrificing to it and saying, "This is your God, O Israel, who led you up out of the land of Egypt."' And Jehovah went on to say to Moses:

Make Sure of All Things—Hold Fast to What Is Fine, 1965, p. 249.

where the propensities or organs of the mind have come to a strict party division; the one the party of truth and righteousness and love, in harmony with the Lord, and the other the party of sin and selfishness, with contrary sentiments. If *conversion* has taken place it means that the higher organs of the mind, sufficient in number or in influence, have gained the control of the mind; that these preponderate in number or in influence; that they constitute the majority, and the evil propensities the minority. Any heart in which the evil propensities are in the majority and in control is an unconverted heart.

And what was found in Congress respecting the disposition of minorities to baffle the will of the ruling majority is found also in our minds, namely, the disposition of our natural mind not only to be heard, but to foil and baffle and render void the will of the new mind, in respect to the control of the affairs of life. What the Scriptures propose to us, therefore, is illustrated again in Congress: the Scriptures propose that the new mind, having obtained the control, shall elect a Speaker, a head,—and that that head or Speaker for our every talent, directing all our interests and all our efforts, shall be Christ Jesus our Lord. They propose that we shall place full authority and power in the hands of the Lord, so that his word and will shall be our will, our law. And how safe it is for us to admit such a Czar, such an autocrat, to control us, since we have learned to know him as the very embodiment of justice, wisdom, and love. Safely we can trust our affairs in his hands.

There are other analogies which might be drawn: for instance, the power of the Speaker of the House rests solely in the fact that it is the power of the majority. If the majority which placed him in power and gave him the authority which he exercises should become a minority, his power would immediately terminate; and the opposition party might give its representative equal power in an opposite direction. So with our hearts; only as our hearts voted to have the Lord in control, did he take charge; and if our wills, the preponderance of our propensities, our judgments, cease to be on the side of the Lord, he no longer retains his power in our hearts and lives, and the evil majority appoint a successor, in line with the selfish propensities, favoring everything selfish.

In Congress, when any matter is brought up, each representative has an opportunity for expressing himself, either directly or indirectly, either on the floor personally, or through representatives in committee. And so with our wills: when a matter is presented by one organ of the mind, the other organs have a chance to respond, and to seek to influence the majority, and to overthrow the rule of righteousness. For instance, a suggestion is made to the mind by the organ of combativeness, to the effect that there is a good, proper cause why the whole being should be angry, and undertake vengeful retaliation; and under the influence of the eloquence of combativeness, various other of the lower organs would most surely be aroused; namely, pride, self-esteem, destructiveness, selfishness, etc., and in addition perhaps some of the higher organs might be temporarily swayed by the old sympathies, prejudice, antipathy, etc., to favor the angry, malicious and resentful course. Conscientiousness might excitedly declare that it was a righteous cause of indignation. Caution might join, and claim that if the thing were not now opposed violently, worse results would follow; even spirituality and veneration might be swayed into favoring the angry course, with suggestions that it was in the service of God, and a duty towards God, and toward righteousness, to be angry and to crush the opponent with retaliation and vengeance. Thus, for a moment the entire mind might be swayed toward the side of evil, yet without previous wilfulness or sin—because of the hereditary tendencies of the mind.

But here the gavel of the Speaker is heard, memory calls attention, and points out that the will of the majority has already been expressed to the contrary of such a course; and calls attention to the rules already adopted;—namely, to put away all anger, malice, hatred and strife, as being in general works of the flesh and of the devil. Memory calls attention to the fact that the majority adopted as the rule of action the words of the Speaker, Christ, "Love your enemies, do good to them that hate you, and speak evil of you." Commit your way unto the Lord, remembering that he has said, "Vengeance is mine, I will recompense." Where the will of the majority of organs is loyal to its own previous decision, the effect of memory's calling attention to that law will be instantaneous: at once conscientiousness, veneration, spirituality, caution, and all the higher organs realize that they were about to make a mistake; and immediately they change front, fully supporting the law of the Speaker, Christ. Selfishness, combativeness, pride, etc., may attempt to argue the point, but immediately they are called to order and reminded that by vote of the majority they are strictly under the law of Christ, and all further discussion of the subject is forbidden.

Similarly, illustrations might be drawn as representing other passions, tastes or desires of the flesh, which temporarily might seem to gain some control; but from the moment that memory calls attention to the proposal as being in conflict with the law of the Master, there should be an instantaneous surrender. Such a course would prove that the will had all along been thoroughly loyal to the Lord, and that he reigns there. It proves the reign of Christ in that heart far better than if no suggestion to the contrary course had come up. And who cannot see that a life thus ordered, and under strictest control of the will of our Head, Christ Jesus, is not only proper life (the only one in which the new mind is properly exercised), but in addition to this the only mind which is a "*sound* mind." People who are continually carried from their moorings by their emotions show that their minds are unsound; such are continually proving to those around them that they have poor judgment. They are frequently angry, troubled, vexed, hurt; or continually falling into one wrong act or another, as they confess afterward. Indeed, the majority of the things at which they take offence, become angry, etc., prove to have been mistakes nothing having been done or intended to anger, hurt, or injure them. And we know, not only from the Scriptures, but also from our own observation, that the world of mankind in general is thus of *unsound* mind; and, as the Apostle explains, the only ones in all the world who have even the spirit or disposition of a sound mind are the new creatures in Christ Jesus, who have the new mind, the new will, in control. These, as we have seen, would be liable to be carried away also, by evil passions, evil surmisings, etc., but those who have put themselves fully and completely under the control of Christ and his law of the New Covenant are kept from the extremes to which otherwise they would be as subject as others.

The Apostle's exhortation to the double minded, is in place, and should be heeded promptly by all who realize that they have a double mind or will which can never please the Lord nor bring joy and blessing either now or hereafter: "Purify your hearts, ye double minded;"—purge your consciences by hearty obedience to the truth, by the washing of water through the Word.

"Grant, Lord, a heart, submissive, meek,
My great Redeemer's throne,
Where only Christ is heard to speak,
Where Jesus reigns alone;

"A heart in every thought renewed,
And full of love divine,
Perfect and right, and pure and good,
A copy, Lord, of thine."

INTERESTING QUERIES

Question. The fact that our Lord received worship is claimed by some to be an evidence that while on earth he was God the Father disguised in a body of flesh and not really a man. Was he *really* worshiped, or is the translation faulty?

Answer. Yes, we believe our Lord Jesus while on earth was really worshipped, and properly so. While he was not *the* God, Jehovah, he was *a* God. The word "God" signifies a "mighty one," and our Lord was indeed a mighty one. So it is stated in the first two verses of the gospel of John. It was proper for our Lord to receive worship in view of his having been the only begotten of the Father, and his agent in the creation of all things, including man.

Besides, he had come to earth under the divine arrangement and accepted the condition of Messiahship, presenting himself to God as fallen man's sin-offering; besides, at his baptism he was anointed of the holy spirit as the Messiah, and authorized to carry out the great divine plan and to receive homage from both angels and men. This alone would have rendered worship proper even aside from his pre-human greatness as "the only begotten of the Father."

CHRISTADELPHIAN PROOF-TEXTS

Question. Some "Christadelphians" offer the following texts in proof that death ends all for a large majority of the human family—that the majority will never be awakened from the sleep of death.—Psa. 88:4, 5; 49:14. Isa. 26:14; 43:16, 17; Obad. 16.

Please let me have your explanation of the meaning of these texts.

The Watchtower, July 15, 1898, p. 216.

those who worship Him in spirit and in truth. The rank and file of religious "Christendom" as well as of "heathendom" are worshiping images, the creations of men's hands. These images are not confined to Catholic religious edifices and heathen temples and shrines. The images that are idolized include also the systems, the organizations, and the leagues that men build up of a political, commercial, social, and religious kind. Such things stand as symbols of concentrated power, rulerships, money-making agencies, and organized clergy and ecclesiasticism.

[28] The various religious denominations, sects, and cults, by which men go through different forms of worshiping according to creeds, are man-made images. To the peoples such religious organizations stand for God and his means of salvation. Likewise, the postwar international organization for peace and security, to which politicians, clergymen and peoples ascribe the powers which belong only to Jehovah God, is an "image". It is death-dealing foolishness now to follow the popular trend toward worshiping these symbolic images. They are nothings when it comes to bringing eternal salvation and a better world and lasting peace. Their worshipers are doomed to ultimate disappointment, shame, and bitter chagrin. Their boastings about the things they idolize will die out. The Word of the true and living God, who does not seek worship by means of any images whatsoever, says: "Let all them be put to shame that serve graven images, that boast themselves of idols: worship him, all ye gods." (Ps. 97:7, *Am. Stan. Ver.*) Or, according to another version: "Put to shame are all they who were serving an image, who were boasting themselves in nothings: all messengers divine, bow ye down to him." (*Roth. Pss.*) By our answer to the question, Whom shall we serve and worship? we must now determine whether we shall harvest eventual shame for ourselves with failure to gain salvation, or shall reap everlasting life in a satisfying relationship with the true God.

[29] Now that Jehovah God has put his capital organization in power, even the angels of heaven are faced with the need to decide as to whom they will worship. Those mighty angels who would abide within Jehovah's universal organization must subject themselves to His capital organization under Christ Jesus and must obey Jehovah's commandment: "Worship him, all ye gods." Or: "All messengers divine, bow ye down to him." The apostle Paul quotes from this verse (Ps. 97:7) according to the Greek *Septuagint Version* (*LXX*) and shows that this command applies to the angels or heavenly messengers. He also shows that this command applies to the time when Jehovah brings his only begotten Son, Christ Jesus, to the throne in 1914, preparatory to the beginning of the New World of righteousness. Quoting the words above, the apostle Paul says, at Hebrews 1:6: "And when he again bringeth in the firstborn into the world he saith, *And let all the angels of God worship him.*" (*A.S.V.*) "But of the time when he is to bring his firstborn Son back to the world he says, '*And let all God's angels bow before him.*"—*Amer. Trans.*

[30] When God's only begotten, firstborn Son was made a man on earth, Jehovah God saw good to "make him but little less than messengers divine", or less than godly angels, *elohim.* (Ps. 8:5, *Roth. Pss.*) Now, at Christ's coming to reign as king in Jehovah's capital organization Zion, to bring in a righteous new world, Jehovah makes him infinitely higher than the godly angels or messengers and accordingly commands them to worship him. This does not mean that Christ Jesus is Jehovah, a "Jehovah-Christ", as certain religionists say; but it simply fulfills what Jesus said on earth: "The Father judgeth no man, but hath committed all judgment unto the Son: that all men should honour the Son, even as they honour the Father. He that honoureth not the Son honoureth not the Father which hath sent him." (John 5:22, 23) Since Jehovah God now reigns as King by means of his capital organization Zion, then whosoever would worship Him must also worship and bow down to Jehovah's Chief One in that capital organization, namely, Christ Jesus, his Co-regent on the throne of The Theocracy. The holy angels gladly obeyed the divine command and they proved their worship of Jehovah's new King and their subjection to him by joining in his "war in heaven" against Satan and his wicked angels. Thereafter, when Christ Jesus came to the temple of God in 1918, to begin judgment at the house of God, many of such angels came along as his loyal, obedient servants. (Rev. 12:7-12; Matt. 25:31; Isa. 6:1-8; Matt. 24:31, 32) At Armageddon they will fight under him to the utter destruction of Satan's entire organization.

VISIBLE THEOCRATIC ORGANIZATION

[31] Satan's visible organization, the present symbolic *earth,* now suffers the pains of the ending of this present evil world and also feels plagued by the declaration of God's judgments against this world. To her this is the worst of times. Satan the Devil has come down, having great wrath because of being ousted from heaven and also because of knowing he has but a short time until the showdown fight at Armageddon; and so he brings great woes upon his earthly organization, to regiment everybody to his side of the controversy. But to those who have turned their backs upon the idolatrous images of the

28. Why is it death-dealing foolishness now to worship such images?
29. To whom does the command apply, "Worship him, all ye gods"? and when?
30. Why do such "gods" obey such command? and how?
31. On earth, to whom is it the worst of times? and to whom is it the best of times?

The Watchtower, Oct. 15, 1945, p. 313.

● Does Stephen's prayer to Jesus, as found in Acts 7:59, show that he understood Jesus to be Jehovah?—W. R., U.S.A.

The prayer offered by Stephen when he was being martyred is recorded at Acts 7:59, 60, which says: "And they went on casting stones at Stephen as he made appeal and said: 'Lord Jesus, receive my spirit.' Then, bending his knees, he cried out with a strong voice: 'Jehovah, do not charge this sin against them.' And after saying this he fell asleep in death." Rather than indicating that Stephen understood both Jesus and Jehovah to be the same person, his prayer shows that he knew they were not, because he differentiates between the two. His request to Jesus he does not address merely to the Lord, but to the Lord Jesus, thus doing away with any ambiguity. Further, his statement shortly prior to this, as recorded in verse 56, indicates two persons: "And he said: 'Look! I behold the heavens opened up and the Son of man standing at God's right hand.'" He does not say the Son of man, Christ Jesus, is Jehovah God, but that he was standing at God's right hand.

Not only does Stephen's request, "Lord Jesus, receive my spirit," not prove the trinity, but Jesus' similar fervent prayer, "Father, into your hands I entrust my spirit," conclusively shows that Jesus is not the same as his Father Jehovah.—Luke 23:46.

In the wording of his prayer Stephen showed that he understood the difference between Jehovah and the Lord Jesus as set out in Psalm 110:1 and applied by Jesus at Matthew 22:42-46. He was not perplexed by Jesus' application of it, as were the Pharisees to whom Jesus spoke and who were silenced by his answer. Jesus had taught his followers that the Father authorized him to raise others to life. (John 5:26; 6:40; 11:25, 26) So it was proper for Stephen to petition Jesus over this matter, and his prayer indicates proper understanding on his part. It does not support the trinity.

ANNOUNCEMENTS

FIELD MINISTRY

During February Jehovah's witnesses will call on persons in all parts of the world, many of whom want to know the divine will concerning world happenings. To aid these persons of good will, they will offer them *The Watchtower* on a subscription basis, together with three Bible booklets, for $1. If you are not now associated with a congregation of Jehovah's witnesses but would like to have a share in this activity, write to this office for further information.

WHEN YOUTH WILL FADE NO MORE

"Utopia" and the "fountain of youth" are two dreams of unending happiness sought by men throughout the world. Such false hopes and disappointment have they brought that most men now believe them nonexistent. But are they? Yes, in the form that men have sought them. But the fondest dreams of men cannot compare with the paradise Almighty God has promised to restore to earth. This hope is real and certain for our generation! Would you like the proof? Then send 75c at once for the beautifully illustrated hard-bound book *From Paradise Lost to Paradise Regained.* It is based on God's unfailing Word, the Holy Bible.

"WATCHTOWER" STUDIES FOR THE WEEKS

March 1: Paradise, ¶1-22. Page 69.
March 8: Paradise, ¶23-30, and Maintaining Our Spiritual Paradise, ¶1-15. Page 75.
March 15: Maintaining Our Spiritual Paradise, ¶16-39. Page 81.

The Watchtower, Feb. 1, 1959, p. 96.

Relative Worship—Can Jesus Receive Indirect Worship?

Let's note how Jay and Chris discuss this question.

Chris: I found a verse I think you'll be interested in, Jay; it's Hebrews 1:6. I think it demonstrates the deity of Christ since God commands all the angels in heaven to worship His Son.

Jay: Well, let's see what it says. My Bible [NWT, 1981 ed.] reads: "But when he again brings his Firstborn into the inhabited earth, he says: 'And let all God's angels do obeisance to him.' "

Chris: To me that shows that Jesus must be God, as the Father even tells all the angels in heaven to worship the Son.

Jay: But my Bible says "do obeisance to"; what it *really* means is just "respectful obeisance," "bowing down" before him as one "honored" by Jehovah. (See p. 171.)

Chris: I agree that's what *The Watchtower* says, but I'm not so sure that's what the Bible means. Remember what we talked about last time? [See "Is Jesus Christ Worthy of Worship?"] We saw this same action was refused by both men and angels (Acts 10:25; Rev. 19, 22). This action of worship belongs only to God himself.

Jay: Well, *The Watchtower* quotes a Greek lexicon (a dictionary of the language used at the time of Christ—words are looked up in Greek and definitions are given in English). It says the word used in Hebrews 1:6 was

> used to designate the custom of prostrating oneself before a person and kissing the feet, the hem of the garment, the ground. (See p. 171.)

In other words, the worship given to Jesus here just refers to a respectful bowing down, like the Society says.

Chris: And which lexicon was that? Maybe we could look it up.

Jay: *The Greek-English Lexicon of the New Testament* (Bauer, Arndt, Gingrich). I have one right here so we can look it up.

Chris: Yes, that's what it says. But notice that description isn't defining any particular New Testament usage of obeisance (*proskuneo*). As we read on several things become clear. The definition, as far as the Watchtower has quoted it, is also used in non-biblical writings,[4] and can refer to the false worship of deified men and holy objects.

---

[4]E.g., Aristotle, Philo, Josephus, Enoch, Herodotus, Testament of the 12 Patriarchs.

Jay: Well, read what the rest of the definition says there.

Chris: Starting where the Watchtower left off, it says:

> . . . the Persians did this in the presence of their deified king, and the Greeks before a divinity or something holy; *(fall down and) worship, do obeisance to, prostrate oneself before, do reverence to, welcome respectfully*. . . .[5]

This looks like *proskuneo* is something more than casual respect, or a salute or calling someone "sir." And certainly this description doesn't imply that real worship isn't to be understood in Hebrews 1:6.

Jay: No, it doesn't. But it doesn't prove that mere respect is to be ruled out either.

Chris: Let's see if Hebrews 1:6 is specifically mentioned further on in the definition. Okay?

Jay: Sure.

Chris: Look, it is. Here under point 2, "to God," item "a." The kind of worship in Hebrews 1:6 is listed as being used "of the God worshipped by monotheists (Christians, Jews, Samaritans)."[6] That kind of narrows it down, doesn't it, Jay?

Jay: Yes, I guess it does.

Chris: I also noticed your lexicon lists this form of worship in Hebrews 1:6 with what Jesus says shall be offered to the Father in John 4:21 and 23, and also of that restricted to Jehovah himself in Luke 4:8 and Matthew 4:10.

Jay: What does Luke 4:8 say?

Chris: This is where the devil tells Jesus:

> "You, therefore, if you do an act of worship before me, it will all be yours." In reply Jesus said to him: "It is written, 'It is Jehovah your God you must worship, and it is to him alone you must render sacred service.' " (Luke 4:7, 8, NWT)

That really narrows down what *proskuneo* can mean. There is no way it could just be referring to obeisance, just respectful bowing.

Jay: No. As a matter of fact the same article in *The Watchtower* that mentioned the Lexicon says:

> It may also signify "worship," which is how some Bibles read at Hebrews 1:6. If that is the correct sense here, it evidently means a relative worship, a worship of Jehovah God directed through his glorified Son. (See p. 171.)

---

[5] *Greek-English Lexicon*, Bauer, Arndt, Gingrich (Univ. of Chicago Press, 1957, Fourth ed.), p. 723.

[6] Ibid., p. 724.

Chris: In other words, they really can't get out of the fact that Jesus is "evidently" worshiped. So when they find a verse like Hebrews 1:6, they say Jehovah is the one receiving the worship even though *Jesus* is in fact the one being worshiped!

Jay: Evidently.

Chris: Since the Watchtower doesn't believe Jesus is really God, I don't see much difference between that worship and idolatry. Maybe the definition isn't so clear for the Watchtower anymore, but they used to be certain of what idolatry was. *The Watchtower* said: "It is the worship of any one or any thing aside from the true God." (See p. 172.)

Jay: I can see what you mean. But it's not really worshiping Jesus if prayers and praise are given *through* Jesus to Jehovah. It's relative worship.

Chris: Unless the Watchtower thinks "less-educated" Witnesses are more educated than Catholics, some of that worship that is supposed to go *through* Jesus must go *to* Jesus himself.

Jay: Why do you say that?

Chris: Because *The Watchtower* said:

> It does no good to argue that such honor given to images is merely "relative," for in actual practice among less-educated Catholics the worship of the image itself is real. (See p. 173.)

By the same token some Witnesses who pray and worship through Jesus must give real worship to Jesus.

Jay: I can't speak for other Witnesses, but I do just what this 1983 article says. I'm "worshiping Jehovah God through or by means of his chief representative, his Son Jesus." (See p. 171.) That is only *relative worship*, and that is okay.

Chris: Jay, I think we can again let the Watchtower respond to that:

> A religionist may not excuse himself by saying that he merely gives the image "relative honor and worship" and is not worshiping the image itself, but the one for whom the image stands. That is the very argument that the pagan heathen gave. . . . Such religious practice is self-deception, and God does not excuse the use of images under this pretext, but calls it a snare and expressly forbids it to those who worship him in spirit and in truth. Even to wave the hand and give a salute and throw a kiss was forbidden by him as idolizing the image or thing. (See p. 174.)

Jay: I can see how what you read applies in principle, but the

Watchtower was really only talking about giving images relative worship. I'm still not convinced relative worship to Jesus is wrong.

Chris: Jay, is worshiping a created being wrong?

Jay: Certainly, that's creature worship. True worship belongs to the true God.

Chris: Okay, we know the kind of worship given to Jesus is the kind that belongs only to God. We also know the Watchtower teaches Jesus was a created being, a creature, even when He was highly exalted after the resurrection. The Society says, "In due time God exalted him to the highest position a creature could be given. . . . (See p. 175.)

Jay: So. . .

Chris: If Jesus is a created being, then the Father commanded all the angels in heaven to engage in creature worship in Hebrews 1:6. Would God really do that?

Jay: Well . . . He shouldn't . . . No, He didn't. He just commanded them to give Jesus relative worship. And they do because "they appreciate that he has been 'crowned with glory and honor' and given authority. . . ." (See p. 171.)

Chris: Then the angels engage in relative creature worship?

Jay: Uhmm, that doesn't sound too good. I don't know.

Chris: All right. Hebrews 1:6 speaks of the kind of worship that belongs to Jehovah. This worship is given to Jesus, at least relatively, according to the Watchtower. They say that Jesus is a creature, an exalted angel. To worship a creature is idolatry, but you think to give Jesus relative worship is okay, right?

Jay: Right.

Chris: Since Jesus is still an exalted angel, a created being, the important question becomes, "Can an angel receive relative worship?" Right?

Jay: Right.

Chris: The Watchtower said:

> *Relative* honor to God through an angel was reproved in these words: "Be careful! Do not do that! . . . Worship God" (Rev. 19:10; 22:8, 9, *NW*). (See p. 176.)

The answer is no! If Jesus was a creature as the Watchtower says He is, the Father would not command all the angels to worship Him.

Jay: Now that's interesting!

Chris: Just one more thing. Notice the Father commands *all* the angels to worship the Son? If Jesus was Michael the archangel like the Society teaches, Hebrews 1:6 would say, "Let all the *other* angels worship Him."

Jay: I never noticed that before. That *is* a problem!

Chris: You probably don't know that the Watchtower once used this very verse to prove that Jesus could *not* be Michael, right?

Jay: They did?

Chris: Yes. *The Watchtower* said:

> His *position* is contrasted with that of men and angels, as he is Lord of both, having "all power in heaven and earth." Hence it is said, "Let *all* the angels of God worship him"; [that must include Michael, the chief angel; hence Michael is not the Son of God] and the reason is, because he has "by *inheritance* obtained a more excellent *Name* than they." (See p. 177.)

Jay: Wow! Maybe I'd better take another look at who Jesus is.

I hope we can all take a good look at who Jesus really is, and as we come to Him in worship, let's tell others and bring them too.

OBEISANCE or WORSHIP

In Hebrews 1:6 the Greek word *proskynéo* may mean:

1. Rendering respectful obeisance, as 'bowing down,' to Jesus as the one whom Jehovah God has honored and glorified
2. Worshiping Jehovah God through or by means of his chief representative, his Son Jesus

part of a triune deity and that the Father, Son and Holy Ghost are equal. Yet, who gets most of their attention? Jesus. He is pushed into the foreground, and the Father is squeezed into the shadows. This poses a challenge for true Christians. At John 14:28 Jesus said that his Father was greater, and Psalm 83:18 states that "you, whose name is Jehovah, you *alone* are the Most High over all the earth." But we must not overreact to the distorted views about Jesus and unconsciously minimize his true position. As with the Hebrew Christians, a balanced and accurate estimation of Jesus will be of immense value as we face the future.

10 The book of Hebrews begins by focusing attention on Christ's superior position. He is now a glorified spirit, "the exact representation of [God's] very being." This does not imply that the Father and the Son are one person or one god, for Hebrews 1:3 adds that Jesus has "sat down on the right hand of the Majesty ["of God," *Today's English Version*] in lofty places." Texts such as Hebrews 2:10 and 5:5, 8 also indicate that Jehovah is superior to the Son. Still, Christ now has "a name [position or reputation] more excellent than [the angels']." —Hebrews 1:4.

11 As the faithful angels do, we also need to recognize Christ's exalted position. Quoting from Psalm 97:7 (Greek *Septuagint Version*), Hebrews 1:6 says: "Let all God's angels do obeisance to him." As other versions render this, the angels "fall before," "bow down before" or "pay homage" to the Son.* The context suggests that this means that even the angels render homage to Jesus as God's chief representative and exalted Son. They appreciate that he has been "crowned with glory and honor" and given authority over the inhabited earth to come.—Hebrews 2:5, 9.

12 How should this affect us? After showing Jesus' superiority over the angels, Paul says: "That is why it is necessary for us to pay more than the usual attention to the things heard by us, that we may never drift away." (Hebrews 2:1) As the Hebrew Christians knew, the Jews long paid attention to God's Word, or Law, given through Moses. It is much more vital for us to pay attention to divine guidance provided through Jesus.

13 Bearing this out, recall what Jesus Christ had said about fleeing when Je-

* Paul employed the Greek word *proskynéo*, which *The Greek-English Lexicon of the New Testament* (Bauer, Arndt, Gingrich) says was "used to designate the custom of prostrating oneself before a person and kissing the feet, the hem of the garment, the ground." (1 Samuel 24:8; 2 Kings 2:15) It may also signify "worship," which is how some Bibles read at Hebrews 1:6. If that is the correct sense here, it evidently means a relative worship, a worship of Jehovah God directed through his glorified Son.—Compare Revelation 14:7; *The Watchtower* of November 15, 1970, pages 702-704.

10. What does Hebrews indicate about Jesus' position?

11. (a) How do God's angels treat Jesus Christ? (b) How is Hebrews 1:6 to be understood?

12. Why is it important for us to pay attention to Jesus' words?

13. How might Christians benefit from attention to Jesus? Illustrate.

The Watchtower, Feb. 15, 1983, p. 18.

CHRISTENDOM'S IDOLATRY FORESHADOWED

Christendom guilty of idolatry?
In what ways?

GOD'S Word, the Bible, is clear and unequivocal on the subject of idolatry. There is no mistaking the words of Jehovah addressed to the Israelites, whom he had just brought out of the land of Egypt, out of the house of slaves: "You must not have any other gods against my face. You must not make for yourself a carved image or a form like anything that is in the heavens above or that is on the earth underneath or that is in the waters under the earth. You must not bow down to them nor be induced to serve them." —Ex. 20:3-5.

Christians, although "not under law but under undeserved kindness," are, nevertheless, explicitly and emphatically likewise warned against idolatry: "Idolaters" will not "inherit God's kingdom." "Neither become idolaters." "Beloved ones, flee from idolatry." "What agreement does God's temple have with idols?" "Now the works of the flesh are manifest, and they are . . . idolatry." "Little children, guard yourselves from idols." And among those barred from the holy city, those to have their destiny in the lake of fire, the second death, are idolaters.—Rom. 6:14; 1 Cor. 6:9, 10; 10:7, 14; 2 Cor. 6:16; Gal. 5:19, 20; 1 John 5:21; Rev. 21:8; 22:15.

What is idolatry? Of course, idolatry includes the worship of literal idols, images, statues, physical representations of a deity. But it is by no means limited to these. It is the worship of any one or any thing aside from the true God. As modernly defined: "The giving of absolute devotion and ultimate trust to something that is not God; immoderate attachment or veneration for something; respect or love that approaches that due a divine power."—*Webster's Third New International Dictionary.*

POPULAR IDOLS

Christendom claims to worship the God of the Bible and it looks down upon what it terms pagan idolaters. However, the facts show that the people of Christendom themselves are guilty of idolatry, and that in ever so many ways. For example, there is the idolatry of political heroes. Today Perón of Argentina has again become an issue. Apparently many still feel as did his wife Evita, when she once exclaimed: "He is God for us, so much so that we cannot conceive heaven without Perón. . . . He is our sun, our air, our water, our life."

There is also the idolatry of movie stars in Christendom, especially by its youth. Certainly the German teen-age girls were guilty of idolatry when they painted on the portals of the Bamberg Cathedral in Munich the words, "Elvis Presley—my God."

Then, again, there are those who become so attached to an animal pet that they put the life of it ahead of their own. Others have lavish funeral services for their pets. All such are likewise guilty of idolatry.

A little more than a year ago twenty-five leading theologians of the United States accused or charged its people with worshiping the false gods of scientism, political demagogues, the Western way of life, sex, physical power, comfort, man's

53

The Watchtower, Jan. 15, 1963, p. 53.

—*Catholic Encyclopedia,* Vol. XII, page 742; and Vol. VII, page 666.

[9] "In the fourth century the Christian Roman citizens in the East offered gifts, incense, even prayers (!) to the statues of the emperor. It would be natural that the people who bowed to, kissed, incensed the imperial eagles and the images of Caesar (with no suspicion of anything like idolatry), who paid elaborate reverence to an empty throne as his symbol, should give the same signs to the cross, the images of Christ, and the altar." (*Catholic Encyclopedia,* Vol. VII, page 667) With this unmistakable pagan background for image worship, it can readily be understood why Cardinal Newman in his book *An Essay on the Development of Christian Doctrine,* page 373, admitted that, among a long list of other things, " . . . images at a later date . . . are all of pagan origin and sanctified by their adoption into the [Roman Catholic] Church."

[10] It does no good to argue that such honor given to images is merely "relative", for in actual practice among less-educated Catholics the worship of the image itself is real. This too is admitted by the *Catholic Encyclopedia,* Vol. VII, page 668, which, speaking of the eighth century, says: "At the same time one must admit that things had gone very far in the direction of image-worship. Even then it is inconceivable that anyone, except the most grossly stupid peasant, could have thought that an image could hear prayers, or do anything for us. And yet the way in which some people treated their holy [images] argues more than the merely relative honour that Catholics

---

10. What actual practice toward images is admitted as carried on among the less-educated Catholic people?

Let God Be True, 1952 ed., p. 150.

[*Elohim*], who brought thee out of the land of Egypt, out of the house of bondage. Thou shalt have no other gods before me. Thou shalt not make unto thee a graven image, nor any likeness of any thing that is in heaven above, or that is in the earth beneath, or that is in the water under the earth: thou shalt not bow down thyself unto them, nor serve them; for I Jehovah thy God am a jealous God."—Exodus 20:2-5, *A.R.V.;* and 31:18.

A religionist may not excuse himself by saying that he merely gives the image "relative honor and worship" and is not worshiping the image itself, but the one for whom the image stands. That is the very argument that the pagan heathen gave as an excuse for using images in their religion and worshiping the sun, moon and stars, and the "queen of heaven", as they called it. (Jeremiah 7:18; 44:17-25) Such religious practice is self-deception, and God does not excuse the use of images under this pretext, but calls it a snare and expressly forbids it to those who worship him in spirit and in truth. Even to wave the hand and give a salute and throw a kiss was forbidden by him as idolizing the image or thing.

Therefore God inspired Moses to utter and write down this warning to God's covenant people: "Take ye therefore good heed unto yourselves; for ye saw no manner of form on the day that Jehovah spake unto you in Horeb out of the midst of the fire; lest ye corrupt yourselves, and make you a graven image in the

The Truth Shall Make You Free, 1943, p. 37.

Gal. 6:3) Not only should a person not think more of himself than he ought to, he should not think more of other humans than he ought to.

There are religious leaders who fail to heed this Scriptural counsel. They ignore Jesus' statement that "whoever exalts himself will be humbled." (Matt. 23:12) They pay no attention to his warning not to be like the scribes and Pharisees who sought the seats of prominence at public gatherings and dinners, who doted on special titles and loved distinctive greetings in the market place. Those religious leaders exalted themselves and encouraged the people to exalt them. They were directing attention to themselves when they should have had the people direct it to God. There are religious leaders today who are doing the same thing. This was not the practice of Christ nor of those who followed him.

Exalting religious leaders is just as bad as hero-worshiping a singer, a cowboy star, a baseball player, a military hero or a political ruler. It is detrimental to a person's spiritual welfare.

Who Should Be Exalted

Jehovah God is the One to be exalted and glorified, not men. He is the One to look up to and to worship. It is his wisdom that is reflected in all creation, not man's. It is his will that determines the future for all living creatures, not the will of egocentric men. "There is One who is dwelling above the circle of the earth, the dwellers in which are as grasshoppers, the One who is stretching out the heavens just as a fine gauze, who spreads them out like a tent in which to dwell, the One who is reducing high officials to nothing, who has made the very judges of the earth as a mere unreality."—Isa. 40:22, 23.

Christ made it clear in his scathing denunciation of the scribes and Pharisees that it is wrong to exalt men and for men to exalt themselves. God is opposed to such a degenerating practice. The apostle Paul pointed this out when he said: "God chose the ignoble things of the world and the things looked down upon . . . in order that no flesh might boast in the sight of God." —1 Cor. 1:28, 29.

Christ did not exalt himself but humbled himself. He directed the people's adoration to the heavenly Father. In due time God exalted him to the highest position a creature could be given and gave him appropriate honors because of his humble devotion and faithful fulfillment of the divine commission given him. "God exalted him to a superior position and kindly gave him the name that is above every other name." (Phil. 2:9) He is the one we should look to as the model to pattern our lives after and not to the heroes and self-important men of this world.

Without a doubt some men have admirable traits or are above average in intellectual achievements, and a person can learn much from them. But that does not mean we should give them hero worship as the famous writer and philosopher Thomas Carlyle thought. It does not mean we should exalt them above ordinary men as if they are supermen. The same can be said of persons who entertain us well. Such abilities do not make them gods. No human is worthy of another's worship no matter how much publicity he may have received. All worship belongs to God alone. Let your praises be for Him and the One he has exalted, Jesus Christ.

With so much hero worship and the exalting of men going on world-wide it is easy to fall victim to creature worship and consequently be alienated from God. Follow the example of Jesus Christ, who refused to be victimized in that manner. He said: "It is Jehovah your God you must worship, and it is to him alone you must render sacred service."—Matt. 4:10.

Awake!, Sept. 22, 1959, p. 7.

are taught to observe toward them. . . . [Images] were crowned with garlands, incensed, kissed. Lamps burned before them, hymns were sung in their honor. They were applied to sick persons by contact, set in the path of a fire or flood to stop it by a sort of magic." This was in the eighth century; and after twelve centuries of unlimited opportunity to educate the people of Italy, yet, in 1944, when Mount Vesuvius erupted, the humble folk placed their images in the path of the flowing lava to prevent disaster. To this very day the unlearned Catholic people of Mexico, Central America and South America do exactly as the Catholic people of the eighth century, even to placing before them daily offerings of food and drink. —Psalm 115:4-8; Habakkuk 2:18, 19.

11 Still, are not prayers addressed through images of angels and saints in *relative* worship allowable? No. Prayer is to be directed to God, who says: "I am Jehovah, that is my name; and my glory will I not give to another, neither my praise unto graven images." (Isaiah 42:8, *AS*) Prayer, instead of being addressed to images of Jesus, saints or angels, is to be addressed to the Father in heaven and through the living invisible Christ Jesus, not through a lifeless object of wood or stone. (Matthew 6:6-15; John 15:16; 14:13) *Relative* honor to God through an angel was reproved in these words: "Be careful! Do not do that! . . . Worship God." (Revelation 19:10; 22:8, 9, *NW*) At Caesarea and Lystra the apostles Peter and Paul likewise rebuked others' bow-

---

11. Is "relative" worship of God through images Scriptural, and how should prayer be addressed to God?

Let God Be True, 1952 ed., p. 151.

THE NAME OF JESUS

"What's in a name?" is often asked, implying insignificance, and it may make but little difference to a man whether he be called Peter, James, John, Moses, Aaron or even Joshua (Jesus) in times when these and other names are used without any reference to their signification. But in Bible study we are impressed with the idea that names are full of meaning. They were given with reference to time, place or circumstance, past, present or future. Some names were as *monuments* to remind of some special dealings of the Lord, and others were *prophetic*. The qualities, work or destiny of an individual was often expressed by his name. When the direction of a life was changed it was sometimes indicated by a change of name. Adam, indicates man's origin—"of the earth, earthy." Cain, is "acquired," and the woman was mistaken in the value of the man she had gotten of the Lord. Abel, is "feeder," a shepherd, and fitly represents the great Shepherd of the sheep, who gave his life for them. Abraham means "father of a great multitude," or "of many nations." His name was changed from Abram to Abraham when God made him the promise. (Gen. 17: 5,) And in reference to the same great plan Sarai was changed to Sarah, i. e., Princess. (Ver. 15) These are prophetic in their character and point to the grand success of the gospel in bringing the nations to God, the Father of all, through the agency of the "seed" of promise —Christ and the church—the antitypes of Isaac and Rebekah. David, means beloved, a type of Christ, the true King of Israel. David as a prophet personifies Christ, and God makes promises to him as if he were Christ.

The excellent language of David—"Thou wilt not leave *my* soul in the grave, neither wilt thou suffer thine holy one to see corruption,"—was fulfilled in the triumphant resurrection of Christ from the dead. The name given is made to refer to position or official relationship, so that the *position is meant* when the word "name" is used. Even in this sense "a good name is rather to be chosen than great riches." The success of the Lord's work is to Him "for a *name*"—an honor. (Isa. lv:13.) To the obedient the Lord promises "an everlasting *name*." (lvi.:5) "but the *name* of the wicked shall rot." (Prov. x:7.) To receive a prophet in the *name* of a prophet certainly refers to his official character. "Thou shalt call his name Jesus because He shall save His people from their sins." Jesus, means Saviour, and we are carried forward from the mere *word* to the exalted official position, on account of which he can "save to the uttermost all who come unto God by him." His *position* is contrasted with that of men and angels, as he is Lord of both, having "all power in heaven and earth." Hence it is said, "Let *all* the angels of God worship him"; [that must include Michael, the chief angel, hence Michael is not the Son of God] and the reason is, because he has "by *inheritance* obtained a more excellent *Name* than they." Michael or Gabriel are perhaps grander names than Jesus, though Jesus is grand in its very simplicity, but the *official* character of the Son of God as Saviour and King is the inheritance from his Father, which is far superior to theirs, for it pleased the Father that in him *all fullness* should dwell. He has given him a *name* which is above every name, that at the *name* of Jesus *every knee should bow* both in heaven and earth. And there is "none *other* name under heaven given among men whereby we must be saved."

With this view before our minds that the name refers to his official position, the importance of taking from among the Gentiles a "people for his *name*" will be appreciated. As the wife takes the name of her husband, so the church takes the name of her Head. The two made one is the fact of importance. Not one in name merely, but in *fact*, as represented by the name—one in spirit, position, aim and work. The difference between the terms Jesu-it and Christian may illustrate a point. The first relates to the *letter*, as Jesus is a proper name; the second relates more nearly to the *spirit*, as Christ means *anointed* and refers to his official position.

We are not here pleading for a *name*, but what appears to be an important *idea*. There is doubtless as much danger in using the name *Christian* as the name of a *sect*, as in using other names. The one body knows *no* divisions. All who have the spirit of Christ are *one* whether they fully realize it or not; one in spirit now and when glorified—married—one in every *possible* sense, even as the Father and Son are one. Jno. xvii:22, 23.

To be baptised into the name of Jesus (or Father, Son and holy Spirit,) as in him all fullness of the Godhead dwells, means far more than a baptismal *formula*. It is by the apostle expressed as being baptised by one spirit into one body. (1 Cor. xii:13.) There are letter and spirit in the subject of baptism as in almost every other part of God's plan. We should not ignore or belittle either. The letter *represents* the spirit, as a symbol or "*likeness* of his death," and "resurrection." (Rom. vi:5.) Those who can appreciate the spirit need not and are not most likely to ignore the letter, but it seems important that we should guard against mere formalism. In *spirit*, to be baptised involves a death to sin, a rising into a new life of obedience, and a consequent formation of a character;—having "your fruit unto *holiness* and the end everlasting life." (Rom. vi:22.) "As many of you as have been baptised into *Christ* have *put on* Christ." (Gal. iii:27.) "Into one body!" "Ye are *members* of Christ," as in the figure used, bone of his bone and flesh of his flesh. (Eph. v:30.) Do not confound the figure with the reality, do not imagine we will lose our individuality. The body of Christ is a body corporate, each individual acting in harmony with each other and under the direction of Christ for the manifestation of God's love in the salvation of men.

The human body is used to *represent* the church, but in this as in all other figures the reality is but dimly foreshadowed. As Jesus is the *anointed*, so are we, and for the same purpose. He is both king and priest, so we are to be kings and priests—kings to rule and priests to bless.

To be baptised into his name is to become sharers in his spirit, his character, his official position and his work. The power given to him will be manifested through his saints. He is *our* Saviour, but the body corporate will save the *world*. He will continue to be our Head, but the church will be the head of the world. Adam was the head of his wife, but *they* were the united head of the race. The natural is the shadow of the spiritual. Our *position* will be higher than the highest angel. We, like them, will *die no more;* but as we for a *little while* have been *lower* than the *angels*, and in an important sense under their influence, they in this world being ministering spirits to the *heirs* of salvation, so in the world to come, the church being then exalted to the throne of him who is Lord of both angels and men, the "saints will judge (rule) angels," and "judge (rule) the world" too. In that day when every knee shall bow to the highest manifested authority—before the Messiah's throne—the Queen as well as the King will be there. Is it a false ambition, to look for such royal honor? The voice of our coming husband sounds sweetly upon our ears as we struggle on amid the trials of this life. The overcomer will sit with me *in my throne*. Will he allure us on by such a hope to *deceive* us? Are the crown, throne and kingdom promised but unmeaning words? Are our hopes in vain? Will they vanish in fulfillment? Away with the doubt, it is Satan's snare; our Lover is true and faithful, and He has "all power." Call it an unworthy ambition and selfish withal, do you? Then God never would have given the inducement. If this hope of ours is selfish, then our Saviour is selfish. For the *joy* set before *him* he *endureth;* but it is a *benevolent* selfishness. His power is exercised to *bless*. The greater *serves* the less.

How else could we enter into the *joy* of our Lord than by reaching a position from which we can pour blessing on the needy? He hath given him a *name* above every name. Oh that we may realize our privilege of sharing it!

Baptised into the Saviour's death,
With him we rise again;
His spirit moves our every breath,
With him we'll live and reign.

J. H. P.

THE DAY OF JUDGMENT

One great reason for the perverted views respecting the Messianic age, is the failure to understand the Bible meaning of the word *judgment*. It has several significations. Sometimes it means simply an examination or investigation of certain facts, testimony or arguments, in order to ascertain truth, or to reach a just decision. We also use the term to express that quality of mind which enables one to correctly grasp the true conclusion; as we speak of a person having *good judgment*. It often means the determination arrived at in the mind; also the results flowing from the trial and decision in the distribution of the rewards or punishments.

We have been taught to associate the word, when found in the Scriptures, with the last mentioned meaning, i. e. the *executive* judgment, which signification it certainly has; nevertheless, it also and frequently refers to the trial itself while in progress. Notice the first occurrence of the word in the New Testament, (Matt. vii:1, 2,) would clearly bear this rendering: "Test not, that ye be not tested. For with what

The Watchtower, Nov. 1879, p. 4.

Jesus, the God of Thomas

According to the Bible, there is only one God. The Watchtower teaches Jehovah's Witnesses that Jesus is not God. But let's drop in on Jay and Chris as they investigate what the Bible teaches.

Chris: Jay, read Galatians 1:1 (NWT) with me. It says, "Paul, an apostle, neither from men nor through a man, but through Jesus Christ and God the Father." Do you see how Paul points out that the source of his apostleship is not through a mere human?

Jay: Sure, Chris. He says it is "through Jesus Christ and God the Father."

Chris: Right. Paul clearly distinguishes Jesus from humans who are created beings, and ranks Jesus with God the Father.

Jay: Well, it does seem like it, but I doubt if that's really what he meant. After all, none of Jesus' other followers ever called Him "God." If somebody actually called Jesus "God," that would be a different story.

Chris: Would it really, Jay?

Jay: Sure. If one of the apostles called Jesus "God"—and Jesus said it was okay, then it would have to be okay by me! But, it never happened.

Chris: Really? Hold onto your hat, and let's read John 20:28, where the risen Lord has just appeared to the Apostle Thomas. It says, "Thomas answered and said to Him, 'My Lord and my God.' "

Jay: I've sure never seen *that* before. It seems like blasphemy!

Chris: Right, Jay. If Jesus is *not* God, that *would* be blasphemy. But let's read on, "Jesus said to him, Because you have seen Me, have you believed?" (John 20:29). Looks like it was okay with Jesus. What do you think?

Jay: Well, it sure looks like it. But the Watchtower says . . . uh, well, let's talk more about it next week.

Chris: Okay, I'm looking forward to it.

The Watchtower says Jesus is *not* God. But the Bible says Jesus *is*. The Watchtower president has said that Jehovah's Witnesses accept "without question doctrines . . . of the Watchtower Bible and Tract Society" (see p. 179). But the Bible encourages us to test *all* things to determine whether they are of God (1 Thess. 5:21).

A directions and commands carried out to-day through the
executive body which in the end of the day is to be
found in the President and Directors of the Watch
Tower Bible and Tract Society? A. Yes. Q. And
we shall hear how that Society is formed and ordered.
B Is that regarded by Jehovah's Witnesses as the
visible agency which Jehovah God is using at the present
time? A. Yes. Q. To conduct and direct the work
which he wishes done on earth to-day? A. Yes.
Q. That is your belief? A. Yes. Q. Is it for
C that reason that Jehovah's Witnesses accepts without
question doctrines and Biblical interpretations as
expounded by the Watch Tower Bible and Tract-Society
through its Directors? A. Yes. Q. In
publications both periodical and in book form?
D A. Yes. Q. Issued by and with the authority of the
President and Directors of that Society? A. Yes.
Q. That brings me to another matter which is
referred to on Record in the Pleadings, and deals
with what in the Pleadings are called the Little
E Flock or the Anointed. In the first place, would you
tell me, what are the Anointed and where do you find
authority for their existence to-day or in the past?
A. In the Sixty-first Chapter of Isaiah, the first
three verses, we find those prophetic words, "The
F "Spirit of the Lord God is upon me; because the LORD",
here/

Douglas Walsh Trial, Scotland, 1954 (1958 ed.), p. 91.

Jesus—"Our God and Savior"

In the last section we saw Jay tell Chris that as a Jehovah's Witness, he believed that Jesus is not God. Like many others, Jay follows the Watchtower because he believes that what the Watchtower teaches agrees with the Bible.

However, Jay told Chris that if the Bible said one of the apostles called Jesus God, it *would* make an important difference to him. Well, as you recall, Jay was surprised when he read John 20:28, where the Apostle Thomas calls Jesus God, and Jesus blesses him for believing. Now Jay and Chris continue their discussion.

Jay: Chris, the Watchtower never told us about Thomas or that Jesus was ever called God by anyone in the Bible. Does the Bible say other apostles called Jesus God?

Chris: Yes, it does. Look here at 2 Peter 1. In the first verse it says, "Simon Peter, a bond-servant and apostle of Jesus Christ, to those who received a faith of the same kind as ours, by the righteousness of our God and Savior, Jesus Christ."

Jay: Wow! Peter actually calls Jesus "our God and Savior."

Chris: That he does, Jay. Perhaps you have heard of William Barclay, whom the Watchtower calls "the noted Bible translator." (See p. 181.) Barclay says, "In the Greek there is only one person involved. . . ." (See p. 182) and "It actually calls Jesus God." (See p. 183.)

Jay: Well, I told you last week that if one of the apostles called Jesus God, it would really make a difference to me—and you've shown me where both the Apostle Thomas and the Apostle Peter clearly say Jesus is God.

Chris: The Apostle Paul said that if you will confess Jesus as Lord and believe that God raised Him from the dead, you will be saved (Rom. 10:9).

Jay: I think I am beginning to really understand what it means to confess Jesus as Lord. I do want to be saved.

garding this point the noted Bible translator William Barclay writes:

"Now normally, except for special reasons, Greek nouns always have the definite article in front of them, . . . When a Greek noun has not got the article in front of it, it becomes rather a description than an identification, and has the character of an adjective rather than of a noun. We can see exactly the same in English. If I say: 'James is *the* man', then I identify James with some definite man whom I have in mind; but, if I say: 'James is man', then I am simply describing James as human, and the word man has become a description and not an identification. If John had said *ho theos ēn ho logos,* using a definite article in front of both nouns, then he would definitely have identified the *logos* [the Word] with God, but because he has no definite article in front of *theos* it becomes a description, and more of an adjective than a noun. The translation then becomes, to put it rather clumsily, 'The Word was in the same class as God, belonged to the same order of being as God'. . . . John is not here identifying the Word with God. To put it very simply, he does not say that Jesus was God." —*Many Witnesses, One Lord* (1963), pages 23, 24.

Hence, in both their translations Dr. Edgar J. Goodspeed and Dr. James Moffatt render the phrase as, "the Word [or Logos] was divine." This reflects the fine distinction in wording that the apostle John used, a distinction that accords with the fact that Jesus was not equal in power and eternity with the Father but was the created Son of the Father. (1 Cor. 11:3) The *New World Translation* accurately renders the verse: "In [the] beginning the Word was, and the Word was with God, and the Word was a god."

"WATCHTOWER" STUDIES FOR THE WEEKS

June 19: The "Tree" Whose Fall Shocks the World. Page 300. Songs to Be Used: 1, 3.

June 26: Get Out from Under That "Pretty" Tree!, ¶1-20. Page 306. Songs to Be Used: 80, 27.

July 3: Get Out from Under That "Pretty" Tree!, ¶21-40. Page 310. Songs to Be Used: 84, 59.

The Watchtower, May 15, 1977, p. 320.

(ii) To call the Christian the *doulos* of God means that he is unqualifiedly at the disposal of God. In the ancient world the master could do what he liked with his slave. He had the same power over his slave as he had over his inanimate possessions. He had the power of life and death over his slave. The Christian belongs to God, for God to send him where He will, and to do with him what He will. The Christian is the man who has no rights of his own, for all his rights are surrendered to God.

(iii) To call the Christian the *doulos* of God means that the Christian owes an unquestioning obedience to God. Ancient law was such that a master's command was a slave's only law. Even if a slave was told to do something which actually broke the law, he could not protest, for, as far as he was concerned, his master's command was the law. In any situation the Christian has but one question to ask: " Lord, what wilt *Thou* have me to do? " The command of God is his only law.

(iv) To call the Christian the *doulos* of God means that he must be constantly in the service of God. In the ancient world the slave had literally no time of his own, no holidays, no time off, no working-hours settled by agreement, no leisure. All his time belonged to the master. The Christian cannot, either deliberately or unconsciously, compartment life into the time and the activities which belong to God, and the time and the activities in which he does what he likes. The Christian is necessarily the man every moment of whose life and time is spent in the service of God.

We may note one further point. Here Peter speaks of the impartial justice of *our God and Saviour Jesus Christ*. The Authorized Version translates, " the righteousness of God and our Saviour Jesus Christ," as if this referred to two persons, God and Jesus; but as Moffatt and the American Revised Standard Version both show, in the Greek there is only one person involved, and the phrase should read, *our God and Saviour Jesus Christ*. The great interest of this is that it does what the New Testament very, very

William Barclay, *The Letters of James and Peter*, Philadelphia: Westminster Press, 1960, p. 346.

seldom does. It actually calls Jesus God. The only real parallel to this is the adoring cry of Thomas, when he recognized his Lord for what He was: " My Lord and my God " (*John* 20: 28). This is not a matter to argue about at all; it is not even a matter of theology; for to Peter and to Thomas to call Jesus by the name of God was not a matter of theology, but an outrush of the adoration of the heart. It was simply that in the depths of the emotion of their heart and in the glory of their wonder they felt that human terms could not contain this person whom they knew as Lord.

THE ALL-IMPORTANT KNOWLEDGE

2 *Peter* I: 2

> May grace and peace be multiplied to you by the knowledge of God, and of Jesus, our Lord.

PETER puts this in an unusual way. Grace and peace are to come from *knowledge,* the knowledge of God and of Jesus Christ, our Lord. What does he mean by this? Is he turning Christian experience into something which is dependent on knowledge? Or, is there some other meaning here? First, let us look at the word which he uses for knowledge. The word is *epignōsis.* This word can be interpreted in two directions.

(*a*) It can mean *increasing knowledge. Gnōsis* is the normal Greek word for *knowledge,* and here it is preceded by the preposition *epi* which means *towards, in the direction of. Epignōsis* then could be interpreted as knowledge which is always moving further in the direction of that which it seeks to know. Grace and peace are multiplied to the Christian, they increase more and more, as he comes to know Jesus Christ better and better. As it has been put: " The more Christians realize the meaning of Jesus Christ, the more they realize the meaning of grace and the experience of peace." The better we know Jesus, the greater

William Barclay, *The Letters of James and Peter,* Philadelphia: Westminster Press, 1960, p. 347.

John 1:1 and the Two Gods

John 1:1 is a favorite passage for both the Christian and the Jehovah's Witnesses. Let's drop in on Jay and Chris as they discuss this fascinating portion of scripture.

Chris: Are you familiar with the passage at Isaiah 43:10?

Jay: Sure. That is where we get our name, Jehovah's Witnesses.

Chris: Right. Please read that verse for me, and tell me what two basic truths we are to be witnesses of?

Jay: My Bible says, " 'You are my witnesses,' is the utterance of Jehovah, 'even my servant whom I have chosen, in order that you may know and have faith in me, and that you may understand that I am the same One. Before me there was no God formed, and after me there continued to be none' " (NWT).

Chris: And what are we to be witnesses of?

Jay: That He is the only God; there were none formed before Him and none after.

Chris: Yes, and that agrees with Isaiah 45:5, "I am the Lord [Jehovah], and there is no other; besides Me there is no God."

Jay: That's right. Jehovah is the only true God.

Chris: The idea that there is only one God is called monotheism. The Jews were monotheists, and so were the first Christians. They believed in the existence of only one God. 1 Timothy 1:17 is an evidence of this doctrine in the early church. It says, "Now to the King eternal, immortal, invisible, the only God, be honor and glory forever and ever. Amen." Is that what you believe, Jay?

Jay: Sure. I don't have any problem with that. It is what Paul said, and what all the Jews and Christians were to believe.

Chris: Right. Even the writers of the New Testament were monotheists. Being Jews who had recently come to believe in Jesus, they had no reason to think differently even when one of them writes "the Word was God."

Jay: You Christians always try to slip in that trinitarian doctrine which says Jesus is God. But you better remember my Bible says, "In [the] beginning the Word was, and the Word was with God, and the Word was a god" (John 1:1, NWT).

Chris: Perhaps we can look at some of the problems with that translation at another time. But for now, let's look at that verse from another angle. The NWT teaches polytheism.

Jay: What? How?

Chris: Polytheism means belief in more than the one God. The NWT makes John 1:1 say there are two Gods—one called "the God" and the second called "a god."

Jay: Well, maybe that's what John wanted to tell us.

Chris: John was a Jewish-Christian monotheist; he believed there was only one God. There is no way he would have said Jesus [the Word] was "a god"—another god. It was against his religion!

Jay: I think I see what you mean. John believed there was only one true God.

Chris: Exactly. Since John believed there was only one true God, if he called Jesus "a god," in effect he would have been saying Jesus was a false god. And since he wouldn't say that—

Jay: Since he wouldn't say "a god," he meant Jesus *was* God? Just like the Father is God?

Chris: That's what he said! *Both* the Father and the Word are the ONE GOD![7]

The Jehovah's Witnesses took their name from Isaiah 43:10, but the Watchtower seems to have forgotten what the verse said they were supposed to be witnesses of, when they mistranslated John 1:1. "Understand that I am He. Before Me there was no God formed, and there will be none after Me" (Isa. 43:10). Strikingly similar to this Old Testament revelation are the words of Jesus, "Unless you believe that I am He, you shall die in your sins" (John 8:24).

John 1:1 and the Watchtower Rule

For the Watchtower Society, the issue of the deity of Christ has always been a choice item of discussion. While ready to debate with Christians on most issues, John 1:1 becomes a special delight—especially since the Society has published their own translation of the Bible. At John 1:1 the Society's *New World Translation* reads, "In [the] beginning the Word was, and the Word was with God, and the Word was a god." "A god?" Yes, suddenly the seemingly in-

[7]"The Word was God," "i.e., The Word partook of the Divine *Nature*, not was identical with the Divine *Person*. The verse may be thus paraphrased, 'The Logos existed from all eternity, distinct from the Father, and equal to the Father . . . neither confounding the Persons nor dividing the Substance' " (A. Plummer, *The Gospel According to St. John*, Cambridge: University Press, 1892, p. 62).

significant article "a" takes on new relevance.

The little addition "a," makes John to say that Jesus was "a god," a second, though inferior deity, and distinct from "the God." Such an interpolation forces the apostle to polytheism, "the belief in or worship of a plurality of gods."[8] While this alone should be enough for even a Witness to reject the translation, the Society argues that "a god" is the preferred translation since the Greek text does not say "*the* god."

We drop in on Chris and Jay in the midst of their discussion on this topic.

Jay: What Bible are you reading, Chris?

Chris: The *New American Standard Bible*. Why?

Jay: Well, I can show you why it's a biased translation. I'll bet it's translated by trinitarians who believe Jesus is God. They have mistranslated John 1:1. Go ahead and read it.

Chris: "In the beginning was the Word, and the Word was with God, and the Word was God."

Jay: If you think about it, that doesn't make sense. The New World Translation Committee points out that if the verse read "the Word was God," "that would mean that the Word was the God with whom The Word is said to be. This is unreasonable; for how can the Word be with the God and at the same time be that same God?"[9] My Bible says the Word was "a god," not "God."

Chris: How do you know John 1:1 should be translated "a god"?

Jay: Well, the Watchtower says some other translations read the Word was "divine" and don't translate the Greek as "God." They say it is the Greek noun *theos* without the definite article. (See p. 188.)

Chris: You mean the first God mentioned is Jehovah because the Greek has the article "the" before God ("*ho*" *theos*)?

Jay: Yes.

Chris: But at John 20:28 Thomas says to Jesus, "My Lord and my God" (KJV), and the Greek says, "The Lord of me and the God of me"! Does that mean Jesus is Jehovah?

Jay: Uh . . . I've never noticed that before.

Chris: Second Corinthians 4:4 says "the" god in the Greek, and that's talking about Satan, "the god of this world" (KJV).

---

[8]*Webster's Third New International Dictionary* (Chicago: Encyclopaedia Britannica, 1966), Vol II, p. 1761.

[9]*The Kingdom Interlinear Translation of the Greek Scriptures*. 1969, pp. 1158–1159.

Does that mean Satan is Jehovah?

Jay: Oh, no! I get your point. I remember now, I think there is some rule that applies to John 1:1, that since there is no indefinite article "a" in Greek, and where there is no definite article "the," then the article "a" is to be inferred. Yes, I know I've heard that before.

Chris: Really? What about right here in the same verse. The Greek reads, "In beginning was the Word." There is no "the" before "beginning" in the Greek, yet the *New World Translation* says, "In [the] beginning . . ." It looks like they think "the" is to be inferred, not "a."

Jay: Well, yes, it does.

Chris: John 1:6 says in your translation, "There arose a man that was sent forth as a representative of God." There's no article "the" in the Greek. According to your "rule," shouldn't the verse read, "There arose a man that was sent forth as a representative of a god"? Yet the verse is talking about *the* God, isn't it?

Jay: Yes.

Chris: Seems like if there is no "the" in the Greek, it doesn't mean "a" should be inferred, at least not in verse 6 when it speaks of God. What happened to the "rule," Jay?

Jay: I don't know. Maybe there's no rule after all. Probably it's the context that determines whether it's "a god" or "the God."

Chris: Context is important. What do you see in the context here that shows John 1:1 should say "a god"?

Jay: It's just that Jesus can't be God! The Bible teaches He isn't.

Chris: Admit it, Jay. You like the Watchtower's "a god" because it fits your theology, not that it is correct grammatically.

Jay: I'll think about it some more and we can talk further.

Chris: Sounds good to me!

with the sense of 'late on.' But Philostratus shows examples where ὀψέ [o·pse'] with the ablative has the sense of 'after' like ὀψὲ τούτων='after these things.' . . . Hence in Mt. 28:1, ὀψὲ σαββάτων may be either late on the Sabbath or after the Sabbath. Either has good support. Moulton is uncertain, while Blass prefers 'after'. It is a point for exegesis, not for grammar, to decide. If Matthew has in mind just before sunset, 'late on' would be his idea; if he means after sunset, then 'after' is correct."

A Greek-English Lexicon, compiled by Liddell and Scott (1948 Reprint), Volume 2, says on ὀψέ [o·pse']: "4. as preposition with genitive, ὀψὲ τούτων *after* these things, Philostratus V A 6.10, compare 4.18; so perhaps ὀψὲ σαββάτων *after* the sabbath day. Evangel Matthew 28:1." As early as 1806 the *Critical Greek-German Lexicon* by J. G. Schneider had determined "after" as a meaning of ὀψέ [o·pse'] saying: "Adverb, late, too late; really, after; hence also with the Genitive, long after," and then he gives examples.

In *The Four Gospels* translated from the Greek with reference to the Aramaic idiom Prof. C. C. Torrey renders Matthew 28:1: "In the night between the close of the sabbath and the dawn of the first day of the week, . . ." Dr. J. Murdock's translation renders the Syriac Peshitto Version: "And in the close of the sabbath, as the first [day] of the week began to dawn, . . ."

Hebrew versions of Matthew also here render ὀψέ [o·pse'] as "after." Our translation does likewise.

John 1:1 — "a god"

(θεός [*the·os'*], Greek)

The Complete Bible—An American Translation renders this expression "divine," making the entire verse read: "In the beginning the Word existed. The Word was with God, and the Word was divine." (1943 Reprint) *A New Translation of The Bible* by Dr. Jas. Moffatt reads likewise: "The Logos existed in the very beginning, the Logos was with God, the Logos was divine." (1935 edition) Every honest person will have to admit that John's saying that the Word or Logos "was divine" is not saying that he was the God with whom he was. It merely tells of a certain quality about the Word or Logos, but it does not identify him as one and the same as God.

The reason for their rendering the Greek word "divine," and not "God," is that it is the Greek noun *the·os'* without the definite article, hence an anarthrous *the·os'*. The God with whom the Word or Logos was originally is designated here by the Greek expression ὁ Θεός, *the·os'* preceded by the definite article *ho*, hence an articular *the·os'*. Careful translators recognize that the articular construction of the noun points to an identity, a personality, whereas an anarthrous construction points to a quality about someone. That is what *A Manual Grammar of the Greek New Testament* by Dana and Mantey remarks on page 140, paragraph vii. Accordingly, on page 148, paragraph (3), this same publication says about the subject of a copulative sentence, that in a copulative sentence sometimes the article makes the subject distinct from the predicate. Xenophon's *Anabasis*, 1:4:6, ἐμπόριον δ' ἦν τὸ χωρίον, *but the place was a market*, corresponds with what is stated in John 1:1. In both examples above the article used differentiates the subject. The market mentioned by Xenophon was not the only market. Correspondingly the same argument could be used respecting the Greek *theós* without the article *ho* in John 1:1.

Instead of translating John 1:1, *and the word was deity*, this *Grammar* could have translated it, *and the word was a god*, to run more parallel with Xenophon's statement, *and the place was a market*.

In the sentence "and the word was a god" the copulative verb "was" and the expression "a god" form the predicate of the sentence. In the original Greek there is no definite article *ho* (*the*) before *the·os'* (*god*), and it is presumptuous to say that such a definite article is to be understood so that the sentence should therefore be translated "and the Word was God." That would mean that the Word was the God with whom the Word was said to be. This is unreasonable; for how

The Kingdom Interlinear Translation of The Greek Scriptures, 1969, p. 1158.

can the Word be with the God and at the same time be that same God?

True, on page 178, Green's *Handbook to the Grammar of the Greek Testament* has this to say on the significance of the article: "206. Hence arises the *general* rule, that in the simple sentence the Subject takes the article, the Predicate omits it. The subject is definitely before the mind, the predicate generally denotes the class to which the subject is referred, or from which it is excluded." Then this *Handbook* adds some sentences to illustrate this general rule regarding an anarthrous predicate, such as, "thy word is truth," "the Word was God," "God is love"; and next the *Handbook* says: "Had the article been employed with the Predicate in the above case, the sentences would have read thus: . . . *Thy Word is the Truth,* and nothing else can be so described; *the Word was the entire Godhead,* and *God and Love are identical,* so that in fact Love is God." Such an explanation is, in itself, an unintended admission that "the Word" of John 1:1 is not the same god as the God with whom the Word is said to be. Hence the omitting of the article in the predicate of a simple sentence is shown to be only a *general* rule, and not one that holds good in *every* case. One such case where that general rule does not hold true is John 1:1. The definite article "the" was there omitted, but not according to that general rule; it was not omitted with the idea that it should be understood by the reader.

Here we agree with Dr. A. T. Robertson when he says: " 'God' and 'love' are not convertible terms any more than 'God' and 'Logos' or 'Logos' and 'flesh.' . . . The absence of the article here is on purpose and essential to the true idea." (Page 768, *A Grammar of the Greek New Testament*) John's inspired writings and those of his fellow disciples show what the true idea is, namely, the Word or Logos is not God or *the* God, but is the Son of God, and hence is *a* god. That is why, at John 1:1, 2, the apostle refers to God as the God and to the Word or Logos as a god, to show the difference between the two. Hence he deliberately left out the definite article in the predicate which describes who or what the Word (Logos) was.

With a reference to the *Grammar* by Dr. Robertson the *Manual Grammar* by Dana and Mantey, page 140, says: "Surely when Robertson says that θεός [*the·os'*], as to the article, 'is treated like a proper name and may have it or not have it' (R. 761), he does not mean to intimate that the presence or absence of the article with θεός has no special significance. We construe him to mean that there is no definite rule governing the use of the article with θεός, so that sometimes the writer's viewpoint is difficult to detect, which is entirely true. But in the great majority of instances the reason for the distinction is clear. The use of θεός in John 1:1 is a good example."

The above disposes of the trinitarian argument that the article was omitted before θεός in the predicate of John 1:1 according to the general rule that it was not needed, but would be understood. On page 761 Robertson's *Grammar* says: "Among the ancient writers ὁ θεός [*ho the·os'*] was used of the god of absolute religion in distinction from the mythological gods." So, too, John 1:1, 2 uses ὁ θεός to distinguish Jehovah God from the Word (Logos) as a god, "the only begotten god" as John 1:18 calls him.

In further proof that the omitting of the definite article in the predicate of John 1:1 by the apostle was deliberately meant to show a difference, we quote what Dr. Robertson's *Grammar* says on page 767: "(*i*) NOUNS IN THE PREDICATE. These may have the article also." In our footnote[a] below we give a list of texts in John alone which have the definite article before the noun in the predicate. Any reader with the Greek text can check these. If a "general rule" made it unnecessary, then why was the definite article used before the noun in the predicate in all these cases? All this shows that the omitting of the definite article in the predicate may be, not according to any general rule, but for a specific purpose outside that rule.

[a] John 1:4, 9, 20, 21, 25, 49; 3:28; 4:29, 42; 5:35; 6:14, 35, 48, 50, 51, 58, 63, 69; 7:26, 40, 41; 8:12; 10:7, 9, 11, 14, 24; 11:25, 27; 14:6; 15:1, 5; 18:33; 20:31; 21:24. In these verses the Greek text uses the definite article.

The Kingdom Interlinear Translation of the Greek Scriptures, 1969, p. 1159.

John 1:1—Clearing Up the Difficulty

While some of the following Jehovah's Witness arguments are not found in Watchtower publications, they arise often in discussions with individual Witnesses. Since these arguments are so popular, it is apparent that the Watchtower Society does little to discourge them.

Chris: Jay, I've been doing some further study in those Watchtower books you loaned me, about the teaching on John 1:1. Most of my homework has been done in the Society's two Greek interlinear translations. I'd like your opinion on my researched conclusion.

Jay: Well, I'm no scholar in biblical Greek, so don't expect too much from me.

Chris: Don't worry. I'm no scholar either. What I'd like to discuss really isn't too complicated. The Society has given various reasons for translating the Greek text, "the Word was 'a' god," in John 1:1. Since this is such an important text to our belief about God, I want to share one of these reasons with you.

Jay: Okay.

Chris: First, let's look at the Society's *Emphatic Diaglott*. The Society explains:

> An interlinear word-for-word English translation appears with this Greek text, and enables the student who is not a Greek scholar to get at the original sense of the Greek Scriptures. This is one of the *Diaglott's* finest features. (See p. 195.)

The translator of the *Diaglott*, Benjamin Wilson, was not a Jehovah's Witness, even though he held the same basic doctrinal beliefs. Reportedly a Christadelphian, he also denied the Trinity. (See p. 196.) The Society says: "We consider this to be among the most accurate translations of the New Testament extant, and believe the book to be an almost indispensable aid to careful study." (See p. 197.)

Jay: Oh, yes. I've used the *Diaglott* a number of times. It's very helpful.

Chris: What if the Jehovah's Witness finds an "error" (something that doesn't agree with Watchtower teaching) in Mr. Wilson's emphatic translation found in the right-hand-column? No problem. All he needs to do is to note the *word-for-word* translation in the left-hand column. (See p. 195.) The Society gives an appropriate example of the value of the left-hand column interlinear rendering:

> That controversial text of John 1:1 well illustrates the value of the features the interlinear and signs of emphasis. In the *Diaglott* John 1:1 reads: "In the beginning was the Logos, and the Logos was with GOD, and the Logos was God." This seems to support the view of trinitarians. But the interlinear translation says: "In a beginning was the Word, and the Word was with the God, and a god was the Word." This clears up the difficulty. (See p. 198.)

But what do they mean by saying, "This seems to support the view of trinitarians"?

Jay: Obviously, they are referring to Wilson's emphatic translation in the right-hand column, where it reads, "And the *Logos* was God." But that translation is not as accurate as the interlinear translation in the left-hand column which reads, "And a god was the Word."

Chris: Therefore, you prefer the interlinear word-for-word translation over the freer translation on the right?

Jay: Yes, this is why they say the "interlinear translation . . . clears up the difficulty" with the freer translation.

Chris: I noted in the booklet *"The Word"—Who Is He? According to John* that there is a discussion on the correct translation of John 1:1. After mentioning various translation renderings, they say:

> Since we have examined so much of what John wrote about Jesus who was the Word made flesh, we are now in position to determine which of those several translations is correct. It means our salvation. (See p. 199.)

Does it mean *your* salvation too?

Jay: Of course. If I don't know who Jesus is, how can I be saved? I believe He is *not* Jehovah, as you claim, but only "a god."

Chris: Well, since it means your salvation, and you respect the interlinear rendering of John 1:1, I have something very interesting to show you. Do you also use the Watchtower's *Kingdom Interlinear Translation* (KIT) in your studies?

Jay: Sure.

Chris: Please turn to John 1:1 in your KIT. How does it read?

Jay: "In [the] beginning the Word was, and the Word was with God, and the Word was a god."

Chris: That's the freer Watchtower translation [NWT in the right margin in the illustration]. Now tell me, what is the *more accurate* interlinear rendering?

Jay: "In beginning was the Word, and the Word was toward the God, and *god was the Word*." (See p. 200, italics mine.) Are you trying to prove from this interlinear that Jesus is God?

Chris: I think it speaks for itself!

Jay: Wait a minute! I've just noticed something important. There is a difference between the first person mentioned as "God" and the second person. The first one is with a capital "G" and the second one is with a lowercase "g". This shows the first one is Jehovah and the second is Jesus—a god.

Chris: Jay, let me explain something to you about capital letters and the Greek manuscripts. According to B. F. Wescott and F.H.A. Hort, the scholars whose Greek text the *New World Translation* is based on (see NWT title page), the early Greek manuscripts of the New Testament were written in only capital letters, called uncials. (See p. 201.) Obviously, the Watchtower Society is quite aware of uncials. See here in their booklet *"The Word"—Who Is He? According to John*, page 54. Here, they illustrate the use of uncials in the early Greek manuscripts of John 1:1. (See p. 202.) Every letter was a capital letter, Jay. The Watchtower decided to put a small "g" for the "Word" because of their theology; they don't want you to believe He is God with a capital "G"!

Jay: Okay, I see your point. But, I've just noticed another difference between the first person called God and the second person. The first person (the Father) has a different looking Greek word for God than the word for the second person (the Word). See what I mean? The Father is θεον (*theon*), yet the Word is θεος (*theos*). The difference is the last letters of the Greek words; one looks like a "v" and the other looks like an "s". Does that show a difference between Jehovah the Almighty God and Jesus a mighty god?[10]

Chris: Not at all. The difference only indicates the grammatical role that the word plays in the sentence. The Watchtower itself says:

> To a person unfamiliar with the Greek language, it might seem that there is a significance indicated by the fact that

[10]See "The Mighty God—A Lesser God?", *From Kingdom Hall to Kingdom Come,* Witness, Inc., for a detailed discussion and refutation of this Watchtower teaching.

> first the word is spelled *theon* and the next *theos*. But the difference is simply a matter of complying with the Greek grammatical case used. (See p. 203.)

If you still think that *theos*, one form of the word "God," is somehow inferior to *theon*, another form of the word "God," then can you explain to me who is the God referred to in John 3:16?

Jay: "For God loved the world so much. . . ." (See p. 204.) Well, that's Jehovah, of course!

Chris: Yes, it is. Now look at the Greek, please. The word for God is none other than *theos*. Now, by what stretch of the imagination should we believe Jesus is an inferior god at John 1:1 because He is *theos*. If He is inferior, then so is the Father! This can't be, Jay. Also, in the Old Testament Greek translation (LXX), *theon*, which refers to the Father in John 1:1, sometimes refers to false gods![11] Isn't it apparent that the particular *form* of the word *theos* for God doesn't necessarily identify which god is under discussion?

Jay: Boy, I'm really confused now.

Chris: Well, let's see if we can summarize. Point #1: The Watchtower's *Interlinear*, a word-for-word translation, says Jesus is God—not a god! The Watchtower itself encourages us to judge their modern translation by their interlinear:

> But under each Greek word is placed its basic meaning, according to its grammatical construction, whether this agrees literally with the *New World Translation* or not. What we as Bible students should want is what the original Greek text says. Only by getting this basic meaning can we determine whether the *New World Translation* or any other Bible translation is right or not.[12] (For further comments on this subject, see p. 205.)

---

[11]See *Septuagint* (LXX), Zondervan, 1975, p. 1069, where θεον (*theon*) refers to false gods in Daniel 11:36–38.

[12]*Watchtower*, November 15, 1969, p. 692. (See p. 205.) Further comment on the difference between the literal interlinear rendering and the modern NWT is noted:

> To aid such seekers of truth and life is the purpose behind the publishing of *The Kingdom Interlinear Translation of the Greek Scriptures*. Its literal interlinear English translation is specially designed to open up to the student of the Sacred Scriptures what the original *koiné* Greek basically or literally says, without any sectarian religious coloration. . . . For the interlinear word-for-word rendering the English word or phrase has not been taken from the modern translation in the right-hand column and transferred to a position under the Greek word to which it corresponds. Rather, the translation under each Greek word sets out what the Greek word itself says according to its

We have checked to see if Jesus is *a* god in the interlinear—He is not. He is *God*.[13]

Jay: Yes, I see that it does say that.

Chris: Point #2: The Watchtower publishes two interlinears. The *Emphatic Diaglott* says Jesus is "a god." *The Kingdom Interlinear* says He is "God." They contradict each other. Which do you accept?

Jay: Do I *have* to make a choice?

Chris: Yes, you do, Jay. After all, the Watchtower says knowledge of the correct translation of John 1:1 "means our salvation."

The Watchtower Society is confused about the identity of Jesus Christ. This has led Jehovah's Witnesses into a spiritual desert of dry theology and works. The truth-seeker doesn't have to be an expert in biblical Greek to know the real Jesus. A look into God's precious Word will reveal Him and clear up John 1:1.

> root meanings (where the Greek word is made up of two or more particles) and according to its grammatical form. So in many cases the reading in the English word-for-word interlinear translation is not the same as that found in the right-hand column. This aids us in determining what the Greek text actually, basically says. (See p. 206.)

It "is *not* the same as that found in the right-hand column." Why? Because the NWT committee employed their theological bias against the deity of Christ in their translation efforts. Consequently, their NWT of John 1:1, unlike the interlinear, is tainted with "sectarian religious coloration."

[13]The student who checks other interlinears will find essentially the same rendering for John 1:1 as in the KIT: "and God was the Word." See the *Interlinear Greek-English New Testament* by Alfred Marshall (Samuel Bagster & Sons, London, 1958) and also that (same title) by Jay P. Green (MacDonald Publishing Co., MacDill AFB, FLA., 1972).

to derive the fullest benefit from this translation of the Greek Scriptures.

A careful study of the *Diaglott* will show the abundance of material it has to offer to the critical student within its own pages, without going to any outside helps on the Greek Scriptures. The provisions within its own covers make possible an exhaustive research on the Christian Scriptures. This, however, means work. It means that if one determines on a certain number of verses that he is going to critically study, then the study of those verses includes not just the emphatic English translation of the given verses in the right-hand column, but embraces the left-hand column of the original Greek text with its interlinear word-for-word rendering in English, the footnotes that are given on the verses within the assignment, any application of the *Diaglott's* introductory matter that may be pertinent; and also the store of information in the Alphabetical Appendix should be tapped for use if it will add force and weight to the theme or argument the verses are developing. Thus the critical student has a tremendous field thrown open to him for analytical study, and his treatment of his assignment should exploit all these *Diaglott* features and show their value.

To forcefully show the values of the *Diaglott* and its superiority in many respects, some comparison with the Authorized Version renderings will be necessary. This, however, does not mean that the student should consume his time in a verse-by-verse comparison, but should limit comparison to disputed texts and those which in the Authorized Version are so erroneously rendered that they seem to give credence to false religious doctrines. All these instructions as to treatment of material will be illustrated before this discussion closes.

Turning to the pages in the main body of the *Diaglott*, one finds the work arranged in parallel columns on the page. The left-hand column contains the Greek text, being Dr. Griesbach's recension of the 18th century. It is based on a comparison of many Greek texts, the older ones being preferred, and particularly does it tend to conform to the Alexandrine Manuscript, of the fifth century. An interlinear word-for-word English translation appears with this Greek text, and enables the student who is not a Greek scholar to get at the original sense of the Greek Scriptures. This is one of the *Diaglott's* finest features.

In the right-hand column is Mr. Wilson's own emphatic or emphasized English translation, the emphasis being shown by typographical style, as explained in the introductory matter on "Signs of Emphasis". His translation is based on the interlinear translation, the renderings of eminent critics, and on the various readings of the Vatican MS. No. 1209, a fourth-century manuscript. If the Theocratic minister, reading along in Mr. Wilson's emphatic translation, finds something that does not agree with what the Bible teaches elsewhere, he can check up on Mr. Wilson by shifting the eye to the left-hand column and noting the word-for-word translation, and even in some cases going to the untranslated Greek text to settle the matter.

For example, the student may open the *Diaglott* at John 1:1 and read: "In the beginning was the Logos, and the Logos was with God, and the Logos was God." This seems to support the view of trinitarians. The minister knows that that impossible three-in-one doctrine is false; so he shifts his eye from the right-hand column to the left-hand column and reads the interlinear translation: "In a beginning was the Word, and the Word was with the God, and a god was the Word." This clears up the difficulty.

This text also supplies a fine illustration of the value of the signs of emphasis which Mr. Wilson uses in his emphatic translation. The introductory matter explaining these signs says: "The Greek article often finds its equivalent in the

Consolation, Nov. 8, 1944, p. 27.

Presenting "This Gospel of the Kingdom"

The Emphatic Diaglott for Analytical Study

(*In Two Parts*—Part One)

ONE of the three Scripture editions published by the Watchtower Society is *The Emphatic Diaglott*. The arrangement of this work and the avenues for critical study which it opens to the Bible student make it the most valuable translation of the Greek Scriptures available for analytical study. This article and the succeeding one will aim at bearing out that assertion. However, in the space allotted, the vast store of material in the *Diaglott* can only be scratched. But as the student pursues an individual and detailed study of its pages the evidence in support of that claim will mount, and in time the accumulated proof will have driven home the incomparable value of *The Emphatic Diaglott* in the field of critical and analytical study.

The history of the *Diaglott* is interesting. It was prepared by Benjamin Wilson, and published by Fowler & Wells Co., New York city, in 1864. In the preface by Mr. Wilson the statement is made, "Scrupulous fidelity has been maintained throughout this version in giving the true rendering of the original text into English; no regard whatever being paid to the prevailing doctrines or prejudices of sects, or the peculiar tenets of theologians." Critical study of the *Diaglott* bears out the general truthfulness of this claim. Even the Alphabetical Appendix is quite free from common religious errors; and this may be attributed to the following fact: Mr. Wilson was reportedly a Christadelphian. Christadelphians believe the organized churches are apostate, do not believe in the "trinity", do not believe in the "inherent immortality of the soul" or in "eternal torment", but hold that eternal death is the punishment awaiting the wicked.

Though free from these basic errors, they are in bondage to religion, and there are isolated instances where Mr. Wilson's religious leanings seem to influence his work to some slight extent. But the very plan and arrangement of his work serves as a check on this score, as we shall later see. Mr. Wilson knew of the truth, and it is reported that he at one time attended some of the meetings of Jehovah's people, but disagreed on certain fundamental issues. His work was used more extensively by Jehovah's witnesses than any other group, and in course of time the copyright and plates and publication rights were bought from Fowler & Wells Co. and presented to the Society, and today *The Emphatic Diaglott* is published exclusively by its owners, the Watch Tower Bible and Tract Society.

The author's preface briefly lists the provisions of the *Diaglott,* saying, "These features are: An approved Greek text, with the various readings of the Vatican Manuscript No. 1209; an interlineary literal word-for-word English translation; a new version, with the signs of emphasis; a copious selection of references; many appropriate, illustrative, and exegetical footnotes; and a valuable Alphabetical Appendix." In addition to the preface, the introductory material of the *Diaglott* contains a concise history of the Greek text, a history of English versions, a statement to the reader (in which it is shown that, due to the availability of older manuscripts, the *Diaglott* translation is able to correct many errors that appear in the Authorized Version), an outline of the plan of the work, an explanation of the signs of emphasis used in the emphatic English translation, and the letters and pronunciation of the Greek alphabet, along with a few elementary rules of Greek grammar. It is a primary requisite for the student to thoroughly study all this introductory material if he is

Consolation, Nov. 8, 1944, p. 26.

BIBLES AND CONCORDANCES

Distributed by
Watchtower Bible and Tract Society of New York, Inc.
117 Adams St., Brooklyn, N.Y. 11201

WATCHTOWER BIBLE EDITIONS

New World Translation of the Holy Scriptures. A revised and refined text of the *New World Translation of the Holy Scriptures*. It is an entirely new translation of Hebrew and Greek texts. While maintaining the accuracy of a literal translation, it follows modern English usage. Of interest is its use of God's revealed name, Jehovah, throughout. This complete Bible edition is printed in clear, legible type, two columns to the page. A sample of the type and style is at the right. It has a comprehensive concordance, appendix and maps; hardbound green cover with gold-embossed title, special Bible paper, 1472 pages, size 7 5/16" x 4 7/8" x 1 1/8".

Bible bi12 .... $1.00
Deluxe edition (Dbi12) Black or maroon $2.50
Pocket edition (bi24) flexible brown cover, 6 1/2" x 4 1/2" x 1" $1.50

New World Translation of the Holy Scriptures (Original edition) (bi8). It has copious marginal references, chain references, footnotes, a foreword, an appendix, maps and illustrations. 2 3/8" thick. 6 volumes in 1. 3648 pages. (A sample of the print is at the right.) $4.50

New World Translation (Individual volumes)
Regular edition $1.00
Deluxe edition $3.00
Volume I (bi4). The first eight books of the Hebrew Scriptures, Genesis to Ruth.
Volume II (bi5). The historical books of the Hebrew Scriptures from 1 Samuel to Esther.
Volume III (bi-ps). The poetic books of the Hebrew Scriptures, Job to The Song of Solomon.
Volume IV (bi-isa). Isaiah to Lamentations of Jeremiah.
Volume V (bi6). Ezekiel to Malachi.
Christian Greek Scriptures (bi7). Matthew to Revelation.

Other languages. **New World Translation of the Christian Greek Scriptures.** Matthew to Revelation. Available in Dutch, French, German, Italian, Portuguese and Spanish. Regular edition only .... 50c.

1289 Critical times. Scriptures inspired **2 TIMOTHY 3:1—4:14**

3 But know this, that in the last days critical times hard to deal with will be here. 2 For men will be lovers of themselves, lovers of money, self-assuming, haughty, blasphemers, disobedient to parents, unthankful, disloyal, 3 having no natural affection, not open to any

ficial for teaching, for reproving, for setting things straight, for disciplining in righteousness, 17 that the man of God may be fully competent, completely equipped for every good work.

4 I solemnly charge you before God and Christ Jesus, who is

ºMt 21:31 •Mt 9:2 Mr 2:5 ⊕Isa 53:3 Mt 9:3 Mr 2:7 Lu 5:21 ⊖Lu 18:8 •Mt 9:22 Mr 5:34 Mr 10:52 Lu 8:48 Lu 17:19 Lu 18:42 ª1Sa 1:17 •Mt 9:35 Lu 4:43 ▭Mt 27:55 Mr 15:40 Ac 1:14

little."º 48 Then he said to her: "Your sins are
forgiven."• 49 At this those reclining at the
table with him started to say within themselves: "Who is this man who even forgives
sins?"⊕ 50 But he said to the woman: "Your
faith⊖ has saved you;• go your way in peace."ª
8 Shortly afterwards he went journeying from
city to city and from village to village,
preaching and declaring the good news of the
kingdom of God.• And the twelve were with
him, 2 and certain women▭ that had been cured

ª One de.nar′i.us equaled 17c or 8d. 2f. Hence five hundred de.nar′i.i equaled $85, or about £17.

Emphatic Diaglott. New Testament only. The Diaglott is a Greek New Testament, built on the Griesbach recension, with footnotes showing variations in the Alexandrine and Vatican No. 1209 texts, two of the oldest MSS. Besides the Greek text there is an interlinear word-for-word translation under each line, and also an arranged translation in a separate column. We consider this to be among the most accurate translations of the New Testament extant, and believe the book to be an almost indispensable aid to careful study. The printing is in a clear though smallface type and on Bible paper. New edition, 7 5/16" x 4 7/8" x 7/8", bound in beautiful blue leatherette, gold-embossed cover.

Diaglott $2.00

Chap. 3:13.] JOHN. [*Chap.* 3:22.

λῆται, ἀλλ'] ἔχη ζωὴν αἰώνιον. 16Οὕτω
be destroyed, but] may have life age-lasting. Thus
γὰρ ἠγάπησεν ὁ Θεὸς τὸν κόσμον, ὥστε
for loved the God the world, so that
τὸν υἱὸν αὐτοῦ τὸν μονογενῆ ἔδωκεν,
the son of himself the only-begotten he gave,
ἵνα πᾶς ὁ πιστεύων εἰς αὐτόν, μὴ ἀπό-
that every one who believing into him, not may
ληται, ἀλλ' ἔχῃ ζωὴν αἰώνιον. 17Οὐ
be destroyed, but may have life age-lasting. Not
γὰρ ἀπέστειλεν ὁ Θεὸς τὸν υἱὸν αὐτοῦ
for sent the God the son of himself
εἰς τὸν κόσμον, ἵνα κρίνῃ τὸν κόσμον, ἀλλ'
into the world, that he might judge the world, but
ἵνα σωθῇ ὁ κόσμος δι' αὐτοῦ. 18'Ο
that might be saved the world through him. He

16 ‡For GOD so loved the WORLD, that he gave •his SON, the ONLY-BEGOTTEN, that EVERY ONE BELIEVING into him may not perish, but obtain aionian Life.

17 ‡For GOD sent not his SON into the WORLD that he might judge the WORLD, but that the WORLD through him might be saved.

18 ‡HE BELIEVING into him is not judged; but HE

American Standard Version Bible of 1901. This version ranks with the best of the modern Bible translations, and the WATCHTOWER edition presents it without any alterations and with all its valuable footnotes. The value and usefulness of this version, however, have been added to in the WATCHTOWER edition in that our edition appends a 95-page cyclopedic concordance of words, expressions and phrases found in the version, and also four new maps (two in color). Our edition is the first to present this concordance feature. The Bible is bound in light-brown leatherette, gold-stamped, 7 5/16" x 4 7/8" x 1 3/8".

Bible bi11 .... $1.00
Bible bi11, thumb indexed $1.75

American Standard, pocket edition, blue leatherette, 6 1/4" x 4 1/8" x 1 1/8".
Bible bi22 .... $1.50

THE ACTS 17.1—24 **152**

Paul and Silas are sent to Berea. Paul at Athens. His Speech

17 Now when they had passed through Ăm-phĭp′ŏ-lĭs and Ăp-ŏl-lō-nī′ā, they came to Thĕs-să-lō-nī′că, where was a synagogue of the Jews: 2 and Paul, as his custom was, went in unto them, and for three ¹sabbath days reasoned with them from the scriptures, 3 opening and alleging that it behooved the Christ to suffer, and to rise again from the dead; and that this Jē′sŭs, whom, *said*

they came thither likewise, stirring up and troubling the multitudes. 14 And then immediately the brethren sent forth Paul to go as far as to the sea: and Sī′lăs and Tĭm′ŏ-thȳ abode there still. 15 But they that conducted Paul brought him as far as Ăth′ĕns: and receiving a commandment unto Sī′lăs and Tĭm′ŏ-thȳ that they should come to him with all speed, they departed.

Authorized (King James) Version. This Bible edition is handsomely bound in maroon leatherette. The size is 7 5/16" x 4 7/8" x 1 1/8". The Bible text is that of the popular King James Version, unchanged, and printed in minion type, with handy marginal references, and with maps. Among other features, it contains an extensive list of Bible names and expressions and their meanings; also a 59-page concordance of key Bible words and phrases, as well as a further section containing fully quoted texts grouped under various headings showing what God's Word teaches on such subjects.

Bible bi10 .... $1.00
Bible bi10, thumb indexed $1.75

Paul preaches at Corinth. **THE ACTS, 18, 19.**

which *was* Dī-ŏ-nȳs′ĭus the Ăr-ĕ-ŏp′-ă-gīte, and a woman named Dăm′-ă-rĭs, and others with them.

CHAPTER 18.

3 Paul labouring with his hands, and preaching at Corinth, 9 is encouraged in a vision.

AFTER these things Paul departed from Ăth′ĕns, and came to Cŏr′inth;
2 And found a certain Jew named

A. D. 65.
CHAP. 18.
ª 1 Cor. 16. 19. 2 Tim. 4. 19.
ᵇ 1 Cor. 4. 12. 1 Thess. 2. 9.
ᶜ ch. 17. 14.
ᵈ Job 33. 16.

and names, and *of* your law, look ye *to it;* for I will be no judge of such *matters*.
16 And he drave them from the judgment seat.
17 Then all the Greeks took ª Sŏs′-thĕ-nēs, the chief ruler of the synagogue, and beat *him* before the judgment seat. And Găl′lĭ-ō cared for none of those things.

C-9 9.64

Printed in U.S.A.

Bibles and Concordances, Sept. 1964, form #C–9.

eminent critics, and on the various readings of the Vatican MS. No. 1209, a fourth-century manuscript. For the most part it is very good. (He frequently uses the name *Jehovah.*) However, if the Theocratic minister, reading along in Mr. Wilson's emphatic translation, finds something that does not agree with what the Bible teaches elsewhere, he can check up on Mr. Wilson by shifting the eye to the left-hand column and noting the word-for-word translation, and even in some cases going to the untranslated Greek text to settle the matter.

That controversial text of John 1: 1 well illustrates the value of the features the interlinear and signs of emphasis. In the *Diaglott* John 1: 1 reads: "In the beginning was the Logos, and the Logos was with GOD, and the Logos was God." This seems to support the view of trinitarians. But the interlinear translation says: "In a beginning was the Word, and the Word was with the God, and a god was the Word." This clears up the difficulty. The introductory matter explaining the signs of emphasis says: "The Greek article often finds its equivalent in the English definite article *the,* but in the majority of cases it is evidently only a mark of emphasis. . . . Those words rendered positively emphatic by the presence of the Greek article are printed in small capitals." The emphatic translation of John 1: 1 prints the first occurrence of the word "GOD" in capital and small capital letters, thereby showing the reader that it is "the God" being referred to; whereas in the second occurrence, "the Logos was God," the word "God" is written with a capital and lower-case letters, thereby showing that the Logos was not "the GOD" but "a God", or mighty one.

How will the Greek text aid in a critical study of the *Diaglott?* The Catholic Hierarchy claims that the church is built on Peter. They cite Matthew 16: 18. Mr. Wilson's emphatic translation in the right-hand column reads (Jesus speaking to Peter): "Thou art a Rock, and on this ROCK I will build my church." The interlinear does not clear up the matter, the term "rock" being used both times.

Theocratic Aid to Kingdom Publishers, 1945, p. 268.

PART 5

BACK TO JOHN 1:1, 2

EVEN at the end of his first letter to Christians the apostle John brings us to the same understanding, namely, that Jesus Christ is the Son of God and that humans begotten of God are children of God with Jesus Christ. *An American Translation* presents the end of John's letter as follows: "We know that no child of God commits sin, but that he who was born of God protects him, and the evil one cannot touch him. We know that we are children of God, while the whole world is in the power of the evil one. And we know that the Son of God has come, and has given us power to recognize him who is true; and we are in union with him who is true." How? "Through his Son, Jesus Christ. He is the true God and eternal life. Dear children, keep away from idols."—1 John 5:18-21, *AT; RS.*

59 Since the One of whom Jesus Christ is the Son is "the true God and eternal life," and since Jesus Christ is "he who was born of God" and who protects God's other children, how are we to understand John 1:1, 2, of which there are differing translations? Many translations read: "And the Word was with God, and the Word was God." Others read: "And the Word (the Logos) was divine." Another: "And the Word was god." Others: "And the Word was a god." Since we have examined so much of what John wrote about Jesus who was the Word made flesh, we are now in position to determine which of those several translations is correct. It means our salvation.

58. To what understanding regarding Jesus Christ does John bring us at the end of his first letter to Christians?
59. How do various translations of John 1:1 read, but now what are we in position to determine?

52

"The Word"—Who Is He? According to John, 1962, p. 52.

ΚΑΤΑ ΙΩΑΝΗΝ

ACCORDING TO JOHN

1 Ἐν ἀρχῇ ἦν ὁ λόγος, καὶ ὁ λόγος
In beginning was the Word, and the Word
ἦν πρὸς τὸν θεόν, καὶ θεὸς ἦν ὁ λόγος.
was toward the God, and god was the Word.
2 Οὗτος ἦν ἐν ἀρχῇ πρὸς τὸν θεόν.
This (one) was in beginning toward the God.
3 πάντα δι' αὐτοῦ ἐγένετο, καὶ
All (things) through him came to be, and
χωρὶς αὐτοῦ ἐγένετο οὐδὲ ἕν.
apart from him came to be not-but one (thing).
ὃ γέγονεν 4 ἐν αὐτῷ ζωὴ ἦν, καὶ
Which has come to be in him life was, and
ἡ ζωὴ ἦν τὸ φῶς τῶν ἀνθρώπων· 5 καὶ
the life was the light of the men; and
τὸ φῶς ἐν τῇ σκοτίᾳ φαίνει, καὶ ἡ
the light in the darkness is shining, and the
σκοτία αὐτὸ οὐ κατέλαβεν.
darkness it not overpowered.
6 Ἐγένετο ἄνθρωπος ἀπεσταλμένος
Came to be man having been sent forth
παρὰ θεοῦ, ὄνομα αὐτῷ Ἰωάνης·
beside God, name to him John;
7 οὗτος ἦλθεν εἰς
this (one) came into
μαρτυρίαν, ἵνα μαρτυρήσῃ
witness, in order that he might witness
περὶ τοῦ φωτός, ἵνα πάντες
about the light, in order that all
πιστεύσωσιν δι' αὐτοῦ. 8 οὐκ ἦν
might believe through him. Not was
ἐκεῖνος τὸ φῶς, ἀλλ' ἵνα
that (one) the light, but in order that
μαρτυρήσῃ περὶ τοῦ φωτός.
he might witness about the light.
9 Ἦν τὸ φῶς τὸ ἀληθινὸν
Was the light the true
ὃ φωτίζει πάντα ἄνθρωπον
which is enlightening every man
ἐρχόμενον εἰς τὸν κόσμον. 10 ἐν
coming into the world. In

1 In [the] beginning
the Word was,
and the Word was
with God, and the
Word was a god.[a]
2 This one was in
[the] beginning with
God. 3 All things came
into existence through
him, and apart from
him not even one
thing came into existence.

What has come into
existence 4 by means
of him was life, and
the life was the light
of men. 5 And the
light is shining in
the darkness, but
the darkness has not
overpowered it.

6 There arose a man
that was sent forth
as a representative of
God: his name was
John.[b] 7 This [man]
came for a witness,
in order to bear witness
about the light,
that people of all sorts
might believe through
him. 8 He was not
that light, but he was
meant to bear witness
about that light.

9 The true light that
gives light to every
sort of man was
about to come into
the world.[c] 10 He

1[a] "A god." In contrast with "the God." See Appendix under John 1:1.
6[b] See Matthew 3:1, footnote[a]. 9[c] World=κόσμος (*kos'mos*), אBA; עולם
(*o·lahm'*), J[17,18].

The Kingdom Interlinear Translation of the Greek Scriptures, 1969, p. 417.

Thus each great class of documentary evidence supplies valuable testimony both for the investigation of the history of the text as a whole and for the determination of the true text in detail.

Greek MSS

The Greek MSS of the New Testament are usually divided into two classes, conventionally known as 'Uncials' and 'Cursives', according as they are written in capital letters or in a more or less running hand. For the sake of brevity it is customary to distinguish Uncials by capital letters (ABC &c.; ΓΔΘ &c.; ℵ), and Cursives for the most part by arabic numerals (1, 2, 3, 4, 13, 22, 33 &c.).

At the head of the list of Uncials stand four great MSS belonging to the fourth and fifth centuries, which contained when complete both the Old and the New Testaments. They are

B, *Codex Vaticanus*, at Rome, containing the whole New Testament except the later chapters of Hebrews, the Pastoral Epistles, Philemon, and the Apocalypse.

ℵ, *Codex Sinaiticus*, at St Petersburg, containing the entire New Testament. Discovered by Tischendorf in 1859 in the convent on Mount Sinai.

A, *Codex Alexandrinus*, in the British Museum, containing all, except about the first 24 chapters of St Matthew's and two leaves of St John's Gospel and three of 2 Corinthians. Preserved at Alexandria from at least the end of the eleventh century. Presented to Charles I in 1628 by Cyril Lucar, Patriarch of Constantinople.

C, *Codex Ephraemi rescriptus*, at Paris, containing nearly three fifths of the whole, part of almost every book being preserved. A 'palimpsest', the original writing having been partially washed out, and Greek translations of works of Ephrem Syrus written over.

B. F. Westcott and F.J.A. Hort, *The New Testament in the Original Greek*, 1885, p. 567.

54 "THE WORD"—WHO IS HE? ACCORDING TO JOHN

tristic Gospels—An English Version of the holy Gospels as they existed in the Second Century," by Roslyn D'Onston. The title page tells how this version was put together. In John 1:1 this version reads: "and the Word was God." But it has this footnote: *"The true reading here is, probably,* of God. *See* Critical Note." —Page 118.*

[63] Now why is it that translators disagree as to what the Word was—"God," or, "god," or, "a god"? It is because the Greek word for "God" is at the beginning of the statement although it belongs to the predicate, and it also does not have the definite article "the" in front of it. Below, to illustrate this, we give on the first set of lines the Greek text according to the fourth-century uncial manuscripts; and then on the second line, how the Greek text is pronounced in our language today; and on the third line a word-for-word English translation. Note Greek abbreviations for "God."

ΕΝ	ΑΡΧΗ	ΗΝ	Ο	ΛΟΓΟϹ	ΚΑΙ	Ο	ΛΟΓΟϹ
EN	ARKHEI	ĒN	HO	LOGOS,	KAI	HO	LOGOS
IN	BEGINNING	WAS	THE	WORD,	AND	THE	WORD

ΗΝ	ΠΡΟϹ	ΤΟΝ	Θ̄Ν	ΚΑΙ	Θ̄Ϲ	ΗΝ	Ο	ΛΟΓΟϹ
ĒN	PROS	TON	THN,	KAI	THS	ĒN	HO	LOGOS.
WAS	WITH	THE	GOD,	AND	GOD	WAS	THE	WORD.

ΟΥΤΟϹ	ΗΝ	ΕΝ	ΑΡΧΗ	ΠΡΟϹ	ΤΟΝ	Θ̄Ν
HOUTOS	ĒN	EN	ARKHEI	PROS	TON	THN.
THIS	WAS	IN	BEGINNING	WITH	THE	GOD.

[*Continued from page 53*] Tenth Century; the 26 Old Latin (Italic) Versions of the Second Century; the Vulgate; 24 Greek uncials and some cursives; the Syriac, Egyptian, and other ancient versions and corrected by comparing all the critical Greek texts from Stephanus (A.D. 1550) to Westcott and Hort, 1881; all the English versions from Wiclif (Fourteenth Century) to the American Baptist Version of 1883; as well as every commentator English and Foreign, who has ever suggested a practicable rendering.—London: Grant Richards, 48 Leicester Square, 1904."

* This Critical Note for John 1:1, found on page 156, says: "There are three distinct reasons for believing 'of God' to be the true reading. First, the manuscripts, as stated in that Note; secondly, the logical argument, because if the Evangelist meant 'was God,' there would have been no occasion for the next verse; thirdly, the grammatical construction of the sentence: for 'was God,' would he not have written *ho lógos ēn theós,* which would, at any rate, have been more elegant? But if we read it, *kai theoû ēn ho lógos,* the *theoû* is in its proper place in the sentence. I have refrained from correcting the text of this passage at the express desire of the late Bishop Westcott."

The Greek word *theoû* means "of God."

63. Why does the wording of John 1:1 in the Greek text make translators disagree as to what the Word was?

"The Word"—Who Is He? According to John, 1962, p. 54.

from one's labor, saying: "Look! The best thing that I myself have seen, which is pretty, is that one should eat and drink and see good for all his hard work with which he works hard under the sun for the number of the days of his life that the true God has given him, for that is his portion."—Eccl. 5:18.

Commenting on the good effect this has upon the individual, Solomon states: "Also every man to whom the true God has given riches and material possessions, he has even empowered him to eat from it and to carry off his portion and to rejoice in his hard work. This is the gift of God. For not often will he remember the days of his life, because the true God is preoccupying him with the rejoicing of his heart." —Eccl. 5:19, 20.

The man who recognizes his prosperity as a gift from God will not hoard riches but will use them to bring joy to others. Such a man has a balanced view of his possessions because of allowing himself to be guided by godly wisdom. Therefore, he gets personal enjoyment from what he has. Jehovah God has empowered him to find pleasure in food and drink in the sense that he grants the individual the wisdom to use material things properly. At the same time such an individual is not unduly concerning himself with the brevity of life and its problems and uncertainties. No, he is getting so much enjoyment from doing good in his life that the negative aspects do not dominate his thinking. He is joyful at heart.

Surely one's striving to get wholesome enjoyment in life is the wise course. It shields one from the disappointment experienced by those whose life is fully occupied by materialistic pursuits.

● In John 1:1 the term "god" is applied to both the Father and the Son, the Word. But in the Greek text the word for "god" (*theos*) is written differently in these two instances. Why? What does it mean?

To a person unfamiliar with the Greek language it might seem that there is a significance indicated by the fact that first the word is spelled *theon* and next *theos*. But the difference is simply a matter of complying with the Greek grammatical case used.

John 1:1 reads: "In [the] beginning the Word was, and the Word was with God [τὸν θεὸν, literally, the god], and the Word was a god [θεὸς]."

Greek has five cases—nominative, genitive, dative, accusative and vocative. How a word is spelled can vary depending on the case in which it is used. Take, as an example, the definite article "the." In the masculine gender "the" is respectively written in the first four of these cases: ὁ, τοῦ, τῷ, τὸν, in the singular number.

Similarly, in John 1:1 the word *theos* is spelled in accord with the particular case being employed. In the first instance ("the Word was with God") it is in the accusative case and thus is spelled θεὸν. But in the second occurrence it is in the nominative case, and so it is spelled θεὸς. The spelling of *theos* does not of itself indicate the person or position of the one designated, as 2 Corinthians 4:4, 6 illustrates. In verse four Satan is identified as θεὸς, "the god of this system of things," and in verse six the Creator is designated θεὸς. The spelling is *theos* in both verses, for the nominative case is used in each. So the fact that *theos* is spelled differently in its two occurrences in John 1:1 does not show any difference in meaning; "god" is the meaning in both instances.

What is interesting is that in John 1:1 the definite article ὁ [*ho*] is not used in front of *theos* when applied to the Son, the Word. Re-

THE WATCHTOWER — MAY 15, 1977 319

The Watchtower, May 15, 1977, p. 319.

JOHN 3: 9—16 428

γεγεννημένος ἐκ τοῦ πνεύματος.
having been generated out of the spirit.
9 ἀπεκρίθη Νικόδημος καὶ εἶπεν αὐτῷ
Answered Nicodemus and he said to him
Πῶς δύναται ταῦτα γενέσθαι;
How is able these (things) to occur?
10 ἀπεκρίθη Ἰησοῦς καὶ εἶπεν αὐτῷ Σὺ
Answered Jesus and said to him You
εἶ ὁ διδάσκαλος τοῦ Ἰσραὴλ καὶ
are the teacher of the Israel and
ταῦτα οὐ γινώσκεις; 11 ἀμὴν
these (things) not you are knowing? Amen
ἀμὴν λέγω σοι ὅτι ὃ οἴδαμεν
amen I am saying to you that which we have known
λαλοῦμεν καὶ ὃ ἑωράκαμεν
we are speaking and which we have seen
μαρτυροῦμεν, καὶ τὴν μαρτυρίαν
we are bearing witness of, and the witness
ἡμῶν οὐ λαμβάνετε. 12 εἰ τὰ
of us not YOU are receiving. If the
ἐπίγεια εἶπον ὑμῖν καὶ οὐ
earthly (things) I said to YOU and not
πιστεύετε, πῶς ἐὰν εἴπω ὑμῖν
YOU are believing, how if ever I should say to YOU
τὰ ἐπουράνια πιστεύσετε; 13 καὶ
the heavenly (things) YOU will believe? And
οὐδεὶς ἀναβέβηκεν εἰς τὸν οὐρανὸν εἰ μὴ
no one has ascended into the heaven if not
ὁ ἐκ τοῦ οὐρανοῦ καταβάς,
the (one) out of the heaven having descended,
ὁ υἱὸς τοῦ ἀνθρώπου. 14 καὶ καθὼς
the Son of the man. And according as
Μωυσῆς ὕψωσεν τὸν ὄφιν ἐν τῇ
Moses put high up the serpent in the
ἐρήμῳ, οὕτως ὑψωθῆναι
desolate [place], thus to be put on high up
δεῖ τὸν υἱὸν τοῦ ἀνθρώπου,
it is necessary the Son of the man,
15 ἵνα πᾶς ὁ πιστεύων ἐν αὐτῷ
in order that everyone the believing in him
ἔχῃ ζωὴν αἰώνιον.
may have life everlasting.
16 Οὕτως γὰρ ἠγάπησεν ὁ θεὸς τὸν
Thus for loved the God the
κόσμον ὥστε τὸν υἱὸν τὸν μονογενῆ
world as-and the Son the only-begotten
ἔδωκεν, ἵνα πᾶς ὁ πιστεύων
he gave, in order that everyone the believing

has been born from
the spirit."
9 In answer Nic-
o·de′mus said to
him: "How can these
things come about?"
10 In answer Je-
sus said to him:
"Are you a teach-
er of Israel and yet
do not know these
things? 11 Most truly
I say to you, What
we know we speak
and what we have
seen we bear wit-
ness of, but YOU
people do not re-
ceive the witness
we give. 12 If I have
told YOU earthly
things and yet YOU do
not believe, how will
YOU believe if I
tell YOU heavenly
things? 13 Moreover,
no man has ascend-
ed into heaven but
he that descended
from heaven, the
Son of man. 14 And
just as Moses lift-
ed up the serpent
in the wilderness,
so the Son of man
must be lifted up,
15 that everyone
believing in him may
have everlasting
life.
16 "For God loved
the world[a] so much
that he gave his
only-begotten Son,
in order that every-
one exercising faith

16[a] World=κόσμος (*kos′mos*), ℵBA; עולם (*o·lahm′*), J[17,18].

The Kingdom Interlinear Translation of the Greek Scriptures, 1969, p. 428.

A NEW INTERLINEAR TRANSLATION

[10] And now, in this year 1969 at the "Peace on Earth" International Assemblies of Jehovah's Witnesses, there is released to the reading public *The Kingdom Interlinear Translation of the Greek Scriptures.* This is a clothbound book of 1,184 pages. The Greek text that it uses is that prepared and published by Westcott and Hort in 1881. Underneath this is printed a literal word-for-word translation. In the right-hand column alongside on each page is presented the modern-day translation as found in the *New World Translation of the Holy Scriptures* in a revised edition. However, in the interlinear literal translation of the Greek the English words are not taken bodily or directly from the *New World Translation* and placed under the appropriate Greek word. No! But under each Greek word is placed its basic meaning, according to its grammatical construction, whether this agrees literally with the *New World Translation* or not. What we as Bible students should want is what the original Greek text says. Only by getting this basic meaning can we determine whether the *New World Translation* or any other Bible translation is right or not.

[11] For example, in Matthew 8:5 the *New World Translation* uses the expression "army officer" but in the interlinear translation under the Greek word you read "centurion," because that is what the Greek text literally calls this army man. In Mark 6:21 the words "military commanders" are found, but under the Greek word you read "chiliarchs," meaning a commander of a thousand soldiers, for that is what the Greek word literally calls this army officer. In Acts 19:41 the *New World Translation* has the word "assembly," but the interlinear reading says "ecclesia," like the Greek. In this particular verse it does not mean a "church" or "congregation," as the word does elsewhere. Thus we learn more specific details.

[12] *The Kingdom Interlinear Translation* contains and preserves for us both the Foreword and the Appendix as found in the *New World Translation of the Christian Greek Scriptures,* as published in the year 1950. These two features are very vital, because *The Kingdom Interlinear Translation* contains footnotes that refer the reader to such Foreword and Appendix and also to an Explanation of the Symbols Used in the Marginal References. For instance, those footnotes will refer you to the Foreword in order that you may learn why, in the *New World Translation,* the divine name Jehovah appears in its translation of the Greek Scriptures.

[13] Of course, the Westcott and Hort text does not contain God's name Jehovah or Yahweh by itself. But in Revelation 19:1, 3, 4, 6 the Greek text does contain the word *Hallelouiá* and beneath this Greek word each time the interlinear translation renders it literally "Hallelujah." This is really a Hebrew phrase and it means "Praise YOU Jah," this word "Jah" being an abbreviation for Jehovah. Hence the *New World Translation* in the right-hand column renders it, "Praise Jah, YOU people!" In other places where the *New World Translation* uses the divine name Jehovah, the interlinear literal translation puts "God," or "Lord," or "the Lord," under the corresponding words in the Westcott and Hort Greek text. But the footnotes

10. (a) What new interlinear translation was released at the "Peace on Earth" International Assemblies of Jehovah's Witnesses in 1969, and what are its features? (b) With it what will we be able to do regarding any translation of the Greek Scriptures?
11. For example, what does the interlinear reading show regarding words such as "army officer," "military commanders" and "assembly"?
12. What features of the *New World Translation of the Christian Greek Scriptures* are preserved in *The Kingdom Interlinear Translation,* and for what vital reasons?
13. What Hebrew phrase does the Westcott and Hort Greek text contain, and how does *The Kingdom Interlinear Translation* render this in its interlinear reading and in the modern-day translation, and with what footnotes?

The Watchtower, Nov. 15, 1969, p. 692.

BY WAY OF EXPLANATION

The inspired Greek Scriptures, completed near the end of the first century of our Common Era, are an indispensable part of the Sacred Scriptures inspired by the Creator of heaven and earth. In fact, the original Greek Scriptures give us the key to the proper understanding of the first and larger part of the Holy Bible, that is, the inspired Hebrew Scriptures commonly called The Old Testament. Comparatively few persons in this latter half of the twentieth century C.E. have studied the original language of the inspired Greek Scriptures so as to be able to pry directly into the basic thoughts of the original written text. The inspired Greek Scriptures were written, not in the ancient classical Greek nor in the modern Greek which dates from the fall of Constantinople in 1453 C.E., but in the common or *koiné* Greek of the first century of our Common Era, the international language of that time. Hence the *koiné* Greek of the divinely inspired Scriptures is a special study in itself.

Sincere searchers for eternal, life-giving truth desire an accurate understanding of the faith-inspiring Greek Scriptures, an understanding that will not be confused by sectarian, denominational religious teachings but that is fortified by the knowledge of what the original language says and means. To aid such seekers of truth and life is the purpose behind the publishing of *The Kingdom Interlinear Translation of the Greek Scriptures.* Its literal interlinear English translation is specially designed to open up to the student of the Sacred Scriptures what the original *koiné* Greek basically or literally says, without any sectarian religious coloration.

In the broad left-hand column of the pages of the main material will be found the original *koiné* Greek text as revised (in 1881 C.E.) by the renowned Greek scholars B. F. Westcott and F. J. A. Hort, and in between the lines of the Greek text will be found the word-for-word English translation. In the slim right-hand column of the page will be found the twentieth-century language translation entitled "New World Translation of the Christian Greek Scriptures," in its latest revision. The word-for-word interlinear translation and the *New World Translation* are arranged parallel on the page, so that comparisons can be made between the two readings and the accuracy of any modern translation can be determined.

For the interlinear word-for-word rendering the English word or phrase has not been taken from the modern translation in the right-hand column and transferred to a position under the Greek word to which it corresponds. Rather, the translation under each Greek word sets out what the Greek word itself says according to its root meanings (where the Greek word is made up of two or more particles) and according to its grammatical form. So in many cases the reading in the English word-for-word interlinear translation is not the same as that found in the right-hand column. This aids us in determining what the Greek text actually, basically says.

5

The Kingdom Interlinear Translation of the Greek Scriptures, 1969, p. 5.

The "Perfect" Translation—John 8:58

John 8:58 reads, "Jesus said to them, 'Truly, truly, I say to you, before Abraham was born, I AM.' " Here we find that Jesus reveals himself to be the eternally existent One. The "I AM" in this verse is what has been called "in the style of deity," as it is found so often on the lips of God in the Old Testament. As we read on, we find Chris and Jay discussing the "special attention" the NWT has given to this verse.

Chris: I noticed that the NWT of John 8:58 is different than my Bible.

Jay: You're right, Chris. While other translations are biased by the doctrine of the Trinity and read, "Before Abraham was, I am," the NWT says, "Before Abraham came into existence, I have been." (See p. 209.)

Chris: That little change from "I am" to "I have been" makes a big difference.

Jay: It sure does, Chris. Instead of what Christendom teaches, that Jesus is Jehovah, the NWT shows the real idea. Jesus was simply saying He had existed for a long time. You see, Jews didn't realize that Jesus had existed as Michael the Archangel before He came to earth.

Chris: Do you think lack of bias is the only reason the NWT has translated the Greek words *ego eimi* as "I have been"?

Jay: I don't mean to boast, but I think the Watchtower answers that very question when it says, "The *New World Translation* gives special attention to conveying the sense of the action of the Greek and Hebrew verbs." (See p. 210.)

Chris: That is really interesting, Jay. But I think you'll be even more interested when I show you the "special attention" the NWT has given to the verb in John 8:58.

Jay: What kind of "special attention"?

Chris: For instance, in the 1950 edition of the NWT, the footnote for John 8:58 explains that *ego eimi* has been "properly rendered in the perfect indefinite tense." (See p. 211.)

Jay: Well, so . . .

Chris: Well, Jay, there is no such thing as a "perfect indefinite tense"! The New World translators made up a phony tense to cover up for their interpretation. I'd call that very special attention.

Jay: I must say, if that's true, I am disappointed. But I don't think our newer translations say that anymore.

Chris: You're right again. In the 1971 large print NWT, the identity of the verb has been changed. Now *eimi* is supposed to be "properly rendered in the perfect tense indicative." (See p. 212.)

Jay: There you are, Chris. One thing I hope you learn is that when the Watchtower makes a mistake, it's not too proud to add something new or make a change.

Chris: Admitting an honest mistake is one thing, but I seriously question their scholastic honesty.

Jay: What do you mean?

Chris: The Society not only invented a phony tense to hide the truth, but it is still lying in order to justify its translation.

Jay: I still don't know what you're talking about.

Chris: What I am driving at is that while there is a perfect tense in Greek, there is no perfect tense form of *eimi* in the entire New Testament!

Jay: Then Jesus couldn't have been saying "I have been" like the NWT says?

Chris: Right. *Eimi* is really a simple present tense of the verb "to be." What Jesus said is "I AM." The NWT correctly translates the verb "to be" in the surrounding verses. (See pp. 213, 214.) It's just here, in verse 58, where they object to Jesus' claim of deity, that they want the reader to think differently.

Jay: Wow! No wonder the NWT is different than other translations.

The Watchtower has gone to great lengths to deny the deity of our Lord Jesus. They have continually dodged the issue in order to justify their abhorrent translation. Perhaps the Proverb is found true, "Every word of God is tested; He is a shield to those who take refuge in Him. Do not add to His words lest He reprove you, and you be proved a liar" (Prov. 30:5, 6).

JOHN 8:55—9:25 **Before Abraham. Blind man healed. Investigation** **1164**

rify myself, my glory is nothing. It
is my Father that glorifies me, he
who YOU say is YOUR God; **55** and
yet YOU have not known him. But
I know him. And if I said I do not
know him I should be like YOU, a
liar. But I do know him and am
observing his word. **56** Abraham
YOUR father rejoiced greatly in the
prospect of seeing my day, and he
saw it and rejoiced." **57** Therefore
the Jews said to him: "You are not
yet fifty years old, and still you have
seen Abraham?" **58** Jesus said to
them: "Most truly I say to YOU, Before Abraham came into existence,
I have been." **59** Therefore they
picked up stones to hurl [them] at
him; but Jesus hid and went out of
the temple.

9 Now as he was passing along
he saw a man blind from birth.
2 And his disciples asked him: "Rabbi, who sinned, this man or his parents, so that he was born blind?"
3 Jesus answered: "Neither this
man sinned nor his parents, but
it was in order that the works of
God might be made manifest in his
case. **4** We must work the works
of him that sent me while it is day;
the night is coming when no man
can work. **5** As long as I am in
the world, I am the world's light."
6 After he said these things, he
spit on the ground and made a clay
with the saliva, and put his clay
upon the [man's] eyes **7** and said
to him: "Go wash in the pool of
Si·lo'am" (which is translated 'Sent
forth'). And so he went off and
washed, and came back seeing.

8 Therefore the neighbors and
those who formerly used to see he
was a beggar began to say: "This is
the man that used to sit and beg, is
it not?" **9** Some would say: "This
is he." Others would say: "Not at
all, but he is like him." The man
would say: "I am [he]." **10** Consequently they began to say to
him: "How, then, were your eyes
opened?" **11** He answered: "The
man called Jesus made a clay and
smeared [it] on my eyes and said
to me, 'Go to Si·lo'am and wash.'
I therefore went and washed and
gained sight." **12** At this they said
to him: "Where is that [man]?" He
said: "I do not know."

13 They led the once-blind man
himself to the Pharisees. **14** Incidentally it was Sabbath on the day
that Jesus made the clay and opened
his eyes. **15** This time, therefore,
the Pharisees also took up asking
him how he gained sight. He said
to them: "He put a clay upon my
eyes, and I washed and have sight."
16 Therefore some of the Pharisees
began to say: "This is not a man
from God, because he does not observe the Sabbath." Others began
to say: "How can a man that is a
sinner perform signs of that sort?"
So there was a division among
them. **17** Hence they said to the
blind man again: "What do you say
about him, seeing that he opened
your eyes?" The [man] said: "He is
a prophet."

18 However, the Jews did not
believe concerning him that he had
been blind and had gained sight,
until they called the parents of
the man that gained sight. **19** And
they asked them: "Is this YOUR son
who YOU say was born blind? How,
then, is it he sees at present?"
20 Then in answer his parents said:
"We know that this is our son and
that he was born blind. **21** But
how it is he now sees we do not
know, or who opened his eyes we
do not know. ASK him. He is of
age. He must speak for himself."
22 His parents said these things because they were in fear of the Jews,
for the Jews had already come to
an agreement that, if anyone confessed him as Christ, he should
get expelled from the synagogue.
23 This is why his parents said:
"He is of age. QUESTION him."

24 Therefore a second time they
called the man that had been blind
and said to him: "Give glory to God;
we know that this man is a sinner."
25 In turn he answered: "Whether
he is a sinner I do not know. One
thing I do know, that, whereas I was

New World Translation of the Holy Scriptures, 1981 ed.

English meaning for each major Greek word, and to be as literal as possible. The word usually rendered 'justify' is generally translated very correctly as 'declare righteous.' The word for the Cross is rendered 'torture stake' which is another improvement. Luke 23:43 is well rendered, 'Truly I tell you today, You will be with me in Paradise.' This is a big improvement upon the reading of most versions." On the translation of the Hebrew Scriptures, the same reviewer makes this comment: "The New World Version is well worth acquiring. It is lively and lifelike, and makes the reader think and study. It is not the work of Higher Critics, but of scholars who honour God and His Word."—*The Differentiator*, April 1952, pages 52-57, and June 1954, page 136.

10 The consistency of the *New World Translation* has won many a technical Bible discussion in the field. On one occasion, a society of freethinkers in New York asked the Watch Tower Society to send two speakers to address their group on Biblical matters, which request was granted. These learned men held to a Latin maxim, *falsum in uno falsum in toto*, meaning that an argument proved false in one point is totally false. During the discussion, one man challenged Jehovah's witnesses on the reliability of the Bible. He asked that Genesis 1:3 be read to the audience, and this was done, from the *New World Translation:* "And God proceeded to say: 'Let light come to be.' Then there came to be light." Confidently, he next called for Genesis 1:14, and this also was read from the *New World Translation:* "And God went on to say: 'Let luminaries come to be in the expanse of the heavens . . .'" "Stop," he said, "what are you reading? My Bible says God made light on the first day, and again on the fourth day, and that is inconsistent." Though he claimed to know Hebrew, it had to be pointed out to him that the Hebrew word translated "light" in verse 3 was *ōr*, whereas the word in verse 14 was different, being *m'o·roth'*, which means "luminaries." The learned man sat down defeated. The faithful consistency of the *New World Translation* had won the point, upholding the Bible as reliable and beneficial.

CAREFUL VERB RENDERINGS

11 The *New World Translation* gives special attention to conveying the sense of the action of the Greek and Hebrew verbs. In doing so the *New World Translation* endeavors to preserve the peculiar charm, simplicity, forcefulness and manner of expression of the original-language writings. It has thus been necessary to use auxiliary verbs to convey carefully the actual states of the actions. It is due to the power of their verbs that the original Scriptures are so dynamic and so full of action.

12 The Hebrew verb does not have "tenses" in the sense that that term is applied to most languages of the West. In English there are quite a number of tenses, the present, past, future, past perfect, future perfect, and so forth. The Hebrew verb, on the other hand, basically expresses just two "states." These are (1) the "perfect" state, used to speak of an action that is completed, and (2) the "imperfect" state, to describe an action that has begun but has not yet been completed. These states of the Hebrew verb may be used with reference to actions in the past or in the future, the context determining the time. The perfect or completed sense of the verb is used to speak of a future action or state as if it had already occurred and were past, this to show its future certainty or the obligation of it to occur.

13 The conveying of the state of the Hebrew verb accurately into English is most important, otherwise the meaning may be distorted and a completely different thought conveyed. For an example of this, consider some of the expressions in Genesis 2:2, 3. In many translations, speaking of God's resting on the seventh day, the expressions "he rested," "he desisted," "he had desisted," "he then rested," "God rested," and "he had rested" are used. From these readings one would conclude that God's resting on the seventh day was completed in the past, and that the Hebrew verb in this case is therefore in the "perfect" state. But this is not so. Note how the *New World Translation* brings out the sense of the imperfect state of the verb used, and so conveys the accurate understanding of the passage: "And by the seventh day God came to the completion of his work that he had made, and he proceeded to rest on the seventh day from all his work that he had made. And God proceeded to bless the seventh day and make it sacred, because on it he has been resting from all his work that God has created for the purpose of making." So the original Hebrew does not convey the thought that God "rested," that is, completed the action back at that time, but rather conveys the idea of an action commenced and still continuing, not yet completed. The expression "he has been resting" thus gives the right sense.

10. Illustrate how the consistency of this translation upholds Bible truth.
11. What dynamic feature of the original Scriptures is preserved in the *New World Translation*? How?
12. (a) In what does Hebrew differ from Western languages? (b) Explain the two "states" of the Hebrew verb.
13. How does proper regard to state of the Hebrew verb help in a correct understanding of Genesis 2:2, 3?

All Scripture Is Inspired of God and Beneficial, 1963, p. 328.

all."[◊] 52 The Jews said to him: "Now we do
know you have a demon.[a+] Abraham died,[⊕] also
the prophets,[×] but you say, 'If anyone observes
my word, he will never taste[#] death at all.'
53 You are not greater[*] than our father Abraham, who died, are you? Also the prophets
died. Who do you claim to be?" 54 Jesus answered: "If I glorify[□] myself, my glory is nothing. It is my Father that glorifies me, he who
YOU say is YOUR God, 55 and yet YOU have not
known him.[△] But I know him.[◊] And if I said I
do not know[+] him I should be like YOU, a liar.[⊙]
But I do know him and am observing his word.
56 Abraham YOUR father rejoiced[○] greatly in the
prospect of seeing my day,[⊙⊕] and he saw it and
rejoiced."[×] 57 Therefore the Jews said to him:
"You are not yet fifty years old, and still you
have seen Abraham?"[b] 58 Jesus said to them:
"Most truly I say to YOU, Before Abraham[○]
came into existence, I have been."[c#] 59 Therefore they picked up stones to hurl them at
him;[*] but Jesus hid and went out of the temple.
9 Now as he was passing along he saw a man
blind from birth.[□] 2 And his disciples asked
him: "Rabbi, who sinned,[△] this man or his
parents,[◊] so that he was born blind?" 3 Jesus
answered: "Neither this man sinned nor his
parents, but it was in order that the works of
God might be made manifest in his case.[+] 4 We
must work the works of him that sent me while
it is day;[⊕] the night[⊙] is coming when no man

◊Joh 5:24
Joh 11:26
Joh 14:23
+Joh 10:20
⊕Ge 25:8
×Zec 1:5
Ac 2:29
Heb 11:13
#Mt 16:28
*Joh 4:12
□Joh 5:41
Joh 13:32
Ac 3:13
△Joh 7:28
◊Joh 7:29
+Mt 26:72
⊙Ro 3:4
○Ac 13:48
⊙Ac 2:17
⊕Ge 17:17
Ge 22:18
Lu 10:24
×Mt 13:17
Heb 11:13
○Ac 3:13
#Pr 8:22
Joh 17:5
Php 2:6
Col 1:17
Heb 13:8
1Jo 2:13
*Lu 4:29
Joh 10:31
Joh 11:8
□Ac 3:2
Ac 14:8
△Lu 13:2
◊Ex 20:5
+Mt 11:5
Joh 11:4
⊕Joh 4:34
Joh 11:9
⊙Ac 16:9

---

[a] Or, "you are demonized." [b] You have seen Abraham? BAVg; has Abraham seen you? ℵSy[s]. [c] I have been = ἐγώ εἰμί (*e.go′ ei.mi′*) after the a′orist infinitive clause πρὶν Ἀβραὰμ γενέσθαι and hence properly rendered in the perfect indefinite tense. It is not the same as ὁ ὤν (*ho ohn′*, meaning "The Being" or "The I Am") at Exodus 3:14, *LXX*.

New World Translation of the Christian Greek Scriptures, 1950 ed.

taste death at all.' **53** You are not greater than our father Abraham, who died,
are you? Also, the prophets died. Who do
you claim to be?" **54** Jesus answered:
"If I glorify myself, my glory is nothing.
It is my Father that glorifies me, he who
YOU say is YOUR God; **55** and yet YOU
have not known him. But I know him. And
if I said I do not know him I should be like
YOU, a liar. But I do know him and am observing his word. **56** Abraham YOUR father rejoiced greatly in the prospect of
seeing my day, and he saw it and rejoiced." **57** Therefore the Jews said to
him: "You are not yet fifty years old, and
still you have seen Abraham?"* **58** Jesus said to them: "Most truly I say to YOU,
Before Abraham came into existence, I
have been."□ **59** Therefore they picked up
stones to hurl [them] at him; but Jesus
hid and went out of the temple.

9 Now as he was passing along he saw a
man blind from birth. **2** And his disciples asked him: "Rabbi, who sinned, this
man or his parents, so that he was born
blind?" **3** Jesus answered: "Neither this
man sinned nor his parents, but it was in
order that the works of God might be
made manifest in his case. **4** We must
work the works of him that sent me while
it is day; the night is coming when no man
can work. **5** As long as I am in the
world, I am the world's light." **6** After
he said these things, he spit on the ground
and made a clay with the saliva, and put
his clay upon the [man's] eyes **7** and said
to him: "Go wash in the pool of Si·lo'am"△
(which is translated 'Sent forth'). And so
he went off and washed, and came back
seeing.

8 Therefore the neighbors and those
who formerly used to see he was a beggar
began to say: "This is the man that used
to sit and beg, is it not?" **9** Some would
say: "This is he." Others would say: "Not
at all, but he is like him." The man would
say: "I am he." **10** Consequently they
began to say to him: "How, then, were
your eyes opened?" **11** He answered:
"The man called Jesus made a clay and
smeared [it] on my eyes and said to me,
'Go to Si·lo'am△ and wash.' I therefore
went and washed and gained sight."
12 At this they said to him: "Where is
that [man]?" He said: "I do not know."

13 They led the once-blind man himself
to the Pharisees. **14** Incidentally it was
Sabbath on the day that Jesus made the
clay and opened his eyes. **15** This time,
therefore, the Pharisees also took up asking him how he gained sight. He said to
them: "He put a clay upon my eyes, and I
washed and have sight." **16** Therefore
some of the Pharisees began to say: "This
is not a man from God, because he does
not observe the Sabbath." Others began to
say: "How can a man that is a sinner perform signs of that sort?" So there was a
division among them. **17** Hence they said
to the blind man again: "What do you say
about him, seeing that he opened your
eyes?" The [man] said: "He is a prophet."

18 However, the Jews did not believe
concerning him that he had been blind and
had gained sight, until they called the parents of the man that gained sight.
19 And they asked them: "Is this YOUR
son who YOU say was born blind? How,
then, is it he sees at present?" **20** Then
in answer his parents said: "We know that
this is our son and that he was born blind.
21 But how it is he now sees we do not
know, or who opened his eyes we do not
know. ASK him. He is of age. He must
speak for himself." **22** His parents said
these things because they were in fear of
the Jews, for the Jews had already come
to an agreement that, if anyone confessed
him as Christ, he should get expelled from
the synagogue. **23** This is why his parents said: "He is of age. QUESTION him."

24 Therefore a second time they called
the man that had been blind and said to
him: "Give glory to God; we know that
this man is a sinner." **25** In turn he answered: "Whether he is a sinner I do not
know. One thing I do know, that, whereas
I was blind, I see at present." **26** Therefore they said to him: "What did he do to
you? How did he open your eyes?"

* You have seen Abraham? BAVg; has Abraham seen you? ℵSy[s]. □ I have been=ἐγώ εἰμί (*e·go' ei·mi'*) after the a'orist infinitive clause πρὶν 'Αβραὰμ γενέσθαι and hence properly rendered in the perfect tense indicative. It is not the same as ὁ ὤν (*ho ohn'*, meaning "The Being" or "The I Am") at Exodus 3:14, *LXX*. △ Si·lo'am, ℵBA; Shi·lo'ah, J[7-14,16-19]. See Isaiah 8:6, *LXX*.

New World Translation of the Holy Scriptures, 1971 ed.

ἐμαυτόν, ἡ δόξα μου οὐδέν ἐστιν. ἔστιν
myself, the glory of me nothing is. Is

ὁ πατήρ μου ὁ δοξάζων με, ὃν
the Father of me the (one) glorifying me, whom

ὑμεῖς λέγετε ὅτι θεὸς ὑμῶν ἐστίν, 55 καὶ
YOU are saying that God of YOU is, and

οὐκ ἐγνώκατε αὐτόν, ἐγὼ δὲ οἶδα
not YOU have known him, I but have known

αὐτόν· κἂν εἴπω ὅτι οὐκ
him; and if ever I should say that not

οἶδα αὐτόν, ἔσομαι ὅμοιος ὑμῖν
I have known him, I shall be like YOU

ψεύστης· ἀλλὰ οἶδα αὐτὸν καὶ τὸν
liar; but I have known him and the

λόγον αὐτοῦ τηρῶ. 56 Ἀβραὰμ ὁ
word of him I am observing. Abraham the

πατὴρ ὑμῶν ἠγαλλιάσατο ἵνα
father of YOU exulted in order that

ἴδῃ τὴν ἡμέραν τὴν ἐμήν, καὶ εἶδεν
he might see the day the mine, and he saw

καὶ ἐχάρη. 57 εἶπαν οὖν οἱ Ἰουδαῖοι
and rejoiced. Said therefore the Jews

πρὸς αὐτόν Πεντήκοντα ἔτη οὔπω
toward him Fifty years not yet

ἔχεις καὶ Ἀβραὰμ ἑώρακας;
you are having and Abraham you have seen?

58 εἶπεν αὐτοῖς Ἰησοῦς Ἀμὴν ἀμὴν
Said to them Jesus Amen amen

λέγω ὑμῖν, πρὶν Ἀβραὰμ γενέσθαι
I am saying to YOU Before Abraham to become

ἐγὼ εἰμί. 59 ἦραν οὖν λίθους
I am. They lifted up therefore stones

ἵνα βάλωσιν ἐπ' αὐτόν·
in order that they might throw upon him;

Ἰησοῦς δὲ ἐκρύβη καὶ ἐξῆλθεν ἐκ τοῦ ἱεροῦ.
Jesus but hid and went out of the temple.

9 Καὶ παράγων εἶδεν ἄνθρωπον τυφλὸν
And going beside he saw man blind

ἐκ γενετῆς. 2 καὶ ἠρώτησαν αὐτὸν οἱ
out of birth. And questioned him the

μαθηταὶ αὐτοῦ λέγοντες Ῥαββεί, τίς
disciples of him saying Rabbi, who

ἥμαρτεν, οὗτος ἢ οἱ γονεῖς αὐτοῦ,
sinned, this (one) or the parents of him,

ἵνα τυφλὸς γεννηθῇ;
in order that blind he should be generated?

myself, my glory
is nothing. It is
my Father that glo-
rifies me, he who
YOU say is YOUR
God; 55 and yet YOU
have not known
him. But I know
him. And if I said
I do not know him
I should be like
YOU, a liar. But I
do know him and
am observing his
word. 56 Abraham
YOUR father rejoiced
greatly in the pros-
pect of seeing my
day, and he saw
it and rejoiced."
57 Therefore the Jews
said to him: "You
are not yet fifty years
old, and still you
have seen Abraham?"
58 Jesus said to them:
"Most truly I say
to YOU, Before Abra-
ham came into exis-
tence, I have been."[a]
59 Therefore they
picked up stones
to hurl [them] at
him; but Jesus hid
and went out of the
temple.

9 Now as he was
passing along he
saw a man blind
from birth. 2 And his
disciples asked him:
"Rabbi, who sinned,
this man or his
parents, so that
he was born blind?"

58[a] I have been=ἐγὼ εἰμί (*e·go' ei·mi'*) after the a'orist infinitive clause πρὶν Ἀβραὰμ γενέσθαι and hence properly rendered in the perfect tense. It is not the same as ὁ ὤν (*ho ohn',* meaning "The Being" or "The I Am") at Exodus 3:14, *LXX.*

The Kingdom Interlinear Translation of the Greek Scriptures,, 1969, p. 467.

JOHN 9: 3—9 **468**

3 ἀπεκρίθη Ἰησοῦς Οὔτε οὗτος ἥμαρτεν
Answered Jesus Neither this (one) sinned
οὔτε οἱ γονεῖς αὐτοῦ, ἀλλ' ἵνα
nor the parents of him, but in order that
φανερωθῇ τὰ ἔργα τοῦ θεοῦ ἐν
might be manifested the works of the God in
αὐτῷ. 4 ἡμᾶς δεῖ ἐργάζεσθαι τὰ
him. Us it is necessary to be working the
ἔργα τοῦ πέμψαντός με ἕως ἡμέρα
works of the (one) having sent me until day
ἐστίν· ἔρχεται νὺξ ὅτε οὐδεὶς δύναται
is; is coming night when no one is able
ἐργάζεσθαι. 5 ὅταν ἐν τῷ κόσμῳ
to be working. Whenever in the world
ὦ, φῶς εἰμὶ τοῦ κόσμου.
I may be, light I am of the world.
6 ταῦτα εἰπὼν ἔπτυσεν
These (things) having said he spat
χαμαὶ καὶ ἐποίησεν πηλὸν ἐκ τοῦ
on the ground and he made clay out of the
πτύσματος, καὶ ἐπέθηκεν αὐτοῦ τὸν πηλὸν
spittle, and he put upon of him the clay
ἐπὶ τοὺς ὀφθαλμούς, 7 καὶ εἶπεν αὐτῷ
upon the eyes, and he said to him
Ὕπαγε νίψαι εἰς τὴν
Be going under wash yourself into the
κολυμβήθραν τοῦ Σιλωάμ ὃ
pool of the Siloam which
ἑρμηνεύεται Ἀπεσταλμένος.
is being translated Having been sent forth.
ἀπῆλθεν οὖν καὶ ἐνίψατο, καὶ
He went off therefore and he washed himself, and
ἦλθεν βλέπων.
he came seeing.
8 Οἱ οὖν γείτονες καὶ οἱ
The therefore neighbors and the (ones)
θεωροῦντες αὐτὸν τὸ πρότερον ὅτι
beholding him the former [time] that
προσαίτης ἦν ἔλεγον Οὐχ οὗτός
beggar he was were saying Not this (one)
ἐστιν ὁ καθήμενος καὶ προσαιτῶν;
is the (one) sitting and begging?
9 ἄλλοι ἔλεγον ὅτι Οὗτός ἐστιν·
Others were saying that This (one) is;
ἄλλοι ἔλεγον Οὐχί, ἀλλὰ ὅμοιος αὐτῷ
others were saying No, but like to him
ἐστίν. ἐκεῖνος ἔλεγεν ὅτι Ἐγώ εἰμι.
he is. That (one) was saying that I am.

3 Jesus answered:
"Neither this man
sinned nor his par-
ents, but it was
in order that the
works of God might
be made manifest
in his case. 4 We
must work the works
of him that sent
me while it is day;
the night is com-
ing when no man
can work. 5 As long
as I am in the
world, I am the
world's light." 6 Af-
ter he said these
things, he spit on
the ground and made
a clay with the sa-
liva, and put his
clay upon the [man's]
eyes 7 and said to
him: "Go wash in
the pool of Si·lo'-
am"[a] (which is trans-
lated 'Sent forth').
And so he went
off and washed,
and came back see-
ing.

8 Therefore the
neighbors and those
who formerly used
to see he was a
beggar began to
say: "This is the
man that used to
sit and beg, is it
not?" 9 Some would
say: "This is he."
Others would say:
"Not at all, but he
is like him." The man
would say: "I am he."

7[a] Si·lo'am, ℵBA; Shi·lo'ah, J[7-14,16-19]. See Isaiah 8:6, *LXX*.

The Kingdom Interlinear Translation of the Greek Scriptures, 1969, p. 468.

Jews Don't Stone Angels—John 8:58

The Watchtower does some pretty fancy footwork to avoid the obvious implication of Jesus' words "Before Abraham was born, I AM." What is the implication? That Jesus here reveals himself as the eternally existing One. While "was born" or "came into being" (*genesthai*) can be applied to even great men like Abraham, Jesus belongs to a different order of being.[14] "Came into being" cannot be applied to Jesus at all. Jesus' being is described by the continuous present "I AM" [*ego eimi*], without beginning and without end.

This was obvious to the Jews to whom Jesus was speaking. This is apparent by their reaction. "The Jews took up stones to stone Him" (v. 59, Williams). The Jews heard in Jesus' words the self-ordained name of Jehovah from their Greek Old Testament.[15] They knew He had claimed to be the eternal God. The only parallel use of verb contrast is Psalm 90:2, "Before the mountains were born [came to exist], or Thou didst give birth to the earth and the world, even from everlasting to everlasting, Thou art [You are] God." Here the temporal mountains which "came to exist" are contrasted to the eternal God, "from everlasting to everlasting, You are." God could not be said to have come to exist, and neither could Jesus. Like the God revealed in the Old Testament, Jesus can be described only in terms of absolute existence—"I AM," or "You are." Never was there a point in time when Jesus could be said to have "come to be." Let's drop in on Chris and Jay, with their conversation already in progress.

Chris: In Jesus' words, the Jews heard what they believed to be *blasphemy*, placing himself on a level with the eternal God.

Jay: Perhaps they just thought He meant He had existed even before Abraham.

Chris: You mean something like the Watchtower teaches, that as the Archangel Michael, He indeed was before Abraham, but that Jesus had not *always* been?

Jay: Right. That's probably what it was.

Chris: I'm afraid that Watchtower teaching is wrong for a couple

---

[14]"His claim is not that He is the greatest of the prophets, or even greater than Abraham himself. He belongs to a different order of being. The verb *genesthai* (came to exist) is not applicable to the Son of God at all. He stands outside the range of temporal relations. He can say *ego eimi*" (C.H. Dodd, *The Interpretation of the Fourth Gospel*, Cambridge: University Press, 1953, p. 261).

[15]LXX: Ex. 3:14; Deut. 32:39; Isa. 43:10, et al.

of reasons. First, the Greek does not say "I was," but "I am."[16] There is a difference in the Greek just like there is in the English. The Jews knew exactly what Jesus was alluding to, and not believing Jesus they interpreted His words as blasphemy. (See p. 217.)

Jay: Yes, they were pretty upset about something. You said you had a couple of reasons?

Chris: Well, if Jesus had only said what the Watchtower says He did, "I have been," Jesus' words would have been meaningless, but the reaction of the Jews would also be left unaccounted for.

Jay: Why, Chris?

Chris: The Jews were angered to the point of stoning Jesus because they understood His words in light of the background of their Old Testament writings. If Jesus had merely said, "I have been," there would have been no background in which His words could have been intelligible—no Old Testament background, no claim of deity, no grounds for blasphemy, no reason to pick up stones. Even if the Watchtower was right, and the Jews did understand Jesus, they had no law prescribing stoning for emotionally disturbed people who thought they were angels!

The Watchtower would twist the Scripture in order to support their own idea of what Jesus should have said. An acceptable translation of John 8:58 must seriously consider what Jesus did say, and account for the violent reaction of the Jews. The Watchtower translation fails on both points.

---

[16]Jesus uses the present tense form of the verb "to be" (*einai*) found in Ex. 3:14. If He had not wanted to draw attention to an eternal existence and the Old Testament background, and instead desired to conform to the Watchtower idea of simple preexistence, He would have used the imperfect tense *ego en* (I was).

Heavenly way. So then, as the Apostle says, in us as New Creatures the righteousness of the Law is fulfilled. Every one of us who is a New Creature is thinking justly, speaking justly and acting justly to the very best of his ability. This is the *will* of the New Creature.

As for the *flesh*, the New Creature controls the flesh so far as he is able; and the merit of Jesus, the merit of the sacrifice of Jesus imputed on behalf of these, covers all the blemishes and shortcomings of the flesh that are unintentional. The Father encourages these to come to the Throne of Heavenly Grace to obtain mercy for all such imperfections and blemishes. If any of the transgressions of a child of God should have a measure of wilfulness, he must suffer "stripes" as an expiation, to the extent of the wilfulness; but upon application to the Lord, he will be forgiven all that was not wilful, and be fully reinstated in the Lord's favor. The child of God should earnestly strive, however, to keep so close to the Lord that there will be no measure of wilfulness in his trespass.

This is a class that is offering sacrifice acceptable to God, as well as serving Him acceptably. It is not that we do the sacrificing ourselves; for that is the work of the great High Priest. We present ourselves, He receives us, and day by day the sacrificing is under His supervision and is acceptable to the Father through His merit. And so the Church of Christ, the Body of Christ, is going grandly on in the footsteps of our Lord, reckoned as absolute in justice and judgment, and sacrificing additionally. Eventually, she will be completed through the grace of God and by this arrangement which He has made. Then will come the time for dispensing God's blessings to all mankind, and this class, so especially called, so especially favored, will be highly exalted and honored to this great office with their Lord, higher than all other offices, next to the Father.

CHRIST JESUS—OUR ILLUSTRIOUS EXAMPLE

"Consider Him who endured such contradiction of sinners against Himself, lest ye be wearied and faint in your minds."—Hebrews 12:3.

THE Apostle's argument in our text is that the Lord's people need to be of good courage, need to remember that they have enlisted in a war on the side of righteousness and against sin, and that the enlistment is for life. The condition of their acceptance by the Lord was to this effect: "Be thou faithful unto *death*, and I will give thee the Crown of Life."—Revelation 2:10.

In the Apostle's day, as in our day, there was a tendency on the part of some to espouse the Cause of the Lord and to run faithfully for a while, and then to become discouraged, disheartened, and turn away to something else. In a previous chapter the Apostle has pointed out that some of those whom he was addressing had been faithful and courageous for a time, had "endured a great fight of afflictions," and then had become as babes, requiring milk, and needed to be taught again by others what were the first principles of the doctrines of Christ. They seemed to have lost their zeal to a large extent, and to have become discouraged in some way. They were not alert as servants of the Truth, and as servants of the Lord, as at first. They had permitted the opposition to wear down greatly their zeal and energy.

In Chapter 11 of this Epistle, the Apostle calls attention to the fact that all through the past there had been noble witnesses to God and His Cause, to whom the Church might well look as patterns of faithful endurance of opposition, and from whose course they might take encouragement. He cites the case of Abraham and his faith in God's promises. He recounts many of those who had endured great sufferings and privations, and were exiles from home—some of whom were even stoned to death or sawn asunder, etc., "of whom the world was not worthy." These were to be considered by the Church of Christ as glorious examples of faithfulness. And now, in our text, the Apostle brings us down to the grandest example of faithfulness to God ever known—our Lord Jesus Christ—and says that we should all especially consider *Him* who endured so much.

The word "consider" is here used in the sense of study, appreciate, take knowledge of. The more we study our Lord's course in life and realize what it cost Him to be faithful to the Father, to the principles of righteousness and truth, the more we see the exaltation of His character. He loved not His life. He withheld nothing, in order that He might do the will of the Father. He made no effort to be sensational, that thus He might attract attention to Himself; but humbly, quietly, went about His Father's business.

RELIGIOUS TEACHERS CHRIST'S CHIEF OPPONENTS

Our Lord Jesus was loyal to the principles of righteousness as expressed in the Law and the Prophets. "In His mouth was found no guile"—no deception. No one found in Him an attempt to curry favor with the multitude by saying something that would please the ear, and yet not be true. We find that He was absolutely faithful to God's Law. When the matter came up as to how this Law should be interpreted, He would give full, plain instruction respecting it, holding nothing back. He was loyal to the Heavenly Father in that He never claimed that anything He said or did was of Himself, but declared that it all came from the "Father who sent Him." He was loyal to the Father and to the Truth in everything. This loyalty brought Him much of opposition; for when He said that He was the Son of God, of "the Father who sent Him," the Jews were angry. "If you, a mere man, make yourself the Son of God," they said, "you are putting yourself on an equality with God. We never claim anything of this kind. We are the children of Abraham." Then they charged that He was fraudulent; whereas He was speaking the plain truth.—John 10:31-39; 8:39.

Thus the opposition to our Lord began—contradiction, as it is called in our text. There was opposition to Him in proportion as He presented the Truth. As the Jewish leaders began to see that the Message Jesus proclaimed was contrary to the one that they had given, or that they had received, antagonism sprang up. He did not make as many disciples as might have been expected, considering that "never man spake like this man." There were only something over five hundred of His followers altogether in the three and one-half years of His ministry. Five hundred seemed a small number from amongst the one nation that had been expecting the Messiah for over sixteen hundred years!

We inquire, How did the Master receive the opposition, the contradiction of sinners, and who were the sinners? The answer is, He received the contradiction with meekness and self-possession. The sinners were those of the Jewish people who, having a measure of light, were not obedient to that light. The Apostle does not wish us to consider how the *Gentiles* failed to receive the Lord,

The Watchtower, Feb. 1, 1917, p. 37.

Ego Eimi, Ho On, and the KIT—John 8:58

Once again we find Chris and Jay discussing John 8:58, where Jesus' claim to be the eternally existent One is met with the violent reaction of the Jews who picked up stones to stone Him.

Jay: I know we've discussed John 8:58 before, Chris, but I just noticed the footnote in my copy of the *Kingdom Interlinear Translation* (KIT). Referring to the Greek words *ego eimi*, "I have been," in my translation, the footnote says, "It is not the same as ὁ ὤν (*ho ohn'*, meaning "The Being," or "The I Am") for Exodus 3:14, LXX." (See p. 220.)

Chris: Yes, I've seen that before. As you know LXX refers to the *Septuagint*, the Greek translation of the Old Testament, popular at the time of Christ. Exodus 3:14 is where God told Moses to tell the Israelites that "I am" had sent him.

Jay: Right, and the Greek for Exodus 3:14 that refers to the name of God is *ho on*, not *ego eimi* as in John 8:58. Since these are different words altogether, you can see Jesus was not saying that He was God, the "I am" of the Old Testament, like trinitarians believe.

Chris: Oh, but, Jay, that's just what the Watchtower would like you to believe. The fact is that *ho on* and *ego eimi* are forms of the same verb "to be." The Exodus verb *ho on* is the present participle meaning "the One who is," or "the being One"; while *eimi* is the present indicative, "I am."[17] Far from being different words altogether, Jay, both are present tense forms of the same verb, and are employed to signify timeless existence.

Jay: You mean what Jesus says is really the same thing as the *ho on* in Exodus 3:14, that Jesus meant he had *always* been?

Chris: Yes. I also think it very likely that Jesus *intended* for us to see the parallel, as the Jews undoubtedly had. Remember, they picked up stones to kill Him. The point of both passages is eternalness of being. While John 8:58 affirms there was a time when Abraham "came to be," the absolute "I am" is in contrast to this, and denies there was ever a time when Jesus "came to be."

Jay: Whew! Jesus describes himself in the same way that Jehovah's name describes Him—"I am." I thought Exodus 3:14

---

[17]The Greek for "I Am" at John 8:58 is *ego eimi*. While *eimi* by itself says "I am," *ego*, the pronoun "I," is also used and gives added emphasis; "I—I am."

and John 8:58 were so different because one said *ho on* and the other said *ego eimi*.

Chris: They really do have parallel thoughts, and teach us a lot about who Jesus really is, don't they?

Jay: Yes, and I can see how "I have been" changes the meaning of Jesus' words. I imagine "I am" is the best translation of *ego eimi*, right?

Chris: Why don't we let the KIT answer that one for you.

Jay: How's that, Chris?

Chris: Look at your KIT at John 8:58 once more, Jay. The right-hand margin has the NWT interpretation "I have been." But look at what the Watchtower's literal translation of *ego eimi* says on the Interlinear side. What does the KIT say the literal translation is—"I have been" or "I am"?

Jay: "I am"!

The Watchtower uses many differing means to obscure the truths of the Gospel. We hope these brief expositions clarify the lines of debate, as well as strengthen you in the grace and the true knowledge of our Lord Jesus Christ.

467 **JOHN 8: 55—9: 2**

ἐμαυτόν, ἡ δόξα μου οὐδέν ἐστιν. ἔστιν
myself, the glory of me nothing is. Is
ὁ πατήρ μου ὁ δοξάζων με, ὃν
the Father of me the (one) glorifying me, whom
ὑμεῖς λέγετε ὅτι θεὸς ὑμῶν ἐστίν, **55** καὶ
YOU are saying that God of YOU is, and
οὐκ ἐγνώκατε αὐτόν, ἐγὼ δὲ οἶδα
not YOU have known him, I but have known
αὐτόν· κἂν εἴπω ὅτι οὐκ
him; and if ever I should say that not
οἶδα αὐτόν, ἔσομαι ὅμοιος ὑμῖν
I have known him, I shall be like YOU
ψεύστης· ἀλλὰ οἶδα αὐτὸν καὶ τὸν
liar; but I have known him and the
λόγον αὐτοῦ τηρῶ. **56** Ἀβραὰμ ὁ
word of him I am observing. Abraham the
πατὴρ ὑμῶν ἠγαλλιάσατο ἵνα
father of YOU exulted in order that
ἴδῃ τὴν ἡμέραν τὴν ἐμήν, καὶ εἶδεν
he might see the day the mine, and he saw
καὶ ἐχάρη. **57** εἶπαν οὖν οἱ Ἰουδαῖοι
and rejoiced. Said therefore the Jews
πρὸς αὐτόν Πεντήκοντα ἔτη οὔπω
toward him Fifty years not yet
ἔχεις καὶ Ἀβραὰμ ἑώρακας;
you are having and Abraham you have seen?
58 εἶπεν αὐτοῖς Ἰησοῦς Ἀμὴν ἀμὴν
Said to them Jesus Amen amen
λέγω ὑμῖν, πρὶν Ἀβραὰμ γενέσθαι
I am saying to YOU Before Abraham to become
ἐγὼ εἰμί. **59** ἦραν οὖν λίθους
I am. They lifted up therefore stones
ἵνα βάλωσιν ἐπ' αὐτόν·
in order that they might throw upon him;
Ἰησοῦς δὲ ἐκρύβη καὶ ἐξῆλθεν ἐκ τοῦ ἱεροῦ.
Jesus but hid and went out of the temple.

9 Καὶ παράγων εἶδεν ἄνθρωπον τυφλὸν
And going beside he saw man blind
ἐκ γενετῆς. **2** καὶ ἠρώτησαν αὐτὸν οἱ
out of birth. And questioned him the
μαθηταὶ αὐτοῦ λέγοντες Ῥαββεί, τίς
disciples of him saying Rabbi, who
ἥμαρτεν, οὗτος ἢ οἱ γονεῖς αὐτοῦ,
sinned, this (one) or the parents of him,
ἵνα τυφλὸς γεννηθῇ;
in order that blind he should be generated?

myself, my glory
is nothing. It is
my Father that glo-
rifies me, he who
YOU say is YOUR
God; **55** and yet YOU
have not known
him. But I know
him. And if I said
I do not know him
I should be like
YOU, a liar. But I
do know him and
am observing his
word. **56** Abraham
YOUR father rejoiced
greatly in the pros-
pect of seeing my
day, and he saw
it and rejoiced."
57 Therefore the Jews
said to him: "You
are not yet fifty years
old, and still you
have seen Abraham?"
58 Jesus said to them:
"Most truly I say
to YOU, Before Abra-
ham came into exis-
tence, I have been."[a]
59 Therefore they
picked up stones
to hurl [them] at
him; but Jesus hid
and went out of the
temple.

9 Now as he was
passing along he
saw a man blind
from birth. **2** And his
disciples asked him:
"Rabbi, who sinned,
this man or his
parents, so that
he was born blind?"

58[a] I have been=ἐγὼ εἰμί (*e·go' ei·mi'*) after the a'orist infinitive clause πρὶν Ἀβραὰμ γενέσθαι and hence properly rendered in the perfect tense. It is not the same as ὁ ὤν (*ho ohn'*, meaning "The Being" or "The I Am") at Exodus 3:14, *LXX*.

The Kingdom Interlinear Translation of the Greek Scriptures, 1969, p. 467.

Who Is the Alpha and the Omega?

One of the toughest jobs the Watchtower organization faces is trying to prove that Jesus Christ is not God. However, the Watchtower slips up occasionally, and, in doing so, actually comes up with a proof of Christ's deity. *Awake!* magazine, August 22, 1978, cites Revelation 22:12, 13, which reads as follows:

> Look, I am coming quickly, and the reward I give is with me, to render to each one as his work is. I am the Alpha and the Omega, the first and the last, the beginning and the end. (See p. 222.)

Awake! attributes these words to Jehovah God. Then just five weeks later, *The Watchtower* magazine for October 1 attributes the very same words to Jesus!

> Jesus again stresses the suddenness with which he comes:
> "I am coming to you quickly . . . I am coming quickly. Keep on holding fast what you have."—Rev. 2:16; 3:11.
> "Look! I am coming quickly. . . . Look! I am coming quickly, and the reward I give is with me. . . . Yes; I am coming quickly." (Rev. 22:7, 12, 20) (See p. 223.)

Christians have always believed that Jesus is the Alpha and the Omega in the book of Revelation. And since Jehovah has claimed this title throughout the book of Isaiah, Jesus is indeed Jehovah, and hence equal with the Father.

Judging from these two contradictory statements, it would appear that the writers of Watchtower literature are unaware of their presentation of contradictory teachings about Christ. Throughout revelation, John speaks of Jesus as the one who is to come, and Jesus calls himself the one who was, who is, and who is to come. Further, we know the Bible *never* speaks of the Father as the one who is to come. In 1917, Watchtower readers were taught in a book called *The Finished Mystery* that Revelation 1:8; 21:6, and 22:12, 13 confirmed that Jesus is the Alpha and Omega (see pp. 224–226). Witnesses of that time were told these Bible interpretations of *The Finished Mystery* book, which was a verse-by-verse commentary on Ezekiel and Revelation, were supplied as "meat in due season from the Lord" (see p. 227).

As we can see, the Watchtower Society is a very confused organization. Years ago they claimed that Alpha and Omega was Jesus Christ. Later they said He wasn't. Then in the October 1, 1978, *The Watchtower* magazine said He was again! As confused as the Watchtower leaders are—at least in some places, at some times, they have told the truth—accidentally yes—but the truth still stands—Jesus IS the Alpha and Omega.

example of this. Moreover, in the very next verse, the writer of the book of Revelation, the apostle John, says: "I . . . came to be in the isle that is called Patmos for speaking about God and bearing witness to Jesus." (Rev. 1:9) This provides additional confirmation that John understood God to be the Father of the Lord Jesus Christ.

In what sense is Jehovah God "the One who is and who was and who is to come"? Being the eternal God, Jehovah has at all times been the Almighty. (Ps. 90:2) So, in the indefinite past, he was the Most High. Furthermore, he continues to be the Almighty God and will come in that capacity to execute his judgment. As shown in other parts of the book of Revelation, Jehovah God will display his all-powerfulness at the time that his Son destroys all opposers of his sovereignty. —Rev. 16:14; 19:13-16.

The next occurrence of the title "the Alpha and the Omega" is found at Revelation 21:6. In the following verse, the One who applies this title to himself says: "Anyone conquering will inherit these things, and I shall be his God and he will be my son." Since Jesus Christ speaks of himself as a "brother" of these conquerors, it is the Father of the Lord Jesus Christ who is referring to himself as "the Alpha and the Omega."—Compare Matthew 25:40; Hebrews 2:10-12.

Finally, at Revelation 22:12, 13, we read: "Look! I am coming quickly, and the reward I give is with me, to render to each one as his work is. I am the Alpha and the Omega, the first and the last, the beginning and the end." This quotation appears among others that are ascribed to an angel and to Jesus Christ. Before these words are quoted in the book of Revelation, the angel who was instrumental in presenting the revelation to the apostle John spoke. (Rev. 22:8, 9) Then, after the quotation that begins with Revelation 22:12 and ends with the words of verse 15, we find the statement: "I, Jesus, sent my angel." (Rev. 22:16) Since the context does not necessitate our attributing the words of Revelation 22:12, 13 either to the angel or to Jesus, they could have originated with another speaker. Consistent with the rest of the book of Revelation, "the Alpha and the Omega" must be the Almighty God. He is the One who comes in the capacity of a judge to reward and to punish individuals according to their works.

The thought expressed at Revelation 22:12 also harmonizes with what the apostle Paul wrote. He stated: "According to your hardness and unrepentant heart you are storing up wrath for yourself on the day of wrath and of the revealing of God's righteous judgment. And he will render to each one according to his works: everlasting life to those who are seeking glory and honor and incorruptibleness by endurance in work that is good; however, for those who are contentious and who disobey the truth but obey unrighteousness there will be wrath and anger, tribulation and distress, upon the soul of every man who works what is injurious, of the Jew first and also of the Greek; but glory and honor and peace for everyone who works what is good, for the Jew first and also for the Greek." (Rom. 2:5-10) Of course, the judgment will be expressed by Jehovah God through his Son, for the apostle also says: "This will be in the day when God through Christ Jesus judges the secret things of mankind."—Rom. 2:16.

The fact that Jehovah God speaks of himself as "the Alpha and the Omega" gives us the assurance that what he has purposed will come to a successful realization. This should prompt us to do our utmost to be found approved by him. Our reward will then be certain, for the Bible tells us: "God is not unrighteous so as to forget your work and the love you showed for his name."—Heb. 6:10.

Awake!, Aug. 22, 1978, p. 28.

"Keep on the watch, for you do not know when the master . . . is coming." —Mark 13:35.

"What I say to you I say to all, Keep on the watch."—Mark 13:37.

"Happy are those slaves whom the master on arriving finds watching!"—Luke 12:37.

"Keep ready, because at an hour that you do not think likely the Son of man is coming."—Luke 12:40.

"Suddenly that day [will] be instantly upon you as a snare. For it will come in upon all those dwelling upon the face of all the earth. Keep awake, then."—Luke 21:34-36.

[6] Also, in his final revelation concerning "the things that must shortly take place," Jesus again stresses the suddenness with which he comes:

"I am coming to you quickly . . . I am coming quickly. Keep on holding fast what you have."—Rev. 2:16; 3:11.

"Look! I am coming quickly. . . . Look! I am coming quickly, and the reward I give is with me. . . . Yes; I am coming quickly." (Rev. 22:7, 12, 20)

In response to these last expressions of our Master, surely each one of us joins with the apostle John in saying: "Amen! Come, Lord Jesus."

[7] Make no mistake! This world is fast

6. What does Jesus stress with regard to "the things that must shortly take place"?

7. Why must we remain alert?

The Watchtower, Oct. 1, 1978.

And they also which pierced Him.—"And I will pour upon the House of David, and upon the inhabitants of Jerusalem [the Jewish people], the spirit of grace and of supplications: and they shall look upon Me whom they have pierced, and they shall mourn for Him, as one mourneth for his only son."—Zech. 12:10.

And all kindreds of the earth shall [wail because of] BEWAIL Him.—"At the time of our Lord's Second Advent the world will be far from converted to God; for 'all kindreds of the earth shall wail because of Him.' Christ comes before the conversion of the world and for the very purpose of converting all mankind."—Z.'16-344.

Even so, Amen.—We cannot stop the clouds of the Time of Trouble, or the tears of disappointment, and later, of repentance; and we would not if we could. The trouble and the tears are a necessary preparation for the blessings which follow.

1:8. **I am THE Alpha and I AM ALSO THE Omega.**—Alpha is the first letter, and Omega the last letter, of the Greek alphabet.

The Beginning and the Ending.—"Our Lord's great honor is shown in that He was not only the *first* of God's creation, but the *last.* From this we are to understand that the great Jehovah did not directly employ His own power in creating either men or angels; but that He delegated His power to His *Only*-begotten Son."—Z.'93-115.

Saith the Lord GOD.—But not the clergy; they will have none of this doctrine.

Which is, and which was, and which is to come, the Almighty.—"It is since His resurrection that the message has gone forth—'All power in Heaven and in earth *is given* unto Me.' (Matt. 28:18.) Consequently it is only since then that He could be called the Almighty."—Z.'93-115; Rev. 1:4; 16:5-7.

1:9. **I John, who [also] am your brother.**—"Instead of adding titles to his name, as Reverend, Bishop, Overseer of all the Churches in Asia Minor, we find John introducing himself as 'your brother.'"—Z. '01-187.

And companion in tribulation.—"He was sharer with Christ, as a member of His Body, in His afflictions, in His endurance; and the brother of all fellow-disciples, sharers of the same sufferings, and prospectively of the same glory."—Z. '01-187; Matt. 20:23.

And [in] the kingdom.—Now, while "the Kingdom of Heaven suffereth violence;" and later, when "the Kingdom and dominion, and the greatness of the Kingdom under the whole heaven, shall be given to the people of the saints of the Most High."—Matt. 11:12; Dan. 7:27.

The Finished Mystery, 1917, p. 15.

and not in full to any previous time in that Age. (John 5:28, 29.)" –Z.'01-200; 1 Cor. 15:26, 54; Rev. 20:14; Isa. 35:10; 51:11; 65:19.

[Neither shall there be any more pain] For the former things are passed away.—The reign of Satan, sin and death will have ended forever. "To gain a place in the earthly phase of the Kingdom of God will be to find the gratification of every desire and ambition of the perfect human heart."—A291.

21:5. **And He that sat upon the Throne said, Behold, I make all things new.**—"This expression does not relate merely to rocks and trees, etc., but to the great work which our Lord undertook; viz., the regeneration of humanity to the complete perfection contemplated in the original Divine Plan."—Z.'01-201; Rev. 20:11.

And He said unto me, Write: for these words are [true and] faithful, AND TRUE.—"Present conditions seem so contrary to all this grand Restitution outcome that it cannot be fully believed and trusted by any except those who have learned to walk with the Lord. To all others these things will appear untrue, and God will appear unfaithful, and the matters which we are here discussing will seem 'idle tales,' as fables and golden fancies: but to us who believe, these promises are precious."—1 Pet. 2:7.

21:6. **And He [said]** SAITH **unto me, [it is done.] I am Alpha and Omega, the Beginning and the End.**—"It was the Father's good pleasure that the Blessed One, the Only Begotten of the Father, should accomplish the entire program of redemption and restitution; and be forever the Associate and Representative of the Father, through whom and by whom all things should continue, as He was the one through whom all things were made that were made." —Z.'01-201; Rev. 1:8; 22:13.

I will give unto him that is athirst of the fountain of the water of life freely.—"It is this one who, during the Millennial Age, will extend to all the willing and obedient the Water of Life, everlasting life—the privilege of perpetual existence. But they must thirst for it, must desire it; and this desire must be manifest in obedience to the terms, the laws, upon which it will be supplied freely."—Z.'01-201; Rev. 22:17; Isa. 55:1; John 7:37.

21:7. **He that overcometh shall inherit [all]** THESE **things.**—These earthly things.—Acts 3:21.

And I will be his God, and he shall be My son.—"Those addressed are not the Bride class, selected during the Gospel Age, (1 John 3:2) but the sheep class of Matt. 25—such of mankind as during the Millennial Age become the Lord's sheep and obey His voice. They shall inherit the

The Finished Mystery, 1917, p. 318.

And he that is holy, let him be holy still.—"The word seems to denote development and crystallization of character, immediately preceding the coming of the great Judge of all." (Weym.) "Love is patient and kind. Love knows neither envy nor jealosy. Love is not forward and self-assertive, nor boastful and conceited. She does not behave unbecomingly, nor seek to aggrandize herself, nor blaze out passionate anger, nor brood over wrongs. She finds no pleasure in injustice done to others, but joyfully sides with the truth. She knows how to be silent. She is full of trust, full of hope, full of patient endurance."—1 Cor. 13:4-7.—Weym.

22:12. **[And] behold, I come quickly.**—See Rev. 16:15; 22:7, 10, 20. The Lord Himself becomes the speaker.

And My reward is with Me, to [give] BE GIVEN **every man.**—Every man in Christ.

According as his work [shall be] IS.—The Church's work is practically finished. The reward is given on the basis of the work already done, in character development and in the natural outgrowth of that development—works.

22:13. **I am Alpha and Omega,** THE FIRST AND THE LAST, **the Beginning and the End, [the First and the Last].**—"Our Lord tells us over and over again (See Rev. 1:8, 11, 17; 2:8; 3:14; 21:6), that He is the Beginning and the Ending, the First and the Last, of the creation of God."—Z.'93-115.

22:14. **Blessed are they that [do His commandments]** WASH THEIR ROBES.—The Great Company class.—Rev. 7:14.

That they may have right to the Tree of Life.—Rev. 22:2.

And may enter through the gates into the City.—"Whose Builder and Maker is God." (Heb. 11:10.) To these dear brethren we would say, The object of your trials is to remove the dross (Ex. 30:7; Mal. 3:2) that you may be fit companions of the Christ. (Ex. 12:8; Heb. 2:17; Rom. 5:3; Col. 1:11.) Do not think it strange. (James 1:12; 1 Pet. 1:7; 4:12; 5:10.) When you get the right viewpoint, you will rejoice in your sufferings. (Deut. 13:3; Psa. 23:4; 119:67.) The trials will not last forever (Psa. 39:1); and in them all you may hear the songs of deliverance. (Psa. 32:6, 7.) There is nothing to turn back to (Heb. 10:38); but there is joy untold to look forward to, and it is nigh.—Rev. 19:9; Psa. 45:14, 15.

22:15. **[For] without are dogs.**—There will be no clergy class, as such, in the Kingdom.—Isa. 56:10; Phil. 3:2; 2 Tim. 3:8, 9.

And sorcerers, and whoremongers, and murderers, and idolators.—See Rev. 21:8.

The Finished Mystery, 1917, p. 336.

THE TABLE OF THE GREAT KING

"Thou preparest a table before me in the presence of mine enemies; thou anointest my head with oil; my cup runneth over."—Psalm 23:5.

TO SERVE in the courts of an earthly monarch has ever been considered a great privilege, and to sit at the royal table is an honor enjoyed by but a favored few. With this thought in mind we can especially appreciate the condescension of Jehovah as illustrated in the beautiful words of our text. Why should he come to this sinful, accursed realm and select even a handful of earth's inhabitants to be his sons and to serve them, as members of the divine family? If the Lord, the great King of the universe, has been pleased to prepare a table laden with "meat in due season" for his household and to invite us to partake thereof, it would be a most ungrateful, unworthy guest indeed who would spurn such a blessing and turn away from the food which God himself had set before him.

Our text indicates that to sit at the Lord's table would be to expose ourselves to the envious gaze of enemies, headed by Satan. "Thou preparest a table before me *in the presence of mine enemies.*" Those who have been enlightened by present truth, who have been privileged to feast on the good things which the Lord has spread before his children during the past forty years, can appreciate the significance of this statement. One by one the harvest saints have left the Babylonish "tables of vomit" (Isaiah 28:8) to partake of the meat of present truth. In each instance it has meant persecution, and oftimes vilification and ostracism which have been very hard to endure; yet in it all our cup of joy at the privilege of feasting upon the truth and of suffering for Christ's sake has literally overflowed.

"NOT IGNORANT OF HIS DEVICES"

With each publication of harvest truth, gladdening the hearts of the Lord's people, there has been manifested a corresponding hatred on the part of all the enemies of the truth; for indeed these "Helping Hands for Bible Students" have been *plagues* to ecclesiasticism.—Revelation 15:5-7.

Satan has been increasingly active in his endeavors to detract and to distract the minds of the Lord's people, and to draw them away from the table of truth which has been prepared for them. In some instances he has succeeded. It seems strange that any one who has once been privileged to enjoy the food of the Lord's providing would on any account leave the King's table and household, and return to the emptiness of the world. Nothing has incensed the adversary more than has the seventh course of "meat in due season," which the Lord in his providence has seen fit to spread before us. While it has strengthened and refreshed thousands of the Lord's faithful children, "the seed of promise," it has been as a grievous plague upon the ecclesiastical lords, "the seed of Satan." Numerous are the insidious arguments that have been propagated by our wily foe to draw away the Lord's people from the food—arguments designed either to nauseate or to frighten them. More than ever has it been true, as expressed by our text, that this last feature of present truth was spread before us "in the presence of our enemies."

To those who are familiar with Satan's tactics it should hardly be necessary to suggest an offset to his arguments. Yet in order to strengthen the faith of those whose hearts are right, but whose minds have become temporarily confused, we are pleased to set forth a few positive evidences that none other than our Lord himself has served us with the truth of Ezekiel and Revelation, which at the same time constitute the last plague upon Babylon. Let us not say: 'Why should we accept it as present truth?' Rather let us say: 'Why should I *not* accept it as meat in due season from the Lord?'

THE "HAIL" OF PRESENT TRUTH

Did not the Laodicean messenger, "that wise and faithful servant," promise us throughout his ministry, and in the very hour of his death, that the church should expect and would receive an exposition of these two prophetic books? Have they not now been explained thoroughly and clearly and in accordance with all other features of the divine plan? Did not the same channel or agency which the Lord has been pleased to use in publishing the preceding messages of the harvest period also publish these truths for the comfort and encouragement of the church in its hour of direst need? Is not the Watch Tower Bible and Tract Society the one and only channel which the Lord has used in dispensing his truth continually since the beginning of the harvest period? Did not this last published message contain the "hail" of truth which the Scriptures indicated it would? (Revelation 16:19, 21; Job 38:22,23) Furthermore, has it not brought to the Lord's consecrated people tremendously rich blessings as they have feasted upon the wonderful symbolisms so confirmatory of the plan of God as explained by the Laodicean servant?

The explained truths of Revelation and Ezekiel are such as to comport with the prophetic description of what the Lord had said he would proclaim in the end of this age. He indicated that he would administer a stinging blow to Babylon, which would cause her to stumble and fall. He said that when the seventh vial was poured out "great Babylon came in remembrance before God....and there fell upon *the* men [the clergy] a great hail." (Revelation 16:19-21) From this it is evident that the burden of the last message of the age would be upon the heads of ecclesiasticism.

"I WILL HAVE THEM IN DERISION"

Again, in Psalm 2:1-4 the Lord prophetically shows that in the end of the age the nations would rage, and that forthwith the great ones of ecclesiasticism would take counsel together against the Lord and his anointed; i. e., against the anointed body of Christ (the feet members), and thus against the Lord himself. Then the Lord said that he will "have them in derision....and vex them in his sore displeasure." Is not the very keynote of the message of St. John and Ezekiel found in the Psalmist's statement that "the Lord shall have them in derision"? The burden of nearly every chapter in these prophetic books is that very message against nominal Christendom, because of their sins against the Lord and against his anointed body. Therefore since the Lord said that this is the message which he would pour out in the end of the age, does it not appear evident that those who find fault with the irony and derision of the explained messages of these prophets are really complaining against the doing of the Lord?

What could be clearer evidence that the Lord himself has served us with the true explanation of Revela-

The Watchtower, April 1, 1919, p. 105.

Chapter Twelve

THE HOLY SPIRIT—ANALYSIS

Is the Holy Spirit a Person?

Christians believe that the Holy Spirit is God himself, partaking of the same divine nature as the Father and the Son. Jehovah's Witnesses are taught that the Holy Spirit is not God. In fact, they are taught He is not even a person, but merely God's "invisible active force" (see p. 229). Our question is: Does the Holy Spirit have a personality?

While denying the personality of the Holy Spirit, the Watchtower attempts to prove that the most *unholy* spirit, Satan the devil, is a personal being, to which we would agree. They say the Bible reveals the following proofs of his being: Satan carries on conversations, and he is called a "manslayer, a liar . . . and a ruler." Based on this "evidence" they say, "Only an intelligent person could fit all those descriptions" (see p. 230).

By using this same type of "logic," we ask, does the Holy Spirit possess personality? What about personal conversations? Yes, the Bible declares that the Holy Spirit *personally* spoke to the church at Antioch. In Acts 13:2 He commands the church to "set apart for *Me* Barnabas and Saul for the work which *I* have called them."

Just as Satan is shown to be a person because he is called a "liar" and a "ruler," likewise the Holy Spirit is a person because He is our "Teacher" and "Comforter" (John 16:7, 13). As a real person He speaks, He wills, He has a mind, and His own power (Rev. 2:7; 1 Cor. 12:11; Rom. 8:27; and 15:19). Hebrews 10:29 teaches that He can be insulted. This holy person surely must be insulted and outraged by the Watchtower's statements! He also can be grieved, as it says in Ephesians 4:30.

Yet, in spite of all this, He desires to be the personal comforter of Jehovah's Witnesses everywhere. This is the will of Jesus. "I will ask the Father, and He will give you another Helper, that He may be with you forever" (John 14:16).

are clearly seen from the world's creation onward, because they are perceived by the things made, even his eternal power and Godship, so that they are inexcusable; because, although they knew God, they did not glorify him as God." (Romans 1:20, 21) In the face of all the evidence, they cannot successfully argue that God does not exist any more than argue that "God is dead." He still lives and has all the dynamic energy and the perfect memory to carry out his stated purposes, which have been declared and published now for six thousand years. How glad we can be for this!

[13] We do not join the modern-day scientists in their denying that God is the Source of all energy now in operation. We know that he is also the Source of something else that scientists deny, not knowing anything about it. What is that? It is "spirit." And why should he not be the Source of spirit? "God is a Spirit," or, "God is spirit," as Jesus Christ pointed out nineteen centuries ago. —John 4:24, and marginal reading.

[14] From God there goes forth an invisible active force by means of which he gets his will done. It is not a mere influence such as a man might exercise over others by his powerful personality. It is a force that is operative, and it issues forth from God who is holy, that is to say, absolutely clean and righteous. He sends it forth to accomplish what is holy. So it is correctly called "holy spirit." It is so spoken of in God's written Word.

13. Of what else, besides dynamic energy, is God the Source, and why?
14. What is "holy spirit," and who gives it?

Holy Spirit, 1976, p. 11.

SATAN THE DEVIL —Personification or a Person?

THE Holy Bible makes frequent mention of Satan the Devil. With reference to the chief adversary of God and man, the Hebrew Scriptures (Old Testament) speak of Satan (meaning "adversary") eighteen times. The Christian Greek Scriptures (New Testament) refer to the same one thirty-four times as Satan and over thirty times by the term Devil (meaning "slanderer").

Many believe that the Devil is a wicked spirit person who can influence man toward evil. Others deny this. They hold that the Devil is not a person, but merely the personification of an abstract principle of evil. According to the New York *Times Magazine* of February 4, 1973, a Catholic Scripture scholar recently said: "No up-to-date theologian believes that Satan is a person."

Which is the truth? Is the Devil a personification or a person? Knowledge of the Bible's view of this matter will prove to be most beneficial. Bible scholar Louis Matthews Sweet explains why: "Not only is the Bible entirely free from the extravagances of popular Satanology, which is full of absurd stories concerning the appearances, tricks, and transformations of Satan among men, but it exhibits a dependable accuracy and consistency of statement which is most reassuring."

The earliest direct references to Satan (literally, "the Satan") in the Bible are found in Job, chapters one and two. These chapters introduce Satan when he is speaking with Jehovah God. (Job 1:6-12; 2:1-7) This alone presents difficulties for any who, while professing belief in the Bible, claim that Satan is simply a personification of evil in someone. If "Satan" is only the evil in any person, the evil must have been in Jehovah God with whom Satan was speaking. But the Bible describes God as one "in whom there is no unrighteousness."—Ps. 92:15.

An experience that Jesus had with the Devil is similar. Matthew 4:1 relates that "Jesus was led by [God's] spirit up into the wilderness to be tempted by the Devil." Was Jesus tempted by evil within himself? Such a view does not harmonize with the Bible's description of Jesus as "a righteous one" who "committed no sin." (1 John 2:1; 1 Pet. 2:22) No, the Satan that appeared before Jehovah God and that tempted Jesus Christ was separate from them.

You will note, too, that these accounts relate conversations between the Devil and God, and between the Devil and Jesus Christ. Both Jehovah God and Jesus Christ are persons. Can an unintelligent 'force' carry on a conversation with a person? Also, the Bible calls Satan a manslayer, a liar, a father (in a spiritual sense) and a ruler. (John 8:44; 14:30) Only an intelligent person could fit all those descriptions. Therefore, M'Clintock and Strong's *Cyclopœdia* states: "All the forms of personal agency are made use of by the sacred writers in setting forth the character and conduct of Satan. . . . Every quality, every action, which can indicate personality, is attributed to him in language which cannot be explained away."

The Scriptures indicate that the Devil was originally a perfect, righteous spirit creature. But he "did not stand fast in the truth." (John 8:44) Only after he willingly

Awake!, Dec. 8, 1973.

Is the Holy Spirit God Himself?

In the previous section we noted that even though Jehovah's Witnesses have been taught that the Holy Spirit is merely an *impersonal force,* the Bible clearly teaches otherwise: He is a holy person. Our question—Is the Holy Spirit *God himself*? The Watchtower Society says no. Again, the Bible claims the opposite. One example is found in Acts 5:3, 4. Here the Apostle Peter said to Ananias, "Why has Satan filled your heart to lie to the Holy Spirit?" If the Holy Spirit was simply an impersonal, unthinking, unfeeling force, how could He be lied to? Peter goes on to say that Ananias lied to a divine, personal being. He said, "You have not lied to men, but to God" (Acts 5:4). This is why the Holy Spirit knew that Ananias had lied. Yes, friends, the Holy Spirit is God himself!

The Bible teaches that God knows all things. The Scripture says in 1 Corinthians 2:10, 11, "The Spirit searches all things, even the depths of God," and further, "Even so the thoughts of God no one knows except the Spirit of God." David exclaimed in Psalm 139:7, "Where can I go from Thy Spirit?" We see that the Holy Spirit is aware of all things.

As God, He has distributed His gifts to each Christian, as 1 Corinthians 12:11 declares: ". . . distributing to each one individually just as He wills." In this way the church is equipped to do His will and baptize in His name. Jesus said in Matthew 28:19: "Go therefore and make disciples of all the nations, baptizing them *in the name* of the Father and the Son and *the Holy Spirit.*"

We would like to end this message with some good news from the Watchtower's own Bible, *The New World Translation.* Second Corinthians 3:17 reads, "Now Jehovah *is the Spirit;* and where the spirit of Jehovah is, there is freedom." Yes, true freedom is knowing the Holy Spirit and knowing Him as He is—as Jehovah God himself.

Chapter Thirteen

SALVATION—ANALYSIS

The Bible teaches that salvation is by *grace* through faith—not as a *result* of works, but with a goal of walking in the good works for which we have been created (Eph. 2:8–10). Thus, for the Christian, salvation is dependent upon acceptance of Christ's finished work at the cross. This is not, however, what is taught by the Watchtower.

For the Jehovah's Witness, "It is necessary that belief be demonstrated by works" (see p. 236). Does this mean that everlasting life is earned? No, the Society would boldly say, "Life cannot be *earned* by imperfect humans but is the free *gift* through faith in Jesus Christ" (see p. 237). Sounds right, doesn't it? Too bad what they *say* is not what they mean.

The Watchtower Society feels the need to give the impression that they are a "Christian" organization. While they profit, numerically, by their works-oriented doctrine, they must maintain the facade of salvation by grace. In order to do this they play word games and use biblical vocabulary like "free gift" from Ephesians 2:8. But upon examination, one finds that what the Christian means is not what the Society means when it uses the same words.

What the Watchtower means by "free gift" is that Christ's death only wiped away the sin inherited from Adam. They teach that without this work of atonement, men could not *work their way toward* salvation. But the "gift" of Christ's ransom sacrifice is freely made available to all who desire it. In other words, without Christ's sacrifice, the individual wouldn't have a chance to get saved. But in view of His work, the free gift which removed the sin inherited from Adam, the individual now has a *chance*.

Watchtower publications teach the doctrine of salvation, the *possibility* that you might be permitted to live on Paradise Earth forever, in this manner. First, the work of Christ—what did it accomplish? "And he gave his life so that he could take away the harm that Adam did to us" (see p. 238). By accepting the gift of Christ's ransom, do men have the opportunity open to them for reconciliation? Yes:

> The ransom and sin-offering open the way for reconciliation, and then the truth of this great fact must be brought to man and man be given the opportunity of accepting the gracious provision or rejecting it. (See p. 239.)

Does "accepting the gracious provision" simply mean faith in God? Is having faith in what Christ has done sufficient? No, the Society clearly says, "However, more than faith is needed." Why? What is lacking? "There must also be works to demonstrate what your true feelings are about Jehovah" (see p. 240). What part do the works play? "Such works will show that you are choosing life" (see p. 241).

Since faith is not sufficient, one has to wonder what works are required of those who hope to live on Paradise Earth forever. The Society teaches that there are four basic requirements. The first is "*taking in knowledge*" of God. The second requirement is "*to obey God's laws*" (see p. 242). The third affirms there is no hope outside the Watchtower organization:

> A third requirement is that we *be associated with God's channel*, his organization. . . . To receive everlasting life in the earthly Paradise we must identify that organization and serve God as part of it. (See p. 242.)

The fourth demand "is connected with loyalty." It insures that Witnesses sell Watchtower publications and keep the membership growing. "God requires that prospective subjects of his Kingdom support his government by *loyally advocating his Kingdom rule to others*" (see p. 242). Faithfulness to the Watchtower organization, and harmony with its teachings and requirements are, for the Jehovah's Witness, *necessary* if he hopes to achieve everlasting life.

Recent trends in evangelical circles have emphasized the personal aspects of a relationship with Christ and inviting Him into one's life through prayer. With the intent of perpetuating a Christian illusion, the Society has disguised its own theology with similar trappings. This is found in their recent book, *You Can Live Forever in Paradise on Earth*:

> You should approach God in Jesus' name and tell him in prayer that you want to be his servant, that you want to belong to him. In this way you dedicate yourself to God. This is a personal, private matter. No one else can do it for you.
>
> After you have made your dedication to God, he will expect you

> to live up to it. So prove that you are a person of your word by sticking to this decision, or dedication, as long as you live. (See p. 241.)

Notice three things: first the *personal* emphasis; next the *prayer;* and then what the witness *receives*. The Christian responds to the voice of Christ who personally comes in to him. "Behold, I stand at the door and knock; if any one hears My voice and opens the door, I will come in to him, and will dine with him, and he with Me" (Rev. 3:20). Jesus comes to the Christian, whereas the Witness makes the decision that he wants to belong to God.

The Christian's prayer is not only in the name of Jesus. It is to His voice that the new Christian responds; so it is also to Jesus that He calls in prayer. Roman 10:13 says, "Whoever will call upon the name of the Lord will be saved." Acts 4:12, speaking of Jesus, tells us, "There is salvation in no one else; for there is no other name under heaven that has been given among men, by which we must be saved." The Witness' prayer may be in Jesus' name, but it *cannot* be to Jesus himself.

The Christian receives salvation and becomes one of God's children. "But as many as received Him, to them He gave the right to become children of God, even to those who believe in His name" (John 1:12). Contrary to this biblical truth, the Witness receives the *opportunity* to live up to His Word, the *possibility* that he may be saved. The Christian receives the *assurance* of eternal life. "These things I have written to you who believe in the name of the Son of God, in order that you may know that you have eternal life" (1 John 5:13).

Why don't the Witnesses see the truth in God's Word? Because they are taught that the "born again" experience, the right of sonship, belongs only to a small group of 144,000 followers. This group is known as the anointed class, having been gathered out of all nations since Pentecost. They believe passages such as 1 John 3:2, "Beloved, now we are children of God," are written *directly* only to this "little flock." All other Witnesses, known as the "great multitude" or "other sheep," are working to develop a special character which Jehovah will one day look upon with approval, giving them the reward of adoption into His family. This, however, will not happen within this lifetime—not until they have proved loyal by passing a test that will take place more than 1000 years from now, at the end of the millennial kingdom:

> Jehovah will give them the opportunity to show their loyalty. How? By releasing Satan and his demons from their condition of restraint in the "abyss" (Revelation 20:7). . . . Those who stay loyal to God will be judged worthy of everlasting life. . . . Any who rebelliously turn against God will be destroyed. . . . (See p. 243.)

It may be helpful to understand that the Witness is taught that all terms the Christian would normally understand as belonging to the believer do not apply to him at all. He is taught that all such titles refer only to the special anointed class, the born-again ones, the 144,000. Two examples are "the Christian congregation" and "the congregation of the first-born who have been enrolled in the heavens." Others would include "the Body of Christ," "God's spiritual children and heirs," "sons" and "spirit-begotten Christians," etc. Therefore, when one reads Watchtower literature referring to any of these titles, one must realize the article is not addressing the average Witness but the "little flock."

To what can this corrupt view of salvation be traced? As men and women search to find God on their own terms, God waits for them to turn to Him, "He is not far from each one of us" (Acts 17:27). So, too, Satan is always at hand to help the person pursue his own desires. But the essential thing affecting the corruption of the doctrine of salvation has to do with a wrong view of the deity of the Lord Jesus.

A false understanding of who Jesus is will always lead to a false understanding of what He has accomplished. Remember, the Watchtower denies the deity of Christ and propagates the lie that He is a created being. Richard Pratt has rightly said, "If Jesus were not God but merely a creature, then salvation would be brought about by a creature rather than by God alone."[1] Such a means of reconciliation could never bring us all the way back to God. As evidenced in the Watchtower's theology, the false view of who Jesus is not only leaves salvation incomplete, but leaves man dependent upon his own righteousness.

---

[1]Richard Pratt, *Every Thought Captive* (New Jersey: Presbyterian & Reformed, 1979), p. 106.

1 Samuel 12:3, the *Septuagint Version*. "It is unthinkable, on my part," exclaimed David, "to thrust my hand out against [Saul] the anointed [*LXX, khri·ston'*] of Jehovah!" (1 Sam. 26:11) Neither would David allow his nephew Abishai to touch Saul. (1 Sam. 26:8, 9) David also had the Amalekite slain because he said he killed Saul "the anointed [*LXX, khri·ston'*] of Jehovah." (2 Sam. 1:13-16) This title and commission to be king was also bestowed on David, and thereafter he spoke of himself as Jehovah's "anointed one [*LXX, khri·stoi'*]." (1 Sam. 16:12, 13; 2 Sam. 22:51) King Zedekiah, who sat on the throne as an heir of David, was also called "the anointed one [*khri·stos'*] of Jehovah." —Lam. 4:20.

The prophets too were titled Jehovah's anointed ones, as indicated by the parallelism in Psalm 105:15. Jehovah gave the command to his prophet Elijah: "Elisha . . . you should anoint as prophet in place of you," though the details of the actual anointing are not recorded.—1 Ki. 19:16.

There are other instances where the *Septuagint* uses *khri·stos'* prophetically. There are ten references to *khri·stos'* in the book of Psalms, the one in Psalm 2:1, 2 being particularly noteworthy: Nations in tumult and kings of the earth massing together "against Jehovah and against his anointed one." The apostles quoted this prophecy and applied the title to the 'holy servant Jesus, whom Jehovah had anointed.' (Acts 4:24-27) A more unusual example is where the term is applied to the Persian king Cyrus. Before his birth, the prophecy of Isaiah (45:1-3) declared: "This is what Jehovah has said to his anointed one [*LXX, khri·stoi'*], to Cyrus, whose right hand I have taken hold of." Cyrus was never literally anointed with holy oil as were the kings of Israel, but, as in other instances in the Bible, the expression "anointed one" is a titled form of address given to him because of his commission and appointment from God.—See ANOINTED, ANOINTING.

CHRISTIAN. The Latinized Greek term *Khri·sti·a·nos'*, found only three times in the Christian Greek Scriptures, designates followers of Christ Jesus, the exponents of Christianity.—Acts 11:26; 26:28; 1 Pet. 4:16.

"It was first in Antioch [Syria] that the disciples were by divine providence called Christians." (Acts 11:26) It is possible, then, that this name was used as early as the year 44 C.E. when the events surrounding this text occurred, although the grammatical structure of this phrase does not necessarily make it so; some think it was a little later. At any rate, by 58 C.E., in the city of Caesarea, nearly 300 miles (482.7 kilometers) S of Antioch, the term was well known and used even by public officials, for, at that time, King Agrippa II said to Paul: "In a short time you would persuade me to become a Christian." —Acts 26:28.

Bible writers in addressing fellow believers or describing followers of Christ used expressions such as "believers in the Lord," "brothers" and "disciples" (Acts 5:14; 6:3; 15:10), "chosen ones" and "faithful ones" (Col. 3:12; 1 Tim. 4:12), "slaves to God" and "slaves of Christ Jesus" (Rom. 6:22; Phil. 1:1), "holy ones," "congregation of God" and "those who call upon the Lord." (Acts 9:13; 20:28; 1 Cor. 1:2; 2 Tim. 2:22) These terms with doctrinal meaning were used primarily as internal congregational designations. To outsiders Christianity was referred to as "The Way" (Acts 9:2; 19:9, 23; 22:4), and opponents called it "the sect of the Nazarenes" or just "this sect."—Acts 24:5; 28:22.

It was first in Syrian Antioch that Christ's followers became known as Christians. It is most unlikely that the Jews first styled Jesus' followers "Christians" (Greek) or "Messianists" (Hebrew), for they would not reject Jesus as being the Messiah or Christ, and then tacitly recognize him as the Anointed One or Christ by stamping his followers "Christians." Some think the heathen population may have nicknamed them Christians out of jest or scorn, but the Bible shows that it was a God-given name; they "were *by divine providence* called Christians."—Acts 11:26.

The Greek verb *khre·ma·ti'zo* in this text is generally rendered simply "were called." A check of some fifty translations in several modern languages reveals that only the *New World Translation* and *Young's* indicate that God had anything to do with selecting the name "Christian"; *Young's* reads: "The disciples also were *divinely called* first in Antioch Christians."

This is an example of careful scholarship, for *khre·ma·ti'zo* as used in the Christian Greek Scriptures is always associated with something supernatural, oracular or divine. Strong's *Greek Lexicon* defines it as "to utter an oracle, . . . i.e. *divinely* intimate." Robinson's *Greek Lexicon* gives the meaning: "Spoken in respect to a *divine* response, oracle, declaration, to give response, to speak as an oracle, to *warn from God*." Thayer's *Greek-English Lexicon:* "to give a *divine* command or admonition, to teach from heaven . . . to be *divinely* commanded, admonished, instructed . . . to be the mouthpiece of *divine* revelations, to promulge the commands of God." Thomas Scott in his *Commentary* on this text says: "The word implies that this was done by divine revelation: for it has generally this signification in the New Testament, and is rendered 'warned from God' or 'warned of God,' even when there is no word for God in the Greek." Clarke's *Commentary* says: "The word [*khre·ma·ti'sai*] in our common text, which we translate *were called*, signifies in the New Testament, to *appoint, warn*, or *nominate*, by *Divine direction*. In this sense, the word is used, Matt. ii. 12. . . . If, therefore, the name was given by *Divine appointment*, it is most likely that Saul and Barnabas were directed to give it; and that, therefore, the name *Christian* is from God."—See Matthew 2:12, 22; Luke 2:26; Acts 10:22; Hebrews 8:5; 11:7; 12:25, where this Greek verb occurs.

The Scriptures speak of Jesus Christ as the bridegroom, the Head and Husband of his anointed followers. (2 Cor. 11:2; Eph. 5:23) Appropriately, then, as a wife is happy to take her husband's name, so this "bride" class of Christ was pleased to receive a name identifying them as belonging to him. In this way observers of these first-century Christians readily recognized them not only by their activity but also by their name as altogether different from the practitioners of Judaism; here was a growing association where there was neither Jew nor Greek but all were one under their Head and Leader Jesus Christ. —Gal. 3:26-28; Col. 3:11.

WHAT IT MEANS TO BE A CHRISTIAN

Jesus extended the invitation to be his follower, saying: "If anyone wants to come after me, let him disown himself and pick up his torture stake and continually follow me." (Matt. 16:24) Those who are true Christians have full faith that Jesus Christ is God's specially Anointed One and only-begotten Son, the Promised Seed who sacrificed his human life as a ransom, was resurrected and exalted to the right hand of Jehovah, and the one who received authority to subdue his enemies and vindicate Jehovah's name. (Matt. 20:28; Luke 24:46; John 3:16; Gal. 3:16; Phil. 2:9-11; Heb. 10:12, 13) Christians view the Bible as the inspired Word of God, absolute truth, beneficial for teaching and disciplining mankind.—John 17:17; 2 Tim. 3:16; 2 Pet. 1:21.

More is required of true Christians than mere confession of faith. It is necessary that belief be demonstrated by works. (Rom. 10:10; Jas. 2:17, 26) Born as sinners, those who become Christians repent, turn around, dedicate their lives to Jehovah's worship and service, and submit to water baptism. (Matt.

Aid to Bible Understanding, 1971, p. 316.

13 When under trial, let no one say: "I am being tried by God." For with evil things God cannot be tried nor does he himself try anyone.

---

the gift of heavenly life. Life cannot be *earned* by imperfect humans but is the free *gift* through faith in Jesus Christ. (Rom. 6:23) The *enduring* Christian has proved that he has that faith. Its quality has been tested and found complete.

which Jehovah promised to those who continue loving him

The "crown" (life itself) is promised to all spirit-begotten Christians who continue loving Jehovah, who prove to be his real friends. This love is shown by obedience to God's commands. (1 John 5:3; contrast with Romans 1:28-32.) God, through Christ, causes the Christian's trials to work together to perfect his servants, if they endure these steadfastly, uncomplainingly and, with his help, triumphantly down till death. (Rom. 8:28; 1 Pet. 5:10)

13 When under trial, let no one say: "I am being tried by God"

When experiencing any kind of affliction or adversity, a person would be wrong in concluding that Jehovah God is trying to induce him to commit sin. If the individual lets something in connection with the trial become a temptation to him—for example, if he turns from resistance to yielding because of some selfish advantage, or because he is seeking a way to avoid facing and enduring the trial—God is not to blame. For God will give strength to endure if the Christian remains steadfast in his own heart. (Phil. 4:13) The divine

How Sin Takes Place in Humans

Commentary on the Letter of James, 1979, p. 27.

to the stake. Then they stand it up so that Jesus is hanging on it. He is bleeding. The pain is very great.

Jesus does not die right away. He just hangs there on the stake. The chief priests make fun of him. They say: "If you are a son of God, come down off the torture stake!" But Jesus knows what his Father has sent him to do. He knows that he must give his perfect life so that we can have the chance to get everlasting life. Finally, about three o'clock that afternoon, Jesus cries out to his Father and dies.—Matthew 26:36–27:50; Luke 22:39–23:46; John 18:1–19:30.

How different Jesus was from Adam! Adam did not show love for God. He disobeyed God. Neither did Adam show love for us. Because he sinned, all of us have been born with sin in us. But Jesus showed love for God and for us. He obeyed God always. And he gave his life so that he could take away the harm that Adam did to us.

Do you appreciate what a wonderful thing Jesus did? — When you pray to God, do you thank him for what his Son did? — That will show you appreciate it. And if we really do what the Great Teacher says, we will show even more how much we appreciate that he gave his life for us.

(To build appreciation for what Jesus did for us, read John 3:16; Romans 5:8, 19; 1 Timothy 2:5, 6; Matthew 20:28.)

166

Listening to the Great Teacher, 1971, p. 166.

through Christ his message of reconciliation, telling the people how man can be reconciled. Jesus laid down his life in death, which constitutes the basis for reconciliation. His death provided the ransom price, which ransom price presented as a sin-offering constitutes the atonement or expiation of the sin of man. The ransom price, however, and the sin-offering do not constitute the reconciliation of man.

The terms "ransom", "sin-offering" and "reconciliation" should not be used synonymously. To be sure, there could be no reconciliation without the ransom price being provided and presented as a sin-offering, but what would that great ransom sacrifice avail man if he knew nothing about it? He must first have knowledge. It is the will of God that all men be saved and then brought to an accurate knowledge of the truth. (1 Tim. 2: 3, 4) The ransom and sin-offering open the way for reconciliation, and then the truth of this great fact must be brought to man and man be given the opportunity of accepting the gracious provision or rejecting it. In support of this the apostle says: "Therefore, as by the offence of one judgment came upon all men to condemnation; even so by the righteousness of one the free gift came upon all men unto justification of life."—Rom. 5: 18.

There could not be a gift without the party to whom the gift is made having knowledge of the offer. A man is in great need of money. Another offers him a gold coin, but the man is blind and deaf and does not know of the offer. The gift fails for that reason. The human race is in great need of life. God is the source of life. 'Life is a gift from God through Jesus Christ our Lord.' (Rom. 6: 23) To be reconciled to God

Reconciliation, 1928, p. 253.

Chapter 30

What You Must Do to Live Forever

JEHOVAH GOD offers you something wonderful—everlasting life in his righteous new system of things. (2 Peter 3:13) But living then depends upon your doing God's will now. The present wicked world, including all who remain a part of it, is about to pass away, "but he that does the will of God remains forever." (1 John 2:17) So you must choose between two courses. One leads to death and the other to eternal life. (Deuteronomy 30:19, 20) Which one will you take?

2 How do you show that you are choosing life? First of all, you must have faith in Jehovah and in his promises. Are you firmly convinced that God exists "and that he becomes *the rewarder of those earnestly seeking him*"? (Hebrews 11:6) You need to trust God as a son or a daughter trusts a loving and merciful father. (Psalm 103:13, 14; Proverbs 3:11, 12) Having such faith, you will not doubt that his counsel is wise or that his ways are right, even if at times you do not understand matters fully.

3 However, more than faith is needed. There must also be works to demonstrate what your true feelings are about Jehovah. (James 2:20, 26) Have you done things to show that you are sorry for any failing in the past to do what is right? Have you been moved to repent or make changes to bring your life course into harmony with Jehovah's will? Have you turned around, that is, rejected any wrong course that you may have been following, and have you begun doing the things God requires?

---

1. (a) What two courses are open to you? (b) How may you choose the right course?
2. (a) If you have true faith, of what will you be convinced? (b) How will trusting God as a child trusts a loving father help you to serve him?
3. (a) In addition to faith, what else is necessary? (b) What works are needed to show that you are choosing life?

250

You Can Live Forever in Paradise on Earth, 1982, p. 250.

Dedicate yourself to Jehovah . . .

and get baptized

(Acts 3:19; 17:30) Such works will show that you are choosing life.

DEDICATION AND BAPTISM

4 What should move you to choose life by doing God's will? Appreciation should. Just think: Jehovah has made possible for you relief from all sickness, suffering, and even death! By the precious gift of his Son he has opened up to you the way to endless life in a paradise earth. (1 Corinthians 6:19, 20; 7:23; John 3:16) When Jehovah's love moves you to love him in return, what should you do? (1 John 4:9, 10; 5:2, 3) You should approach God in Jesus' name and tell him in prayer that you want to be his servant, that you want to belong to him. In this way you dedicate yourself to God. This is a personal, private matter. No one else can do it for you.

5 After you have made your dedication to God, he will expect you to live up to it. So prove that you are a person of your word by sticking to this decision, or dedication, as long as you live. (Psalm 50:14) If you keep close to God's visible organization, you can be helped by fellow Christians who will gladly give you loving encouragement and support.—1 Thessalonians 5:11.

6 However, you must do more than privately tell Jehovah that you want to belong to him. You need to show before others that

4. (a) What should move you to do God's will? (b) When you decide you want to serve God, what is it proper to do?

5. (a) After you make your dedication to God, what does he expect you to do? (b) What help is available to you in living up to your dedication?

6. (a) When you dedicate your life to God, what step then is necessary? (b) What is the meaning of baptism?

You Can Live Forever in Paradise on Earth, 1982, p. 251.

Four Requirements

Jesus Christ identified a first requirement when he said in prayer to his Father: "This means everlasting life, their *taking in knowledge* of you, the only true God, and of the one whom you sent forth, Jesus Christ." (John 17:3) Knowledge of God and of Jesus Christ includes knowledge of God's purposes regarding the earth and of Christ's role as earth's new King. Will you take in such knowledge by studying the Bible?

Many have found the second requirement more difficult. It is to *obey God's laws,* yes, to conform one's life to the moral requirements set out in the Bible. This includes refraining from a debauched, immoral way of life.—1 Corinthians 6:9, 10; 1 Peter 4:3, 4.

A third requirement is that we *be associated with God's channel,* his organization. God has always used an organization. For example, only those in the ark in Noah's day survived the Flood, and only those associated with the Christian congregation in the first century had God's favor. (Acts 4:12) Similarly, Jehovah is using only one organization today to accomplish his will. To receive everlasting life in the earthly Paradise we must identify that organization and serve God as part of it.

The fourth requirement is connected with loyalty. God requires that prospective subjects of his Kingdom support his government by *loyally advocating his Kingdom rule to others.* Jesus Christ explained: "This good news of the kingdom will be preached in all the inhabited earth." (Matthew 24:14) Will you meet this requirement by telling others about God's Kingdom?

Perhaps you are well acquainted with these requirements. Yet many persons are ignorant of God's purposes and of what he requires. Now we have a marvelous instrument to help such ones. It is the book *You Can Live Forever in Paradise on Earth.* Have you used it to help others learn what God requires of them?

An Effective Teaching Aid

The new *Live Forever* book contains knowledge that leads to everlasting life. It discusses important Bible truths that people need to understand in order to dedicate their lives to Jehovah God and to serve him acceptably. In expressing appreciation for this new Bible study aid, a Witness from Ohio, U.S.A., wrote:

"In June I had no Bible studies. As of this day, I have three Bible studies and a fourth one ready to start. All three studies are in this new publication. All three are regular and exciting. The book answers the student's questions in a precise and understandable way. . . . I cannot say 'Thank you' enough for making Bible studies easy to conduct, as well as covering every essential aspect needed by the student for gaining a lasting and heartfelt appreciation for Jehovah and his organization."

Also pointing to the book's effectiveness is the following letter: "I have been able to start three Bible studies in this book and what I have found is that the book is very good for any age group. I have a study with a woman who is 83 years old, also with two girls who are 11 years old and another one with a wom-

The Watchtower, Feb. 15, 1983, pp. 12, 13.

tunity to show their loyalty. How? By releasing Satan and his demons from their condition of restraint in the "abyss." (Revelation 20:7) By this test each one in God's earthly family may individually have the privilege of giving a personal answer to the challenge made to their heavenly Father by Satan.

26 Those who stay loyal to God will be judged worthy of everlasting life. Jehovah will give this right to them, writing their names in his "book of life." Any who rebelliously turn against God will be destroyed in the "second death." Then, Satan the Devil, along with his demons, will be destroyed forever. (Revelation 20:7-10, 15) Never, no, never, will the earth, or any other part of God's vast universe, be disturbed again by sin and rebellion. Made into a paradise where righteousness prevails, the earth will serve for all time to come as a jewel of praise to Jehovah's name.

27 Does God's purpose for a righteous rule over a paradise earth deepen your respect for his righteousness? Does it increase your appreciation of his wisdom? Does it move you to express your love for him? If so, then you should do all you can now to serve him wholeheartedly. Share in telling others of Jehovah's name and purpose. (Psalm 89:14-16 [88:15-17, *Dy*]; 1 John 4:19) Live now according to God's righteous principles, and so prepare for life eternal in the paradise earth under the Kingdom's righteous rule.

---

26. What will be the outcome for (a) those who stay loyal to God? (b) those who turn against God? (c) Satan and his demons?
27. If we really want life in the paradise earth, what should we do now?

The Truth That Leads to Eternal Life, 1968, pp. 112, 113.

The Distinction Between Watchtower Believers

In Romans 3:22 we learn that God's righteousness is through faith in Jesus—for all who believe. There is NO distinction. The Bible teaches that *all* who believe are without distinction—they are children of God. Yet the Watchtower teaches another gospel—a gospel of partiality. Only a few special persons are said to be God's children. The Watchtower's gospel excludes the great majority of true believers from God's promise of sonship. In fact, they say God will not be the Father of most believers until they attain actual perfection! The Watchtower says only "by virtue of the prospect of eventually becoming Jehovah's perfect sons, they address him *prospectively* as 'Our Father' " (see p. 245, italics mine).

The Watchtower gospel of partiality is not the same gospel found in the Bible. The Bible says "God shows no partiality" (Gal. 2:6). The first epistle of John is written to believers and says, "Now we are the children of God" (1 John 3:2). It also says in chapter 5, verses 11–13, "The witness is this, that God has given us eternal life, and this life is in His Son. He who has the Son has the life; he who does not have the Son of God does not have the life. These things I have written to you who believe in the name of the Son of God, in order that you may know that you have eternal life."

The Apostle John says that eternal life is the promise Jesus gave to us who believe. But Jehovah's Witnesses are told that believers *do not* have assurance of eternal life. This is the same lie that false teachers tried to bring into the early church. But John, writing to the believers, says this, "Let that abide in you which you heard from the beginning. If what you heard from the beginning abides in you, you also will abide in the Son and in the Father. And this is the promise which He Himself made to us: eternal life. These things I have written to you concerning those who are trying to deceive you" (1 John 2:24–26). Don't let the Watchtower deceive you! You can be assured of your salvation and *know* that you have eternal life if you will receive Jesus as your Lord and Savior.

and natural Israel. Just so, Christ Jesus now mediates the new covenant between Jehovah God and spiritual Israel. (Gal. 3:19, 20; Heb. 9:14-24) When Christ reigns together with these spiritual Israelites of that new covenant, he reigns over his obedient subjects on the earth, and will do so as a "priest upon his throne", a "priest for ever after the order of Melchizedek". (Ps. 110:4; Zech. 6:13; Rev. 20:4, 6) Christ Jesus as the Greater Moses now mediates the new covenant toward his remnant of spiritual Israel, but he is not yet begetting earthly children. That is, he is not yet giving the "other sheep" the standing of sons of his, sons of "The everlasting Father". (Isa. 9:6) But these faithful ones will become such during his thousand-year reign after Armageddon; and now, by virtue of the prospect of eventually becoming Jehovah's perfect sons, they address him prospectively as "Our Father".

AS CONCERNS THE DEAD

[15] Concerning the dead in the graves, Christ Jesus said that the hour would come in which they would hear his voice, and would come forth from the tombs. Those that have done evil coming forth "unto the resurrection of judgment", they will come forth on earth as humans. (John 5:28, 29, *Am. Stan. Ver.*) An automatic justification of them in advance while they are still in the graves is not possible for them, neither is such a thing necessary for them, before they can be awakened from the sleep of death. (Note *The Watchtower,* November 1, 1904, page 334.) Such a thing is no more necessary for them in order to bring them forth than it is necessary in order for Satan the Devil to be brought forth from the abyss at the end of the thousand-year reign of Christ. Now you will note that these humans who have done evil are brought unto the "resurrection of judgment", which shows they are not yet justified. They are brought forth that they may avail themselves of the benefits of their King's ransom sacrifice and attain to justification by receiving life through him as "The everlasting Father". The death, which is due to inheritance from Adam, is to be wiped out during the millennial reign of this "everlasting Father." —Rev. 21:4.

[16] The faithful men and women of old time prior to Christ now come under consideration. It is written that they endured all manner of trials of faith, endurance and integrity, some of them being tortured at enemy hands, but not accepting deliverance by a compromise. Why not? "That they might obtain a better resurrection." (Heb. 11:35) The Scriptures indicate that they will be resurrected in human perfection toward the beginning of Christ's thousand-year reign, in order that they may be the "new earth", the righteous visible earthly organization, to represent the kingdom of heaven.—Heb. 11:39, 40.

[17] Their being brought forth in human perfection is not an automatic justification, nor an arbitrary affair, effected unilaterally by God. They are not able to get this resurrection before the church of God has been rewarded with "some better thing", the heavenly resurrection to be with Christ Jesus in the temple. (Heb. 11:39, 40) Furthermore, they underwent great provings of their faith at much privation and suffering, in order that they might obtain a resurrection better than that to be obtained by the rest of mankind. When they awake from death's sleep to life on earth under the Kingdom, they will still have the faith and integrity with which they died. And on seeing then the realization of the things to which they once looked forward according to God's promises and prophecies, they will at once vow and render allegiance to the reigning King Christ Jesus and will accept life at his hands. This will qualify them, so that the King will make them "princes in all the earth".—Ps. 45:16.

[18] At the end of Christ's millennial reign all then living on earth will be perfect, by the uplifting power of the Kingdom. But will they all be justified? That all depends upon God, who is the One that justifies. Hence, by God's permission, they will be tested by Satan the Devil, who will be loosed for just a short time before his everlasting, uninterrupted destruction takes place. Those who yield to Satan will be destroyed. Those of perfect humankind who keep their integrity toward God and his King and universal sovereignty will be the ones that Jehovah God will then justify to everlasting life as human sons of God, by his wondrous grace through Jesus Christ their King. Then right to eternal life on the Paradise earth will be theirs, on a permanent basis. Justification will be complete.

15. Are those dead in the graves that have done evil automatically justified before being brought forth? and unto what opportunity do they come forth?
16. When and how will the faithful ones of old come forth?
17. Why will this not be an automatic justification of them in a one-sided action by God?
18. How will justification of the earth's inhabitants finally be completed?

FROM PRISON TO FOOD ADMINISTRATION

A SHEPHERD boy was the first one to be named "Joseph", dutifully giving attention to his father's flocks. Jacob, his father, who dwelt in tents in the land of Canaan, sent Joseph to a distant town to ascertain the condition of the flocks which Joseph's ten half-brothers were attending. In the prophetic drama which here begins Joseph pictures another good shepherd, namely, Christ Jesus, the Son of Jehovah God, and whom Jehovah sent to

The Watchtower, Aug. 15, 1945, p. 253.

Is Jehovah God Your Heavenly Father?

Dear Jehovah's Witness,

How often have you prayed these words, "OUR Father in the heavens, let your name be sanctified" (Matt. 6:9, NWT)? Wouldn't it be a tragedy to know that no matter how hard you tried to please Him, He did not hear your prayers? Have you ever doubted whether Jehovah acknowledged you as His child?

Perhaps most of you have simply taken it for granted that you are truly God's adopted spiritual sons and daughters. Here is some shocking news! The Watchtower leaders say that most of you are definitely not children of God! Your leaders say that not only are you not God's children now, but that you *cannot* be His children until you have passed a test. When does this test take place? Over one thousand years from now! If you pass the test, then and only then can you call God your Father. Your leaders say:

> Hence, before adopting them [this means you] as his free sons through Jesus Christ, Jehovah God will subject all these perfected human creatures to a thorough test for all time. (See p. 248.)

The Watchtower claims that you can get into God's family by working for it:

> Jehovah God will justify, declare righteous, on the basis of their own merit all perfected humans who have withstood that final, decisive test of mankind. He will [future] adopt and acknowledge them as his sons through Jesus Christ. (See p. 249.)

What a heavy burden! Your own leaders say that you are not God's children and unless you measure up to the standards of righteousness as defined in Watchtower publications, He will never accept you. How is your service for Jehovah? Do you meet His standards? Could you be doing more? If you really tried, don't you think you could put more hours in the witnessing work? How much is enough?

We have seen how the Watchtower says to reach God. What does the Bible say?

> Everyone believing that Jesus is the Christ has been born from God, and everyone who loves the one that caused to be born loves him who has been born from that one. (1 John 5:1, NWT)

Do *you* fall into this category of "everyone"? Do *you* love the Heavenly Father and Jesus Christ? If so, the Bible says you have been "born from God." Unfortunately the Watchtower leaders disagree. They say that only a small number of their group actually are "born from God."[2] Do you want to follow the Bible or the Watchtower?

Do you have the *assurance* of everlasting life? The Bible says:

> And this is the witness given, that God gave us everlasting life, and this life is in his Son. He that has the Son has this life; he that does not have the Son of God does not have this life. I write you these things that you may know that you have life everlasting, you who put your faith in the name of the Son of God. (1 John 5:11–13, NWT)

According to verse eleven, God has *already* given some everlasting life. Are *you* among this group? The Watchtower says that you are not! Do you have the "Son of God," Jesus? If you do, the Bible says you have everlasting life. Again, the Watchtower disagrees. Do you know that the very reason John wrote this letter was to inform Christians that they already had everlasting life? Those who put their faith in Jesus *have* everlasting life (v. 13). Do you?

Today many Jehovah's Witnesses who leave the Watchtower are finding a real relationship with Jehovah God through Jesus. Would you like to be able to call God your father and *know* you are really secure in His family?

---

[2]See *Aid to Bible Understanding*, 1971, p. 1529.

of Christ's earthly human subjects will be uplifted to human perfection. All traces of sin and of death that mankind has inherited by birth from the sinner Adam will have been wiped out; the "law of sin and of death" will have been abolished from all living inhabitants of the earth. This will mark the realization of the apostle John's vision: "And the sea gave up those dead in it, and death and Ha′des [Sheol] gave up those dead in them, and they were judged individually according to their deeds. And death and Ha′des [Sheol] were hurled into the lake of fire. This means the second death, the lake of fire." Ah, yes, because of the priestly, governmental work of God's Messianic kingdom over mankind on earth, "death will be no more, neither will mourning nor outcry nor pain be any more. The former things have passed away." (Revelation 20:13, 14; 21:4) With what freedom the glorious earthly paradise will then ring!

[36] All mankind will then be, like the perfect man Adam in the garden of Eden, free moral agents, with no inborn sin or weakness or bad inclination to enslave them to a certain course of action. Now, without any disability but with vaster understanding and experiences, they can demonstrate to God directly that their unchangeable choice, their unbreakable decision, is to worship and serve the only living and true God forever on their paradise earth. Hence, before adopting them as his free sons through Jesus Christ, Jehovah God will subject all these perfected human creatures to a thorough test for all time. To this end Jesus Christ will turn over the kingdom to God the heavenly Father. (1 Corinthians 15:24-28) The thousand years of Christ's

36. (a) How will all mankind then be as the perfect man Adam was, and what decision will they be in position to demonstrate to God? (b) Through what test must they pass successfully before Jehovah adopts them as his sons?

Life Everlasting in Freedom of the Sons of God, 1966, p. 398.

lead the entire race of restored mankind into destruction, Satan and his demons will be hurled into that "lake of fire" that symbolizes endless death. He has failed to undo the blessing and sanctifying of God's great seventh creative day. (Genesis 2:1-3) In utter defeat Satan the great Serpent and his viperous brood will lie prone, his head crushed under the heel of Jesus Christ and his heavenly brothers, the Seed of God's woman, whom Jehovah God will use as his executioner of the Serpent and his seed.—Hebrews 2:14; Romans 16:20; Genesis 3:15.

[39] What a rapturous result follows this! All the realm of the living, both the limitless invisible heavens and the paradise earth, are forever free of wickedness in action, free of the presence and activity of wicked angels and men. Jehovah God will justify, declare righteous, on the basis of their own merit all perfected humans who have withstood that final, decisive test of mankind. He will adopt and acknowledge them as his sons through Jesus Christ. (Romans 8:33) They will be ushered into the glorious freedom of the sons of God. All earth perfected will be a paradise of freedom for humans sons of God.

[40] O, then, may there soon come, in God's due time on this his seventh creative day, the "revealing of the sons of God" in the heavens! O may there now be an early satisfaction of the "eager expectation" with which all human creation has been waiting for so long, since the loss of the earthly paradise about six thousand years ago!—Romans 8:18, 19.

---

39. How and when will perfected humans on earth be ushered into the glorious freedom of the sons of God?
40. The fulfillment of what hopes do we earnestly expect soon to come?

Life Everlasting in Freedom of the Sons of God, 1966, p. 400.

Born Again. Can Jehovah's Witnesses Be "Born Again"?

Physical life begins by birth. When we were born, we came alive physically. Spiritual life also begins by birth. When we are born again, we come alive spiritually. Unless you have been made alive spiritually, you are still in your sins (see Eph. 2:5). When one is born again, it means he has come alive spiritually.

Who can be born again? The Watchtower teaches that the experience of being born again is only for a small group of people called the "anointed class." They say most people do not have to be born again. But in John 3:3 Jesus says "unless one is born again, he cannot see the kingdom of God." According to Jesus, everyone who hopes to see the kingdom *must* be born again. Do you want to see God's kingdom? Then you need to be born again.

The Watchtower says that only 144,000 can be born of God. But the Watchtower is wrong, for the Bible says in 1 John 5:1, "*Whoever* believes that Jesus is the Christ is born of God." "Whoever" can include *you*! How can you be born again? John 1:12 says, "But as many as have received Him, to them He gave the right to become children of God." You can be born again by receiving Jesus Christ as your personal Lord and Savior.

The president of the Watchtower has agreed that "a witness has no alternative." He has "to accept as authoritative and to be obeyed instructions issued in the "Watchtower". . ." (see p. 251). The Watchtower teaches that you are not among those who need to be born again. The Watchtower is wrong, and you do have an alternative. You can turn to Jesus right now and trust Him for your salvation. Romans 10:13 says, "Whoever will call upon the name of the Lord will be saved."

A in support of the statement, that is why it is put there.
Q.- What does a man do if he finds a disharmony between
the Scripture and those books? A.- You will have to
produce me a man who does find that, then I can answer,
or he will answer. Q.- Did you imply that the individual
B member has the right of reading the books and the Bible
and forming his own view as to the proper interpretation
of Holy Writ? A.- He comes - - - Q.- Would you say
yes or no, and then qualify? A.- No. Do you want me
to qualify now? Q.- Yes, if you wish? A.- The
C Scripture is there given in support of the statement,
and therefore the individual when he looks up the
Scripture and thereby verifies the statement, then he
comes to the Scriptural view of the matter, Scriptural
understanding as it is written in Acts, the seventeenth
D chapter and the eleventh verse, that the Bereans were
more noble than those of Thessalonica in that they
received the Word with all readiness, and they searched
the Scipture to see whether those things were so, and
we instruct to follow that noble course of the Bereans
E in searching the Scripture to see whether these things
were so. Q.- A Witness has no alternative, has he,
to accept as authoritative and to be obeyed instructions
issued in the "Watchtower" or the "Informant" or "Awake"?
A.- He must accept those. Q.- Are those books in a
F different position from these magazines? A.- "Watchtower"
is/

Douglas Walsh Trial, Scotland, 1954 (1958 ed.), pp. 122, 123.

Who Is the Christ—A Person or a Group?

This must seem a strange question to Christians who believe Jesus is the Christ. However, Jesus warned us that in the last days there would be counterfeits—false Christs. He said in Matthew 24:23, 24, "Then if anyone says to you, 'Behold, here is the Christ,' or 'There He is,' do not believe him. For false Christs and false prophets will arise."

The Watchtower Society teaches a false Christ. They do not believe that Jesus is the Christ by himself. They teach He is merely one member of a Christ class—only one—of the anointed members. They say there are 144,000 more members of this Christ class. These members are called the "anointed class."

For some years, this doctrine of a Christ class has not been emphasized in Watchtower publications. This is probably because it is extremely controversial and many witnesses would not accept it. However, it has never been changed or rejected; it is still a basic Watchtower doctrine. You might call it the secret doctrine of the Watchtower.

The Watchtower has claimed this class is the Savior, and is worthy of the same titles Jesus has in Isaiah 9:6. They said in *The Watchtower* of November 1881, " . . . the whole body of Christ [is] the 'Mighty God' . . . [and will] rule and bless the nations. . . . Members of that company . . . as a whole will be the *Everlasting Father* to the restored race" (see p. 253).

The Watchtower has also taught that members of this Christ class are actually gods! They said in December of 1881: "Our high calling is so great, so much above the comprehension of *men*, that they feel that we are guilty of blasphemy when we speak of being '*new* creatures'—not any longer human, but 'partakers of the *divine nature*' . . . it is claiming that we are divine beings—hence all such are Gods. Thus we have a family of God . . . When Jesus said he was *a son of God* . . . he was making himself to be also a God, or of the God family. [Just what we claim. . .]" (see pp. 254–256).

propriate to Our Lord Jesus Christ. And we might add that so perfectly is his Bride—body—church, associated with him, both in filling up the measure of the sufferings—being joined in *sacrifice* and also in the Glory that shall follow, that the same titles are applicable to the Church as his body—for "He that hath freely given us Christ, shall he not with him also freely give us all things?" "Therefore all things are yours, and ye are Christ's and Christ is God's."

After the sacrifice—soon follows the power which will, under him as our head, constitute the whole body of Christ the "Mighty God" (*el*—powerful one) to rule and bless the nations—and the body with the head, shall share in the work of restoring the life lost in Adam, and therefore be members of that company which as a whole will be the *Everlasting Father* to the restored race.

PRACTICAL PREACHING

It is objected that practical preaching is the right kind of preaching, and that prophecy is not practical. **Is this true?** It is not true. The preaching of the Ten Commandments, the social virtues, and the neighborly and moral duties may be called practical preaching by some, but it is not so in the Christian sense of the word. The most successful preaching is the preaching of the cross in which Paul gloried, and the crown for which he waited. The two advents are the poles around which the orb of duty rolls—the strong foundation on which the morality of the new man reposes. Faith lays hold of the cross, the fountain of divine mercy, and out of love to Him that first loved us, brings forth in the heart and life of the believer the fruits of righteousness. Hope looks forward to the crown and the kingdom, and the promised inheritance, to nerve us for the trials and duties of life, and make us victorious over all our spiritual enemies. This is practical religion. Doctrine is the root and basis and motive of practice; and in the whole range of theology there is not a more practical doctrine than the second advent—no, not one. I challenge you to show me a duty of which it is not in one way or another made the motive.

Read, and consider the following texts of Scripture. It is the motive for patient waiting, 1 Thess. 1:10; for divine hope, Titus 2:13; for moderation in all things, Phil. 4:5; for prayer to be counted worthy to stand before the Son of man, Luke 21:36; for long-suffering patience, James 5:8; for heavenly-mindedness, Luke 21:34; for perseverance in spite of persecution, 1 Pet. 1:7; of godliness and holy conversation, 2 Pet. 3:11, 12; it is the motive for earnest preaching, 2 Tim. 4:1-3: for fighting the good fight of faith, 2 Tim. 4:7, 8; for reverence and godly fear, Heb. 7:26-28; for sobriety and watching unto prayer, 1 Pet. 4:7. This is practical preaching; but if you preach these duties without the Advent, which is their chief motive and strength, you are asking the people for bricks without giving them the straw—the steam is taken from the engine and the train stops.—*Messiah's Herald.*

If the belief of the coming of the Lord has so much power to mould and influence the child of God, what indescribable power and influence should and does the belief that he *has come*—is now present a spiritual being—the "*harvest*" now progressing under his supervision as the chief reaper, and the gathering of the ripe wheat now being in progress and soon to be finished and the righteous then made to shine forth as the Sun in the kingdom of their Father—what effect as a separator and sanctifying power, should this truth have we enquire? What preaching can be so powerful?

FROM BRO. J. B. ADAMSON

DEAR BRO:—Your letter received. I shall try to go on in strong faith in all circumstances, believing the "many and exceeding precious promises" "so Christ shall be magnified in my body" by life or by death. Am working more each day, for delivering personally, calls for more preaching to twos and threes, and is very precious to them and me. I avoid those "wise" men who know it all, whose creed is all and in all for them, and go to those really truth hungry, among whom I find Christ's most precious people and *also many infidels.* Some days do not get far and then have appointments for the evening. Truly the views we hold are *true Gold* to a large and increasing class. Most timely was the tract project from every point of view. As the poor teaching and want of teaching among the clergy increases, many look out to gather rays of light. I am asked to come Sunday at one o'clock to make the third meeting with an intelligent couple, members of the M. E. church who let me talk by the half hour and hour, seeming to drink in the doctrine and rejoice in it. Last night I spent an hour with them before prayer-meeting when I was asked to go along and testify *there* of these precious things. I had to remind them I dare not do so *fully*, and of the opposition and even abuse I met almost everywhere. I may give you some incidents in detail again that will rejoice your heart.

Found the Free Methodist's very fair. The treatment better than I got *anywhere else.* Gave the pamphlet to sixteen preachers and one hundred of the most intelligent of the church membership, attending the conference from all over the state, beside in a large number of cases, also adding a word that will make the book more living for the personality attaching to it. That is the reason I talk to so many that I give the books to; so I get their attention to the book more fully. Am generally asked for explanations of our views. and though neither powerful nor eloquent of speech, I get attention to the book by complying. Thank God for the wider field thus opening. May the will of God be done in poor me, and His name get honor and blessing forever.

Yours in Christ,
J. B. A.

YOUR LETTER

We have been so much engaged by the tract work during the past three months that the issuance of the last two numbers of the W. T. has, of necessity, been considerably delayed. Our apology must be found in article under the head of "In the Vineyard."

To many who may have written important letters or ones requiring some answer, the same apology must be offered. The distribution of the pamphlets and papers has brought from their readers hundreds of letters, asking questions or requesting back numbers of the paper, etc. We answered quite a good many of these, but they come so fast, and our time has been so limited, that nearly a thousand letters and postal cards have now accumulated—unopened and unread, and probably *your letter* is among them.

The Lord has provided more office help (for it is difficult to get suitable assistance), and we hope to get caught up soon.

Let us here remark that we do not send *receipts* for regular subscriptions—the amount is too small. You know when and what you send, and we keep a careful record of all receipts. If subscriptions are lost in the mail we will be responsible for it, and be the losers. If your paper fails to come to hand any month, inform us by card if you have paid in advance, or if, as one unable to pay, you have requested to be put on the "*Lord's poor list.*"

NO BACK NUMBERS

The demand recently has exhausted our supply of back numbers of the WATCH TOWER except a few of the July number.

For the benefit of our many new readers we will republish a few articles which appeared in our columns about a year or two ago. Among others in next number will be an article on "The Beast and Image of Rev. 13."

ROME AND JERUSALEM.—The Roman Church maintains a steady attention to the Holy Land. At Jattha they have erected a new hospital, they have established a branch nunnery at Ramleh, and a nunnery and schools at Bethlehem. It would appear that the Franciscans have a new establishment at Emmaus, in addition to the large hospice at Jerusalem. On the Mount of Olives a grand sanctuary and an extensive nunnery have been erected and endowed by the Princess de la Tour d'Auvergne, who, with great devotion, spent several years on the spot, in order personally to superintend the work.

The Watchtower, Nov. 1881, p. 10.

NOTTINGHAM, ENGLAND,
November 8th, 1881.

MY DEAR SIR—Permit me though a stranger to assure you, that I can never feel sufficiently thankful that out of the thousands of copies of your book, "*Food for Thinking Christians*" distributed in this town—a copy fell into my hands: apparently it was the merest accident; but really I regard it as a direct providence. It has thrown light upon subjects which have perplexed me for years; and has made me feel more than ever, what a glorious book the Bible is, how worthy of our profoundest study. At the same time, I came from the study of your book with the conviction that a very large proportion of the Theology of our Churches and Schools, is the merest scraps of human notions, and that our huge *systems of Theology* upon the study of which, some of us have spent so many laborious years—only to be the worse confused and perplexed—are infinitely more the work of mistaken men, than the inspiration of the allwise God.

However I may differ from the book in a few minor details, I found the main argument to be resistless, commending itself to both my head and my heart. Again let me thank you on my own behalf, for the good I have received.

I find at the close of it, you make an offer to send copies to any who have reason to believe they can make a good use of them. In my church and congregation, there is a number of intelligent persons who are interested in the second coming, and who would be only too glad to read your book, I could distribute 60 or 70 copies with advantage, you say, "ask and ye shall receive"—I have faith in your generosity. Believe me to remain yours, Most faithfully ———.

LOUISVILLE, KENTUCKY,
November 22, 1881.

GENTLEMEN—Having read with the most profound interest your publication entitled; "Food for Thinking Christians," and being fairly dazzled by the wonderful light it reveals on the great "subject," I find myself thirsting for more knowledge from this seemingly inspired pen.

Therefore in accordance with the invitation extended by you on the cover of this little work I ask that you send me a few copies of "The Tabernacle and its Teachings," if in print.

With reference to the first named book, permit me to say, that I have never yet read or heard anything equal to that little volume in its influence upon my heart and life; and to my mind, it answers most grandly and conclusively the great question, "Is life worth living." Such views as it sets forth, are bound to find response in the minds and hearts of all unbiased thinking christians, for they bear the stamp of something greater than mere human conception. I only wish we could hear it from the pulpits; but I think this must shortly follow. It is good seed and in its "*due time*" will come forth.

Believe me, I am
Very Truly Yours ————

"A LITTLE WHILE"

A little while, our fightings shall be over;
A little while, our tears be wiped away;
A little while, the presence of Jehovah
Shall turn our darkness into Heaven's bright day.

A little while, the fears that oft surround us
Shall to the memories of the past belong;
A little while, the love that sought and found us
Shall change our weeping into Heaven's glad song

A little while! His presence goes before us,
A fire by night, a shadowy cloud by day;
His banner, love-inscribed, is floating o'er us;
His arm almighty is our strength and stay.

A little while! 'Tis ever drawing nearer—
The brighter dawning of that glorious day,
Blest Saviour, make our spirits' vision clearer,
And guide, oh, guide us in the shining way.

A little while! Oh, blessed expectation!
For strength to run with patience, Lord we cry;
Our hearts up-leap in fond anticipation.
Our union with the Bridegroom draweth nigh.

—*Selected.*

"YE ARE GODS"

"I have said, Ye are Gods; and all of you are children of the Most High. But ye shall die like men, and fall like one of the princes" [literally heads]. Psa. 82:6.

Our high calling is so great, so much above the comprehension of *men*, that they feel that we are guilty of blasphemy when we speak of being "*new* creatures"—not any longer human, but "partakers of the *divine nature.*" When we claim on the scriptural warrant, that we are begotten of a divine nature and that Jehovah is thus our father, it is claiming that we are divine beings—hence all such are Gods. Thus we have a family of God, Jehovah being our father, and all his sons being brethren and joint-heirs: Jesus being the chief, or first-born.

Nor should we wonder that so few discern this grand relationship, into the full membership of which, we so soon hope to come. The apostle tells us that "the *natural* man receiveth not the things of the Spirit of God . . . . *neither can he know them* because they are spiritually discerned." (1 Cor. 2:14). Just so it was, when our great Head and Lord was among men: He, having consecrated the human at 30 years of age was baptized of the spirit, and became a part-taker of the divine nature. When Jesus said he was *a son of God* the Jews were about to stone him, reasoning thus, that if a son of God, he was making himself to be also a God, or of the God family. [Just what we claim. "Beloved, now are we the sons of God"—"The God and Father of our Lord Jesus hath begotten us."] (1 John 3:2 and 1 Pet. 1:3).

Jesus does not deny that when he said he was a son, it implied that he was of the divine nature, but he quotes to them the above passage from the Psalms as being good authority and it seems as though it satisfied them, for they did not stone him. Jesus said, "Is it not written in your law, I said, Ye are Gods"? Then he proceeds to show that the "Gods" there mentioned, are the ones who receive obediently his words and example, and concludes his argument by asking whether if God calls such ones as receive his (Jesus,) teachings, Gods, whether they think that he the teacher, whom the Father had specially set apart as the head of *those Gods* could be properly said to blaspheme, when he claimed the *same* relationship as a son of God. (John 10:35).

These sons of God, like him from whom they heard the word of truth by which they are begotten, are yet in disguise; the world knoweth us not for the same reason that it knew him not. Our Father puts no outward badge or mark of our high relationship, but leaves each to walk by faith and not by sight all through the earthly pilgrimage—*down into* death. His favor and love and the Glory and Honor which belong to our station, we can now see by the eye of faith, but soon it will be realized in fact. Now we appear like *men*, and all die naturally like *men*, but in the resurrection we will rise in our true character as Gods.

"It doth not yet appear
How great we must be made;
But when we see him as he is,
We shall be like our Head."

How forcibly this is expressed by the prophet and how sure it is too, Jesus says—It cannot be broken: "I have said ye are Gods, all of you sons of the Most High. But *ye shall die like men*, and fall like one of the princes." [lit. *heads*—Adam and Jesus are the two heads.]

Then the whole family—head and body are addressed as *one*, as they will be under Christ their head, saying—"Arise O God, judge [rule, bless] the earth: for thou shalt inherit all nations." The Mighty God, and everlasting Father of the nations, is Christ whose members in particular we are. He it is that shall inherit all things and He it is that promised his body that they too should have power over the nations, and of whom Paul says "Know ye not that the saints shall judge the world?"

How forcible this scripture in connection with the thought that *all* must die like men—like the (last) one of the heads. [See article "Who Can Hear It."—*November Number, 1881, Z. W. T.*]

The Watchtower, Dec. 1881, p. 3.

with Jehovah's people helps him to understand that Jehovah has, not only a heavenly, but also an earthly, visible organization of people doing his will. Jesus foretold that among his people there would be a "faithful and discreet slave" class who would be providing the spiritual food to God's family of devoted servants on earth, acting as his channel of communication and overseeing the carrying out of the Kingdom interests world wide. (Matt. 24:45-47) These anointed overseers serve as though being guided in their activities by the right hand of Christ. They take the same viewpoint as Jesus had when he said to Jehovah, "Let, not my will, but yours take place." (Luke 22:42) To illustrate the harmony that would prevail in Jehovah's organization, Jesus likened it, in John 15:1-10, to a vine with branches. Jehovah is the Great Cultivator, Jesus is the vine and those coming into spiritual union with him are the branches. Clearly this necessitates a recognition of Jehovah's organization in the earth today. This vine is a productive one bearing fruit that will last through Armageddon.—Heb. 13: 7, 17.

15 What kind of fruit is it that those attached to the vine must bear in order to have God's favor and to avoid being pruned off as unproductive sprouts? Actually the Scriptures mention two kinds of fruitage that a Christian would endeavor to cultivate. One is the fruitage of the spirit, including love, joy, peace, long-suffering, kindness, goodness, faith, mildness and self-control. (Gal. 5:22, 23) To stay in harmony with Christ and to be pleasing to Jehovah, these qualities must be produced. But we want to see such fruitage, not only in ourselves, but also in others. Those who are disciples of Christ understand that it is Jehovah's will that they make disciples of others also. As Proverbs 11:30 says, "The fruitage of the righteous one is a tree of life, and he that is winning souls is wise." This was the work to which Paul and the early Christians devoted themselves. Paul wrote to the Romans (1:13) that he hoped to come to minister among them that he 'might acquire some fruitage also among them even as among the rest of the nations.' By this he referred to Kingdom fruitage or Christian disciples. Each one who dedicates himself to Jehovah has a responsibility in this regard to endeavor to acquire fruitage by discipling people of the nations.

16 Paul felt so strongly about this responsibility, that he said: "If, now, I am declaring the good news, it is no reason for me to boast, for necessity is laid upon me. Really, woe is me if I did not declare the good news!" (1 Cor. 9:16) This work is not one we do just in our own strength, but we can be assured of the assistance of Jehovah's spirit as long as we prepare and do our part. It is Jehovah who brings the fruitage and the increase as a result of the activities of his servants throughout the earth. Each one who dedicates himself to Jehovah has a serious responsibility before his Creator. As Ezekiel 33: 8 says, if "you actually do not speak out to warn the wicked one from his way, he himself as a wicked one will die in his own error, but his blood I shall ask back at your own hand." How much happier a course to share actively in giving the warning and as a result have the joy of rescuing many honest-hearted ones for life in Jehovah's paradisaic new system! To such ones Jesus declared: "I say, then, to you, Everyone that confesses union with me before men, the Son of man will

15. What good fruits should all Christians endeavor to produce?

16. How do the Scriptures point out a Christian's responsibility and the wise course to follow?

The Watchtower, Jan. 15, 1969.

at the time of his consecration Jesus was made surety or guarantor of the new covenant and that the new covenant was made at the time of his death. Since it must be made with him as Mediator for Israel and all mankind, it follows that he became the Mediator of the new covenant at the time of his death at Calvary. Therefore just before he went to Calvary, and on the same day, he exhibited to his disciples the cup of wine and said to them: "This is [representatively] my blood [representatively] of the new testament [covenant], which is shed for many for the remission of sins." (Matthew 26:28) The blood of Jesus therefore provided the ransom price and at the same time is the blood for making firm the new covenant.

BODY MEMBERS TAKEN IN

29 As used herein the word "inaugurate" is intended to be understood as meaning to ratify and confirm, and cause to begin to operate or function, to establish, to initiate or begin with the first act of operation. It seems quite certain from the Scriptures that when the new covenant is inaugurated and begins to function, the church, which is the body of Christ, will have part in the mediatorial work. And why this conclusion? Because the body members have been taken into the Covenant by Sacrifice and offered up by Christ Jesus as a part of his sacrifice, and therefore become of Christ, the body members functioning with him in the ministration of the new covenant.

30 God through his prophet says: "In an acceptable time have I heard thee, and in a day of salvation have I helped thee: and I will preserve thee, and give thee for a covenant of the people, to establish the earth." (Isaiah 49:8) Paul quotes this prophetic utterance and applies it to the church. (2 Corinthians 6:2) This is proof that the body members of Christ are a part of The Servant and they, together with Christ Jesus the Head, are given "for a covenant of the people, to establish the earth". It also proves that the body members will participate with the Head Christ Jesus in the administration of the covenant. Paul also shows that the prophecy has an application to the body members during the time of the selection and development of the church. In that time they are members of The Servant and are ambassadors for Christ to preach the message of reconciliation. Therefore they should see to it that this great favor from God is not received by them in vain, says the apostle.

31 Do the Scriptures teach that the church, which is the body of Christ, has anything to do with the making or sealing of the new covenant? The body members have nothing to do with making the new covenant for the obvious reason that the covenant was made between God and Jesus Christ as the representative of man before any man was begotten as a member of the church of Christ. The Scriptures say nothing about the sealing of the new covenant and certainly not that the church has anything to do with it. Referring again to Paul's argument, in Hebrews 9:17 he states that a covenant is of force or made firm over the dead victim. The man Christ Jesus was the victim of death whose blood made firm the covenant. The covenant became effective from the moment of his death. It is sure, firm, and steadfast for ever thereafter. There is no occasion then for such a thing as the sealing as that word is used in connection with the execution of documents between earthly contracting parties.

32 Beginning at Pentecost, which was several days after the new covenant was made, men began to be brought into the Covenant by Sacrifice. The disciples were there accepted as a part of Christ's sacrifice. This has been true of Christians since. Being brought into Christ these have committed to them a ministry of reconciliation, and it becomes their privilege and duty to serve that which is the spirit of the new covenant, to wit, proclaim to the people God's message of reconciliation. They are therefore ministers of the spirit of the new covenant because the spirit of it is reconciliation.—2 Corinthians 3:5, 6.

33 The law covenant was made in Egypt. Egypt is a type of the world or Satan's organization. The law covenant foreshadowed the new covenant. It is therefore appropriate that the new covenant be made in the world, and the facts show that it was made while Jesus was in the world but not a part of it. Jesus Christ on earth offered himself as the antitypical passover lamb. At the time he was slain as the antitypical lamb Jesus alone assumed the obligations of the covenant for its beneficiaries. The covenant became effective at that time. From Pentecost forward the first-borns have been passed over and delivered, not by reason of the new covenant, but by virtue of the sacrifice of the Lamb of God that takes away the sin of the world.

PARTICIPATE IN INAUGURATION

34 The body members of Christ will have part in the inauguration of the new covenant as indicated by the Scriptures. The ceremony of the inauguration of the law covenant at Mount Sinai is described by the apostle in this language: "For when Moses had spoken every precept to all the people according to the law, he took the blood of calves and of goats, with water, and scarlet wool, and hyssop, and sprinkled both the book, and all the people." (Hebrews 9:19) Both calves and goats were sacrificed on that occasion, and the blood of both sprinkled on the book of the law and upon the people. That would indicate that Moses represented there the One pictured by the animals that were sacrificed; to wit, the calf (bullock), representing Jesus, and the goat, representing the body members of the church. Once each year the law covenant was renewed with the blood of the bullock (calf) and the goat which were sacrificed on the day of atonement. Consistently, the calf and the goat would represent the same persons on both the oc-

The Watchtower, May 1, 1928, p. 135.

SECTION THREE

MINOR DOCTRINE

Chapter Fourteen

THE CROSS—ANALYSIS

Seeking to set itself apart from the traditions of "Christendom," the Watchtower declares the cross to be a pagan symbol, and teaches that Christ was put to death on an upright stake. Interestingly, early publications of *The Watchtower* bore the image of the cross (see p. 259). But after 1928, the use of the cross was felt to be "Babylonish" by the Society's second president and the "cross and crown emblems were shown to be not only unnecessary but objectionable."[1] Therefore, "some three years thereafter, beginning with its issue of October 15, 1931, *The Watchtower* no longer bore the cross and crown symbol on its cover."[2] While the use of a cross can be abused, it reminds the Christian of the shame and the suffering of Christ on his behalf.

The actual shape of the cross is a matter of debate. But the weight of the evidence seems to be standing against the Watchtower's position. Regarding the use of the cross in the first century, Michael Green has made this observation:

> Some experts doubt whether the cross became a Christian symbol so early, but the recent discoveries of the cross, the fish, the star and the plough, all well known from the second century, on ossuaries of the Judaeo-Christian community in Judaea put the possibility beyond reasonable cavil.[3]

---

[1] *1975 Yearbook of Jehovah's Witnesses*, 1974, p. 148.
[2] Ibid.
[3] Michael Green, *Evangelism in the Early Church* (Grand Rapids: Eerdmans, 1970), pp. 214–215.

At any rate, the accusation that the cross is a pagan symbol does nothing to show that Christ was crucified on something else. Would the fact that the Romans were pagans prove they could not have put Him to death?

More than all this, the Watchtower has removed the word "cross" from their translation of the New Testament. The Greek word for "cross" can refer to a pole, but the *New World Translation*'s substitution of "torture-stake" is a far cry from improvement when it comes to accuracy. Supposing the replacement of "stake" for "cross" does something to make clearer the truth, the Society's substitution of "impaled" for "crucified" is *completely* without warrant and destroys whatever advance was brought about by the use of "stake" over "cross."

The cross has no religious meaning apart from that assigned to it by those who make reference to it. It was the instrument by which the Son of God was put to death on our behalf. If some worship the image of a cross, that is without doubt outside of the will of God. But if some recall the love of God at the sight of the symbol, it makes little difference whether the "stake" has a crossbeam or not. What it means to the Christian and what it calls to mind ought not to be considered pagan, nor outside the bounds of true Christianity.

> But may it never be that I should boast, except in the cross of our Lord Jesus Christ, through which the world has been crucified to me, and I to the world. (Gal. 6:14)

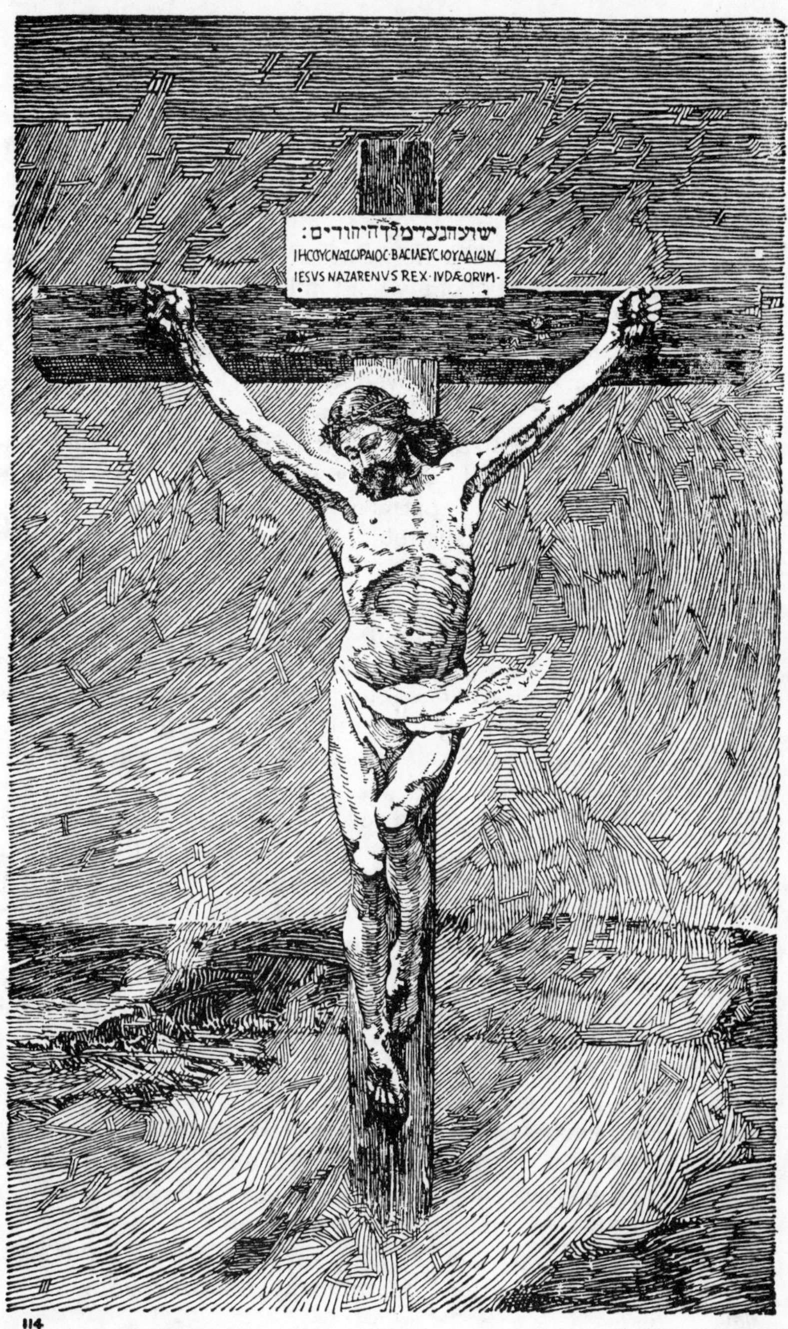

114

The Harp of God, 1921, p. 114.

Dialogue on the Christian Cross

Jehovah's Witnesses say that Jesus Christ did not die on a cross at Calvary. The Watchtower Society has taught them that Jesus was not crucified but rather died on an upright pole or stake. Is the Watchtower Society right? What does the Bible say? To get the answer, let's imagine we are listening to the following conversation.

Jay: Chris, I see that you are wearing a cross around your neck.

Chris: Yes, it is a symbol of my faith in Jesus Christ.

Jay: Don't you know that the cross is a pagan symbol and that Jesus died on a single stake without a crossbeam? Let me show you a picture of how Jesus died. This *Awake!* magazine shows Jesus with His hands over His head with one large nail through both of them. (See p. 261.) There was no crossbeam. Jesus didn't die on a cross.

Chris: Jay, what if the *Bible* disagrees with the Watchtower Society and proves that Jesus couldn't have died on a stake, in the way they claim He did?

Jay: What do you mean?

Chris: The Bible tells us in John 20:25 that the Apostle Thomas desired to see the physical proof of Christ's resurrection and he said: "Unless I shall see in His hands the imprint of the nails . . . and put my hand into His side, I will not believe." So, Jay, how many nails does the Bible say were in the hands of Jesus?

Jay: Well, it says "nails." I've never noticed this scripture before!

Chris: That's because if there is more than one nail, as this scripture shows, then the Watchtower would be wrong when it shows that there was only one nail in the hands of Jesus. In fact, the Society has unwittingly admitted that Jesus had more than one nail in his hands! In *The Watchtower* magazine they say: "In one instance, he invited Thomas to inspect the wounds inflicted in his hands by means of the *nails*." (See p. 262, italics mine.)

Jay: I see, but were crosses used at the time of Christ?

Chris: Sure, even secular sources like *Time* and *Newsweek* magazines printed articles about how Jewish archeologists had unearthed evidence of a crucifixion during the time of Christ.[4]

Jay: I must say that I am really shocked at this information.

Chris: Jay, your very life depends on learning what the Bible teaches about Jesus Christ. Would you like to know more?

Jay: Yes.

---

[4]Articles in *Time* and *Newsweek*, January 18, 1971.

urrected. This man, though being justly executed for some crime, expressed faith in Christ's coming kingdom, and this prompted Jesus Christ to promise that he would have opportunity for life there. —Luke 23:39-43.

Note also some of the other promises of God, many of which he already fulfilled in a typical or miniature way in the sixth century B.C.E., for our faith, hope and comfort:

> "The wilderness and the waterless region will exult, and the desert plain will be joyful and blossom as the saffron. Without fail it will blossom, and it will really be joyful, with joyousness and with glad crying out. . . . For in the wilderness waters will have burst out, and torrents in the desert plain." —Isa. 35:1, 2, 6.

Jesus' promise to an evildoer dying next to him was that he would be resurrected and have an opportunity for life on a paradise earth

These promises proved true in a small-scale way when Israel returned from Babylon. Their land had been utterly desolate, no humans or domestic animals, only wild beasts, having inhabited it for seventy years. Most of the land was like a desert wilderness. Yet God, pleased with their return to true worship, caused waters to break out, and in a short while the land began to blossom and to produce abundantly.

Jehovah promises permanent blessings for those who obey him under Kingdom rule, blessings like those he provided repatriated Israelites:

> "For them I shall certainly conclude a covenant in that day in connection with the wild beast of the field and with the flying creature of the heavens and the creeping thing of the ground, and the bow and the sword and war I shall break out of the land, and I will make them lie down in security."—Hos. 2:18.

If Israel had remained faithful, their peace would have endured. But they were rebellious toward God. Under Christ's heavenly rule, such rebellion will not take place. Why not? Because, on the basis of his atonement sacrifice for mankind, he will gradually bring obedient ones to perfection, wiping out selfishness and greed from the earth. This is the great difference between the basis for peace that his Kingdom rule brings as compared with that which the worldly leaders attempt to establish.

Now, by applying Bible principles, we can partially overcome bad traits and hold them generally under control. But with the full application of the merit of Christ's sacrifice, obedient ones will achieve full spiritual, mental and physical healing, with *full control* of all their faculties, completely overcoming all their imperfections. —Compare Romans 7:18-25.

Awake!, April 8, 1974, p. 14.

● In what way were the evildoers who were impaled alongside Jesus Christ fastened to the torture stake? Were they nailed or tied? —R. P., England.

It is possible that they were tied to the stake. Regarding Roman methods of impalement, *The Imperial Bible Dictionary* (Vol. I, page 377) states: "When the place of doom was reached, the criminal was stripped nearly naked, and either bound or nailed to the cross, which was then hoisted and set up." If Jewish impalement procedures had been followed in the case of Christ and the evildoers, they would first have been killed and then their corpses would have been placed on the stake. (Deut. 21:22, 23; Josh. 10:26) However, they were impaled while alive. (Luke 23:32-46) Hence, their impalements were performed according to Roman methods, which included either tying or nailing.

We know that Jesus Christ was nailed to the torture stake. On occasions following his death and resurrection, Jesus materialized fleshly bodies bearing the marks of such impalement. In one instance, he invited Thomas to inspect the wounds inflicted in his hands by means of the nails. (John 20:19-29) Yet, while the Scriptures show that Jesus was nailed to his torture stake, they do not specifically say whether the evildoers impaled beside him were nailed or tied to their stakes. So, on page 141 of its book *From Paradise Lost to Paradise Regained,* for example, the Watch Tower Society has shown regard for Biblical indications as well as acknowledgment of the fact that Roman impalement methods included both nailing and tying. There Jesus is depicted as nailed to his torture stake, whereas the illustration shows the evildoers fastened by the simplest method, by tying.

● Why is Matthew 17:21 omitted from the *New World Translation of the Holy Scriptures*? —L. F., U.S.A.

This and some other texts, or portions thereof, in the Christian Greek Scriptures are not included in the *New World Translation* because they are not found in the Greek text prepared by Cambridge University scholars B. F. Westcott and F. J. A. Hort. This master text was the one principally used by the New World Bible Translation Committee in rendering the Greek Scriptures into English in the 1950 and 1961 editions of the *New World Translation*.

Consideration of Matthew 17:21 will prove to be enlightening. While this text is not included in the *New World Translation,* there is a helpful footnote on it in the *New World Translation of the Christian Greek Scriptures,* 1950 edition. There one finds a translation of the reading of this text according to the Codex Ephraemi rescriptus of the fifth century C.E. and the Cambridge Manuscript (Cantabrigensis) of the sixth century C.E. It reads as follows: "However, this kind does not come out except by prayer and fasting." This is given as part of Jesus' answer to his disciples when they asked why they had been unable to expel a demon in a certain case. It is noteworthy, though, that various important manuscripts omit these words. Among them are the Sinaitic Manuscript and the Vatican Manuscript No. 1209, both of the fourth century C.E., and hence older than the sources just quoted. Therefore, verse 21 of Matthew, chapter 17, lacks adequate ancient textual support.

It might be observed in passing, however, that some authorities have viewed it as an interpolation from Mark 9:29. This chapter of Mark contains a parallel account of the same incident and includes this detail omitted by Matthew.

The *New World Translation* is not alone in omitting Matthew 17:21, or in showing its questionable nature in an explanatory footnote. Among other translations doing so are the *American Standard Version, An American Translation, Revised Standard Version* and *The New English Bible.*

Evidently, then, copyists made some additions to the Greek text of the Bible at times, being more prone to do this than to omit material. However, careful Biblical research has resulted in uncovering such scribal elaborations. Consequently, the most dependable Greek texts are found to be the most condensed.

From this we should not take the view that the text of the Christian Greek Scriptures has suffered measurably in transmission. Scholar Jack Finegan has stated: "The total number of New Testament manuscripts is very impressive. . . . No other Greek book has anything

The Watchtower, Jan. 15, 1966, p. 63.

Chapter Fifteen

CHRISTMAS—ANALYSIS

Christmas is a day set aside on the calendar for remembering the birth of the Savior. The world has commercialized this occasion to the point that for many, the day brings to mind little of the holy event. Yet for the Christian, the day is a special time of the year wherein the spirit the believer is to have all year is brought to focus. The concept of self-giving and placing others above self is brought to life in remembering God's wonderful gift to us. Just as John 3:16 says, "For God so loved the world, that He gave His only begotten Son," so, too, we give of ourselves in a special way during the Christmas season.

Christmas for the Jehovah's Witness is much different than it is for the Christian. While Christians are gathering together in the name of the Lord to celebrate the first advent of Christ, Witnesses must abstain not only from the celebration itself, but from everything associated with the season. They are taught Christmas is part of the false religious system and given specific commands regarding religious celebrations:

> Do you want to be part of Satan's world? Or are you for God's new system? If you are for God's new system, you will be separate from the world, including its false religion. You will heed the command: "Get out of her [Babylon the Great], my people." (Rev. 18:4.) However, getting out of Babylon the Great, the world empire of false religion, includes more than simply cutting off connections with false religious organizations. It also means having nothing to do with the religious celebrations of the world. (2 Cor. 6:14–18.)
>
> Christmas is a prominent religious holiday today.[1]

The Watchtower consistently places the birth of Jesus in contrast to the "memorial of His death." They claim that Jesus told His followers to observe a memorial of His death, not of His birth.[2] Although Scripture itself never makes such a contrast, the Society

[1]*You Can Live Forever in Paradise on Earth*, 1982, p. 212.
[2]Ibid., p. 213.

does so in order to substantiate an argument from silence, teaching Witnesses not to observe His birth.

The truth is, regardless of the actual date of the historic event, the birth of the Savior is worthy of celebration and remembrance. The birth of Jesus was brought to the attention of the Wise Men by means of a star in the heavens. But it was not on the actual day of His birth, but sometime thereafter when they received the opportunity to honor Christ's birth, and then they "fell down and worshiped Him" (Matt. 2:11). On the day of Jesus' birth it was the angels who first celebrated. The message the angel of the Lord brought was, "I bring you good news of a great joy which shall be for all the people" (Luke 2:10). While Christians rejoice in the good news, the Witnesses are forbidden to take part.

Should We Celebrate the Birth of Christ?

Should we celebrate the birth of Christ? Note how Chris and Jay handle this question.

Jay: Chris, you seem to be excited about the holiday season.

Chris: Yes, for Christians it is a wonderful time because we celebrate the birth of our Lord.

Jay: Chris, I know you are sincere in your faith, but Christians are not supposed to observe Christ's birth.

Chris: But, Jay, did you know that the Watchtower used to teach the *opposite* of what you are saying?

Jay: What do you mean?

Chris: Well, let me explain. They once claimed:

> . . . the celebration of our Lord's birth is not a matter of divine appointment or injunction, but merely a tribute of respect to him. . . . (See p. 266.)

Past Watchtower presidents have given and received presents on Christmas Day. (See p. 267.) They have even requested Jehovah's Witnesses to give Watchtower books as presents. (See p. 268.) Jay, if the Watchtower was God's spokesman to men when they taught this, then God wanted Christians to celebrate Christmas at that time.

Jay: But we don't teach that anymore. Now we have new light about Christmas.

Chris: How can you trust the Watchtower's new light about Christmas when there is an absolute contradiction between the former Watchtower teaching and what they say today? On one hand, they said we should celebrate the birth of Jesus, and on the other hand, we shouldn't. The Bible says, "God is not a God of confusion" (1 Cor. 14:33).

Jay: Well, I know the Bible doesn't tell us to celebrate Christ's birth.

Chris: That's true, but it does tell us in John 5:23, ". . . in order that all may honor the Son, even as they honor the Father." This is what happened at His birth. In Luke 2:11–14, we find these words of the angels to the shepherds:

> "For today in the city of David there has been born for you a Savior, who is Christ the Lord. 'And this will be a sign for you: you will find a baby wrapped in cloths, and lying in a manger.' And suddenly there appeared with the angel a multitude of the heavenly host praising God, and saying, 'Glory to God in the highest, and on earth peace among men with whom He is pleased.' "

Jay, that was the greatest celebration of all time! Don't you think Jesus deserves to be honored?

Jay: I guess so. I'll do some thinking about what you have said.

Pekah and Hoshea. On one slab from his palace Sargan tells the story of the capture of Samaria. The Taylor Cylinder, found in Nineveh in 1830, and now in the British Museum, describes Sennacherib's conquest of Judah in the time of Hezekiah. The stone records of Assyrian history, called the 'Eponym Canon,' discovered in 1862, in Nineveh, by Sir Henry Rawlinson, help us to gain a more exact knowledge of the dates of this period."

Our Golden Text, which constitutes the caption of this article, contains a valuable thought for any occasion, but one especially suited to this review. Looking at the history of God's earthly people, Israel after the flesh, we can readily see that all of their difficulties and failures to attain to the blessings that were before them, were closely associated with neglect of the truth set forth in our Golden Text. They did not sufficiently sanctify the Lord God in their hearts and let him be the only fear and only dread—fear to displease him, dread to come under his reproof. On the contrary, they were prone to forget the Lord and all the blessings and mercies they had received from him and the obligations they were under to him.

They forgot, too, that a part of the Covenant entered into between the Lord and them was that if as a people they would honor him and serve him he would bless and honor them, but if as a people they rejected or neglected him, they were to have special disciplines and corrections. Their neglect of the Lord, their seeking without the Lord to establish themselves and to have the assistance and co-operation, and to adopt the manners, customs, etc., of foreign nations, all these were a part of their failure to properly worship the Lord and serve him alone. How great was their mistake! And yet we are to remember that a remnant did not make this mistake, though they were few. This remnant already received a blessing in the present life and are to have a still greater share in the favors of God in the coming age.

Similarly nominal spiritual Israel has neglected the counsel of this Golden Text, and, instead of having the Lord first, has been disposed to forget the Lord and to affiliate with the world, to seek worldly favor and co-operation. Fear to displease the world has largely controlled Churchianity; desire to have the world's favor and approval has apparently been more important before the mind of Churchianity than the approval of the Lord and a fear of the loss of his favor.

As a result we see today worldly customs in the professed Church of Christ, and note that these worldly customs have drawn into the nominal Church, as they were intended to do, large numbers of the world, unjustified, unsanctified, "tares," and that these now quite overwhelm the few who are loyal to the Lord and the spirit of his Truth. Nevertheless there is today, and has been all throughout the Gospel age, a "little flock" a 'remnant," which did indeed trust the Lord, and which did indeed sanctify the Lord God in their hearts and make him alone their fear and him alone their dread—fear to displease him, dread to lose the light of his kindness, his favor. We trust, dear friends, that the majority of those who read these words are of the latter class. If so all things are working together for good to such, because they love the Lord and have been called according to his purpose, and are seeking to make their calling and election sure by so running as to obtain the prize.

"THE PRINCE OF PEACE."

—ISAIAH 9:1-7.—DECEMBER 25.—

Golden Text:—"His name shall be called Wonderful, Counsellor, Mighty God, Everlasting Father, Prince of Peace."—R. V.

EVEN though Christmas day is not the real anniversary of our Lord's birth, but more properly the annunciation day or the date of his human begetting (Luke 1:28), nevertheless, since the celebration of our Lord's birth is not a matter of divine appointment or injunction, but merely a tribute of respect to him, it is not necessary for us to quibble particularly about the date. We may as well join with the civilized world in celebrating the grand event on the day which the majority celebrate—"Christmas day." The lesson for the occasion is a most happy choice, fitting well to the series of lessons it follows.

The first verse seems much better translated in the Revised Version, thus: "But there will be no gloom in her that was in anguish. In former time he brought into contempt the land of Zebulun and the land of Naphtali, but in the latter time hath he made it glorious, by way of the sea, beyond Jordan, Galilee of the nations." The Prophet penned these words probably shortly after the ten-tribe kingdom known as Ephraim had gone into captivity to Assyria. Zebulun and Naphtali were the names of the principal districts of Ephraim; and Isaiah, prophetically looking from those desolated lands of his time, under the guidance of the holy Spirit, points out that in the latter time a great blessing is coming to those very lands.

It was centuries after Isaiah's prophecy that our dear Redeemer appeared among men and spent most of his time, did most of his mighty works, and performed most of his mighty miracles in these lands of Zebulun and Naphtali, called Galilee, which in the time of Isaiah had been denuded of its Jewish population and had been settled by Gentile emigrants, "Galilee of the Gentiles." Subsequently these Gentiles gathered more particularly in the vicinity of the city of Samaria, and became known as Samaritans, and, noting the hopes of the Israelites, were inclined to claim a certain share in the blessings belonging to the people into whose lands they had been introduced. The Jews, however, disowned them as being still Gentiles, and would have no dealings with the Samaritans, as the Apostle pointed out.

Our Lord himself instructed the apostles to go not in the way of the Gentiles nor into any city of the Samari-

The Watchtower, Dec. 1, 1904, p. 364.

of the divine will—love. Not that we can walk up to the spirit of the law, but that when we walk after it with our best endeavors God counts it unto us as though we actually walked up to its requirements, the merit of Christ our Lord and Head being imputed to us and compensating for all our unwilling imperfections.

Nevertheless, although the new creatures are not under the Mosaic law, yet they may gain valuable lessons from an examination of that law; for the study of its precepts will open wider and wider their eyes of understanding to perceive what are the particular and exact requirements of the divine law and what are our own natural shortcomings. Our study of the Mosaic law, however, will not bring us condemnation. We are not under that law, but under grace. We are not condemned because unable to fulfil every requirement of the Mosaic law, but justified before God and the law through the merit of our Lord Jesus Christ when we put forth our best efforts to the accomplishment of the divine will. In the declaration of the law designed for Israel we see the outlines of the perfect will of God; and the more clearly we discern this, the more will it enable us to fulfil the desire of our hearts and to come into the fuller accord with God's perfect will in thought, word and deed. But let us to whom the Lord has given the royal law of love remember well that it is much more searching, much more strict, than the law of the Ten Commandments given to Israel; for our law relates to us according to the mind, the heart, as new creatures in Christ, and not merely to the flesh and its appetites. Thus we see the necessity of a daily scrutiny of thought, word and deed, as suggested by our Morning Resolve.

LETTERS AFIELD

A MESSAGE OF GRATITUDE

TO THE DEAR FRIENDS EVERYWHERE:—

Grace, mercy and peace be multiplied unto you!

Am taking advantage of an opportunity to dictate this note to extend to all the dear friends throughout the United States and Canada my heartfelt thanks for the great love bestowed upon us and manifested in the numerous Christmas presents which I and my associates have received, as well as cards, letters and messages of love. May the Lord bless you one and all!

I am unable to write you personally, and so am asking that this general message be given you. I am overwhelmed by your expressions of love, dear brethren. May the Lord reward you richly!

Your brother and servant by his grace,
J. F. RUTHERFORD.

CONVINCED OF HIS MISTAKEN ACTION

DEAR BRETHREN:

It is with deep regret for my action taken about a week ago that I humbly write this letter, acknowledging that I have made a grievous mistake in supposing for one moment that THE WATCH TOWER was no longer being guided of the Lord. I attended a meeting of opponents, at which were some hitherto prominent brethren. Their arguments were so convincing that upon my return I immediately sent the copy of the letter to you, without any meditation or without looking to the leading of the Lord in the matter.

However, since that time I have meditated very much over the matter, looking up various Scriptures. Now I am fully convinced of my mistake, and beg to apologize for being so hasty in such an important matter and for any inconvenience or trouble I may have caused there. Hoping that my name will again be placed among the readers of THE WATCH TOWER, and also as a member of the International Bible Students Association, I remain

Your brother in the service of the Lord,
G. W. V. B.—*Wash.*

OUR PASTOR'S WORDS AS TRUE NOW AS EVER

DEAR BRETHREN IN CHRIST:

The TOWER is certainly grand; and we believe the words of our dear Pastor are just as true now as they ever were (See F 658) and that THE WATCH TOWER will be used of the Lord in the future as well as in the past. (Luke 12:37; Revelation 8:3; 14:18) The "Mizpah" of Jeremiah seems to teach the same thing, Mizpah meaning "watchtower."

We ask an interest in your prayers that we may stand ever faithful, and assure you of ours in harmony with the Vow.

Yours in the one hope, Bro. and Sr. K. F. B.—*Ohio.*

THE FATHER'S BOUNTIFUL TABLE

DEAR BRETHREN:

We just want to tell you something about our appreciation of the last two issues of THE WATCH TOWER. We feel sure we have never enjoyed a TOWER as we have that of Nov. 1st. particularly the first article and the reproduction from one of the old TOWERS—"Divine Providences." We have read and re-read these articles, and it seems to us they are just about the finest we have ever had the good fortune to see, and we are grateful to our heavenly Father for his abundant and delicious spread. Every article in the TOWER of Nov. 1st is a gem; and the issue of Nov. 15th is also fine as far as we have read, particularly the first article. The dear Father is certainly setting a most wonderful and bountiful table before us, and it seems that the food gets better as the end of the way draws nearer.

Be assured that it is our daily prayer that our heavenly Father will guide and direct you in the work you are doing; and we ask also that you remember us in your petitions.

Your brother by his grace, P. A. G.—*Tenn.*

COULD NOT MAKE DEAF EARS HEAR

DEAR BRETHREN:

How may I become a member of the Church of Present Truth? I was converted to the belief last winter when a copy of one of your publications was placed in my hands; and I believe that it was by divine providence that I received the volume. I had long struggled with and argued against theories on the Bible as expounded by the Sunday School journals of various churches, until at times I was ashamed of myself, and thought that perhaps the devil was inspiring me to argue against God's Word. But now I see that I was blindly struggling for truth and light.

At the time when I got the volume I was teacher of the men's Bible class in the First Methodist Church here. I realized that it taught me to leave the erring church; but I was so desirous of bringing the light to those whom I had learned to love that I continued to teach the class, discarded theories of the journals and substituted as much present truth as I knew. I was the president of the Gospel Team; and I gave it to them there and tried to lead them to the real truth. But this was all in vain. In a little while I despaired and quit. So at last I have given up all hope of making a deaf ear hear. I am "done." Have you any advice for me?

Sincerely yours, A. E. J.—*Kans.*

GRATEFUL APPRECIATION OF THE TOWER

BRETHREN BELOVED IN THE LORD:

Grace and peace be multiplied unto you! Many times have I had in mind to write to you to tell you of my deep love for you, and of how much I appreciate what you are doing for me in the way of strengthening my faith and increasing my joys in the Lord through THE WATCH TOWER; but I have refrained from so doing because I know that you are all quite busy. But when I read the last TOWER (Dec. 1st issue) I could refrain no longer, as it contained just the subjects that I have been considering for the past three months, using the same references—the back numbers of the TOWER. From the TOWER of 1911, pages 180-182, the article on "The Rewards of Sacrifice," together with the subject, "The Two Parts of the Harvest," I am fully assured, dear brethren, that the Lord is using the same channel in giving the necessary food for the upbuilding of his people. Our prayers have been, and are yet, on your behalf that the dear Lord may continue to guide and direct your work and labors of love to the praise of the God of all grace. In the Nov. 15th issue the article on "Self-Denial"—in fact, all the articles are excellent; and we feel that we could not do without the "meat in due season," "things new and old," from the storehouse.

With love to all at the Watch Tower office, I remain

Your brother in Christ, J. C.—*Ohio.*

I. B. S. A. BEREAN BIBLE STUDIES
FOR MONTH OF FEBRUARY

QUESTIONS FROM
MANUAL ON SERIES SIXTH
"STUDIES IN THE SCRIPTURES"
STUDY VII—"THE LAW OF THE NEW CREATION"

Week of Feb. 2	Q. 7-13	Week of Feb. 16	Q. 20-26
Week of Feb. 9	Q. 14-19	Week of Feb. 23	Q. 27-32

Question Manuals on Vol. VI., Studies in the Scriptures, 10c each, postpaid.

The Watchtower, Jan. 15, 1919, p. 31.

ment of the reign 473 or 474 B. C. This would give the date of 454 or 455 B. C. as his twentieth year and the date of the commission."

It appears that Archbishop Ussher was the first to establish the date of Nehemiah's commission as 454 B. C. as a result of lecturing on the 70 weeks of Daniel in Trinity College, Dublin, in 1613. Other critics who support the date given in DAWN II. are Vitringer, Kruger and Hengstenberg, as well as Tregelles, above quoted. With much love, I remain,

Yours in the Lord, J. P. BURNS,—*England.*

"SCRIPTURE STUDIES" AS CHRISTMAS GIFTS

DEAR FRIENDS:—

It might interest you to know that we are already offering the books for "Christmas gifts." We find that many secure their Christmas presents several months ahead, and that this month is the one in which many are very pleased to secure "*such a beautiful, appropriate, and above all such a reasonable* [in price] *gift!*" Often we can get orders for several sets in one home, in view of the fact that the books make such splendid gifts. Today we got more than one order on this account. We mention this because we think it might help wonderfully during the next six weeks in securing orders from people who would perhaps not buy for their own use. We say, "Many are taking them for gifts, and it is of course a compliment to a friend's intelligence to give him a book, and especially a work of this kind, and you get the entire three for only 98c!"

With much Christian love and appreciating more and more the great privilege of laboring in the harvest field, we are, Yours in Him,

J. AND L. HUTCHINSON,—*Colporteurs.*

THE WATCH TOWER BIBLES

DEAR BROTHER RUSSELL:—

I wish to thank you for the copy of the new Bible you have so kindly sent me. It is needless for me to tell you that I am delighted with it, not only because of its elegant binding and compact form (such that it will easily go into the side-pocket of an ordinary coat), but especially because of the extraordinary helps for Bible study that it provides. In the 220 pages of abbreviated DAWN comments there are 11,608 references to the DAWNS and booklets; or, in other words there are that many Scripture explanations utilized. 4793 texts are examined—about one-seventh of the total number in the Bible.

Just here let me say that I have been deeply impressed in gathering and compiling these explanations to note how perfectly they are in accord with each other and with the Word itself. This beautiful harmony of thought and expression speaks very significantly of the fact that the Lord of the Harvest has exercised close supervision of his message. Few works have ever been subjected to such a critical analysis, and nothing but the TRUTH could stand before the word-by-word and clause-by-clause method which was used. It now remains to be seen whether the Truth people, with their sharp eyes, will find that my representation of your works has been as faithful and as accurate as your representation of the Scriptures has been! If they find a whole lot of mistakes I will take refuge in the thought that I did the best I could and that it was a hurried job —only about 1400 hours of labor altogether.

Sister Seibert has done a grand work in the "Epitome of the Faith." The first thing I did when I got the Bible was to read every word of it. I cannot conceive how it could be more complete in plan, orderly in arrangement or concise in statement. I have already made use of it on two occasions with excellent results, and am sure it will be greatly appreciated.

I feel sure this new Bible will have a very rapid sale, as I do not see how any one who is really in the Truth can afford to go without it.

Your brother and servant in Christ,

CLAYTON J. WOODWORTH.

CHARITY BEGINS AT HOME

DEAR BROTHER RUSSELL:—

Being my Pastor in a very special sense to me, and knowing of your deep interest in all who understand, even to a limited degree, the Harvest Message, I am taking the liberty to write you on a subject that has been on my mind for a long time.

I am sorry, very sorry to say it, but many times I have found, on close acquaintance with the brethren in the Truth, men who professed full consecration, that they neglected their families so very badly relative to the Truth. Seemingly anxious to spread the Truth amongst their friends and neighbors, yet they made no provision for their wives, so that they could attend the meetings, and would even talk before their families in such a way as to leave the impression that maybe the Truth was not for their wives and children.

I confess this is beyond my comprehension—how a man with brains enough to comprehend the Truth, and after reading the six volumes of MILLENNIAL DAWN and the TOWER, could or would do or say such!

A man can leave all the cares of the home and the care of the children to a perhaps not too strong wife, and spend all of his spare time while at home reading; and Sunday morning, instead of helping his wife and encouraging her, just get up and eat, dress and leave, and let her know he expects a hot dinner when he returns from the class, and it is no wonder she cannot go. It certainly doesn't look fair to me. Just nominal Church people do better than that.

From the depths of my heart I pity the man who has the Truth and objects to his children attending the nominal Church Sunday school and makes no effort to teach his children and never has family prayer unless some of the Colporteurs or Elders call on him. These things are so. I wish I could believe otherwise.

Several cases have come to my personal knowledge where the wife was really hungering for fellowship with the class and believed all the Truth she could understand, and whose husband, while himself attending the class every Sunday, was the real cause that hindered her. I feel confident a special, pointed article from your pen would do good to many.

Yours in the service of the King, ——, —*Tenn.*

The Watchtower, Nov. 15, 1907, p. 351.

Does the Christmas Date Matter?

Does it matter which date we celebrate the birth of Christ? Let's look at a further discussion between Chris and Jay as they talk about Christmas.

Jay: Hi, Chris. I've been thinking about what you said the other day about Christmas. You mentioned some good points, but some things are still bothering me.

Chris: What's on your mind?

Jay: Well, what time of the year do you think Jesus was born?

Chris: Jay, I'm not really sure; I celebrate it in December. Christians are not honoring a date, but an *event*. It really doesn't matter when Jesus was born, just *that* He was born.

Jay: But, *The Watchtower* says it really does matter.

Chris: Yes, they do, but *The Watchtower* only teaches the opinion of the Watchtower leaders concerning the importance of the Christmas date.

Jay: Oh, no! The Society speaks for Jehovah God.

Chris: How long do you think they have been speaking for Jehovah?

Jay: Since the Watchtower began—about 100 years ago.

Chris: Jay, let me read you a few statements about the Christmas date from past *Watchtowers*. You be the judge whether these statements show *The Watchtower* is a confusing magazine. In a December 1903 issue they say, "It is quite immaterial upon what day that event, of so great importance to all, is celebrated. Upon this day, so generally celebrated, we may properly enough join with all whose hearts are in the attitude of love and appreciation toward God and toward the Savior." (See p. 271.)

Then they said in December 1904, ". . . it is not necessary for us to quibble particularly about the date." (See p. 272.)

And look at this. *The Watchtower* from December 1926 said, "The event is so important that it is always appropriate to call it to the minds of the people, regardless of the date." (See p. 273.)

The Watchtower, which claims to speak for God, has taught Jehovah's Witnesses that Christ's birth should be honored and the date *doesn't matter*. Now, they say the date *does* matter. Has God changed His mind?

Jay: No, God doesn't change His mind.

Chris: Jay, do you think men change their minds?

Jay: Yes, but do you mean the Society is making up these doctrines from their *own* opinions?

Chris: That is exactly what I mean. It is obviously not from Jehovah God, right?

Lord had established in Israel, were continued through David's career, and these very properly represent the warfare which all the Lord's beloved ones must endure faithfully if they would abide in his favor. Loyalty to the principles of the divine government is of prime importance; the royal banner must be lifted high; our lives must be risked and be given in defence of the divine character and teachings if we would be counted worthy of the Kingdom of glory, if we would belong to the house of David, the beloved, which the Lord has promised shall be established forever—the house of Christ, the house of sons.

We review Solomon's peaceful reign and note how its opening years were typical of the blessings of the noontide of the Millennial Kingdom. The glories and wisdom and wealth of Solomon were but trifles in comparison to the wisdom, honor and riches which God has promised to those who love him. Respecting the faithful overcomers, we remember it is declared that they shall know even as they are known by God, that they shall share the glory, honor and immortality of their glorious Head and Master.

We remember, too, the typical temple, and its construction from materials previously prepared during the Levitic reign, and how this prefigured our preparation as living stones for the glorious temple of the future, in which God shall make his presence known to all the families of the earth for their blessing and uplifting, and for the joy of all those who shall respond to the blessed influences of the Millennial Kingdom. The thought of the preparation of these stones causes us much comfort and joy respecting the trials and difficulties of this present time, as we realize that they are working out for us and in us preparation for the far more exceeding and eternal weight of glory which will be ours if we are faithful when we shall be brought together in glory as the spiritual temple of the Lord.

This review is perhaps as appropriate a lesson for the closing Sunday of the year as any, especially when we remember that all of these glories and blessings and privileges are ours because of the great redemptive work accomplished by him whose entrance upon the work is celebrated by Christmas day. Although we cannot agree that this is the proper day for celebrating the birth of our dear Redeemer, but must insist that it was about October first, nevertheless since he did not intimate his desire that we should celebrate his birthday it is quite immaterial upon what day that event, of so great importance to all, is celebrated. Upon this day, so generally celebrated, we may properly enough join with all whose hearts are in the attitude of love and appreciation toward God and toward the Savior.

The habit of giving little remembrances one to another at this time of year seems to us specially appropriate. God is the great giver of every good and perfect gift. He is continually giving and we are continually receiving from him; but amongst all his gifts the one of greatest importance to us is the gift of his Son to be our Redeemer. While, therefore, thanking the Lord for this great gift and for the great plan which centered in it, it is appropriate that we cultivate in our hearts the spirit of liberality, generosity, and that we allow this spirit to exercise itself to some extent—according to our conditions and circumstances—toward those with whom we have contact, especially to the members of our own households. We recommend that every little gift on this occasion should, so far as possible, represent or be accompanied by some little remembrancer of the great gift—something to draw the mind of the recipient to the fact that the great gift of God in Christ is and should be in the minds of all who give or who receive the trifling exchanges of the season.

THE BOYHOOD OF JESUS.

—LUKE 2:40-52.—JANUARY 3.—

FOR the first six months of the new year the International Lessons turn again to the New Testament, beginning appropriately enough with the childhood of Jesus.

The more we think of it the more marvellous it seems that the Gospel narratives record so many of the particulars of our dear Redeemer's ministry—miracles, teachings, etc.—yet never once descend to the discussion of commonplace events, nor of our Lord's sayings or doings other than those directly connected with his ministry. This is one of the strongest internal evidences that these books were written under divine supervision. Our experience with the writings of men in all ages assures us that it would be almost impossible for four men to write biographies of one person, such as these four Gospels are, without entering into social features and events. Our Lord's mother is barely mentioned, and this only where her life touched particularly with that of Jesus. Her husband, Joseph, was probably dead at the time our Lord's ministry began, yet no mention is made of this fact either.

Respecting our Lord's life, previous to his consecration at thirty years of age, we know scarcely anything. The four Gospels merely bring to our attention his miraculous birth, Herod's jealous fury, and the escape of the child before the massacre of the innocents, followed by the little incident of our lesson, which occurred in his twelfth year, and the declaration that he increased in wisdom and stature and favor with God and man. How brief the record, yet how sugges-

The Watchtower, Dec. 15, 1903, p. 457.

Pekah and Hoshea. On one slab from his palace Sargan tells the story of the capture of Samaria. The Taylor Cylinder, found in Nineveh in 1830, and now in the British Museum, describes Sennacherib's conquest of Judah in the time of Hezekiah. The stone records of Assyrian history, called the 'Eponym Canon,' discovered in 1862, in Nineveh, by Sir Henry Rawlinson, help us to gain a more exact knowledge of the dates of this period."

Our Golden Text, which constitutes the caption of this article, contains a valuable thought for any occasion, but one especially suited to this review. Looking at the history of God's earthly people, Israel after the flesh, we can readily see that all of their difficulties and failures to attain to the blessings that were before them, were closely associated with neglect of the truth set forth in our Golden Text. They did not sufficiently sanctify the Lord God in their hearts and let him be the only fear and only dread —fear to displease him, dread to come under his reproof. On the contrary, they were prone to forget the Lord and all the blessings and mercies they had received from him and the obligations they were under to him.

They forgot, too, that a part of the Covenant entered into between the Lord and them was that if as a people they would honor him and serve him he would bless and honor them, but if as a people they rejected or neglected him, they were to have special disciplines and corrections. Their neglect of the Lord, their seeking without the Lord to establish themselves and to have the assistance and co-operation, and to adopt the manners, customs, etc., of foreign nations, all these were a part of their failure to properly worship the Lord and serve him alone. How great was their mistake! And yet we are to remember that a remnant did not make this mistake, though they were few. This remnant already received a blessing in the present life and are to have a still greater share in the favors of God in the coming age.

Similarly nominal spiritual Israel has neglected the counsel of this Golden Text, and, instead of having the Lord first, has been disposed to forget the Lord and to affiliate with the world, to seek worldly favor and co-operation. Fear to displease the world has largely controlled Churchianity; desire to have the world's favor and approval has apparently been more important before the mind of Churchianity than the approval of the Lord and a fear of the loss of his favor.

As a result we see today worldly customs in the professed Church of Christ, and note that these worldly customs have drawn into the nominal Church, as they were intended to do, large numbers of the world, unjustified, unsanctified, "tares," and that these now quite overwhelm the few who are loyal to the Lord and the spirit of his Truth. Nevertheless there is today, and has been all throughout the Gospel age, a "little flock" a 'remnant," which did indeed trust the Lord, and which did indeed sanctify the Lord God in their hearts and make him alone their fear and him alone their dread —fear to displease him, dread to lose the light of his kindness, his favor. We trust, dear friends, that the majority of those who read these words are of the latter class. If so all things are working together for good to such, because they love the Lord and have been called according to his purpose, and are seeking to make their calling and election sure by so running as to obtain the prize.

"THE PRINCE OF PEACE."

—ISAIAH 9:1-7.—DECEMBER 25.—

Golden Text:—"His name shall be called Wonderful, Counsellor, Mighty God, Everlasting Father, Prince of Peace."—R. V.

EVEN though Christmas day is not the real anniversary of our Lord's birth, but more properly the annunciation day of the date of his human begetting (Luke 1:26), nevertheless, since the celebration of our Lord's birth is not a matter of divine appointment or injunction, but merely a tribute of respect to him, it is not necessary for us to quibble particularly about the date. We may as well join with the civilized world in celebrating the grand event on the day which the majority celebrate—"Christmas day." The lesson for the occasion is a most happy choice, fitting well to the series of lessons it follows.

The first verse seems much better translated in the Revised Version, thus: "But there will be no gloom in her that was in anguish. In former time he brought into contempt the land of Zebulun and the land of Naphtali, but in the latter time hath he made it glorious, by way of the sea, beyond Jordan, Galilee of the nations." The Prophet penned these words probably shortly after the ten-tribe kingdom known as Ephraim had gone into captivity to Assyria. Zebulun and Naphtali were the names of the principal districts of Ephraim; and Isaiah, prophetically looking from those desolated lands of his time, under the guidance of the holy Spirit, points out that in the latter time a great blessing is coming to those very lands.

It was centuries after Isaiah's prophecy that our dear Redeemer appeared among men and spent most of his time, did most of his mighty works, and performed most of his mighty miracles in these lands of Zebulun and Naphtali, called Galilee, which in the time of Isaiah had been denuded of its Jewish population and had been settled by Gentile emigrants, "Galilee of the Gentiles." Subsequently these Gentiles gathered more particularly in the vicinity of the city of Samaria, and became known as Samaritans, and, noting the hopes of the Israelites, were inclined to claim a certain share in the blessings belonging to the people into whose lands they had been introduced. The Jews, however, disowned them as being still Gentiles, and would have no dealings with the Samaritans, as the Apostle pointed out.

Our Lord himself instructed the apostles to go not in the way of the Gentiles nor into any city of the Samari-

The Watchtower, Dec. 1, 1904, p. 364.

The WATCH TOWER
AND HERALD OF CHRIST'S PRESENCE

Vol. XLVIII DECEMBER 15, 1926 No. 24

EARTH'S RIGHTFUL GOVERNOR

"For unto us a child is born, unto us a son is given, and the government shall be upon his shoulder; and his name shall be called Wonderful, Counseller, The mighty God, The everlasting Father, The Prince of Peace."—Isaiah 9: 6.

WITH the coming of the Christmas season all Christians have something to say about Jesus. That is supposed to be the time of his birth. Most of the professed Christians at this season of the year give the three wise men wide advertisement by highly colored cards picturing them, by cantatas, and by divers and numerous other ways. Satan has ever been on the alert to see to it that he and his agents are to the fore and get plenty of advertisement. By this means he turns the minds of the people away from the Lord. He has deceived most of the people about Christmas as well as about many other things. Students of the Bible know that the wise men were not representatives of the Lord but were tools of Satan, used by him to carry out his conspiracy.

² The Scriptural account of the wise men is set forth in Matthew 2: 1-16. This record, together with corroborative facts, shows that the vision had by the wise men, and the light which they followed, were approximately two years after the birth of the child Jesus. Satan seized upon the incident and has worked it overtime for the purpose of turning the minds of men away from God and his beloved Son and from the true facts concerning the birth of the Savior and God's great plan of redemption.

³ Students of the Scriptures also know that the birth of the babe Jesus did not take place in December; yet because of the general belief upon this point by most people, it seems to be an appropriate time to speak the truth concerning his birth and the purpose thereof. The Scriptural testimony, supported by extraneous facts, shows that the birth of Jesus occurred approximately October 1st. The event is so important that it is always appropriate to call it to the minds of the people, regardless of the date.

HIS LOVING KINDNESS

⁴ It is written: "God is love." Few of earth's creatures have ever understood the full import of that statement. Love is the perfect expression of unselfishness. God's love for man has been made manifest in many marked ways. The Scriptures were written for the benefit of men who love God, that all such may be thoroughly furnished unto all good works. (2 Timothy 3: 17) God desires his people to learn and to have their hearts comforted by a knowledge of his plan, and for this reason he caused the Scriptures to be written. (Romans 15: 4) Unselfishness prompted the Lord God to do this. The making of the record is no profit to him. He did it for man's benefit. After having written his Word he then makes man acquainted with it, and permits the light from his countenance to shine upon that Word with increased brilliancy for man's benefit as man makes progress in the narrow way.—Prov. 4: 18.

⁵ In the early days of man's experience God provided that his beloved Son should eventually come to earth and be born of a woman in order to become man's Redeemer. It has been his loving kindness for man that has caused God to unfold his purposes gradually and to show man the outworking of his plan to redeem and bless him. As man comes to understand the Word of the Lord his faith in God increases and his desire also grows to be unselfish and to be devoted wholly to the Lord.

A PROPHECY

⁶ When Isaiah wrote the above text, "Unto us a child is born," the Child had not been born. The words he wrote applied to a future time; hence these words constituted a prophecy. Isaiah could not understand the full meaning or import of his own words, nor could any man prior to the giving of the holy spirit. Isaiah did not know about that. Why then did the prophet say, "Unto us a child is born"? Whom did he mean by "us"? Primarily he meant the natural house of Israel, which house constituted God's chosen people, whom God had selected and set aside for his own purposes. Israel after the flesh foreshadowed spiritual Israel, and the prophecy had more particular reference to the latter.

⁷ Certain faithful Jews before the birth of the Child

The Watchtower, Dec. 15, 1926, p. 371.

Chapter Sixteen

BLOOD TRANSFUSIONS—ANALYSIS

Jehovah's Witnesses are taught that they must abstain from blood transfusions for any and all reasons. Therefore, many Witnesses carry cards directing doctors not to administer blood in order to sustain their lives should an emergency arise. This position is erroneously based upon the prohibition in the Old Testament, and issued to several churches on the behalf of the Jewish believers in the New (Lev. 17:14; Acts 15:20, 23). The Watchtower tells Witnesses that it would be better to die than to consent to a transfusion. They are told that a transfusion "may result in the immediate and very temporary prolongation of life, but that at the cost of eternal life for a dedicated Christian" (see p. 277).

In view of the number of people with medical needs who through accident, disease, or surgery require blood transfusions, the potential for turning casualty into fatality is frightening. But the teaching becomes even more horrifying when the doctrine touches upon the *children* of Watchtower adherents. The Society reminds parents that "they know that if they violate God's law on blood and the child dies in the process, they have endangered that child's opportunity for everlasting life in God's new world" (see p. 276).

While the hope of eternal life can rest upon one's receiving a transfusion, in the Watchtower, such an idea has no basis in the Bible. In the Bible, salvation is by grace, through faith, apart from works (Eph. 2:8, 9). Also, it is a mistake to think that eating blood is synonymous with receiving a transfusion. Even the most orthodox Jew, today, does not refuse blood transfusions on the basis of the Old Testament prohibition.[1]

In the book of Acts a decree is sent out to the Gentile churches, and the decision is to "facilitate social intercourse between Jewish and Gentile Christians."[2] Here one finds compromise in the gospel

---

[1]See Havor Montague, *Jehovah's Witnesses and Blood Transfusions* (Santa Ana: CARIS, 1979), p. 4ff. The authors heartily recommend this work.

[2]F.F. Bruce, *Paul: Apostle of the Heart Set Free* (Grand Rapids: Eerdmans, 1977), p. 185ff.

as Peter says in Acts 15:9, "He made no distinction between us [Jews] and them [Gentiles], cleansing their hearts by faith." On the contrary, the decree is a concession judged to be good by this Jerusalem council, in view of the background of the "weaker brethren." In 1 Corinthians 8:1–13, the "stronger brother" is asked to restrict himself on the behalf of the "weaker brother." In 1 Corinthians the weaker brother has a past wherein certain acts, which now have little consequence for the stronger brother, may cause the weaker brother to stumble. Similarly in Acts 15, the Gentile believer is to restrict himself in respect for his Jewish brother's scruples regarding food laws. The respect for scruples is born out of the past of the Jew, the weaker brother, not of the Gentile now.[3] This principle regarding food laws is again repeated in Romans 14:1ff., where the Apostle says, "Now accept the one who is weak in faith, but not for the purpose of passing judgment on his opinions."

Furthermore, when one turns to the Levitical law, the context is not blood. The context is sacrifice. The priority of the law is the sanctity of life. David, in his time of need, was permitted to eat the shewbread belonging only to the priest (1 Sam. 21:6). If the prohibition did apply to transfusions, so much more would the law be loosed to save a life.[4]

Again Jesus demonstrates the function of the law in Matthew 12:1–15. The disciples are hungry and they pick grain and eat. The Pharisees cry, "Your disciples do what is not lawful to do on a Sabbath" (v. 2). Jesus reminds them of David who ate the shewbread, and quotes the scripture to them: "I desire compassion, and not a sacrifice." He tells them if they had known what this meant, they "would not have condemned the innocent" (v. 7).

---

[3]F.F. Bruce, *The Book of Acts*, "New International Commentary on the New Testament" (Grand Rapids: Eerdmans, 1979), p. 311ff.

[4]Also see 1 Sam. 14:31–35, where the soldiers in hunger eat without complying to the ritual. The punishment is not loss of everlasting life but compliance to the law.

If such maneuvers to overrule parental rights continue to have the approval of judges and the public, it is wise for all parents to consider what it can lead to. Are they prepared to accept the thesis that, when parents disagree with a physician on any form of treatment, their child has in the eyes of the law become a "neglected" child, and can for that reason be taken by the state and subjected to the treatment in spite of parental protest? Is the right of parents to exercise their good judgment in the upbringing of their children going to be offered up in sacrifice before the ancient Spartan theory that children are the property of the State? The application of this rule in Nazi Germany meant that boys were taken from their parents to be trained for the "Hitler Youth," and young girls were used for breeding, out of wedlock, what the rulers proclaimed would be a scientifically superior race. Those considered unfit were sterilized; many were even put to death. When doctors and the courts conspire together to override family rights and force the application of certain medical procedures that are currently in vogue, it is but one step in the destruction of freedom. Once the God-given rights of Jehovah's witnesses to exercise their discretion in harmony with God's Word in the upbringing of their children have been trampled underfoot, whose rights will be next?

Jehovah's witnesses do not reject blood for their children due to any lack of parental love. They have sincere love for their children and will do anything within their means to help them, but they are not foolish enough to think that they do good for their offspring by turning their back on God. They know that if they violate God's law on blood and the child dies in the process, they have endangered that child's opportunity for everlasting life in God's new world. Their love is not moti-

Blood, Medicine and the Law of God, 1961, p. 54.

vated by overriding emotion that seeks satisfaction only at the moment, but their love is deep, seeking the everlasting welfare of their loved ones.

MAINTAINING INTEGRITY TO GOD

Realistically viewed, resorting to blood transfusions even under the most extreme circumstances is not truly lifesaving. It may result in the immediate and very temporary prolongation of life, but that at the cost of eternal life for a dedicated Christian. Then again, it may bring sudden death, and that forever. (Matthew 10:39) How much better to abide by the law of Jehovah God, the Source of life, and abstain from blood than to incur his disapproval as a lawbreaker. At all times, and certainly when one's life forces are ebbing, the course of wisdom is to put confidence in the One in whose hands rests the power of life. God will not forsake those who lovingly obey his commands concerning the sanctity of life. He will reward their confidence in his means of salvation by extending to them the life-giving benefits of the blood of his Son—benefits that will sustain them, not for mere days or years, but forever. They know that none who trust in Jehovah God and his now-glorified Son "will by any means come to disappointment."—1 Peter 2:6.

Even if blood could be administered with absolutely no danger from a medical viewpoint—which cannot be done—would it show love for the patient for others to insist that he accept it in an endeavor to extend his present life, when disobedience to God means the forfeiture of the reward of everlasting life? No! It is a time when all interested persons, whether doctors or friends or relatives, can show their sincere concern for the patient and their fear of God by encouraging the patient to hold fast his faith, not to fear, but to trust in God, who is Almighty.

Blood, Medicine and the Law of God, 1961, p. 54.

Does the Bible Forbid Blood Transfusions?

The Watchtower Society teaches Jehovah's Witnesses that blood transfusions are unbiblical. An inquiry made to the American Red Cross shows that one hundred people per thousand, or ten percent, need blood in some form every year (see p. 279). With the need for blood transfusions so great and with numerous cases of Jehovah's Witnesses sacrificing their lives for this Watchtower teaching, we should indeed seriously search the Scriptures for God's truth in this matter.

The Watchtower uses three main Scripture references in support of its theory. We will examine each one. The first verse is Genesis 9:4. Here a command is given that refers to eating blood, certainly not receiving transfusions. Noah is commanded not to eat flesh that still has the blood in it; in other words, don't eat living animals, or animals not properly drained of blood. Their second "proof text" is found at Leviticus 17:10–16. Again we find reference to the actual eating of the blood of *animals*. These verses are in no way connected with transfusions between humans.

The final reference examined is Acts 15:20. Here it says to "abstain from things contaminated by idols and from fornication and from what is strangled and from blood." We read in Acts 15:21, "For Moses from ancient generations has in every city those who preach him, since he is read in the synagogues every Sabbath." It now becomes clear that abstaining from these four items is referred back to the law of Moses in Leviticus 17. Therefore, we see that the abstaining from blood does in no way refer to receiving blood transfusions as the Watchtower's interpretation wishes it to.

It is important to understand that eating and transfusing are two different bodily processes. Blood which is eaten is digested and destroyed. Blood which is transfused is not eaten, digested, or destroyed. Why? Because eating blood involves the body's digestive system, and transfusion involves the circulatory system.

A similar Watchtower teaching regarding the rejection of vaccinations was classified as biblical truth in the 1930s (see p. 280). However, Jehovah's Witnesses today are free to receive vaccinations and even encouraged to do so (see p. 281). Will the doctrine on blood be changed also? The saddest fact is that because of its present teaching on blood transfusions, the Watchtower has led many to a premature grave.

IS THERE A LAW IN THE BIBLE FORBIDDING BLOOD TRANSFUSION? NO

AT MARK 7:14 JESUS SAID: "NOTHING THAT GOES INTO A MAN FROM THE OUTSIDE CAN MAKE HIM UNCLEAN:"

SINCE THERE IS NO LAW IN THE SCRIPTURES FORBIDDING BLOOD TRANSFUSIONS, THE SCRIPTURAL RULE APPLIES: "FOR WHERE THERE IS NO LAW THERE IS NO TRANSGRESSION." ROMANS 4:15

IF THERE WERE A LAW FORBIDDING BLOOD TRANSFUSION, DO YOU BELIEVE JESUS WOULD SET IT ASIDE AS HE DID THE SABBATH LAW IN ORDER TO SAVE A LIFE? YES

THE PRESIDENT OF JEHOVAH'S WITNESSES LIKE THE SCRIBES AND PHARISEES OF OLD, DOES NOT UNDERSTAND THE MEANING OF JESUS WORDS: "WHAT I WANT IS MERCY, NOT SACRIFICE". MATT. 12:8

FORBIDDING THE SAVING OF LIFE VIA BLOOD TRANSFUSION IS A DOCTRINE OF DEMONS. SATAN'S GOAL IS TO 'STEAL AND KILL'. JEHOVAH'S WITNESSES DOCTRINES WILL NOT ONLY TAKE THIS FROM YOU BUT MORE IMPORTANTLY TAKE AWAY YOUR 'REAL LIFE' YOUR 'ETERNAL LIFE.' JESUS CALLED THESE LYING FALSE PROPHETS "RAVENOUS WOLVES." MATT. 7:15

Are Jehovah's Witnesses a 'Killer Cult'? ——

SIX MILLION JEHOVAH'S WITNESSES ATTENDED THEIR ANNUAL COMMUNION IN 1982.

AMERICAN RED CROSS ESTIMATES 10% OF THE POPULACE NEED BLOOD EVERY YEAR.

1,000 JEHOVAH'S WITNESS' LIVES PER WEEK ARE PLACED IN JEOPARDY STATISTICALLY.

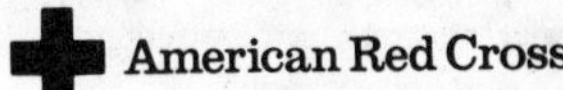

National Headquarters
Washington, D.C. 20006

Thank you for your interest in the American Red Cross. In answer to your request, please see the statement(s) checked:

✓ We enclose information or publications covering the subject of your request.

___ The following organization(s) may be able to furnish you with the information you desire:

✓ The ARC supplies half the blood needs of the nation or 10.5 million blood products. It would appear that 100 people per thousand or 10% need blood in some form every year.

Rudy Clemen
Library

American Red Cross Form 5477 (Rev. 3-80)

Questions for Jehovah's Witnesses, W. & J. Cetnar, 1982.

on the earth as water. Thou shalt not eat it; that it may go well with thee, and with thy children after thee, when thou shalt do that which is right in the sight of the Lord.

What About Armageddon?

When we see these scriptures, and note the emphasis with which these commands not to mingle human blood and animal blood are repeated over and over, we can but wonder what part the violation, the general and impudent violation, of the spirit of this command will play in the battle of Armageddon. Will those who have made and injected and suffered the injection of calf and horse serums into the human blood stream go scot free? We doubt it.

Quite likely there is some connection between the violation of human blood and the spread of demonism. We cannot suppose that the Creator had no reason for associating the two, and He has done so at least twice in His Word. One of these passages is in Leviticus 19:26 and reads: "Ye shall not eat any thing with the blood; neither shall ye use enchantment, nor observe times."

Can it be that the general corruption and violation of human blood by serums of various sorts has provided a garden out of which, in Armageddon, will grow, and do now grow, the most monstrous conditions of accord with the Devil and his angels, with their vibrations, their ways of doing things, if you please, that have ever taken place on this planet? It looks as if it might be so, and as if we were just beginning to find it out.

Let no one hide behind the thought that the laws given to the Jews have no application to anybody now. In the New Testament it is deserving of particular notice that at the very time when the holy spirit declared by the apostles that the Gentiles are free from the yoke of circumcision, abstinence from blood was explicitly enjoined (Acts 15:28, 29), and the action thus prohibited was classed with idolatry and fornication. This plainly suggests that much of the looseness of our day along sexual lines may be traceable to the easy and continued violation of the divine commands to keep human and animal blood apart from each other. With cells of foreign blood racing through his veins man is not normal, not himself, but lacks the poise and balance which make for self-control.

The Sacredness of Human Blood *By Charles A. Pattillo (Va.)*

(REASONS WHY VACCINATION IS UNSCRIPTURAL)

SINCE vaccination has become a topic for discussion, I cannot restrain myself from writing you in regard to this great evil. The vaccination law cannot be a just law. Every father and mother ought to have a right to say what should be done to the body of their own child; yet the vaccination law reduces the father and mother to mere slavery, almost as bad as the colored people were in, when their children were put up on the block and sold. In many slave sale cases the mother and father were even forbidden to shed tears.

Vaccination is a direct violation of the everlasting covenant that God made with Noah after the flood. In Genesis 9:1-17 we read: "And God blessed Noah and his sons, and said unto them, Be fruitful, and multiply, and replenish the earth. And the fear of you, and the dread of you, shall be upon every beast of the earth, and upon every fowl of the air, upon all that moveth upon the earth, and upon all the fishes of the sea; into your hand are they delivered. Every moving thing that liveth shall be meat for you; even as the green herb have I given you all things. But flesh with the life thereof, which is the blood thereof, shall ye not eat. And surely your blood of your lives will I require; at the hand of every beast will I require it, and at the hand of man; at the hand of every man's brother will I require the life of man. Whoso sheddeth man's blood, by man shall his blood be shed: for in the image of God made he man. And you, be ye fruitful, and multiply; bring forth abundantly in the earth, and multiply therein. And God spake unto Noah, and to his sons with him, saying, And I, behold, I establish my covenant with you, and with your seed after you: and with every living creature that is with you, of the fowl, of the cattle, and of every beast of the earth with you, from all that go out of the ark, to every beast of the earth. And I will establish my covenant with you; neither shall all flesh be cut off any more by the waters of a flood, neither shall there any more be a flood to destroy the earth. And God said, This is the token of the covenant which I

The Golden Age, Feb. 4, 1931, p. 293.

have received an injection of horse serum, and have become sensitive to it, are given another injection of it at some later time.

Use of a serum can often be avoided by being inoculated with a vaccine well in advance of trouble. An injection with a tetanus vaccine, for example, gives a person protection from the danger of the lethal poison of tetanus organisms, should he receive a wound from something that has tetanus spores on it. A vaccination for tetanus could mean that tetanus serum would be unnecessary. This is a factor a person might want to consider since tetanus serum presents a greater risk of bad side effects than the vaccine and also is produced from blood.

In view of the hazards accompanying vaccinations, persons opposing them should be given the right to decline to take the risk of those hazards. Some public officials have shown a disregard for these hazards, possibly because of not being aware of them, and have tried to compel people to be vaccinated. Parents often are confronted with such officials in public schools, who may refuse to let unvaccinated children stay in school. When such officials adamantly refuse to respect their right to refuse vaccinations for their children, the parents must decide whether to let their children be vaccinated so as to remain in school or to find some other way to get them educated. The issue for such persons is not a religious one but one of health risks.

The view held by persons believing that a healthy body does not need vaccinations was presented by *Prevention* magazine of October 1958. It stated: "A basic element in the case against artificial immunization is this: just as outward sanitation has helped rid us of some basic causes of diphtheria, so internal cleanliness of the child's system would surely take care of the rest of the problem. A clean and healthy bloodstream, achieved by a good diet of unrefined foods, healthful exercise and use of food supplements has a high immunity of its own to all infections. There is no need then to inject a new immunizing factor to combat each contagious disease, for the body will manufacture its own as the need to defend itself arises."

Are They Necessary?

There can be little doubt that vaccinations appear to have caused a marked decrease in the number of people contracting certain contagious diseases. During the first thirty years of this century there were thousands of smallpox cases in the United States. From 1920 to 1930 alone, they ran from 30,000 to 100,000 annually, but in recent years there have been only about 55 cases of smallpox annually, with no deaths. Vaccinations also appear to have caused a decline in polio.

Strange as it may seem, epidemic poliomyelitis seems to be a disease peculiar to this sanitary twentieth century. As late as 1887, it was unknown; and in places where the standards of hygiene are low it does not seem to be present. An explanation for this might be in what opponents of vaccination say. *Prevention* magazine of June 1964 mentions that a polio epidemic in one locality was stopped when the children there were put on a diet that eliminated refined sweets such as ice cream, soda, candy and pastry that caused a lowering of their blood sugar. Such things are not eaten to any great extent where standards of living are low.

The highest incidence of polio in the United States was in 1952, when there were 57,879 cases of it. After that the Salk polio vaccine began to be used. Since then polio cases have dropped precipitously. In 1957 they had fallen to 5,000, and for the years 1961 and 1962 there were fewer than 1,000 cases.

Awake!, Aug. 22, 1965, p. 20.

Chapter Seventeen

MILITARY SERVICE—ANALYSIS

While the Old Testament often has the follower of God engaged in war in a physical sense, the New Testament does not. In the Old Testament much history is given to the searching for, and the holding onto, an earthly inheritance, the "Promised Land." This is first seen in the theocracy of the wandering nation of Israel, and later in the established kingdom sustained by a kingship rule. Yet in the New Testament the believer is to learn from Abraham, who "by faith lived as an alien in the land of promise, as in a foreign land," and those who died in faith seeking a "better country, that is a heavenly one" (Heb. 11:8–16).

In the New Testament, the issues of war and military service are never directly addressed, though as in all areas of life the principal ethic would be to love one's neighbor (Matt. 5:43). Is military service wrong for the Christian? The Watchtower would say, "Yes, without a doubt." But the Scripture gives no such statement.

The Old Testament leaves no doubt as to the answer; many of the faithful served as leaders in the military. But what of the New Testament? While the question is not directly addressed, we do have some insight. In Matthew 8:5–13, a man in the service speaks with Jesus about a servant who is in great pain. The man is a leader, a centurion, with soldiers under him. Jesus makes no mention of his vocation. Rather He says, "Truly I say to you, I have not found such great faith with anyone in Israel." In Acts 16:27–34, we find the Philippian jailer, someone again in the employment of the government. This man and his household were saved without mention of a needed change of vocation. It would seem a person could serve in the service of his country without contradicting his Christianity. As in any circumstance, the rule would be that obedience to God must take priority.

What about the early church?

Protestant historians have also noted that only two, and possibly three, Church Fathers were openly opposed to Christians participating in the military. The grounds of their rejection of military life is clearly seen to rest on the military's involvement with idolatry. The military required an oath and certain garments of clothing, ceremonies and symbols, which were idolatrous in nature. . . . As soon as those idolatrous circumstances were changed by Constantine, there no longer remained any reason why Christians should hesitate to be in the army.[1]

Our final word would be that each man must judge for himself as the Lord leads.

War and Jehovah's Witnesses—Part I

Let's drop in on Jay and Chris as they discuss the issue of war.

Jay: Chris, I hear that your son is going into the Army next week.

Chris: Yes, he figures it's a good place to get some training in electronics.

Jay: How can your son claim to be a Christian and go into the military?

Chris: I'd like to answer your question by showing you some things your own organization has said.

Jay: Well, that sounds fine.

Chris: How long has the Watchtower Society been used as God's channel of communication to men?

Jay: Since its first *Watchtower* in 1879. (See p. 285.)

Chris: Well, then, your organization said back in 1951:

> Jehovah's Witnesses show courage to follow their conscience. . . . It is only due to conscience that they have . . . objected before draft boards. . . . (See p. 286.)

Jay: That's right. I would be disfellowshiped if I went into the Army. It's against my conscience.

Chris: Then I guess *your* conscience is different than the conscience of Watchtower leaders who lived some years ago.

Jay: What do you mean?

Chris: At one time, God's channel said:

> There could be nothing against our conscience in going into the Army. . . . Wherever we would go we would find opportunities to serve Him. . . . (See p. 287.)

Jay: But, we don't believe that anymore.

---

[1]Robert A. Morey, "The Christian's Response to Tyranny," unpublished manuscript, 1983, pp. 64–67.

Chris: Yes, but if you were living before World War I, you sure would, because the Watchtower told you that was the *Bible's* view. Also, they said if Jehovah's Witnesses were drafted in war, they could "help to terrify the enemy, but need not shoot anybody." (See p. 288.)

Jay: You mean they said we couldn't fire our weapons?

Chris: No, they said, ". . . it would be quite right to shoot, not to kill." They said, "You need not be a good marksman." (See p. 289.)

Jay: You're kidding!

Chris: No, and in the same article they also said, ". . . there is no command in the Scriptures against military service."

Jay: Wow! I can't believe they ever said that! Can you tell me more next week?

Chris: Sure, I'll be here.

Do those associated with your organization seek political positions or reforms? Those in the early congregation had a more permanent hope centered in God's kingdom. (2 Pet. 3:13, 14) Do national or racial barriers exist within your organization? There were none in first-century congregations. (Gal. 3:28; Rev. 7:9) Is discrimination practiced? Early Christians abided by the principle that "there is no partiality with God" but his "will is that all sorts of men should be saved and come to an accurate knowledge of truth." —Rom. 2:11; 1 Tim. 2:4; Jas. 2:1-4.

IDENTIFYING THE THEOCRATIC ORGANIZATION

[18] Those in the apostolic organization did not fulfill these requirements for the Christian congregation in just a token way. They viewed their position in Jehovah's chosen visible channel as sacred and would allow nothing to jeopardize their standing with God. They had no fear of this world. (Matt. 10:26-28) Their only concern was to provide for the safety and well-being of the flock of God. Jesus pointed to this mark of the true visible organization in connection with a detailed prophecy relating to this time of the end. He said: "Who really is the faithful and discreet slave whom his master appointed over his domestics, to give them their food at the proper time? Happy is that slave if his master on arriving finds him doing so. Truly I say to you, He will appoint him over all his belongings."—Matt. 24:45-47.

[19] Evidences are now conclusive that Jesus Christ was enthroned in heaven in 1914 C.E. and that he accompanied Jehovah to his temple in 1918 C.E., when judgment began with the house of God.* (1 Pet. 4:17) After cleansing those belonging to this house who were alive on earth, Jehovah poured out his spirit upon them and assigned them the responsibility of serving as his sole visible channel, through whom alone spiritual instruction was to come. Those who recognize Jehovah's visible theocratic organization, therefore, must recognize and accept this appointment of the "faithful and discreet slave" and be submissive to it.

[20] Today those thus charged with this grand privilege and responsibility are called Jehovah's witnesses, and have been since 1931. As a group they have been separated more and more from the sectarianism of Christendom from the 1870's onward. Since 1879 the *Watch Tower* magazine has been used by this collective group to dispense spiritual food regularly to those of this "little flock" of true Christians. (Luke 12:32) In 1884 they formed a legal servant, a corporation, called Zion's Watch Tower Tract Society, now known as the Watch Tower Bible and Tract Society of Pennsylvania. By 1919, having survived the fiery trials of World War I, this "faithful and discreet slave" class was no novice organization. True, the apostles were no longer in its midst, but they had left behind written instructions as part of Jehovah's great Record Book. Additionally, the modern-day members of this 1900-year-old Christian congregation had received from the days of the apostles onward a rich heritage of Christian loyalty and integrity, long and patient suffering of persecution, abiding faith in Jehovah's precious promises, con-

18. What mark of the true visible organization did Jesus identify, and what reward did he say he would give?
19. What must those who recognize Jehovah's visible organization accept?

* See the book *You May Survive Armageddon into God's New World,* Chapter 6, entitled "A·do·nay' Comes to His Temple." Published by the Watch Tower Bible & Tract Society in 1955.

20, 21. Who today are charged with the responsibility of representing Jehovah's King, and what record provides their recommendation?

The Watchtower, Oct. 1, 1967, p. 590.

armaments race will be at last halted for all time.

[20] After Armageddon those who have survived on the winner's side, Jehovah's side, will enjoy a perfectly guaranteed peace. Then they will "beat their swords into plowshares, and their spears into pruninghooks: nation shall not lift up sword against nation, neither shall they learn war any more".—Isa. 2:4.

20. After what will guaranteed peace come? What will survivors do?

HAVING a good conscience toward God does not make a person a weakling or a coward. Jehovah's witnesses show courage to follow their conscience in these martial times. It is only due to conscience that they have personally and legally objected before draft boards to participating in the armed conflicts and defense programs of worldly nations. In this course their consciences are not warped, but are instructed in what is right, for they are instructed in the Scriptures, God's Word. With the apostle Paul they say: "I am exercising myself continually to have a consciousness of committing no offense against God and men." (Acts 24:16, *NW*) So their consciences are clear, no matter how the militaristic minds of this world may criticize them.

[2] Well, then, if not pacifists, what Scriptural reasons have they given for refusing all part in international war? Repeatedly President Truman of the United States has said he believes in the "sermon on the mount" and that he wants the world to know that Americans believe in the sermon on the mount. Jehovah's witnesses trust that the American president and his colleagues mean the entire sermon. Why? Because it includes not only the so-called "Golden Rule" but also Jesus' words: "You heard that it was said, 'Eye for eye and tooth for tooth.' However, I say to you: Do not resist him that is wicked; but whoever slaps you on your right cheek, turn the other also to him. And if a person wants to go to court with you and get possession of your undergarment, let your outer garment also go to him; and if someone under authority impresses you into service for a mile, go with him two miles. Give to the one asking you, and do not turn away from one that wants to borrow from you without interest. You heard that it was said: 'You must love your neighbor and hate your enemy.' However, I say to you: Continue to love your enemies and to pray for those persecuting you; that you may prove yourselves sons of your Father who is in the heavens, since he makes his sun rise upon wicked people and good and makes it rain

1. How do we show courage of conscience? Why do we, and like whom?
2. In what sermon do officials claim to believe? What does it contain?

The Watchtower, Feb. 1, 1951, p. 73.

ordained of God," we are not to understand the Apostle to mean that they are endorsed by God, nor that their decisions, rules, etc., are approved by him or are in harmony with his rules and laws. The Apostle's intimation means simply that in divine providence things are as they are, and our God, who knows all the circumstances and conditions, permits them to be as they are, though he could overthrow and overturn and substitute his own Kingdom of righteousness. Nevertheless, this is not his plan; but rather for the time being he permits the kingdoms of this world, whose rulers are under the prince of this world, and largely blinded by his deceptions, to take much their own course—subject only to certain limitations by which the Lord hinders Satan and any of his misguided dupes from doing real injury to the best interests of the Lord's people or to the thwarting of the divine plan. His divine power overrules the wrath of man and makes it to praise him, and the remainder, which will not accomplish anything of good, but which would be subversive of the divine arrangements, he will restrain.—Psa. 76:10.

"Render, therefore, to all their dues"—to all men as well as to all rulers—in financial as well as political matters. A great mistake, we believe, is being made along these lines today. The general sentiment amongst Christian people is that Christian citizenship implies engaging in political strife—and endeavoring to determine who shall be the rulers, striving to better the laws and have them obeyed, and putting forth efforts to oppose and rebuke bad laws. It will be noticed that the Apostle gives no such advice. On the contrary, he elsewhere declares, "Your citizenship is in heaven." (Phil. 3:20, R. V.) We are strangers and foreigners in the kingdoms of this world. Our Kingdom is yet to come; it is promised, and we are praying for it, "Thy Kingdom come; thy will be done on earth," and we are expecting it; but meantime, as foreigners, "not of this world" (John 18:36), it is our business to render obedience to the laws, customs, usages, of this world, in so far as these do not infringe upon our conscientious obligations to the Lord and the truth; but this does not mean that we are to become partizans in political strifes, and contentions amongst men. Let the world elect its own rulers in whatever way it sees best; we put up with whatever it provides with thankfulness, with gratitude to God for whatever may come, with the realization that he will guide and care for us under all circumstances, and that in any event our highest interests are being conserved. Obedience to the laws of the land might at some time oblige us to bear arms, and in such event it would be our duty to go into the army, if unable in any legal and proper manner to obtain exemption, but it would not be our duty to volunteer. We are soldiers in another army, which battles not with carnal weapons, and whose contests are from an entirely different standpoint and in an entirely different spirit. There could be nothing against our consciences in going into the army. Wherever we would go we could take the Lord with us, the Captain of our salvation, and wherever we would go we could find opportunities to serve him and his cause. If it came to the point of battling we above all others need have no fear of death, but we, assuredly, would be obliged to draw the line when commanded to fire, and we could not, in harmony with the divine program, fire upon a fellow-creature with the intention of taking his life. If we fired we should be obliged to fire either into the air or into the ground. All this army service would come in under this heading, "Render to all their dues." The governor of the state has the right, under the laws, to call for and to conscript, if necessary, soldiers for the defense of the state and of the nation; and if such requisition be enforced upon us we must render our dues and take our share in the trials and difficulties of the service, whatever they may be. The Apostle, however, stipulates more particularly what he means by dues, showing that he does not mean that we owe it to others to vote, to participate in political strifes. He had particularly in mind the paying of tribute, custom, fear, honor, to whom these are due. Tribute was the tax payable by a subject nation to the principal power, as, for instance, by the Jewish nation to the Roman Empire while its vassal. Custom is a tariff duty, or tax, levied in one form or another for the support of government, by a tax upon imports or exports or by direct taxation. Fear, or reverence, is differentiated from honor, or respect, in the sense that it may be the duty to salute an officer or representative of the government, by baring the head or bowing the knee, or otherwise, thus showing him honor or respect, not necessarily as a man, but as an officer, regardless of his personal character. The fear that is to be rendered is in the sense of obedience, as we elsewhere read, "Fear the judge." The commands of the judge or court are to be obeyed—whatever others might be disposed to do, Christians are never to be found in contempt of court, but are to obey its rules to the very letter, whether they consider them just or unjust, because the judge is the representative of the law, and God permits the law and the judge, and commands us to be subject to whatever he permits. If, therefore, as our Lord explained, some one shall sue us at the law, and take away our coat, or if it include our cloak also, all that we had, we are not to resist; we are to be obedient to the powers that be. This does not mean, however, that we shall willingly submit to the coat or cloak or other articles being taken from us illegally or unjustly without process of law.

The Watchtower, April 15, 1903, p. 120.

highway of holiness then opened up to them "shall be *destroyed* from among the people"—"the second death."—Compare Isa. 35:8; 62:10; Acts 3:23; DAWN I., Chap. 11.

WAS THE TEMPLE CLEANSED TWICE?

Question. From the various accounts would it not appear that the Temple was cleansed twice? I see that DAWN and WATCH TOWER always refer to the matter as tho there had been but one cleansing.—See Mark 11:15; John 2:13-17; Matt. 21:12, 13.

Answer. Many take the view suggested—that there were two cleansings; but we do not share it. It will be noticed that Matthew, Mark and John each mention the matter only once; and each mention once our Lord's riding upon the ass in fulfillment of Zechariah's prophecy (9:9-12); but only one of them *connects* these two events—Matthew. Moreover, since all agree that the riding on the ass was in fulfillment, of Zechariah's prophecy, and that *there* our Lord assumed for the first time his title as *King*, it is but reasonable to suppose that the use of force in cleansing the temple followed and did not precede that assertion of regal authority. For the same reasons we accept that *same* day as the one in which our Lord wept over Jerusalem and said "Your house is left unto you desolate!" Note the Prophet's expression—"Even *today* do I declare I will render [the second half of thy] double unto thee;"—the day of the riding on the ass as King.

The disconnection so noticeable in the gospels may be accounted for (1) By remembering that the Apostles were "unlearned men," not regularly educated historians, men who recorded the wonderful words and works of their wonderful Teacher, but apparently saw little necessity for order or sequence. (2) By assuming that in this matter our Lord designed the confusion of the record, that only the faith-full and zealous might, under the leading of the holy Spirit be led to "rightly divide the Word of truth" and to get from it "meat in due season."

CHRISTIAN DUTY IF DRAFTED

Question. There are possibilities of a still greater war and of a draft which might include some of us who understand our Lord's commands to forbid our engagement in carnal warfare. What then, would be our duty?

Answer. "We know that all things shall work together for good to those who love God—to the called ones according to his purpose." If, therefore, we were drafted, and if the government refused to accept our conscientious scruples against warfare (as they have heretofore done with "Friends," called Quakers), we should request to be assigned to the hospital service or to the Commissary department or to some other non-combatant place of usefulness; and such requests would no doubt be granted. If not, and we ever got into battle, we might help to terrify the enemy, but need not shoot anybody. Meantime what an opportunity we might thus have for preaching "Jesus and the resurrection;"—for being "living epistles known and read by all" the camp:—examples of good soldiers of the Lord Jesus Christ, drilled and thoroughly equipped with the armor of God, loyal and courageous in the Christian warfare, against the world, the flesh, and the devil.

"JEHOVAH, HE IS THE GOD"

JULY 17.—1 KINGS 18:30-40.

"And when all the people saw it they fell on their faces, and they said: Jehovah, he is the God."—1 Kings 18:39.

The three and a half years of drouth no doubt had an humbling effect upon King Ahab, as well as upon the people of Israel. No doubt they began to wonder where the matter would end; and to recognize it as more than an accident—as a judgment. The question would be whether it was a judgment from Baal or a judgment from Jehovah; for the people, as a result of their extended acquaintance with idolatry had a comparatively weak faith respecting the unseen Jehovah, who permitted no image or likeness of himself to be made or to be worshiped. The Lord's time had come for awakening Israel, and starting a reformation movement amongst them, and Elijah, who had been sought by the King throughout the surrounding nations, was instructed to present himself before Ahab, with a promise that rain should follow; and was permitted to be the Lord's agent in drawing the attention of the people to the true God, who alone has power over the elements.

Altho Ahab realized that the famine was a judgment of the Lord, nevertheless, after the custom of the natural man, he ignored personal responsibility, and affected to charge the evils to Elijah, saying to him, "Art thou he that troublest Israel?" It is always so with the faithful mouthpieces of the Lord. Since they cannot prophesy smooth things, but must present the truth in reproof of unrighteousness, therefore the world and the nominal Israelite hate them. They do not seem to realize that the difficulty lies in themselves, and their sins, and their separation from the Lord. But Elijah, humble yet unabashed, did not hesitate to tell the king the truth of the matter, assuring him that the trouble in Israel came from his own wrong course.

The drouth had so humbled Ahab that he did not resent the Prophet's arraignment of his sin: perhaps also he hoped that through the prophet's favor the embargo of the drouth and famine might be lifted. At all events he very promptly complied with Elijah's request that the people of Israel be assembled at Mount Carmel, together with the priests of Baal. Accordingly there was a great concourse to the flat, table-top of Mount Carmel, where Elijah awaited them, the king also coming with them; but Queen Jezebel sullenly remained at the palace in the capital city of Samaria.

Elijah, full of zeal for the Lord, and full of indignation against the idolatry, and probably counseled respecting his course by the Lord, had a plan prepared by which to demonstrate to Israel which was the true God and which the false one. In the presence of the people he made a proposition to the priests of Baal for a contest to prove the question. This proposition was so reasonable, and the interest and expectation of Israel so great, that the priests of Baal dare not refuse. They, four hundred and fifty in number, were to build an altar and to make a sacrifice thereon to their god, Baal, while Elijah would build an altar and offer a sacrifice thereon to Jehovah, and whichever god would answer by fire would thus be attested as the true God. If Baal were powerful enough to answer the prayers of his priests and to accept the offering of the altar, then the people might understand that it was because Baal was offended with them that they had experienced the drouth and the famine. But if Jehovah had the power, and would answer with fire, it would be proof to the people that the drouth and the famine were from him, and signs of his indignation because they had forsaken him and worshiped Baal.

The proposition could not be rejected: the priests of Baal prepared their altar and their sacrifice, and had the advantage of the noon-day heat of a tropical sun, sufficient almost of itself to ignite the fat of the sacrifice. They desired and prayed that the test might be granted; they cut themselves with stones until the blood gushed out, claiming that it must be because some of them, as priests of Baal, had trespassed against him, that their prayers were not heard. They kept this up for hours, until near sunset—Elijah meantime, in the hearing of the people, pouring upon them the sharpest sarcasm—the sarcasm of truth, not of falsehood. He suggested that they pray louder, as peradventure their god might be a little deaf; he urged them to keep it up, peradventure Baal might be on a journey, or attending to other business, or asleep. Thus he was giving to Israel in general the most telling lesson possible, considering their lethargy on religious subjects. He was preparing them for the final demonstration which he was about to give, that Jehovah is the true God, the only God who had power to answer both by fire and by water.

Mark how thorough the Prophet's faith in God, and how thoroughly he demonstrated that there could be no room for deception in connection with his offering. Twelve stone crocks of water were poured upon the sacrifice and the wood, and filled the trench around about it; the sun was losing its power, and the offering was thoroughly drenched, and all things were thus ready for a thorough test of Jehovah's power to send down fire.

Elijah stated the matter to the people: "How long halt ye between two opinions? If Jehovah be God, follow him; but if Baal be God, then follow him." The test was to show which was the true God, and which was the false god, and incidentally which the true and which the false prophets. Then Elijah prayed a beautiful and proper prayer. He did not say, "O Lord, cause Israel all to know how great, I Elijah, am, as a prophet of the Lord," but "Hear me, O Lord, hear me, that this people may know that thou are Jehovah God, and that thou hast turned their heart back again [—recalling them again by their experiences and these signs to be thy people]."

The answer by fire was prompt, and the effect upon the people great. They promptly acknowledged Jehovah, and slew the priests of Baal. Then, while Ahab and the people

The Watchtower, July 1, 1898, p. 204.

do some good things in harmony with the divine law, and that to that extent their conduct meets with the divine approval. But the Apostle clearly shows that neither the Jews nor the heathen do all things in harmony with the divine law, nor can they, because of inherited imperfections. Hence, neither the Jews nor the heathen would be justified under the Law. God, however, has provided through Christ a justification, under the terms of the New Covenant, which excuses and forgives whatever is not wilful sin, on the part of both Jews and heathen, who receive Christ, and through his merit. Thus it is that God will justify the heathen through faith—not all the heathen, but all the heathen who will exercise the faith when the knowledge of Christ shall reach them, in God's *due time.*

Question. I was surprised to note your advice to any who might be drafted into the army. Would not your advice seem like *compromising* to avoid trouble?

Answer. It is proper to avoid trouble in a proper manner. It is proper to compromise when no *principle* is involved, as in the case mentioned. Notice that there is no command in the Scriptures against military service. Obedience to a draft would remind us of our Lord's words, "If any man compel thee to go a mile, go with him twain." The government may compel marching or drilling, but cannot compel you to kill the foe. You need not be a good marksman.

Question. You suggested in a recent WATCH TOWER that, if drafted and in the army, we need not shoot to kill. Would such a course be right? Would it not be fraudulent?

Answer. No; it would be quite right to shoot, not to kill. You forget, perhaps, our provisos, which were that we explain our conscientious scruples against war, and seek to be excused: if not excused, that we seek non-combatant positions, as nurses, etc.; but if *compelled* to go a mile or many miles as a soldier, we still need not kill anybody.

Question. Will we know each other in the kingdom?

Answer. When the Apostle says (1 Cor. 13:12), "Now we see through a glass darkly [*i. e.*, as through an obscured glass], but then face to face; now I know in part, but then shall I know, even as I also am known," he undoubtedly included in the future knowledge the recognition of friends, even as he realized himself already known of God. If we are to be partakers of "the divine nature" and inheritors of all things, we must expect to be acquainted with the beings who form a considerable part of our heritage for a thousand years as well as with our associates in that inheritance.

Question. Were not the Psalms inspired specially for song service; and is it not therefore improper to use other hymns?

Answer. David's thought in writing the Psalms may have been merely their use in song; but the Lord's object was to give *prophecy* to assist his people of a later period. See what Peter says on this subject. (1 Pet. 1:10-12) Other prophecies of the Old Testament are written in poetical form, particularly Isaiah and Job. Our Lord quoted from both, as did also his apostles, and showed that in some of the Psalms David typified the Lord.

While some of the Psalms seem to us very suitable for singing, others we regard as less appropriate than hymns of praise of modern date. When the apostles said that we should sing "psalms and hymns and spiritual songs" (Eph. 5:19), he recognized a distinction between the three kinds of songs and commended all. We believe it is safe to follow his instructions, remembering the instruction, "Be not wise above what is written." However, on this subject we believe each one should follow his own conscience. Doubtless the Lord accepts the offering of song, whatever its form, so long as it comes from the heart,—just as with prose prayers; for hymns and psalms should be regarded as union or concert prayers.

ELISHA DOING RESTITUTION WORK

AUG. 14.—2 KINGS 4:25-37.

"Cast thy burden upon the Lord, and he shall sustain thee."—Psa. 55:22.

Elisha did receive a double portion of Elijah's spirit, or power. Not only did Jordan part before him, in obedience to his faith and at the stroke of the mantle, but other important works followed. Coming to a school of the prophets, they found that in preparing the dinner of vegetables something had gotten into the stew which they recognized to be poisonous, and the dinner was spoiled; but Elisha miraculously antidoted the poison, and made the dinner wholesome. Again, the people of Jericho complained that the fountain of water which supplied them was brackish, and he healed the waters so that the fountain became known as the fountain of Elisha, and the place is so known today.

These may be considered as typical of the restitution works which the Elisha class will introduce to the world. What do people who are religiously disposed, and who seek to understand the Word of the Lord, need, as the first feature of restitution blessings? Will it not be that something shall be put into their mess of pottage, that will destroy its poisonous errors, and make it health-giving, nutritious? Surely the peoples of civilized lands have God's Word in their hands, and its contents are good and nourishing and health-giving; but some of the theological cooks have unintentionally added doctrines of the evil one so that it is made to the people a poisonous dinner, injurious, as represented in the various creeds of Christendom. And what does the world in general need more than that the springs of the water of life (which have become corrupted and brackish, through false theories and misinterpretations of the divine Word and plan) should be corrected, healed, made sweet and pure and refreshing? And such restitution work will be accomplished, we understand, by the successors of the Gospel church in a much larger measure than the church itself is able to accomplish it now, the church's work being specifically the making of herself ready,—Rev. 19:7.

Further, we have the record of how the poor widow and her sons were helped by the prophet Elisha, to whom she appealed in her distress. A debt was upon her, and, according to the terms of the law, her sons would be bound to serve the creditor until the indebtedness had been discharged, or until the Jubilee year should be ushered in; and as she was a widow she needed her sons' assistance at home. The prophet saw her distress, sympathized with her, and assisted: the assistance being rendered in a manner which helped to develop her faith in the Lord. The only merchantable thing she had in her house was a pot of oil; and the prophet directed her to send among her neighbors and borrow all the empty vessels that she could obtain, and to pour all full of oil, which then she could sell, and from the proceeds pay the debt and have something left; and so she did, according to directions. Does not this act of relieving the poor illustrate restitution powers and work also? Are we not told that in that time the Lord will "lift up the poor and the needy, and him that hath no helper?" There is in this a lesson of the Lord's sympathy with us in our earthly difficulties; a lesson of his willingness to assist us to pay our honest debts; and a lesson of the propriety of paying honest debts. And there is another lesson respecting how God is pleased to bless the use of the things which we have, rather than to send us other things, or to miraculously put the money into our pockets. There is also a lesson for faith, because it was in proportion to her faith that the woman gathered a large or small number of vessels, and therefore got a larger or a smaller evidence of divine bounty and mercy. Let us, when dealing with the Lord, remember that all the gold and silver are his, and the "cattle on a thousand hills," and let our works be in harmony with our faith.

We come now to the particular feature of this lesson, the Shunammite woman and her son: and this also contains a suggestion of the great restitution blessing of awakening the dead. This Shunammite has the record of the Scriptures that she was "a great woman." Apparently she and her husband were comfortably situated in life; perhaps indeed the greatness referred in part to wealth, but evidently she was a more than ordinary woman in other respects, as is indicated by the narrative. She may have been superior to her husband in intelligence, as the narrative seems to indicate. She had the kind of greatness, too, which recognizes goodness, and reverences the Lord, and those who are his. Seeing the prophet pass her place occasionally, probably on his way to the schools of the prophets, she hospitably urged him to take dinner with her, and so, apparently, every time he passed that way he stopped to partake of her hospitality. And the more this great woman saw of the Lord's prophet the more she realized that it was a favor to have him under the roof, so she said to her husband, "Behold now, I perceive that this is an holy man of God, which passeth by us continually. Let us make a little chamber, I pray thee, on the wall, and let us set for him there a bed, and a table, and a stool and a candlestick: and it shall be when he cometh to us that he shall turn in thither." Altho apparently the

The Watchtower, Aug. 1, 1898, p. 231.

War and Jehovah's Witnesses—Part II

Jay and Chris continue to discuss war.

Jay: Chris, you really surprised me last week with your proof that the Watchtower Society had formerly told Jehovah's Witnesses that they could go into the military. But, today they teach the opposite.

Chris: You know, Jay, I think each man has to live with his own conscience. But I'd like to explain why many Christians feel that it's their duty to defend their country. By the way, you do believe in self-defense, don't you?

Jay: Of course, but I don't see what that has to do with it.

Chris: Let me illustrate. Your own Watchtower Society teaches that to protect yourself you have a right to strike an intruder with "hard blows" (see p. 291) and use "whatever is at hand." (See p. 292.) They also say that you may even decide to get a gun for protection in advance of an attack. After all, according to Luke 22:38, "Jesus' apostles were known to have at least two swords." (See p. 292.)

Jay: O.K., but what does that have to do with the military?

Chris: Jay, this country is filled with people who are our families and friends. The Watchtower says the government acts as "God's minister, an avenger to express wrath upon the one practicing what is bad." (See p. 293.) One of the biggest dangers to the people is from foreign attack, wouldn't you agree?

Jay: Sure, that's what I read in the papers.

Chris: Then if this country is attacked and we refuse to defend it, the government can't perform its God-assigned duty to protect the people from harm. Both your family and friends, and mine, will suffer the consequences. All because we didn't obey God and let government do its duty. Jay, if you knew right now that your own family was going to be attacked and killed by ruthless criminals, and you didn't have time to get the police, what would you do?

Jay: I would defend them the best I could.

Chris: I'm sure you would. Do you know what John the Baptist's advice was to the soldiers of his day? Did he tell them to leave the military?

Jay: I don't know. What did he say?

Chris: In Luke 3:14 he said, "Be content with your wages."

Jay: I see. They could be content with their wages only if they remained soldiers. Well, Chris, I guess I get your point.

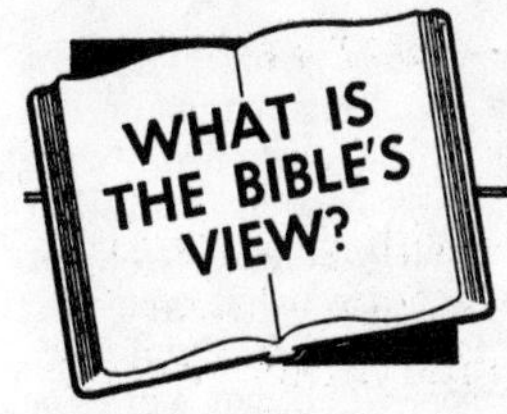

Should You Defend Yourself?

IN MANY parts of the earth crime and violence are on the increase. Especially in the larger cities, people do not feel secure even in their own homes. What if you were threatened with violence? Should you 'turn the other cheek'?

Jesus Christ did speak about 'turning the other cheek.' But we need to consider whether he was actually talking about serious threats to a person's life. He said: "Do not resist him that is wicked; but whoever slaps you on your right cheek, turn the other also to him." (Matt. 5:39) Now, a slap is an insult, often designed to provoke a fight. By not retaliating when subjected to insulting speech or action, the Christian may prevent trouble. "An answer, when mild," says the Bible, "turns away rage."—Prov. 15:1.

The situation, however, is very different when one is threatened with serious bodily harm. In his Law to Israel, Jehovah God revealed that the individual had the right of self-defense. For example, regarding a thief who broke into a house at night, the Law stated: "If a thief should be found in the act of breaking in and he does get struck and die, there is no bloodguilt for him." (Ex. 22:2) At night it would be very hard to determine the intentions of the intruder. To protect himself from possible harm, the homeowner had the right to inflict hard blows. And if these blows proved fatal, he was considered to be free from bloodguilt.

Actually, it is inherent in man to prevent injury to his body. If an object is hurled at him, he instinctively tries to get out of the way or, if that is impossible, to shield the head from injury. Similarly, if a beloved relative—wife or child—comes under attack, a man will instinctively do what he can to help, even if doing so could cost him his life. Such action is also in harmony with what Jesus Christ himself did in sacrificing his life for the congregation.—Eph. 5:25.

So if you or one of your loved ones were confronted by a man or a woman carrying a weapon, what could you do? To the extent that time and human ability allow, you must assess matters, judging whether the individual merely wants money and other valuables or is bent on inflicting serious bodily injury. It would certainly be foolhardy to sacrifice one's life in an effort to protect perishable material possessions. Giving up money or other valuables without putting up resistance may well remove any threat to life. Then, too, the Mosaic law considered as bloodguilty the person taking the life of a thief in the daytime. (Ex. 22:3) Why? Evidently because, in the daytime, the thief could be identified to the Law. Since the Mosaic law sets forth God's view, we can appreciate that a Christian could not claim self-defense if, in reality, only property defense against an identifiable criminal was involved.

On the other hand, the armed person may definitely want to kill. What then?

When flight is possible, that is to be preferred. The Bible relates a number of instances involving Jesus' doing just that. There was the time when certain Jews 'picked up stones to hurl at him; but Jesus hid and went out of the temple.' (John 8:59) Regarding another occasion, we

Awake!, Sept. 8, 1975, p. 27.

read: "They tried again to seize him; but he got out of their reach."—John 10:39.

If flight is impossible, the individual may be able to reason with the assailant. But, at other times, trying to reason with a person determined to inflict injury may lead to loss of valuable time. The situation may be such that the only thing a person can do is to use whatever is at hand to protect himself or others. As a result, the attacker may receive a fatal blow. From the Scriptural standpoint, the one acting in self-defense would not thereby incur bloodguilt.

In view of increasing crime and violence, some Christians may wonder whether they should not arm themselves in preparation for a possible attack. Jesus' apostles were known to have had at least two swords. (Luke 22:38) This was not something unusual, for Jews at that time were under the Mosaic law that allowed for armed conflict. Also, swords were of value in warding off wild beasts. And they could serve a utilitarian purpose, much like that of an ax or a large knife.

However, as developments on Nisan 14, 33 C.E., show, Jesus Christ did not want his Jewish followers to use swords under circumstances that might provoke armed resistance against authorities of the land. When Peter, for example, used one of the swords against the mob that had come to arrest his Lord, Jesus commanded: "Return your sword to its place, for all those who take the sword will perish by the sword." (Matt. 26:52) Peter's action in this case was not a matter of self-defense, but, rather, resistance to authorities and even against God's will. The intent of the mob was to arrest Jesus and to bring him to trial.

It is good to keep in mind that we simply cannot prepare ourselves for everything that might happen. The Christian, therefore, is wise when he does not become overanxious about his material needs and safety. Jesus Christ cautioned: "Stop being anxious about your souls as to what you will eat or what you will drink, or about your bodies as to what you will wear." (Matt. 6:25) Jesus was not here saying that a person should not work for life's necessities, but he was simply pointing out that this should not become a matter of undue concern. Similarly, it is right to take precautions about one's personal safety, but it is an entirely different matter when one allows this to become a cause for great anxiety.

A Christian, therefore, should give serious consideration to the potential dangers that come with procuring a deadly weapon, such as a gun, for self-defense. Not infrequently availability of a gun, coupled with panic or overreaction, has led to needless deaths. There was the forty-year-old man in Arkansas who loaded his shotgun for the first time in four years. Because of robberies that had been taking place in the neighborhood, he was determined to protect his property. Early the next morning he heard what he thought to be a prowler stumbling outside his home. He took hold of his gun and fired at the front door. Then he turned on the light. There in the doorway lay his thirteen-year-old daughter—dead.

Accordingly, before buying a deadly weapon, one should certainly weigh both aspects—one potential danger against the other potential danger. He must decide which would be the greater risk.

From the foregoing it is evident that the Scriptures give a person the right to defend himself or others against bodily harm. However, they give no authorization for armed conflicts or the taking of human life in efforts during daytime to protect material possessions.

Awake!, Sept. 8, 1975, p. 28.

mental "superior authorities" to act as "God's minister, an avenger to express wrath upon the one practicing what is bad." Hence, "it is not without purpose that it [the authority] bears the sword." —Rom. 13:1, 4; 1 Pet. 2:13, 14.

The apostle Paul showed his recognition of this "sword" of the State, even when his own life was at stake. When facing Governor Festus on false charges that could have brought the death penalty, he did not dispute the government's right to act. On the contrary, Paul said: "If, on the one hand, I am really a wrongdoer and have committed anything deserving of death, I do not beg off from dying."—Acts 25:11.

A Deterrent?

Does the death penalty deter persons from committing murders? Man's Maker, who knows human thinking well, says that it does. Speaking of a false witness whose testimony might even bring death to his victim, God's law said that "you shall treat him as he intended to treat his fellow . . . You shall show no mercy." "Life for life" was to be the penalty. Noting the deterrent effect of this certain justice, the Law states: "The rest of the people when they hear of it will be afraid."—Deut. 19: 16-21, *NE;* 13:6-11.

Some may respond that the deterrent value of capital punishment is unproved. But consider: If it would deter even a few potential murderers, yet it is not used, who is to answer for the lives of their innocent victims? On the other hand, if the death penalty is carried out, only the lives of murderers are lost. Which lives do you consider more valuable?

Too often murderers kill again, both inside and outside of prison. "The going price for murder [within the prison is] two cartons of cigarettes," testified a former inmate of the U.S. Federal Penitentiary in Lewisburg, Pennsylvania. A number of murders had occurred within that prison and others. Why is life there so cheap? Murderers serving long terms "have nothing to lose," he said.

"Rehabilitated" murderers also continue to take innocent lives. In one recent typical case, the murderer, "who went to prison for more than five years for the murder of a young woman and was later paroled in 1973 because he was a 'model inmate,'" reports the New York *Times,* "has been sentenced to life in prison for the nearly identical slaying [of an] aspiring actress." Clearly, it is not the death penalty, but the lack of it that makes innocent lives cheap!

Does unequal application of the law in favor of certain groups make capital punishment invalid? According to this reasoning, because unequal sentences are often handed out by different judges for the same crimes, all criminals should be set free! However, in 1971 a black Illinois state senator declared, in support of capital punishment: "I realize that most of those who would face the death penalty are poor and black and friendless. I also realize that most of their victims are poor and black and friendless and *dead.*"

Discriminatory punishment under the present human judicial system merely il-

Awake!, July 22, 1977, p. 7.

BIBLIOGRAPHY

A. Primary Source Material: WTBTS Publications (and publications written by WT representatives for JWs). Periodicals are noted by "P." Some sources listed here are not quoted in this volume.

Aid to Bible Understanding, 1971.

Atonement Between God and Man, Studies in the Scriptures, Series V, 1899.

All Scripture Is Inspired of God and Beneficial, 1963.

Awake!, 1946 to date, various issues, P.

Babylon the Great Has Fallen—God's Kingdom Rules!, 1963.

Battle of Armageddon, The, Studies in the Scriptures, Series IV, 1897.

Blood, Medicine and the Law of God, 1961.

Bibles and Concordances, Watchtower Publications Advertisement List, Form c–9, 9/64.

Commentary on the Letter of James, 1979.

Consolation, 1937 to 1946, various issues, P.

Creation, 1927.

Defending and Legally Establishing the Good News, 1950.

Emphatic Diaglott, Benjamin Wilson, 1864, 1942 edition.

Face the Facts, 1938.

Faith on the March, A.H. Macmillan, Englewood Cliffs, N. J.: Prentice Hall, Inc., 1957.

Finished Mystery, The, Studies in the Scriptures, Series VII, 1917.

God's Eternal Purpose Now Triumphing, 1974.

God's Kingdom of a Thousand Years Has Approached, 1973.

Golden Age, The, Feb. 4, 1931, P.

Harp of God, The, 1921.

Holy Spirit—The Force Behind the Coming New Order!, 1976.

Informant, 1936 to 1956, various issues, P.

Jehovah's Witnesses in the Divine Purpose, 1959.

Jehovah's Witnesses in the Twentieth Century, 1978.

Jehovah's Witnesses—The New World Society, Marley Cole, N.Y.: Vantage Press, 1955.

Judge Rutherford Uncovers Fifth Column, 1940.

Kingdom Interlinear Translation of the Greek Scriptures, 1969.

Kingdom Is at Hand, The, 1944.

Kingdom Ministry, 1956 to 1975, various issues, P.

Kingdom, the Hope of the World, The, 1932.

Let God Be True, 1946 and 1952 editions.

Life, 1977.

Life Everlasting in Freedom of the Sons of God, 1966.

Listening to the Great Teacher, 1971.

Light II, 1930.

Make Sure of All Things—Hold Fast to What Is Fine, 1965.
Messenger, The, published irregularly 1927 to 1946, various issues.
Millions Now Living Will Never Die, 1920.
New World Translation of the Christian Greek Scriptures, 1950.
New World Translation of the Holy Scriptures, 1961, 1971, and 1981 editions.
Our Kingdom Service, 1976 to 1981, various issues, P.
Pastor Russell's Sermons, 1917.
Qualified to Be Ministers, 1955 and 1967 editions.
Reconciliation, 1928.
Religion, 1940.
Riches, 1936.
Theocratic Aid to Kingdom Publishers, 1945.
Theocratic Ministry School Guidebook, 1971.
Things in Which It Is Impossible for God to Lie, 1965.
Thy Kingdom Come, Studies in the Scriptures, Series III, 1891.
Time Is at Hand, The, Studies in the Scriptures, Series II, 1888.
Truth Shall Make You Free, The, 1943.
Truth That Leads to Eternal Life, The, 1968.
Vindication I, 1931.
Vindication III, 1932.
Watchtower, The, 1879 to date, various issues, P.
Watch Tower Publications Index (1976–1980), 1981.
Watch Tower Reprints, containing *Watchtowers* July 1879 to June 1919.
What Do You Really Know About God?, tract, c1971.
Word—Who Is He? According to John, The, 1962.
Yearbook of Jehovah's Witnesses, 1927 to date, various years.
You Can Live Forever in Paradise on Earth, 1982.

B. Primary Source Material: Containing statements of important Watchtower representatives.

Douglas V. Walsh, The Right Honorable James Latham Clyde, M., P. C., etc., Scotland, 1954 (1958 edition).
J.F. Rutherford to Olin R. Moyle, letter, March 31, 1938.
Olin R. Moyle, v. *F.W. Franz*, et al. Libel suit testimony, May 10th to May 27th, 1943, New York Supreme Court, Appellate Division.

C. Secondary Source Material: Witness, Inc.

Eyes of Understanding, 1980 edition.
From Kingdom Hall to Kingdom Come, 1982 edition.
Who Is the Faithful and Wise Servant?, 1979, 1981 edition.

D. Secondary Source Material: Biblical Commentaries, Lexicons, etc.

Barclay, William. *The Letters of James and Peter*. Philadelphia: Westminster Press, 1960.
Barrett, C.K. *First Epistle to the Corinthians*. N.Y.: Harper & Row, 1968.
Bauer, Arndt, Gingrich. *Greek-English Lexicon*. Chicago: University of Chicago Press, 1957.

Bruce, F.F. *Paul: Apostle of the Heart Set Free.* Grand Rapids: Eerdmans, 1977.

Bruce, F.F. *The Book of Acts,* International Commentary on the New Testament. Grand Rapids: Eerdmans, 1979.

Cetnar, W. & J. *Questions for Jehovah's Witnesses,* 1982.

Dodd, C.H. *The Interpretation of the Fourth Gospel.* Cambridge: University Press, 1953.

Fortman, Edmund. *The Triune God.* Grand Rapids: Baker, 1972.

Franz, Raymond. *Crisis of Conscience.* Atlanta, Ga: Commentary Press, 1983.

Greber, Johannes. *Communication with the Spirit World of God.* Teaneck, N.J.: Johannes Greber Memorial Foundation, 1932 and 1958.

Green, Jay P. *Interlinear Greek-English New Testament.* MacDill AFB, Fla.: MacDonald Publishing Co., 1972.

Green, Michael. *Evangelism in the Early Church.* Grand Rapids: Eerdmans, 1970.

Gruss, Edmund. *Apostles of Denial.* Presbyterian Reformed Publ. Co., 1970.

Hislop, Alexander. *The Two Babylons.* A & B Black, 2nd American ed., 1959.

History of Christianity, The. Tim Dowley Gen. ed. Grand Rapids: Eerdmans, 1977.

Marshall, Alfred. *Interlinear Greek-English New Testament.* London: Samuel Bagster & Sons, 1958.

McClintock, John, and Strong, James. *Cyclopaedia of Biblical, Theological, Ecclesiastical Literature.* New York: Harper and Brothers, 1881.

Montague, Havor. *Jehovah's Witnesses and Blood Transfusions.* Santa Ana, Ca.: CARIS, 1979.

New Catholic Encyclopedia, Vol. XIV, Catholic University of America, 1967 ed.

Newsweek, January 18, 1971.

Newman, B. and Nida, E. *Translators Handbook on the Acts of the Apostles.* United Bible Societies, 1972.

New York Times, October 5, 1914.

Plummer, A. *The Gospel According to St. John.* Cambridge: University Press, 1892.

Pratt, Richard. *Every Thought Captive.* New Jersey: Presbyterian & Reformed, 1979.

Roberts, Rev. Alexander, and Donaldson, James. *The Ante-Nicene Fathers,* Vols. 1 and 3. Grand Rapids: Eerdmans, 1969.

Sanday, W. and Headlam, A. *The Epistle to the Romans,* The International Critical Commentary. Edinburgh: fifth ed., T. & T. Clark, 1902.

Septuagint (LXX), Zondervan, 1975.

Stevens, Leonard A. *Salute!* New York: Coward, McCann & Geoghagan, Inc., 1973.

Time magazine, various issues.

Vincent, Marvin. *The Epistles to the Philippians and to Philemon,* The International Critical Commentary. Edinburgh: T. & T. Clark, first printed 1897.

Webster's Third New International Dictionary. Chicago: *Encyclopaedia Britannica.* Vol. II, 1966.

Webster's Seventh New Collegiate Dictionary. Springfield, Mass.: G. C. Merriam Co., 1965.

Westcott, B.F. and Hort, F.J.A. *The New Testament in the Original Greek*. Cambridge & London: Macmillan and Co., 1885.

Williams, Charles B. *The New Testament—A Private Translation in the Language of the People*. Chicago: Moody Press, 1955.

SCRIPTURE INDEX

Gen. 9:4 . . . 278
Ex. 3:14 . . . 215, 216, 218
Lev. 17:10-16 . . . 278
17:14 . . . 274
Deut. 6:4 . . . 123, 126
29:29 . . . 118
32:39 . . . 215
1 Sam. 14:31-35 . . . 275
21:6 . . . 275
Ps. 90:2 . . . 215
96:4 . . . 123
110:1 . . . 156
139:7 . . . 231
Prov. 30:5, 6 . . . 208
Isa. 9:6 . . . 252
43:10 . . . 123, 185, 215
45:5 . . . 123, 184
45:21 . . . 125
45:22 . . . 126
55:9 . . . 118
Jer. 23:16 . . . 63
30:22 . . . 123
Dan. 11:36-38 . . . 193
Matt. 2:11 . . . 264
4:10 . . . 167
5:43 . . . 282
6:9 . . . 246
8:5-13 . . . 282
12:1-15 . . . 275
24:23,24 . . . 252
24:45 . . . 25
28:9 . . . 161
28:19 . . . 129, 149, 156, 231
Mark 9:35 . . . 43
16:12 . . . 119
Luke 2:10 . . . 264
2:11-14 . . . 265
3:14 . . . 291
4:8 . . . 167
22:38 . . . 290
24:36 . . . 109
24:39 . . . 109
John 1:1 . 124, 126, 184-187, 190-194
1:12 . . . 234, 250
2:18-22 . . . 112
2:19 . . . 116
2:21 . . . 116
3:3 . . . 250
3:16 . . . 193, 263
3:36 . . . 116
4:21, 23 . . . 167
5:23 . . . 265
8:24 . . . 185
8:58 . . . 207, 208, 215, 218, 219
8:59 . . . 215
14:16 . . . 228
16:7, 13 . . . 228
20:25 . . . 260
20:27 . . . 113
20:28 . . . 126, 178, 180, 186
20:29 . . . 178
Acts 4:12 . . . 234
5:3, 4 . . . 231
7:59 . . . 161
10:25-26 . . . 161,166
13:2 . . . 228
15:19 . . . 275
15:20 . . . 274, 278
15:21 . . . 278
15:23 . . . 274
16:27-34 . . . 282
17:22-31 . . . 10
17:27 . . . 235
17:29 . . . 118
17:31,32 . . . 102
26:23 . . . 103
Rom. 1:19 . . . 124
1:20 . . . 124
1:21 . . . 149
1:21, 22 . . . 124
1:25 . . . 36
3:22 . . . 244
8:27 . . . 228
10:8,9 . . . 109, 180
10:13 . . . 234, 250
15:19 . . . 228
1 Cor. 2:10, 11 . . . 231
8:1-13 . . . 275
8:4-6 . . . 125
10:20 . . . 125
12:4-6 . . . 129
12:11 . . . 228, 231
14:33 . . . 265
15:1-4 . . . 102

15:14 103
15:17 . . . . 109, 112
2 Cor. 3:17 231
4:4 . . . . 125, 186
6:14-18 263
13:14 129
Gal. 1:1 178
2:6 244
4:8 125
6:14 258
Eph. 2:5 250
2:8, 9 274
2:8-10 232
4:30 228
5:11 9
Phil. 2:4-8 119
1 Thess. 5:21 . . . . 64, 178
1 Tim. 1:17 . . . . 149, 184
2:5 . . . . 109, 112
Titus 2:13 126
Heb. 1:6 166-170
10:29 228
11:8-16 282
2 Pet. 1:1 . . . . 126, 178
1 John 2:24-26 244
3:2 . . . . 234, 244
5:1 . . . . 246, 250
5:11-13 . . . . 244, 247
5:13 234
5:20 126
Rev. 1:8 221
2:7 228
2:16 211
3:11 221
3:20 234
16:14 63
18:4 263
20:7 235
21:6 221
22:7 221
22:12, 13 221
22:20 221

SUBJECT INDEX

Abbreviations: JW—Jehovah's Witnesses; NWT—New World Translation; WT—Watchtower; WTBTS—Watch Tower Bible and Tract Society.

Alpha and Omega, See Jesus Christ.
Angels
  messages, deliver to WT, 19, 20
  worship of, idolatry, 161
  worship of Jesus, commanded, 166, 170
Anointed class
  authority over JWs, 25
  born again, 234, 235, 250
  Christ, a member of, 252
  little flock, 234, 235
  members called gods, 252
  144,000, 234, 235, 250, 252
  Savior, claimed to be, 252
Armageddon, 63, 64, 65
Apostles' Creed
  affirmation of resurrection, 102
Athanasian Creed
  statement on Trinity, 128
Authority, (WT)
  over JWs, 42, 50, 250
Blood transfusions
  biblical view, 274, 275, 278
  forbidden by JWs, 274, 278
Born again, See Anointed class.
Christmas
  biblical view, 264, 265
  date of celebration, 269, 270
  early WT view, 264
  false religious celebration, 263
Cross, the
  pagan symbol, 257, 260
  stake or cross?, 257, 258, 260
Dates, prophetic
  1874 (Second Coming), 64
  1914 (key WT date)
    Armageddon, 63, 64
  1925
    Abraham, Isaac, and Jacob, resurrection of, 64, 66
  1940
    destruction of British Empire predicted, 66
  1941
    Armageddon connected with WWII, 66
  1942
    Abraham, Isaac, and Jacob, resurrection of, 66
  1975
    year of doom, 66
  1976
    change in power structure, 58
Devil, 167
  See also Satan
Faithful and Wise Servant
  definition of, 25
  God's spokesman, 25
  Russell, Charles Taze, 25, 26, 35
Franz, Fred, 14, 57
  presidency, assumed, 58
Franz, Raymond, 58
Governing Body
  earthly leaders, 42, 43, 50
  Russell's opposition to, 42, 43
Holy Spirit, 228ff.
  denial of personhood by JWs, 228, 231
  Jehovah, equal to, 231
Ignatius, bishop of Antioch, 102
Inspiration
  Jehovah, editor of *The Watchtower*, 14
  Supreme Court, 19
Jehovah
  Holy Spirit, equal to, 231
  Jesus Christ, equal to, 126
  Supreme Court, 19
  worship of, 167
Jesus Christ,
  Alpha and Omega, 221
  a god?, 126, 184–187, 190–194
  called God, 178, 180, 193
  created being, 169, 235
  deity denied by JWs, 101, 178, 180
  exalted angel, 169
  See also Jehovah
  See also John 8:58, "I AM"
  member of anointed class, 252
  Michael the Archangel, 170, 207, 215

mighty god, 192
prayer to, 161
See also Resurrection of
See also Spirit person
revealer of WT prophecies, 19, 63
worshiped equally to the Father formerly by JWs, 161
Jesus' second coming, See Dates, prophetic, 1874.
John 1:1, 124, 184ff.
view of NWT Committee, 186
John 8:58
"I AM," 207, 208, 215, 216, 218, 219
Kingdom Interlinear Translation, 191
Jesus' diety, affirmed, 193
Knorr, Nathan, 14, 58
Michael, Archangel, 170, 207, 215
Military service
biblical view, 282, 283
former WT view, 284
present WT view, 282, 283, 291
Monotheism
biblical view, 123
New Testament, 124, 184, 185
Old Testament, 124
definition of, 123, 125, 184
Mormons, See Polytheism.
Obeisance, 161, 167
definition of, 161, 166
144,000, See Anointed class.
People's Pulpit Association, See WTBTS.
Peter, Apostle
deity of Christ, affirms, 180
deity of Holy Spirit, affirms, 231
Polytheism
definition of, 123, 185
Mormons, 124, 125
NWT's teaching, 184
Prayer,
form of worship, 161
in Jesus' name, 234
to Christ, 161, 168
President of WTBTS
Franz, 14, 57, 58
Knorr, 14, 58
Russell, 25, 26, 35, 42, 43, 50, 51, 57, 64
Rutherford, 51, 57, 58, 66
Proskuneo, 166, 167
See also obeisance
Prophet, false
biblical definition, 63
JW's definition, 64
Resurrection of Christ, bodily
biblical, 102, 112
denial by JWs, 109, 112
annihilation of body, 109, 117
not physical, 103, 116
Russell, Charles Taze, 50, 51
death of, 51
See also Faithful and Wise Servant
founder, 25, 42, 43
mouthpiece of God, 50, 57
view of WWI, 64
worship of, 35, 36
Rutherford, J. F.
Judge, 57, 58, 66
presidency, assumed, 51
Salvation
assurance, 234, 244, 246, 247
biblical view, 101, 116, 232, 234
correct understanding of John 1:1, 191, 194
jeapordized by blood transfusions, 274
works, depends on, 232, 233, 244, 246, 247
Satan, 65, 235
a god, 123, 125
god of this world, 186
originator of the doctrine of the Trinity, 101
personal being, 228
Spirit person, invisible, 109, 112, 116
Christ, resurrection of, 103
Supreme Court
interprets prophecy, 63
See also Jehovah
Theocracy, See Governing Body.
Thomas, Apostle, 260
bodily resurrection, affirms, 113
deity of Christ, affirms, 178, 180, 186
Trinity
definition of, 118-120
denial by JWs, 126, 127

misrepresentation of doctrine, 119, 120, 126ff.
Satan, author of, 101, 118, 119
Uncials, 192
Vaccinations
early JWs view, 278
revised view, 278
War, See Military service.
Westcott, B. F., and F.H.A. Hort
Greek scholars explain "uncials," 192
Wilson, Benjamin, (translator of the *Diaglott*), 190, 191
Works, See Salvation.
Worship
angels, 161
creature, 35, 169
Jehovah, 167
relative, 168-170
See also Russell, Charles Taze
WTBTS,
original name, 35
WWI
Armageddon, beginning of, 64
See also Date, prophetic, 1914
WWII
Armageddon, beginning of, 65
See also Date, prophetic, 1940s

WITNESS, INC.

The Watchtower Files are the result of a ministry of evangelism to Jehovah's Witnesses with an emphasis on the research of their beliefs, history and organization. This ministry is called Witness, Inc., and is publishing *witnessing aids* for concerned Christians. Each publication is designed to deal with a different aspect of sharing truth with JWs and exposing the serious error they have been taught. Witness, Inc., publishes books which expose the Watchtower Society as being a false organization, *by utilizing the Society's own statements to do so.*

In an ordered presentation, the book *Who Is the Faithful and Wise Servant*? provides proof that the Watchtower leaders have no right to teach JWs anything at all. *Eyes of Understanding* examines the Society's claim to being God's "prophet" and their numerous predictions for the end of the world. *Bible Students*? proves *from the Society's own claims* that Jehovah's Witnesses are not students of the Scriptures, but rather only students of men, the Watchtower leaders. The book *From Kingdom Hall to Kingdom Come* is a step-by-step procedure of how to use the Bible to lead a JW to Jesus—in one meeting! Another publication, *Where Is Michael*?, exposes the Society's false doctrine that Michael the archangel was born to the Virgin Mary. Witness, Inc., has also published many booklets and tracts for the purpose of sharing the truth with Jehovah's Witnesses. The ministry address is:

Witness, Inc.
P.O. Box 597
Clayton, CA 94517